NEW

Langua
LEADE

UPPER INTERMEDIATE

COURSEBOOK

DAVID COTTON | DAVID FALVEY | SIMON KENT

CONTENTS

Listening	Speaking / Pronunciation	Scenario	Study Skills / Writing	Video
Five people talking about communication habits (1.1) Radio programme about gender conversation styles (1.3) Conversation between two student counsellors (1.4)	Discussing communicating (1.1) Discussing non-verbal communication (1.1) Talking about current trends considering consequences (1.2) Thinking of advice for men/women (1.3)	Key language: outlining problems, offering solutions, reacting to suggestions Task: solving communication problems Scenario: flat sharing	Writing a list of advice for communicating in your country (1.1) Study skills: Note-taking from listening to a talk structure of talks note-taking Writing skills: Writing and checking written communication register peer-checking	Study Skills video: James Hammond gives a lecture about public speaking James H 23r Public Face y
3 people talking about their local area (2.1) Lecture about volcanoes (2.3) Phone conversation about a proposed wind farm (2.4) Conversation with a lecturer about questionnaires (2.5)	Collocations (2.1) Discussing solutions to problems (2.1) Discussing the environment (2.2) Talking about volcanoes (2.3) Making a short presentation; presenting (2.3)	Key language: agreeing and disagreeing politely, polite questions Task: Attending a formal meeting Scenario: Sparrow Hill Wind Farm	Writing a short summary to a solution (2.1) Study skills: Designing a Questionnaire question types Writing skills: Writing a questionnaire	Meet the expert: an interview with Dr Andrew McGonigle about active volcanoes.
Interview with a karate teacher (3.2) Presentation about Yuna Kim (3.4) Lecturer answering questions about essay writing (3.5)	Weak forms of the (3.3) Using idioms to talk about experiences (3.1) Ranking characteristics (3.3)	Key language: Using emphasis and comparison Task: giving a presentation Scenario: Who is the Greatest?	Study skills: Understanding Essay Questions; understanding key words, essay writing Writing skills: A For and Against Essay: introductions, formal expressions	Meet the expert: an interview with Dr Elizabeth Pummell about the science of sports Psychology
Doctor talking about her work (4.1) A professor talking about malaria (4.2) Six doctors talking about future medical developments (4.3) Business consultant talking about using the internet (4.5) Lecturer advising students about internet resources (4.5)	Stressed syllables (4.1) Discussing medicine and the medical profession (4.1) Planning a fund-raising day (4.2) Talking about hopes for the future (4.3)	Key language: discussing implications Task: making difficult decisions Scenario: Medical dilemmas	Study skills: Evaluating resources on the internet Writing skills: A short report; making recommendations	Meet the expert: an interview with Dr Tina Chowdhury, about medical bionics.
People talking about transport (5.1) News report on transport of the future (5.2) Discussion on transport problems (5.4)	Discussing road safety (5.1) Making future predictions (5.2) Describing a memorable journey (5.3)	Key language: the language of meetings - summarising Task: Evaluating proposals Scenario: Beauciel	Writing a short report on road safety (5.1) Study skills: Graphs, charts and tables Writing skills: Describing information in a table; comparison and contrast	Meet the expert: interview with Monisha Rajesh about her Indian train journey (5.3)
Discussion about a book (6.1) Four people talking about books (6.2) Five people talking about reading habits (6.3) Conversation about a film proposal (6.4) Five people describing a memorable presentation (6.5)	Used to (6.3) Describing a book or film (6.1) Discussing influential books (6.2) Talking about childhood (6.3)	Key language: persuading Task: making a persuasive presentation Scenario: the new film project	Study skills: making an effective presentation, rhetorical techniques Writing skills: An online review; adjectives, adverbs	Study skills video: a presentation about The Girl with the Dragon Tattoo

CONTENTS

Listening	Speaking / Pronunciation	Scenario	Study Skills / Writing	Video
Architect answering questions (7.2) Three architects discussing a hotel design (7.4)	Word stress (7.1) Describing a building (7.1) Discussing the issue of young people living at home (7.2) Sharing information on bridges (7.3)	Key language: talking about requirements Task: deciding on facilities in a hotel Scenario: on the horizon	Describing a well-known building (7.1) Study skills: identifying fact and opinion Writing skills: an opinion-led essay; avoiding repetition	Meet the Expert: an interview with Laura Mark about innovative designs
Five people talking about globalisation (8.1) Radio programme about working internationally (8.2) Radio interview about supermarket expansion (8.4)	Discussing globalisation; Assessing results and consequences (8.1) Sharing information about global projects (8.3)	Key language: clarifying Task: taking part in a debate Scenario: supermarket superpower	Writing your opinion on globalisation (8.1) Study skills: Summarising; topic sentences, paraphrasing Writing skills: a summary	Meet the Expert: an interview with Richard Cook about working in a global workplace (8.1)
Three people talking about art (9.1) Conversation about an art gallery (9.4) Lecture about writing a blog (9.5)	Discussing what is art; justifying opinions (9.1) Describing a work of art (9.1) Describing a photo (9.2) Discussing public art (9.3)	Key language: discussing implications, offering counter-arguments Task: deciding on an action plan Scenario: The Russell Drake Gallery	Study skills: Expanding your vocabulary; collocations Writing skills: An online review	Meet the Expert: an interview with Yulia Podolskaya about her work as a sculptor
Lecture about group dynamics (10.1) Radio advice phone-in (10.4)	Stress patterns (10.1) Planning a newspaper (10.1) Discussing peer pressure (10.2) Talking about famous criminals (10.3)	Key language: giving and reacting to advice Task: an advice phone-in Scenario: What's on your mind?	Summarising an article (10.3) Study skills: writing a bibliography, referencing Writing skills: An advantages and disadvantages essay; complex sentences, conclusions	Meet the Expert: an interview with Dr Jack Lewis, a neuroscientist, about psychological profiling (10.3)
Six people talking about what they miss about their culture (11.1) Radio discussion about culture shock; (11.2) Two people talking about cultural mistakes (11.3) Presentation about Toronto (11.4) Radio lecture about reading (11.5)	Deciding what to put in a time capsule (11.1) Discussing culture shock; justifying answers (11.2) Describing a person (11.2) Discussing cultural issues (11.3)	Key language: creating impact in a presentation Task: giving a formal presentation Scenario: Kaleidoscope World	Describing a person in culture shock (11.2) Study skills: Improving reading skills; reading and chunking, guessing unknown words, reading linkers Writing skills: Formal correspondence; letter layout, formulaic language	Meet the Expert: an interview with Anna Colquhoun, about the cultural importance of food. (11.3)
Three people talking about gadgets (12.1) Conversation between two workers (12.4) Conversation between two managers (12.4)	Discussing technology (12.1) Discussing living without technology (12.2) Debating technology (12.3)	Key language: persuading, making a case for something Task: conducting a problem-solving meeting Scenario: conducting a problem-solving meeting	Writing your opinion (12.1) Study skills: Plagiarism – what it is and how to avoid it Writing skills: An opinion article; stylistic features	Study skills video: a lecture about plagiarism

1 Communication

1.1 CONNECTIONS

The more elaborate our means of communication, the less we communicate. J.B. Priestley, 1894–1984, British novelist

SPEAKING AND LISTENING

1 Discuss these questions in small groups.

1 How do you communicate with the people below, and how often?
- friends
- neighbours
- online/virtual friends
- followers (on social media)
- family members
- colleagues

2 When did you last …
- send an SMS/text message?
- send an email?
- write a letter (on paper)?
- send a greeting card?
- make a phone call?
- use social media to contact someone?
- speak to someone face to face?
- make a presentation/speech?

3 How do you prefer people to communicate with you?

4 Which forms of communication do you use most often?

5 Which forms of communication are most common in your country?

2a 1.1 **Listen to five people talking about their communication habits and answer the questions.**

Which person/people (1–5):

1 prefers conversations?
2 met someone by accident?
3 sometimes has technical problems with communication?
4 was suddenly contacted by someone?
5 thinks they are not up-to-date in their habits?
6 is interested in famous people?

2b Which forms of communication does each person mention?

3 Which person is most like you and least like you?

VOCABULARY
PHRASAL VERBS

4 Match the phrasal verbs from the listening with their meanings.

1 get in touch with   a meet by accident
2 track down   b maintain a relationship with
3 bump into   c follow what is happening
4 lose touch with   d find
5 stay in touch with   e have no contact with
6 keep track of   f exchange the latest news
7 catch up with   g contact

5 Complete these sentences to make them true for you. Compare your ideas with a partner.

1 The best way to track down a person who doesn't use social media is …
2 I like to stay in touch with people who …
3 If I bumped into an old friend after ten years, I'd …
4 I like to keep track of what my friends are doing by …
5 A person I have lost contact with who I wish I hadn't is …
6 It is easier to get in touch with people when …
7 The best time of day to catch up with people is …

READING

6a Read the title of the article. What do you think it will be about? What do you think are the 'Six degrees of separation'?

6b Now read the article and check your predictions.

7 Complete the sentences with no more than three words and/or a number.

1 The majority of our communication is with _____ people.
2 The 'Six degrees of separation' idea dates from ___1929___.
3 In the 1960s, an American sociologist attempted to _____.
4 The participants only had knowledge of the name, _____ location of the target.
5 The average number of steps to deliver the packets was between ___5-7___.
6 The results of the experiment appeared in _____.
7 A recreation of Milgram's experiment took place in ___2003___.
8 The most recent experiment looked at the connections between _____ social-media users.

8 Find verbs and nouns in the article that are connected to scientific study.

9 Reacting to the text Discuss these questions in small groups.

1 What is your opinion of the ideas in the article about how closely people are connected?
2 How do you think the internet has improved communication?
3 What are the negative aspects of the internet in relation to communication?
4 Is any communication really 'private' these days?

SPEAKING AND WRITING

10a Work in small groups. Discuss these questions about non-verbal communication in your culture.

• **Greetings and saying goodbye** – What do people do (shake hands, kiss, bow, wave, etc.)? Does age or gender make a difference?
• **Personal space** – How near do people usually stand when talking? Do they ever touch?
• **Silence** – How important is this?
• **Body language** – Do people use a lot of gestures? Which gestures are common? Are there any gestures you should avoid?
• **Eye contact** – Is this important at all times?

10b How important are the above in more formal situations (giving a presentation/speech, taking part in a seminar/meeting, etc.)?

11 Write a list of the most important things to consider when communicating with people from your country.

'Think for a minute … interesting ideas you need to know about'

HOW CLOSELY CONNECTED ARE WE? or 'SIX DEGREES OF SEPARATION'

Research shows we have regular communication with between seven and fifteen people, and that most of our communication is in fact with the closest five to ten people. However, perhaps we are closer to the rest of the world than we think. 'Six degrees of separation' is the theory that any person on Earth can be connected to any other person through a chain of not more than five other people.

The concept goes back to a 1929 book of short stories called *Everything is Different* by Hungarian author Frigyes Karinthy. He was very interested in friendship networks and his ideas influenced many of the early ideas about social networks.

In the 1950s, two scientists tried to prove the theory mathematically, but after twenty years, they still had not been successful. In 1967, an American sociologist called Stanley Milgram tried a new method to test the theory, which he called the 'Small-world problem'. He chose at random a sample of people in the middle of America and asked them to send packages to a stranger in the state of Massachusetts. The people sending the packages only knew the name, job and general location of the people. Milgram told them to send the package to a person they knew personally who they thought might know the target person. This person would then send the parcel onto a contact of theirs until the parcel could be personally delivered to the correct person. Amazingly, it took only between five and seven people to get the packets delivered, and the results were published in the magazine *Psychology Today*. It was this research that inspired the phrase 'Six degrees of separation'.

In the last few decades, the theory and the phrase has appeared again. It was first the title of a play and then a film. Then, in the mid-1990s, two college students invented the game 'Six degrees of Kevin Bacon'. They wondered how many movies the actor had been in, and how many actors he had worked with. The idea of the game is to link any actor to Kevin Bacon through no more than six links.

In 2003, Columbia University tried to recreate Milgram's experiment on the internet. This became known as the Columbia Small World project. The experiment involved 24,163 email chains with eighteen target people in thirteen different countries. The results confirmed that the average number of links in the chain was six.

Most recently, an experiment in 2011 at the University of Milan analysed the relationship between 721 million social media users and found that 92 percent were connected by only four stages, or five degrees of separation.

So, think about it for a minute. How might you be connected to a celebrity, politician or sports star?

READING

1a Work in groups and discuss how you feel when you have to do these things.

- give a presentation
- participate in a seminar or meeting
- meet new people

1b What advice would you give to people who are nervous about all the situations above?

2 Read the leaflet quickly. Are any of the points similar to your answers to Exercise 1b?

3 Read the leaflet again. Match these extracts from Anika Bhaskar's course handouts with the weeks in the leaflet.

A

Decide what you want to say before the seminar. Review it in your mind. Keep rehearsing it until you can say it confidently. There's truth in the old saying, 'Think before you speak'.

B

People from Britain and the USA often leave more space around them than other nationalities. They are more likely to move away when they feel that others are invading their space.

C

People judge you very quickly, so it is very important to make a good first impression. You look much more confident and capable when you have made an effort to smarten your appearance.

D

Your voice gives people a clear indication of how you are feeling. If we are stressed, our voices can crack under pressure and get louder – giving away our emotions.

E

Even when you are sitting still, your body is communicating with everyone in the audience. Aim to look confident. Remember, 'Actions speak louder than words'.

---

4 Are these sentences true, false or not given?

This course will:

1. help you if you have a speech impediment such as a stammer.
2. teach you how to walk properly.
3. teach you how to be assertive and aggressive.
4. teach you to understand and be aware of your listeners.
5. teach you how to interact successfully with other participants in a seminar.
6. not help you to prepare for a presentation.
7. help you to show your true nature.

5 Which communication skills mentioned in the leaflet are you good at? Which areas do you need to develop?

Do you want to

communicate confidently?

The world of communication is changing rapidly.

The need for people to do public speaking in their work and studies is rising, be it face to face or via the web.

Stress in the workplace is increasing dramatically – and one of the main reasons given by people is their lack of confidence in giving presentations.

More and more people are taking communication courses these days to help them in both work and home life.

If you find it difficult to speak up during seminars, or if you feel you can't get a word in edgeways when others are talking, then this small, friendly group will help you to manage these situations with more ease and confidence.

The course lasts for twelve weeks and aims to help you communicate more effectively.

Week	Aim
1	Remain in control of your emotions and your voice
2	Maintain good posture
3	Prepare what you want to say before the event
4	Use tone to engage people with interest and excitement
5	Dress smartly to make a good impression
6	Communicate in an assertive and not a passive or aggressive style
7	Stay calm and polite at all times
8	Participate actively in seminars
9	Consider your potential listeners
10	Be a good listener
11	Understand cultural differences
12	Be yourself

Facilitator: Anika Bhaskar

Anika is currently carrying out research for her doctorate on communication barriers. She became interested in communication skills while she was studying for her MBA at Edinburgh University.

VOCABULARY
IDIOMS

6a Match these idioms with their meanings.

1 actions speak louder than words
2 think before you speak
3 get a word in edgeways
4 hear it on the grapevine
5 be on the same wavelength
6 get straight to the point
7 have a quick word with someone

a talk about the most important thing immediately
b share similar ideas
c hear about a rumour passed from one person to another
d get a chance to say something
e talk briefly to someone
f what you do is more important than what you say
g don't start talking until you have thought about what you want to say

6b Work with a partner and discuss the questions.

1 Does it irritate you when people do not get straight to the point?
2 When was the last time you felt you were really on the same wavelength as someone else?
3 Who was the last person to ask to have a quick word with you?
4 What have you heard on the grapevine recently?

GRAMMAR
THE CONTINUOUS ASPECT

7a Underline the seven continuous forms in the leaflet and course handouts.

The world of communication is changing rapidly.

7b Look again at the leaflet and answer these questions.

1 Is the amount of stress in the workplace changing?
2 Is the number of people taking communication courses staying the same?
3 Has Anika finished her research?
4 Is Anika's research for her doctorate temporary or permanent?
5 When did Anika become interested in communication skills?

8 Work with a partner and look at the verb forms in the sentences below. What is the difference in meaning between each sentence?

1 a I'm writing an email to my parents.
  b I write a letter to my parents every week.
2 a I work in London.
  b I'm working in London, but I'm looking for a job in Paris.
3 a When my colleague arrived, we were having dinner.
  b When my colleague arrived, we had dinner.
4 a Everyone around me cried and screamed.
  b Everyone around me was crying and screaming.
5 a I live in Istanbul.
  b I am living with my parents at the moment.
6 a I walk to work every day.
  b I am walking to work this week, as my car is broken.

→ Language reference and extra practice, pages 126–149

9a Read the beginning of the leaflet and answer these questions.

1 How is the world of communication changing?
2 How is stress in the workplace increasing?

The present continuous is often used to talk about trends. Below are some of the most frequently used verbs, together with the adverbs they most commonly collocate with in academic texts.

change	constantly, dramatically, rapidly, frequently
increase	constantly, dramatically, rapidly
occur	frequently
expand	constantly, dramatically, rapidly
behave	differently

9b Think of as many sentences as possible about these topics using verbs and adverbs from the Grammar tip box.

The web is changing our lives dramatically.

1 The web
2 The use of tablets
3 The universe
4 Hurricanes
5 Men/behave
6 The population
7 Identity fraud

SPEAKING

10a Work in groups and talk about current trends in communication. Think about the following topics.

- reading
- texting
- the internet
- tablets
- telephoning
- writing letters
- writing emails
- smartphones
- using Twitter

People are reading fewer novels these days because they're using computers more.

10b Considering consequences **Choose the trend you think is most important, worrying or interesting, and explain why. Say how it affects different groups or parts of society (e.g. large families, business people, students, publishers, libraries, etc.).**

People are texting more and more these days because they find it so convenient. I find this worrying because it affects family relationships. I have even seen people texting at the dinner table or when they are out for a meal together. Personally, I find it very rude.

LISTENING

1 Discuss this statement in small groups.

'Men don't know how to listen properly.'

2 [1.2] **Listen to two extracts about men and women communicating. In each case say who the people are and what the situation is.**

3 Listen again and answer these questions.

1 What are the following books about?
 • *Talking from 9 to 5*
 • *You Just Don't Understand*
 • *You Were Always Mom's Favorite!*
2 What is the essay *Would You Please Let Me Finish* about?
3 What are the different factors that can affect conversational style?
4 What have recent surveys shown?
5 How long has May been married?
6 Why is May feeling sad?
7 How does May get on with her mother-in-law?
8 Does May interrupt her husband a lot?

GRAMMAR
THE PERFECT ASPECT

4a Look at this extract from the listening and answer the questions.

M: We've had so many arguments recently and he has moved out.
R: Oh, when did he leave?
M: This evening. He phoned me from a café at 5 p.m. and asked me to meet him there after work to talk about our problems. But by the time I arrived at the café, he had left.

1 Is May's husband living in her house now?
2 Did he live in her house at some time in the past?
3 Who was at the café first, May or her husband?
4 Were they at the café at the same time?
5 What did the husband do before May arrived?

4b Look at the extract again. Which tense do we use when we want to suggest a connection between these things?

1 a past event and the present
2 an earlier and a later past event

4c Look at Audio script 1.3 on page 168 and underline examples of the present perfect simple, the past perfect simple and the past simple.

➡ Language reference and extra practice, pages 126–149

5 Seven sentences contain a mistake. Find the mistakes and correct them.

1 Tannen wrote many books.
2 In 2009, Tannen has written *You Were Always Mom's Favorite!*
3 Have you read any of Tannen's books?
4 When has this book been published?
5 I realised that we met before.
6 Is this the first time she spoke in public?
7 Last night there have been an all-women panel on the show.
8 When I arrived at the conference, the main speaker already finished.

6 Work with a partner to ask and answer questions about the following topics. Try to develop the conversation. Use the words and phrases in the box.

Have you ever?	How long ago?	When?	Who?

A: Have you ever sent an aggressive email?
B: Yes, I have.
A: When did you do that?
B: In my first year at university.
A: Who did you send it to?

1 send an aggressive email
2 raise voice in a meeting
3 interrupt
4 upset a friend when just joking
5 have dream in which …
6 tell lie
7 write a difficult letter
8 use sign language

READING

7a Do you agree with these statements?

1 Women talk far more than men.
2 Men talk about sport. Women talk about their feelings.
3 Women and men communicate differently.

7b Read the two extracts from *You Just Don't Understand* by the academic Deborah Tannen. What does the author say (if anything) about the statements above?

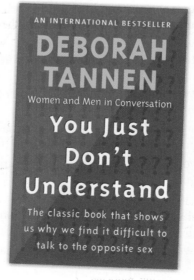

AN INTERNATIONAL BESTSELLER
DEBORAH TANNEN
Women and Men in Conversation
You Just Don't Understand
The classic book that shows us why we find it difficult to talk to the opposite sex

Extract 1

YOU JUST DON'T UNDERSTAND

'Put down that paper and talk to me!'

I was sitting in a suburban living room, speaking to a women's group that had invited men to join them for the occasion of my talk about communication between women and men. During the discussion, one man was particularly talkative, full of lengthy
5 comments and explanations. When I made the observation that women often complain that their husbands don't talk to them enough, this man volunteered that he heartily agreed. He gestured toward his wife, who had sat silently beside him on the couch throughout the evening, and said, 'She's the talker in our family.'
10 Everyone in the room burst into laughter. The man looked puzzled and hurt. 'It's true,' he explained. 'When I come home from work, I usually have nothing to say, but she never runs out. If it weren't for her, we'd spend the whole evening in silence.' Another woman expressed a similar paradox about her husband:
15 'When we go out, he's the life of the party. If I happen to be in another room, I can always hear his voice above the others. But when we're home, he doesn't have that much to say. I do most of the talking.'

Who talks more, women or men?
20 Women are believed to talk too much. Yet study after study finds that it is men who talk more – at meetings, in mixed-group discussions, and in classrooms where girls and young women sit next to boys or young men. For example, communication researchers Barbara and Gene Eakins recorded and studied seven university faculty meetings.
25 They found that, with one exception, men spoke more often and, without exception, spoke for a longer period.

Extract 2

YOU JUST DON'T UNDERSTAND

'Put down that paper and talk to me!'

For most women, the language of conversation is primarily a language of rapport: a way of establishing connections and negotiating relationships. Emphasis is placed on displaying similarities and matching experiences. From childhood, girls
5 criticise peers who try to stand out or appear better than others. People feel their closest connections at home, or in settings where they feel at home – with one or a few people they feel close to and comfortable with – in other words, during private speaking. But even the most public situations
10 can be approached like private speaking.

For most men, talk is primarily a means to preserve independence and negotiate and maintain status in a hierarchical social order. This is done by exhibiting knowledge and skill, and by holding centre stage through
15 verbal performance such as storytelling, joking or imparting information. From childhood, men learn to use talking as a way to get and keep attention. So they are more comfortable speaking in larger groups made up of people they know less well – in the broadest sense, 'public speaking'.
20 But even the most private situations can be approached like public speaking, more like giving a report than establishing rapport.

8a Read the two extracts again and complete these statements with M (men) or W (women).
1 _M_ like to stand out.
2 _W_ prefer private speaking.
3 _M_ often speak for longer.
4 _M_ are concerned about their rank and position in society.
5 _W_ like to find things that are almost the same between people.
6 _M_ often don't say much at home.

8b Underline the sections in the extracts that gave you this information.

9 Identifying stylistic devices Look at the two extracts again and underline examples of the following stylistic devices.
* anecdotes (short interesting stories about a person or event)
* using questions to raise interest
* using contrast
* direct speech

VOCABULARY
COLLOCATIONS

10a Underline the nouns in Extract 2 which collocate with verbs 1–6.
1 establish (x2) 4 maintain
2 negotiate (x2) 5 exhibit
3 display 6 impart

10b Complete the sentences using the collocations in Exercise 10a.
1 Many businesses have _____ with local universities.
2 Psychology students need to _____ of the differences in gender communication.
3 This book looks at the difficulties young people can have when they _____ with friends and family.
4 The Nordic countries _____ as well as differences in terms of culture.
5 In sharp contrast to the communication style of men, which seeks to establish and _____ and dominance, women's communicating is more equal.
6 Communication is the art and technique of using words effectively to _____ or ideas.

SPEAKING

11a Work with a partner to think of three pieces of advice for men communicating with women, and women communicating with men. Use the information in this unit, and your own ideas.

11b Work with another pair to share your ideas. Choose the three best pieces of advice.

SITUATION

1 Look at the poster below and discuss the questions with a partner.

1 What services does the Advice Centre offer?
2 Have you ever used a service like this? Would you use it?
3 What kind of problems do you think the Advice Centre has to deal with?

2 [1.3] Two counsellors from the Advice Centre are discussing the financial problems of Marco, a student at the university. Listen and answer the questions.

1 What are the reasons why Marco cannot pay his rent?
2 Why is Marco in a 'difficult situation'?
3 What solutions does Carol propose to solve Marco's problems?

Westfield University

Student Advice Centre

Got a problem? We're here to help.
Come and see us with any problem, big or small.

We deal with emotional matters, financial difficulties, problems with studies, problems between flatmates ... anything you want.

Just make an appointment

W
university

KEY LANGUAGE
OUTLINING PROBLEMS, OFFERING SOLUTIONS, REACTING TO SUGGESTIONS

3a Listen to the counsellors again and tick the expressions in the list that you hear.

1 The problem is, he's been spending too much money.
2 Well, the way to sort it out, surely, is to tell him to get a loan.
3 I'm not sure it's the right thing to do, Carol.
4 The trouble is, it's the third time he's run out of money.
5 He can't go on like that.
6 One way of dealing with this could be to look at his weekly expenses.
7 Mmm, great suggestion.
8 Well, there's an obvious solution.
9 We could talk to the owner of the flat.
10 That seems the best way to deal with it.

3b Match the expressions in Exercise 3a with these language functions.

• outlining problems
• offering solutions
• reacting to suggestions

3c Practise saying the expressions.

3d Match expressions a–g with the functions in Exercise 3b.

a That seems to be the best way forward.
b It's a tricky situation because …
c The best way to deal with it is to …
d It's a vicious circle.
e That might well solve the problem.
f The trouble is …
g That makes sense to me.

4 Work with a partner to discuss the situation below and suggest solutions. Try to use some of the expressions from the Key language.

Marco works every evening in a cafe to make more money. As a result, he often oversleeps and misses early-morning lectures.

TASK
SOLVING COMMUNICATION PROBLEMS

5 Martin, Paul, Stewart and Carlos are students sharing a flat for a year. Read about them and discuss what problems could arise because of their different personalities.

6a The students are having problems living together. Work in groups of four. You are counsellors at the Advice Centre and are helping the students to sort out their problems. Each of you has met one of the flatmates. Read the notes of your conversation.

Counsellor A: look at page 155.
Counsellor B: look at page 157.
Counsellor C: look at page 161.
Counsellor D: look at page 163.

6b In your group, share information about the four students. Explain the point of view of the student you met.

6c Discuss the flatmates' problems and suggest solutions. Think about the questions below to help you.

1   Why are the students having so many problems?
2   Do they need more rules to improve relations in the flat?
3   Should they continue to live together?
4   Should they try to cancel their contract with the owner of the flat?
5   What is the best solution to their problems?

6d As a class, discuss the solutions you have thought of. What is the best solution?

7 Discuss which student you would most like to share a flat with, and give reasons. Which one would you least like to live with?

Stewart (English), aged 20, is the youngest flatmate. He is studying Modern Languages. Shy and lacking confidence, he is a typical introvert. He loves travelling and spends his vacations going all over Asia, alone. He is continually saving money for these trips and eats little food. An unemployed friend of Stewart, Tom, has been staying in the flat for over two weeks. Stewart does not like face-to-face communication or telephoning.

Carlos (Brazilian), aged 21, is studying Media. Easy-going, confident, he is always happy and relaxed. He spends a lot of time late at night telephoning his family in Rio de Janeiro, Brazil. He loves talking and chatting to friends. An untidy person, his favourite pastime is playing Brazilian music as loudly as possible.

Martin (English), aged 21, is studying Engineering. A strong personality, he is extrovert and sociable. He can often upset people because he usually speaks his mind. He likes to organise things and plans his life carefully. A tidy person, he has already put up several notices reminding his flatmates to keep the flat clean.

Paul (American), aged 26, is a postgraduate student. He comes from a very wealthy family – both his parents are top lawyers in the United States. Encouraged by his parents, he is also studying Law. Ambitious and very hard-working, he spends most of the day and night reading law books and writing assignments. He likes to communicate by email and often sends messages to his flatmates.

STUDY SKILLS
NOTE-TAKING FROM LISTENING TO A TALK

1 You are going to watch someone giving a lecture about public speaking. Discuss these questions in small groups.

1 Have you ever made a speech? How did you feel?
2 What tips do you think will be given?
3 What would you like to know about?

2a Structure of talks Formal talks, such as lectures, are usually structured in a very clear way, with 'signposts' to help listeners. Match headings 1–5 with examples a–e.

1 Introducing what is to come
2 Sequencing
3 Signalling the main point
4 Rephrasing
5 Exemplifying

a For instance, …
b I intend to discuss …
c In other words, …
d The most important thing …
e Firstly, I want to …

2b What other phrases do you know for each heading?

3 ▶1.1 Note-taking Watch the first part of the lecture by James Hammond and make notes of the main points.

4a Compare your notes with a partner and discuss the questions.

1 Did you note the same information?
2 Did you make notes in the same way?
3 Which of the phrases from Exercise 2 did you hear? Which did you find most useful for your notes?

4b Which of these techniques did you use in your note-taking?

- arrows
- using headings/colours
- using a lot of space
- underlining key words
- using capital letters for very important ideas and points
- your own system of abbreviations and short forms (e.g. using one letter to mean a word or topic, S = speech, C = communication)

5 ▶1.2 Watch the second part of the talk and make notes of the main points. Use techniques from Exercise 4 which you think might be useful.

James Ham
23rd M

Public spe
Face your

6 Compare your notes with the notes you made in Exercise 3. Is the second set of notes better or clearer?

7 Work in small groups and reconstruct what you heard using your notes. Look at the Video script on page 168 and check your ideas.

8 Discuss these questions.

1 Do you agree or disagree with any of the advice given by James?
2 Can you add anything else?
3 What is your opinion of the communication style of James?

WRITING SKILLS
WRITING AND CHECKING WRITTEN COMMUNICATION

9 Work with a partner to discuss these questions.

1 How often do you write emails?
2 How often do you send letters (either on paper or attached to emails)?
3 Do you write more emails for formal or informal situations?
4 Can you remember the last three emails you wrote? Who were they to? What was their purpose?

10 Register Read the two emails sent to the lecturer James Hammond. In each case, what is the relationship between the writer and James? How do you know this?

Dear Mr Hammond,

I attended your lecture on public speaking at the Communication Skills conference in London last week and I was very impressed. I am involved in organising something similar and I would like to invite you to speak at our conference in Milan, Italy, on 15 May. The talk would need to last for 60 minutes (45 minutes for the talk and 15 minutes for questions).

Please find attached a document giving full details of the programme.

Should you have any further questions, please do not hesitate to contact me.

I look forward to hearing from you.

Yours sincerely,
Elena Conti
Conference Organiser

Hi James,
Great talk last week on public speaking. I really enjoyed it. Do you want to give a talk at an industry thing I'm getting together in Italy in May?
The session needs to be an hour (45 mins for the talk and 15 mins questions).
See attached for the full prog.
Any problems or queries, just let me know.
Hope to hear from you soon.

Best,
Lisa

11 Complete the table with expressions from the emails.

	Formal/Neutral	Informal
Greeting		
Request		
Mention of attachment		
Additional information		
Future contact		
Ending		

12 The replies to the two emails are below, but they are jumbled. Decide which sentences go with which email and put them in the correct order.

	1	2	3	4	5	6	7
Email 1 (formal)	a						g
Email 2 (informal)	h						n

a Dear Ms Conti,
b Sorry, but I won't be able to make it this year as I've already got something on.
c Once again I would like to apologise for not attending this year and for any inconvenience caused.
d I am afraid that I will be unable to attend the conference this year due to a prior engagement.
e If you want, I can see if I can find someone to step in.
f Anyway, sorry again for not coming and I hope it doesn't put you out too much.
g Yours sincerely, James Hammond
h Hi Lisa,
i Thank you for your email of 5 February inviting me to speak at the conference in Milan, Italy.
j Please let me know about any other stuff you are doing in the future.
k If you wish, I could recommend one of my colleagues to speak in my place.
l Thanks for the invite to talk at the conference in Italy.
m Please do not hesitate to contact me should you organise another conference in the future.
n Best, James

13 Complete the table with expressions from the two replies in Exercise 12.

	Formal/Neutral	Informal
Thanking		
Giving bad news		
Offering help		
Apologising		
Future contact		

14 From your analysis of the four emails, list the general features of formal and informal language.

In informal language: missing out words, …

15a Work with a partner. Choose one situation each and write an email.

1 Your college or workplace is opening a new building. Last week, you saw a television news item about the project. There was an interview with a former employee who worked in the old building for fifty years. Write an email inviting him/her to make a speech as part of the opening ceremony.
2 A friend is returning soon from a study trip abroad. Write an email inviting him/her to give a talk to a group who will go on the same study trip this year. The talk should be about his/her experiences, and give some 'survival' tips.

15b Peer-checking Exchange your email with your partner. Check your partner's email for mistakes, using the system below.

Unlike notes which are only for you to understand, writing needs to be accurate to communicate effectively. People will also judge you on the accuracy of your writing, whereas they may judge speaking on communicative ability alone. Readers need to GRASP your message:

> **G** – Grammar: check it!
> **R** – Register: is the level of formality correct and consistent?
> **A** – Appropriacy of vocabulary: is it the right meaning and register?
> **S** – Spelling
> **P** – Punctuation (commas, full stops, capital letters, etc.)

15c Write a suitable reply to your partner's email.

2 Environment
2.1 LOCAL ENVIRONMENT

The environment is everything which isn't me. Albert Einstein, 1879–1955, German-born physicist

LISTENING AND VOCABULARY
LOCAL ENVIRONMENT COLLOCATIONS

1 Work with a partner and answer the questions.

1   What sort of area do you live in? Choose words from the box.

| urban | rural | suburban | residential | traditional |
smart   inner-city   coastal   up-and-coming
long-established   recently developed

2   How would you describe your area to a visitor?

2 2.1 Listen to three people taking part in a survey about their local area. Complete the table.

	1	2	3
Type of building			
Where they live			
What they like			
Problems			

3 Complete collocations 1–20 with the words in the boxes. Listen again to check.

| atmosphere | hour | house | area | pollution |
| rate | environment | farm | points | activities |

1 detached _____
2 rush _____
3 desirable _____
4 noise _____
5 natural _____
6 wind _____
7 cultural _____
8 cosmopolitan _____
9 crime _____
10 recycling _____

| abandoned | friendly | apartment | mindlesss | traffic |
| transport | renewable | environmental | urban | open |

11 _____ neighbourhood
12 _____ spaces
13 _____ connections
14 _____ vandalism
15 _____ congestion
16 _____ energy
17 _____ issue
18 _____ cars
19 _____ block
20 _____ environment

PRONUNCIATION

4 `2.2` **Collocations** Underline the main stress in each collocation in Exercise 3. Then listen and check.

READING

5 Work with a partner and discuss this list of problems. Which are the worst, do you think? Can you add any others?

- noise from traffic
- people drinking in the street
- young people/children misbehaving
- abandoned vehicles
- noise from neighbours
- graffiti
- litter/rubbish
- dog mess
- vandalism

6 Read the article and answer the questions.

1 How many people took part in the survey?
2 Which groups of people have a particular problem with noisy neighbours?
3 According to the survey, how many people have protested to their local government, the police or to their neighbours?
4 According to the article, why is transport noise not a bigger problem?

7a Match words or phrases in the article with their meanings 1–8.

1 results (paragraph 1)
2 survey (paragraph 1)
3 subjects often discussed or argued about (paragraph 2)
4 size/level (paragraph 3)
5 become unaffected by (paragraph 4)
6 closely connected with (paragraph 4)
7 not thinking about other people's feelings (paragraph 4)
8 something very important (paragraph 5)

7b Match the highlighted phrases in the article with functions 1–4.

1 introduce who asked for the survey (2 phrases)
2 gives the purpose of the survey (1 phrase)
3 compare two results of the survey (2 phrases)
4 introduce facts from the survey (3 phrases)

8a Identifying similarities and differences Look again at the facts in the article and make notes on the similarities and differences between the article and your country in general, and your local area.

8b Work with a partner to summarise your ideas.

SPEAKING AND WRITING

9 Work with a partner to discuss solutions to the problems you identified in Exercise 5.

10 Write a paragraph summarising your solution to one of the problems.

NEWS

Noisy neighbours and all the things that drive us mad

BY ROSS LYDALL

Noisy neighbours, uncollected litter and graffiti are among the things that really annoy us, according to a new survey. The findings come from a Mori poll of more than 2,000 residents in three UK cities – London, Dundee and Newcastle.

The government-commissioned survey revealed that other issues, such as dog mess and abandoned vehicles, also cause so much anxiety that they can affect our quality of life. Designed to measure how people respond to noise, the survey also established the extent to which we are troubled by other anti-social problems.

While almost one in three people said noisy neighbours were a problem, they placed it eighth on a list of what troubled them most. They were more than twice as concerned about litter and rubbish – the main problem to affect their quality of life. They said noise was a problem of similar scale to abandoned cars and drinking in the street. However, the effect of noisy neighbours ranked much more highly among residents already dissatisfied with their home – jumping to second place. It is also the second biggest quality-of-life issue among residents in medium- or high-rise flats.

The study – carried out for the Department for Environment, Food and Rural Affairs – found that loud music, shouting and banging attracted far more complaints than noisy parties. As many as two in five people annoyed by noise have complained to their council or the police, while one in four have complained directly to neighbours. The survey finds that while people are able to develop 'immunity' to traffic and trains, they see neighbourhood noise as being synonymous with a 'lack of consideration'.

The Environment Minister said tackling noise pollution was a government priority.

READING AND VOCABULARY
THE ENVIRONMENT

1 Work in groups and discuss these questions.

1 Can you give an example of extreme weather in your country?
2 What are the causes of climate change?
3 What effects of global warming can be seen today?

2 Match words 1–10 with their meanings a–j.

1	emissions	6	habitat
2	fossil fuels	7	ecosystem
3	deforestation	8	glaciers
4	species	9	drought
5	extinction	10	famine

a a group of animals or plants of the same kind
b when a type of animal or plant stops existing
c the natural environment in which a plant or animal lives
d a long period of weather when there is not enough water
e fuels such as coal or oil that are produced by animals or plants decaying over millions of years
f when a large number of people have little food for a long time and some people die
g all the animals and plants in an area and their relationship to each other and their environment
h substances that are sent out into the air
i a large mass of ice that moves slowly down a mountain valley
j when all the trees in an area are destroyed

3 Read the article and complete gaps 1–8 with headings a–j. There are two extra headings.

a	Melting glaciers	f	More wildfires
b	Spread of disease	g	Sea level rise
c	Arctic sea ice is shrinking	h	Increased flooding
d	Decline in polar bears	i	More intense hurricanes
e	Increased drought	j	Threats to forests

4 Read the article again and decide what these numbers refer to.

1.1–6.4	20–30	two-thirds	2005	442
90	2000–2009	50		

5 Identifying sources Underline all the sources in the article and answer the questions.

1 What information are they linked to?
2 What phrase (e.g. *according to*) is used?

6 Work with a partner and discuss the questions.

1 Which of the effects of global warming do you think is the most dramatic?
2 If you could save one species at threat from extinction (e.g. polar bears, tigers, gorillas, giant pandas), which would it be?
3 'Global warming is a myth.' Do you agree?
4 What can people do to be more environmentally friendly?

Climate change impacts

The effects of warming on our world can be seen today

The Earth could warm between 1.1 and 6.4°C this century if we fail to reduce emissions from burning fossil fuels and deforestation – devastating the natural world we love.

Impacts on the world around us

Loss of species

Thousands of species risk extinction from disappearing habitat and changing ecosystems. According to the IPCC, climate change will put some 20–30 percent of species globally at an increasingly high risk of extinction, possibly by 2100.

1 _____

Arctic sea ice is the polar bear's feeding habitat. As sea ice disappears, the death rate of bears rises. The US Geological Survey has warned that two-thirds of the world's polar bear populations could be lost by the mid-century as sea ice continues to retreat.

Coral whitening

Coral reefs are highly sensitive to small changes in water temperature. Heat causes corals to lose the algae that feed them, which leaves coral white. Continued warming could cause coral whitening to become an annual event within the next few decades, destroying many reef ecosystems.

2 _____

The US Geological Survey reports that slight changes in the climate may result in sudden changes in ecosystems. These may be impossible to reverse. The Rocky Mountains in Canada and the US have been losing their forests at a worrying rate since 2000 due to the increase of tree-killing insects.

Thinning ice, rising seas

Rising seas are one of the most certain effects of global warming, as warming ocean waters expand and melting glaciers, ice caps and ice sheets add more water to the oceans.

3 _____

Satellite images show that the extent of Arctic summer sea ice has been melting at an increasing rate and almost 9 percent of it has disappeared per decade since 1979.

4 _____

A recent IPCC report predicts that sea levels could rise 25–38 centimetres by 2100 if current warming patterns continue.

5 _____

A 2005 survey of 442 glaciers from the World Glacier Monitoring Service found that 90 percent of the world's glaciers are shrinking as the planet warms.

Threats to people around the globe

Extreme weather will become more frequent – and more dangerous. The World Meteorological Organisation reported that 2000–2009 was the hottest decade on record, with eight of the hottest 10 years having occurred since 2000.

6 _____

The recent IPCC report concludes that very heavy rain has increased in frequency during the last 50 years and that global warming has been a factor.

7 _____

There have also been increased periods of drought, particularly in parts of Africa and Asia suffering from famine. According to the National Centre for Atmospheric Research, the percentage of the Earth's surface suffering drought has more than doubled since the 1970s.

8 _____

Diseases such as malaria could become more difficult to control in areas where it is currently too cold for them to spread year round. As temperatures rise, diseases can grow.

GRAMMAR
PRESENT PERFECT SIMPLE AND CONTINUOUS

7a **Read these sentences that describe a similar situation and answer the questions.**

a   I've been working for the US Geological Survey for the last three months on a temporary contract.

b   I've worked for the US Geological Survey for three months now and this is my last day in the office.

1   Which sentence uses the present perfect simple? Which uses the present perfect continuous?
2   Do both sentences refer to the same period of time?
3   Do both sentences refer to a time starting three months ago and lasting up to now?
4   Which sentence emphasises a completed action?
5   Which sentence sees the action as temporary and incomplete at the moment that it is talked about?

7b **Underline examples of the present perfect simple and the present perfect continuous in the article. Why has the writer used these forms in each case?**

➥ **Language reference and extra practice, pages 126–149**

8 **Complete the sentences with the present perfect simple or present perfect continuous form of the verbs in brackets. Sometimes both forms are correct.**

1   In Iceland, the ice _____ (disappear) at an alarming rate.
2   The Dead Sea _____ (shrink) at the rate of one metre per year.
3   Rising sea levels mean that some reclaimed land in low-lying areas _____ (already/vanish).
4   I _____ (work) on the environmental project all year.
5   The Environment Agency _____ (send) over 115,000 warnings to people at risk of flooding.
6   The environmental lobby _____ (try) to get the government to reduce CO_2 emissions for ages.
7   Some scientists _____ (question) the impact of climate change.
8   The IPCC _____ (just/publish) their latest report.

SPEAKING

9 **Work in groups. Talk about your environment using the present perfect simple and continuous. Discuss some of these topics.**

- the weather
- wildlife
- sea levels
- the seasons
- endangered species

Our class has been paying a lot of attention to local environmental news over the past couple of years, and we now know that honey bees have been disappearing at an alarming rate. A top scientist has warned that these bees could be wiped out in a few years.

SPEAKING AND LISTENING

1 Work with a partner to brainstorm everything you know about volcanoes in two minutes.

2 Guess the answers to this quiz.

What do you know about Volcanoes?

Decide if these statements are true or false.

1   Volcanoes are a natural way that the Earth and other planets have of cooling off.
2   The biggest volcano on Earth is Mauna Loa in Hawaii.
3   Most volcanoes are found around the rim of the Atlantic Ocean.
4   There are volcanoes around the coastline of Antarctica.
5   There are no underwater volcanoes.
6   About fifty volcanoes erupt each year.
7   The temperature of lava flows can reach 1,250°C.
8   People can never go inside volcanoes.
9   There is a large volcano under Yellowstone Park in the USA.
10 Vesuvius is a famous active volcano in Italy.

---

3 [2.3] **Listen to someone talking about volcanoes and answer the questions.**

1   What is the situation?
2   What is the relationship between the speaker and the listeners?
3   How many questions are asked?

4 **Listen again and check your answers to the quiz.**

GRAMMAR
INDIRECT QUESTIONS

5a **Look at the direct questions below. Then look at Audio script 2.3 on page 169, find exactly how they were asked and write them in the table.**

Direct questions	Indirect questions
1 What is the biggest volcano in the world?	*Can I ask what the the biggest volcano in the world is?*
2 Can people go inside volcanoes?	
3 Is Vesuvius an active volcano?	
4 Why do volcanoes stop erupting?	
5 Is the Chilean Copahue volcano safe for local people?	

5b **Why does the professor use a direct question (*What is a volcano?*) and the students use indirect questions?**

5c **Look again at the indirect questions in Exercise 5a. Are these statements true or false?**

1   We use the word order of affirmative statements in indirect questions.
2   We use *if* or *whether* to introduce indirect *yes/no* questions.
3   We do not use the auxiliary *do* in present simple indirect questions.
4   Indirect questions always end with a question mark.

➥ Language reference and extra practice, pages 126–149

6a **Change the direct questions into indirect questions. Use introductory phrases from Exercise 5a.**

1   How high is Mauna Loa?
    I'd like to know how high Mauna Loa is.
2   How many volcanoes erupt each year?
3   What causes a volcano to erupt?
4   What is the biggest volcano in the USA?
5   Which volcano has been showing a lot of activity recently?
6   When did Vesuvius destroy Pompeii?
7   When did Vesuvius last erupt?
8   Do a lot of people live near Vesuvius?

6b **Work with a partner. Ask and answer the indirect questions in Exercise 6a. Look at Audio script 2.3 on page 169 to help you.**

READING

7 **Read the extracts from Bill Bryson's *A Short History of Nearly Everything* on page 21 quickly and number the topics in the order they are mentioned.**

a   a famous Italian volcano
b   the evacuation of Yellowstone
c   the width and thickness of the Yellowstone volcano
d   the author meeting the park geologist
e   earthquakes

8 **Read the extracts again and answer the questions in your own words.**

1   What does the title, *dangerous beauty*, mean?
2   What are the approximate dimensions of Yellowstone Park?
3   Why, if Yellowstone blew, is 'the cataclysm pretty well beyond imagining'?
4   Does Doss know how much warning would be given if Yellowstone was 'going to go'?
5   Why does Doss say that warning signs of an eruption would not be easy to predict at Yellowstone?
6   Why would evacuating Yellowstone 'never be easy'?

VOCABULARY
ADVERBS

9 **Match the highlighted adverbs in the extracts with adverbs in the box with a similar meaning.**

deliberately   mainly   normally   perhaps   relatively
slowly and carefully

Yellowstone:
DANGEROUS BEAUTY

YELLOWSTONE, IT TURNS OUT, IS A SUPERVOLCANO. It sits on top of an enormous hot spot, a reservoir of molten
5 rock that begins at least 2,000 kilometres down in the Earth and rises to near the surface, forming what is known as a superplume. The heat from the
10 hot spot is what powers all of Yellowstone's vents, geysers, hot springs and popping mud pots. Beneath the surface is a magma chamber that is about
15 72 kilometres across – roughly the same dimensions as the park – and about 13 kilometres thick at its thickest point. The pressure that such a pool of
20 magma exerts on the crust above has lifted Yellowstone and its surrounding territory about half a kilometre higher than they would otherwise be. If
25 it blew, the cataclysm is pretty well beyond imagining.

'It may not feel like it, but you're standing on the largest active volcano in the world,' Paul Doss,
30 Yellowstone National Park geologist, told me soon after climbing off an enormous Harley-Davidson motorcycle and shaking hands when we met at the
35 park headquarters at Mammoth Hot Springs early on a lovely morning in June.

I asked him what caused Yellowstone to blow when it did.
40 'Don't know. Nobody knows. Volcanoes are strange things. We really don't understand them at all. Vesuvius, in Italy, was active for three hundred
45 years until an eruption in 1944 and then it just stopped. It's been silent ever since. Some volcanologists think that it is recharging in a big way, which
50 is a little worrying because two million people live on or around it. But nobody knows.'
'And how much warning would you get if Yellowstone was going
55 to go?'
He shrugged. 'Nobody was around last time it blew, so nobody knows what the warning signs are. Probably you would
60 have swarms of earthquakes and some surface uplift and possibly some changes in the patterns of behaviour of the geysers and steam vents but,
65 nobody really knows.'

'So it could just blow without warning?'
He nodded thoughtfully. The trouble, he explained, is that
70 nearly all the things that would constitute warning signs already exist in some measure at Yellowstone. 'Earthquakes are generally a precursor of
75 volcanic eruptions, but the park already has lots of earthquakes – twelve hundred and sixty of them last year. Most of them are too small to be felt, but they
80 are earthquakes nonetheless.'

Evacuating Yellowstone would never be easy. The park gets some three million visitors a year, mostly in the three peak
85 summer months. The park's roads are comparatively few and they are kept intentionally narrow, partly to slow traffic, partly to preserve an air of
90 picturesqueness, and partly because of topographical constraints. At the height of summer, it can easily take half a day to cross the park and
95 hours to get anywhere within it.

Extract from Bill Bryson's *A Short History of Nearly Everything*

SPEAKING

10a Work in groups of three. Read one short text each about a volcano and make notes on the key points.

Student A: look at page 155.
Student B: look at page 157.
Student C: look at page 161.

10b Presenting Take turns to give a one-minute presentation on your volcano from your notes. At the end of each presentation, ask the presenter polite questions about their volcano.

▶ MEET THE EXPERT

Watch an interview with Dr Andrew McGonigle, a volcanologist, about active volcanoes.
Turn to page 150 for video activities.

SCENARIO
SPARROW HILL WIND FARM

SITUATION

A British power company has identified a good site for a wind farm in the north of England. The proposal is for a wind farm of eighty turbines over a large area. Each tower will be 60 metres tall and have a turbine which is 35 metres in diameter. The wind farm will cover an area of several kilometres and take five years to complete.

As fossil fuels such as coal, gas and oil are being used up, governments are keen to find alternative sources of energy, especially those that do not emit carbon dioxide. Nuclear power is one possible source, but many people have doubts about its safety. Renewable energy sources include solar, wave and wind power. The UK Government is keen to use these sources of power, and hopes to generate 15 percent of its energy needs from renewable sources by 2020. However, some people feel that onshore wind farms spoil the landscape, particularly in countryside areas where they are usually sited. Many people argue that they are unpleasant eyesores which damage the enjoyment of areas of outstanding natural beauty. Other people argue that wind power is simply not reliable as an energy source, as wind is variable and unpredictable.

1 Read the situation and background information above and answer the questions.

1   What sources of energy are mentioned? What advantages and disadvantages are given for the energy sources?
2   Which facts and figures indicate that the wind farm will be large?

2 2.4 **Listen to a government official talking to a power company representative. They are discussing the proposed wind farm. Answer the questions.**

1   What is the attitude of each speaker to a public meeting?
2   What is John Reynolds worried about?
3   What do they decide in the end?

KEY LANGUAGE
AGREEING AND DISAGREEING POLITELY, POLITE QUESTIONS

3a Put words from the conversation in the correct order. Use contractions where necessary.

1   looking / one / it / way / is / but / at / that / of
2   are / because / right / you / absolutely
3   like / I / know / to / would
4   point / you / have / but / a / think / do / not / you
5   interested / I / knowing / am / in
6   very / is / true / that / because
7   go / there / I / because / you / along / would / with

3b Listen again and check your answers.

4 Practise saying the expressions. Pay careful attention to pronunciation and use contractions.

TASK
ATTENDING A FORMAL MEETING

PUBLIC MEETING

To discuss the **Sparrow Hill wind farm** proposals

Date: 15 July | **Time:** 7 p.m.

Venue: Merlin Sports Centre

All welcome

committed to greener energy

5a Work in groups of five. You are going to attend the public meeting. Read your role cards and prepare for the meeting. You can add your own ideas.

Student A: look at page 155.
Student B: look at page 157.
Student C: look at page 161.
Student D: look at page 163.
Student E: look at page 163.

5b Hold the meeting. Ask your questions and give your opinions. Try to persuade the other people at the meeting to accept your ideas.

5c Meet as a class. Report back on the result of your meeting.

6 What do you think would happen in your country with a similar proposal?

USEFUL PHRASES

Asking polite questions

Could you tell me (if/what) … ?
I was wondering (if/what) …

Putting your point of view across forcefully

I'm absolutely certain that …
I really believe that …
There's no doubt in my mind that …
I'm totally convinced that …

Being diplomatic

That's a good point, but …
Yes, I see what you mean, but …

STUDY SKILLS
DESIGNING A QUESTIONNAIRE

1 Questionnaires are used to gather data for surveys and reports. They usually provide up-to-date information or find out people's attitudes and behaviour.

1 If you have answered a questionnaire recently, what was it about?
2 Which organisations frequently use questionnaires to gather information?
3 Which of the following are you most likely to answer: postal, telephone, or online questionnaires? Why?

2 `2.5` **Listen to a lecturer giving a presentation about questionnaires. Answer the questions.**

1 What two key points does she mention about designing questionnaires?
2 What two types of question are mentioned?
3 Which type of question will provide more information?

3 Listen again and complete the sentences. Use a maximum of three words for each sentence.

1 Short questions are better because if you ask long ones, people won't bother _____.
2 Open questions allow people to answer _____.
3 With closed questions, the person answering has _____.
4 It takes a lot longer to analyse the answers to _____.
5 When using open questions, it is important to ask for only one _____.
6 Questions should be clear and well structured so that people can see the point _____.
7 At the start of a questionnaire, you should ask _____.
8 When designing a questionnaire, you need to look ahead and consider how you're going to _____.

4a Question types **Look at extracts A–G from a questionnaire and match them with the descriptions 1–7.**

Descriptions of question types

1 Closed questions requiring the answer 'yes' or 'no'.
2 Questions which require a respondent to indicate how frequently they do something.
3 Questions requiring respondents to tick items in lists or boxes.
4 Questions requiring a choice between alternatives.
5 Questions which require a figure or limited number of words.
6 Open questions beginning with *what, who, why*, etc.
7 Questions which require the respondent to choose a number on a scale.

A What department are you in? ....
How many students are in your class? ....

B Tick the boxes which apply to you.
  1 undergraduate ☐
    postgraduate ☐
    other ☐

  2 course ☐
    research ☐

C Do you feel stressed during your studies?
Yes ☐
No ☐

D Put a cross (×) on the scale to indicate your level of stress.
(1 = no stress, 5 = average stress, 10 = very stressed)
|...|...|
① 5 ⑩

E What do you think are the main causes of stress for students?

F Which would you prefer?
  a fewer course assignments and more tests and examinations
  b fewer tests and examinations and more course assignments

G How often do you feel stressed? Circle the appropriate letter.
  a never
  b rarely
  c sometimes
  d often
  e always

4b Work with a partner and discuss the advantages and disadvantages of using each type of question.

5a Look at these questions from a questionnaire. Tick the good questions and cross the poor questions.

5b Work with a partner and discuss how to improve the 'poor' questions. Suggest alternatives.

ENERGY QUESTIONNAIRE

1 How old are you? Tick the appropriate box.
15–20 ☐   20–30 ☐   30+ ☐

2 Do you believe it is necessary to save energy in the home? Tick the appropriate box.
Yes ☐   No ☐

3 Do you have a gas boiler and is it new and fuel-efficient?

4 Do you replace light bulbs in your house/flat?

5 Which of the following energy-saving activities are you doing? Tick the appropriate boxes.

Wearing jumpers and cardigans in the house to keep heating at a low temperature. ☐

Having fewer baths and more showers. ☐

Driving an energy-saving car (e.g. a hybrid car). ☐

Using as few lights as possible and turning them off as soon as you don't need them. ☐

Installing solar panels to light and heat your house. ☐

WRITING SKILLS
WRITING A QUESTIONNAIRE

6 Read about the Save Our Earth organisation. What issues do you think SOE will list in the questionnaire they are going to prepare? Note down a few key environmental issues.

Save Our Earth (SOE) is an environmental organisation founded two years ago. It aims to raise awareness among young people of environmental issues and to encourage them to take action to protect the environment.

Members of SOE are meeting to prepare a questionnaire which will be sent to young people aged 15–30. The questionnaire will gather information about young people's attitudes to a number of environmental matters.

7 **2.6** Listen to the first part of an SOE meeting. What basic information about respondents will SOE ask for?

8 Listen again. Note down the issues they plan to include in their questionnaire. Are they the same as the ones you chose in Exercise 6?

9 **2.7** Listen to the next part of the meeting and tick the questions which will be included in the questionnaire.
1 How important each issue is for them.
2 Why they chose the most important issue.
3 What they do to protect the environment.
4 How aware and worried respondents are about each issue.
5 If respondents are able to give money to SOE.
6 If respondents are willing to join SOE's campaigns.

10a Work in groups of four and choose one of these tasks.
1 You work for SOE. Each student chooses one issue from Exercise 8. Write six questions to find out the respondents' attitude to your issue.
2 You are going to do a questionnaire about issues in your place of study/work. Each student chooses one issue that interests them (e.g. sports/catering/parking facilities, how clean the building is, etc.). Write six questions to find out the respondents' attitudes to your issue.

10b Show your questions to other members of your group. Correct the questions if there are any errors.

10c Suggest two more questions for each issue.

10d Prepare the questionnaire, adding the basic questions about the respondents from Exercise 7.

3 Sport

3.1 FAIR PLAY

Serious sport has nothing to do with fair play. George Orwell, 1903–1950, British author

SPEAKING

1a Work with a partner. You have three minutes to think of a different sport for each of these categories.

Name a sport where:

1 people often get injured
2 people wear special clothes
3 people have physical contact
4 you can only do it indoors
5 you can only do it outdoors
6 you usually compete as an individual
7 you are part of a team
8 you compete against the clock
9 animals are involved
10 men and women compete together

1b Work with a different partner to compare your ideas.

2 Discuss the questions about the sports you listed in Exercise 1a. Give reasons for your answers.

1 Which sport is the most competitive?
2 Which is the most dangerous?
3 Which has the most complicated rules?
4 Which is the most difficult to be good at?
5 Which is the most exciting to watch?
6 Which would you like to take up?

READING

3 Read the article about football quickly and match headings a–h with paragraphs 1–6. There are two extra headings.

a More than a player
b Breaking the rules
c Taking football further
d A football education
e A final honour
f The world's favourite sport
g The best player in the world
h Only for pleasure

4 Read the article again. Are these statements true, false or not given?

1 Miller played football professionally.
2 Miller was educated in England.
3 Miller scored a lot of goals.
4 Brazil first played against England in 1914.
5 Miller played for several teams in England.
6 Brazil has won the World Cup four times.
7 Miller has a football move named after him.
8 Miller started a football club in Brazil.

5 Underline all the words in the article which refer to people in sport. Match the words with these people.

Someone who:

1 watches sport
2 loves sport
3 teaches sport
4 makes sure rules are followed
5 plays a sport without being paid

6 Justifying opinions **Work with a partner to discuss these questions.**

1   Do you think football is 'the beautiful game'? Why?/Why not?
2   Which other sports do you think are beautiful? Why?
3   Miller felt football is about participation and doing your best, not money. Do you think this is still true today?

VOCABULARY
IDIOMS

7a Many idioms are based on sport, and on football in particular. Complete the idioms with the words in the box.

ball	eye	field	game	goal	goalposts

1   be on the _____
2   move the _____
3   take your _____ off the ball
4   a level playing _____
5   a whole new ball _____
6   score an own _____
7   start the _____ rolling

7b Match the idioms with their meanings.

a   a completely new or different situation
b   able to think or react very quickly
c   start something happening
d   change the rules/limits, making something more difficult
e   lose concentration
f   do or say something which has the opposite result to your intention
g   a fair situation

8 Work in groups of three. Pick two or three idioms from Exercise 7 to talk about experiences you have had.

I remember a time when someone moved the goalposts on me. A lecturer gave me an essay title and I did a lot of work on it. Then two weeks later he completely changed the title!

Charles Miller
Father of the beautiful game

1 _____

Football is the most popular spectator sport in the world – possibly the only global sport – and Brazil is arguably the greatest footballing nation in the world, having won the World Cup more times than any other country. Even people who are not keen on football have heard of Pelé, often considered the world's greatest player. However, how many football fans are familiar with the name of Charles Miller and his contribution to what Pelé called 'the beautiful game'?

2 _____

Known as the father of Brazilian football, Charles William Miller was born on 24 November 1874 in São Paulo to a Scottish father and Brazilian mother. In 1884, young Charles was sent to school in England, where he learned to play both football and cricket. Miller became skilled in running with the ball, heading and taking free kicks.

3 _____

In 1894, Miller returned to Brazil with two footballs and a copy of the rules of football. The São Paulo Athletic Club (SPAC) had been formed in 1888 by a group of British men who played mainly cricket. Miller persuaded them to take up football. He was also instrumental in setting up the Liga Paulista, the first football league in Brazil. Over the first twenty years of the next century, state championships were formed throughout Brazil and in 1914 the first national side played against Argentina.

4 _____

Miller was not only a great player, but also an excellent coach and administrator. In Brazil, he spent a lot of time and effort teaching and coaching Brazilians. After retiring as a player, he continued to be a referee until the age of fifty.

5 _____

When football became professional in Brazil in 1933, Miller was disappointed and decided to have no more contact with the game. He felt that sportspeople should be amateurs – he didn't like the introduction of money and business into sport. For Miller, football was a game, and about participation and doing your best, not money.

6 _____

Charles Miller's memory lives on in the skilful individual game which is Brazilian football. It is also kept alive in another way. When the São Paulo sports writers association brought out a dictionary of football terms in Portuguese, only one word survived from the vocabulary of the past: the *charles* or *chaleira*. Named after Charles Miller, it is a clever pass with the heel of the foot. The exciting ball skills of all the great Brazilian players, including Pelé, owe something to the pioneering spirit of Charles Miller and his passion for the game of football.

LISTENING

1 Work with a partner to tell each other about any martial arts you know. Think of five reasons for doing martial arts.

2 [3.1] **Listen to Kevin Coles talking about his experiences. What is his connection to martial arts?**

3 Listen to Kevin Coles again and put the topics in order.

a   when he got his black belt
b   how often he trains
c   how long he has been doing karate
d   how children react to getting a belt
e   his oldest student
f   different belts
g   having an impact on people
h   how adults react to getting a belt

4 [3.2] **Now listen to the second part of the interview. Answer the questions.**

1   Is karate a hobby or a way of life for most people?
2   Give at least two reasons why people start karate.

5 Reacting to the topic **Work with a partner to discuss the questions.**

1   After listening to this interview, are you motivated to take up a martial art? Why?/Why not?
2   How inspirational do you find Kevin Coles as a teacher?

READING

6 Read the leaflet quickly. What is its purpose?

University Shotokan Karate Club

Learn karate – the ultimate in self-defence and fitness

The university karate club was founded in 1962 and several members of our club have gone on to compete at national level.

5   All grades from beginners to advanced are welcome. The classes are suitable for both men and women.

TUESDAYS AND THURSDAYS | 6–8 p.m.
WEAVER HOUSE GYM
FIRST LESSON FREE

10   Unfortunately, over the last few years, assaults on innocent people have increased. Each of us has some ability to defend ourselves, but by learning a form of self-defence, we are not only increasing that ability, but also doing something to build our own sense of self-respect. Karate will show you a lot of simple and effective techniques
15   to protect yourself, giving you increased self-confidence.

Far too many people think martial arts are about violence. Martial-arts training is based on a lot of respect, self-discipline, self-control and non violence. We learn basic etiquette, courtesy and tolerance. Good manners and consideration for others are expected at all times.

20   Karate is the practice of blocking and striking techniques for the purpose of self-defence, health and self-development. Karate exercises the entire body. Techniques are practised on both sides of the body, therefore muscle imbalances do not occur and the strength, coordination, flexibility and agility of both sides of the
25   body are improved. Regular training in karate improves the body's physical stamina and suppleness. It also helps concentration and produces the mental calm and assurance that come from knowing we can defend ourselves.

Karate has many benefits, but they do not come easily or overnight.
30   Training requires ongoing commitment and hard work. Some of you will give up, but a few of you will get your black belt!

7 Read the leaflet again. Are these statements true, false or not given? Correct the false statements.

1 Benefits from karate come very quickly.
2 It is important to train on both sides of the body.
3 There has been an increase in violence recently.
4 The founder of karate was Gichin Funakoshi.
5 There is a free introductory lesson.
6 There is a karate championship every year.
7 The word *karate* means 'empty hand'.
8 Self-defence classes increase our ability to defend ourselves and build self-respect.

8 Read the leaflet again and cross out the options below that are *not* correct. (You can cross out one, two or three options.)

1 Classes are suitable for
 a beginners.
 b intermediate students.
 c women.
 d children.
2 Martial arts are based on
 a violence.
 b self-defence.
 c respect.
 d self-discipline.
3 Which of the following does karate improve?
 a stamina
 b concentration
 c politeness
 d aggression
4 Which of the following relate to the physical aspects of karate?
 a flexibility
 b agility
 c courtesy
 d suppleness

VOCABULARY
SELF-, ABSTRACT NOUNS

9a Find all the words beginning with *self-* in the leaflet and match them with these meanings.

1 being happy about your character and abilities
2 the certainty that you can do something successfully
3 behaving calmly and sensibly even when you are angry, excited or upset
4 the use of force to protect yourself when you are attacked
5 making yourself do the things you should do
6 becoming better at something

9b Underline the most appropriate combination with *self-* in each sentence.

1 He shot her in *self-defence / self-respect*.
2 He lost his *self-control / self-development* and screamed.
3 It is difficult to keep your *self-respect / self-control* when you have been unemployed for a long time.
4 He can only develop *self-defence / self-confidence* if he is told he is good and clever.
5 The children are so badly behaved. They have no *self-confidence / self-discipline*.

10a Find the abstract nouns in the leaflet related to the following adjectives.

agile   calm   coordinated   courteous
flexible   tolerant

10b Which three of the words in Exercise 10a are related to the body? Which two of the words are related to polite behaviour?

GRAMMAR
QUANTIFIERS

11a Look at the quantifiers in the box. Then find and underline the quantifiers in the leaflet.

almost no   almost none   far too much   hardly any
(a) little   much   none

11b Divide the quantifiers into three groups: those used with plural countable nouns, those with uncountable nouns and those used with both.

> **GRAMMAR TIP**
> All of the quantifiers can be used with *of + the/my/ these*, etc. + noun/pronoun.
> *Hardly any of my friends are taking exams this year.*

➥ Language reference and extra practice, pages 126–149

12 In which sentences does the phrase in bold mean 'not many/much'? In which does it mean 'some'?

1 I'm pleased to say that **a few** of you will get your black belt next year.
2 Unfortunately, **few** of you are likely to pass the exam.
3 There's **little** time to practise for the grading next week.
4 We've got **a little** time left. What shall we practise?

13 Correct the mistakes in the sentences.

1 Several my friends have taken up volleyball recently.
2 Far too much children lack discipline these days.
3 Could you give me little help?
4 A little of the parents take up martial arts with their children.
5 Hardly any the spectators left before the end of the game.
6 It's great that we managed to get few tickets.
7 This sport is so new that we have a little information about it.

14 Make sentences from the prompts that are true for your country by adding a quantifier. Compare your answers with a partner.

1 people do karate
2 women play football
3 people spend money watching sport in stadiums
4 children do regular exercise
5 children eat healthily
6 children spend time doing sport

Children spend a lot of time doing sport in my country.
Not many people in my country do karate.

READING

1 **Work with a partner to discuss the questions.**

1   Which sportswoman/women do you most admire? Why?
2   How do you think they got to the top of their sport?

2 **Read the article quickly and answer the questions.**

1   What is it about?
2   What is the main point?
3   Is it from an encyclopaedia entry, an academic book or a blog?
4   Who do you think the writer is?

3a **Read the article again and match questions a–d with gaps 1–4 in the article.**

a   Why am I doing this?
b   Why do Olympic athletes push themselves to the limit?
c   Can this become obsessive?
d   Don't they know what it takes to get there?

3b **The writer uses nine questions in the article. Why do you think she does this? What is the effect?**

4 **Inferring** **Based on the article, which sentences are true about the writer in real life, do you think? Why?**

1   She is a professional triathlete.
2   Her first sport was rugby.
3   She started competing for the British and Scottish triathlon team at the age of fourteen.
4   She once said, 'Anyone that knows me knows I train all hours of the day.'
5   She usually trains four to six hours a week.
6   She has retired from triathlons and now plays for the Scottish Women's rugby team.

5 **Work with a partner and answer the questions.**

1   Do you admire the writer, or do you think her obsessiveness is unhealthy? Why?
2   Have you ever made sacrifices in order to achieve something? If so, what?

SPORT › GETTING TO THE TOP

[1] _____ We miss birthday parties, ruin family holidays and skip nights out, but there is a very good reason for making such sacrifices.

'We're worried about you,' said my friend from across the table. He was worried that I had no longer become fun to train with and that I was in danger of being left with only a world championship jersey and no one to share it with.

I could have become angry or defensive. Don't they know how hard it is to be at the top in sport? [2] _____ However, deep down I knew elements of what he was saying were right. I was always tired and every workout had a mental intensity that seemed too much for most to handle. I was pushing the limits and extremes beyond what most thought were healthy.

These are the demons I face as a professional athlete on a day-to-day basis. Who am I doing this for? How much is too much?

[3] _____ How can I be so selfish? What are the sacrifices for?

I think of countless birthday parties I have missed or nights out I have sidestepped, ruining a family holiday in France because of the endless search for a swimming pool to train in, almost missing my brother's wedding because I was too busy hiring a car in downtown Johannesburg and driving through the 'no-go' areas in order to do a group ride with the local triathletes. The list is endless.

It boils down to this: I was born with an inordinate amount of drive and determination. From a small girl, I would stay in at lunchtime just to get ahead on class work rather than go out and play; I would get the bus on my own at ten years old and go to swim 100 lengths of the pool while other kids played on floats; I was the only girl in a rugby club of 250 boys. I have always lived my life to extremes. Call it unhealthy if you want, but that is the way I roll, no matter what it is I'm applying myself to.

Being a professional athlete is no different. If you want to be an Olympic champion, it's all about that little extra thing you have done in your preparation that will set you apart from your competitors.

[4] _____ Absolutely. But if your dream is to be the best and reach the podium, you had better be obsessive about your sport. In the words of the British triathlete Alistair Brownlee even if it means getting injured, 'I'd prefer to have three or four cracking years of winning stuff than having ten years of being average.'

6a Find words or phrases in the article with these meanings.

1   when you give up something important in order to get something more important
2   strength
3   something that is much greater than usual
4   the refusal to let anything prevent you from doing what you have decided to do
5   to make someone different from or better than other people
6   thinking about something all the time

6b Complete the sentences using words or phrases from Exercise 6a.

1   Esther Vergeer was so dominant in her sport due to her _____ and mental toughness.
2   Her parents _____ a lot of _____ to give her a good education.
3   Serena Williams says she is a perfectionist and _____ about tennis.
4   Usain Bolt's speed _____ him _____ from other competitors.
5   The reporter was surprised by the _____ of Mike Tyson's emotions.
6   Some athletes cannot deal with the _____ of sporting success and failure.

GRAMMAR
DEFINITE AND ZERO ARTICLES

7a Find the phrases from the box in the article.

the table	the sacrifices	push the limits	the best
drive	Johannesburg	the only girl	birthday parties

7b Complete the rules about the definite and zero articles using the phrases in Exercise 7a.

We use the definite article *the*:
• when we mention a noun a second time (e.g. *the pool*). *The* may be used on a first mention if it is when we refer to something unique (e.g. ¹_____).
• for superlatives (e.g. ²_____).
• with known things that are local and very familiar to most people in the context and do not need to be introduced or explained (e.g. ³_____).
• with certain idioms (e.g. ⁴_____).
• with countries which include Republic, Union, Kingdom, States, Emirates (e.g. *the United Arab Emirates*) and plural names (e.g. *the Philippines*).

We use the zero article:
• with proper nouns, i.e. the names of people and places (e.g. ⁵_____).
• with plural countable nouns referring to things in general (e.g. ⁶_____).
• with uncountable nouns referring to something in general (e.g. ⁷_____).

➥ Language reference and extra practice, pages 126–149

8 Edit the text about Esther Vergeer. Find and correct seventeen mistakes in the use of articles.

According to Richard Krajicek, Esther Vergeer is, 'maybe most successful athlete of all the time'. The wheelchair tennis champion from Netherlands retired in 2013 after going over ten years unbeaten, ending one of most amazing careers in any sport.

Last time she lost was on 30 January 2003 in the Sydney. She went on to win her next 470 matches.

She took number one spot in her sport in 1999 and won first of her four gold Olympic medals in Sydney in 2000. She won her last Olympic gold beating Aniek van Koot in Paralympics final in the London in 2012. She will not now surpass longest run of wins in sport – 555 by the Pakistani squash legend, Jahangir Khan.

Vergeer started playing the wheelchair tennis at age of eight after losing the use of her legs following the spinal surgery.

She is an ambassador of the Laureus foundation for the children with disabilities. The children are encouraged to develop and express themselves.

Roger Federer praised her, 'She is an astonishing athlete, a huge personality, and she has achieved one of most amazing feats in our sport.'

PRONUNCIATION

9 3.3 Weak forms of *the* Listen carefully to five sentences. Is there a definite article before these nouns in the sentences? Use the context to help you.

1   university
2   university
3   game, captain
4   tennis players, wrist injuries
5   tennis players, courts

SPEAKING

10a Work with a partner. Choose the four most important things you need to get to the top in sport. Then rank them 1 (most important) to 4.

aggression	intelligence	stamina	patience
mental toughness	strength	positivity	humility
concentration	self-discipline		

10b Work with another pair to explain your choices.

▶ MEET THE EXPERT

Watch an interview with Dr Elizabeth Pummell, a sports psychologist, about the science of sports psychology.
Turn to page 150 for video activities.

SITUATION

1a Work with a partner. Write the names of two famous sportspeople for the sports in the box.

athletics	baseball	basketball	boxing	football
golf	ice hockey	motor racing	swimming	tennis

1b Work with another pair to compare your choices.

2 Read the situation and answer the questions.

1 Why has the sports channel decided to have a competition?
2 What does the channel mean when it says 'modern sportsperson'?
3 How will the winner be chosen?

A new television channel, Global Sports, has just started broadcasting. To attract viewers' interest, it has announced a competition to decide the greatest modern sportsperson, male or female. The channel has invited viewers to email the sportsperson they consider to be the greatest in the last ten years. They have to make a case for their chosen sportsperson. The writers of the most interesting emails will be invited to the studio to take part in a debate. They will present their case and attempt to persuade the audience that their sportsperson should win the competition. Finally, a vote will be taken and the winner announced.

3a Work in small groups. What should be used as the criteria for choosing the greatest modern sportsperson? Choose the six things which you consider to be most important.

- age
- nationality
- achievements
- exceptional qualities
- strengths compared to the competition
- charisma
- status as a role model
- fame
- ability to overcome difficulties
- contribution to their sport

3b As a class, agree on six criteria to be used in the competition. Then transfer your criteria to the scorecard in Exercise 8b.

4 ⬛ 3.4 Listen to a short talk about Yuna Kim, the Korean ice skater. Listen and answer the questions.

1 Why did Yuna have problems practising her skating when she was young?
2 How successful were her skating programmes in the 2010 Olympic Games?
3 Besides skating, what other talents does Yuna have?

Pelé

Carl Lewis

KEY LANGUAGE
USING EMPHASIS AND COMPARISON

5a Listen again. Note the words and phrases that the presenter uses to emphasise her points. Think about the language below.

- adjectives – *an outstanding achievement*
- adverbs – *a truly remarkable sportswoman*
- expressions – *Above all*

5b Check your answers in Audio script 3.4 on page 171. The emphatic words/phrases are in bold.

5c Look at Audio script 3.4 again and underline words or phrases which are used to make comparisons.

the greatest

6 Put the sentences in order.

1 Pelé / Brazilian / was / footballer / a / fantastic / truly
2 incredibly / Jessica Ennis / sportswoman / is / talented / an / versatile / and
3 considered / female / best / player / soccer / history / in / is / the / Mia Hamm / to / be
4 What's / Serena Williams / about / is / determination / her / extraordinary
5 Usain Bolt / perhaps / greatest / the / is / modern / athlete / times / in
6 Compared / Federer / tennis players / are / not / versatile / to / other / most / as
7 Lionel Messi / skilful / than / most / footballers / more / is / far / other
8 Li Na / unbelievable / to / win / the / US Open Championship / tennis / played
9 Yuna Kim's / performance / was / about / What / its / elegance / remarkable / was
10 is / so / Yi Shiwen / about / her / amazing / What / youth / is
11 Babe Ruth / all / was / baseball / arguably / the / player / greatest / of / time
12 In / Ayrton Senna / a / far / driver / Michael Schumacher / was / than / better / opinion / my

TASK
GIVING A PRESENTATION

7a You are attending a television debate on the greatest modern sportsperson. You are going to give a short talk (two to three minutes) on your outstanding modern sportsperson. Choose one of the options below.

1 Choose one of the personalities on page 164.
2 Choose a sportsperson you know well. (Someone active in the sport within the last ten years.)

7b Prepare your talk by making notes. Organise your talk so that you cover as many of the criteria as possible.

8a Work in groups of four and make your case for your sportsperson. When you listen to the other presentations, ask questions at the end of each one. Then fill in the scorecard for each sportsperson (see below). Do not put a score for your own choice.

8b After the presentations, add up the scores and decide on the winner.

Criteria	Sportsperson's name		
1			
2			
3			
4			
5			
6			
TOTAL			

Marking code: 4–5 = outstanding, 2–3 = good, 0–1 not good

If you have no information about a sportsperson for one of the criteria, give a score of 3.

Martina Navratilova

Mohammed Ali

Babe Ruth

STUDY SKILLS
UNDERSTANDING ESSAY QUESTIONS

1 What makes a good essay? Make a list.

It should have a clear structure ...

2a Understanding key words Work with a partner. Look at the essay questions and discuss what you think each question is asking. Underline the key words.

1 <u>Analyse</u> the reasons why the bad behaviour of spectators at sports events has increased in recent years.
2 Compare and contrast the achievements of two sports stars.
3 To what extent is winning the most important aspect of sport?
4 Account for the success of Association Football around the world.
5 Outline the benefits of children doing sport at school.
6 Top sportsmen and women are paid too much. Discuss.
7 Describe the role of a captain in team sports.

2b Match words and expressions from the essay questions in Exercise 2a with meanings a–g.

a give reasons for, explain
b give a description of the main features or characteristics of something
c look at in detail
d talk about how far something is true or not
e give both sides of an argument (e.g. for and against)
f briefly give (the positive aspects)
g show how two or more things are similar or different

3a `3.5` **Essay writing Listen to a lecturer who has just finished a study skills workshop and is answering questions. What questions do the students ask?**

3b Listen again and complete the notes about essay writing using one word for each gap.

Notes

Preparing to write
1 _____ the title – 2 _____ the key words.
3 _____ what kind of structure the title indicates.
4 _____ some notes.
5 _____ your ideas.
6 _____ yourself questions.
7 _____ your notes.

Writing
Use the beginning, 8 _____ and 9 _____ approach.
In the first paragraph you should 10 _____ the question in your own words and 11 _____ the topic.
In the final paragraph you should 12 _____ back to the question and 13 _____ your own opinion (if needed).

Language
Academic writing tends to be 14 _____ in tone.
Try to leave 15 _____ out of your writing.
16 _____ structures are common.
Avoid 17 _____ and contractions.

---

4 Work with a partner. Choose one of the essay titles from Exercise 2a, analyse it and discuss what you would include in it.

Top sportsmen and women are paid too much. Discuss.

1 In recent years, the amount of money earned by top sportsmen and women has risen and attracted a lot of media attention. Stars of high-profile sports such as football, golf, tennis, boxing and motor racing often feature in lists of the world's richest people. The objective of this essay is to decide if these sportspeople should receive such large amounts of money.

2 It is true that not all sports stars are very well paid, but certain individuals do earn an enormous amount. The earnings of these sports stars come from a number of sources. Firstly, there are the huge salaries for some stars, for instance footballers. Secondly, there is the prize money available for winning major sporting competitions and trophies. Finally, and perhaps most lucrative for many top sports stars, are sponsorship deals and advertising contracts.

3 Many people argue that these stars deserve their earnings for a number of important reasons. Sports players provide entertainment, like any well-known actor or pop star. They are professional people at the top of their chosen career. In simple terms, they are the best at what they do, and should be paid accordingly. They have put in years of training to be as good as they can be at their sport.

It can also be argued that most sports stars have a relatively short career, and so need to earn a lot of money in a short time to support them when they retire. In some sports, there is a risk of serious injury and death. Sportsmen and women should be compensated for this risk.

4 In contrast, some people argue that it is wrong to pay sports stars these huge amounts of money when there is so much poverty in the world. Sports stars do not save lives or really contribute much to society, apart from providing entertainment, which can be seen as unnecessary. It is also clear that these sports stars often have extravagant lifestyles, appearing in celebrity magazines and generally not using their wealth in a positive way. Some, even though they are role models for young people, actually behave very badly.

5 In conclusion, it is obvious that there are differences not only between sports, but also between individuals in the same sports. On balance it can be said that sports stars are worth the money they earn, as they have the ability to enhance people's lives by their achievements. They manage to unite whole countries during significant competitions, which is something even politicians are rarely able to do.

WRITING SKILLS
A FOR AND AGAINST ESSAY

5 Work with a partner. How do you feel about the amount of money top sportspeople earn?

6 Read the essay and answer the questions.
1 Which sports are mentioned?
2 What sources of income are mentioned?
3 What is the writer's opinion?

7 Read the essay again and match ideas a–e with paragraphs 1–5.
a arguments against the proposition
b conclusion and opinion
c introduction and restatement of question
d arguments for the proposition
e background information

8a Introductions Which of the following might you find in the opening paragraph of this type of essay?
1 your opinion
2 a context for the question, or background information
3 your aim/target (i.e. what you are going to argue in the essay)
4 a restatement of the question
5 arguments and examples
6 a recommendation

8b Look at the introduction of the essay and check your answer.

9a Two common ways of starting an introduction are to talk about changes over time or to generalise about the current situation. What do opening expressions 1–7 do? Which tenses are used with each?
1 Over the last twenty years, …
2 Many people nowadays, …
3 In the past decade, …
4 Since the late 1990s, …
5 These days, …
6 For centuries, …
7 At the present time, …

9b Look again at the essay questions in Exercise 2a and write some opening sentences using phrases from Exercise 9a.

10 Formal expressions Match formal expressions in the essay with meanings 1–8.
1 My aim here is to look at … (paragraph 1)
2 like (paragraph 2)
3 A lot of people feel … (paragraph 3)
4 In other words, … (paragraph 3)
5 On the other hand, … (paragraph 4)
6 It also seems to me that … (paragraph 4)
7 To sum up, … (paragraph 5)
8 Overall, … (paragraph 5)

11a Work with a partner to discuss the essay questions.
1 There is too much emphasis on winning in sports today. Discuss.
2 Sports involving animals should be banned. Discuss.
3 Men are more interested in sport than women. Discuss.

11b Choose one essay to plan together. Then write your essays individually, using the notes you made in Exercise 3b, the structure in Exercise 7 and expressions from Exercise 10.

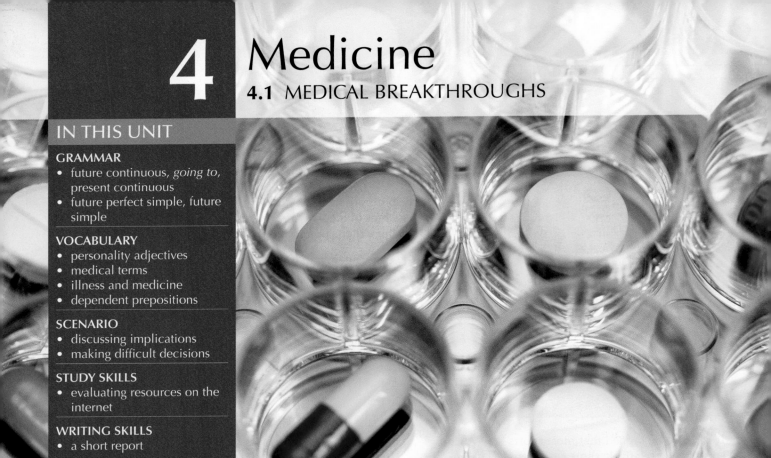

4 Medicine
4.1 MEDICAL BREAKTHROUGHS

Always laugh when you can. It is cheap medicine. Lord Byron, 1788–1824, English poet

SPEAKING AND LISTENING

1 **What do you think are the most important personal qualities for someone who works in the medical profession? Choose your top three from the box. Can you add any others?**

authoritative	calm	efficient	knowledgeable
objective	open-minded	patient	reassuring
sensitive	sociable	sympathetic	

2 **4.1** **Listen to an interview with a doctor. Tick the points that he mentions.**

A good doctor:
1   knows the names of all his/her patients.
2   uses everyday language rather than medical terms in discussions with patients.
3   considers using alternative treatments such as hypnosis, acupuncture and aromatherapy.
4   tells people how to live a healthy life.
5   listens with sympathy to people who are not really ill.
6   usually prescribes medication (e.g. anti-depressant tablets).
7   thinks carefully about the cost of any treatments.

3 **Work with a partner to discuss the statements. Which do you agree with? Give reasons.**

VOCABULARY
MEDICAL TERMS

4a **Look at the words in the box and find the following.**
1   six people who work in medicine
2   six treatments or types of drug
3   six medical conditions

Alzheimer's	anaesthetist	antibiotic	arthritis
cancer	chest infection	diabetes	heart disease
injection	midwife	morphine	painkiller
pharmacist	physiotherapy	psychiatrist	
radiologist	surgeon	transplant	

4b **Complete the sentences with words in the box.**
1   A doctor writes a prescription, but you need to take it to a _____ to get the medicine.
2   After my operation, I had _____ twice a week for three months until I could walk again.
3   They found an organ donor in time, so it looks like the _____ will go ahead as planned.
4   People who suffer from _____ need to take insulin or regulate their diets.
5   People with eating disorders, like anorexia and bulimia, are usually treated by a _____.
6   Some drugs are best given to patients by _____.
7   Often caused by poor diet, _____ is the biggest killer in the western world.

PRONUNCIATION

5 4.2 Stressed syllables Mark the stressed syllable on the words in Exercise 4a and decide what the stressed vowel sound is. Listen and check your answers.

READING

6 You are going to read about some important medical advances: X-rays, penicillin, aspirin, anaesthesia. Work with a partner. What do you know about these medical breakthroughs (e.g. what they are and when they were discovered)? Share your ideas.

7a Work with a partner. You will each read two texts. Make notes about the medical advances, using the questions below. You may not find answers to all the questions.

- what?
- where?
- who?
- when?
- how?
- results/benefits?
- problems?

Student A: look at the texts on this page.
Student B: look at page 165.

7b Using your notes, tell your partner about the two breakthroughs.

8a Ranking by importance Work with a partner. Agree on a ranking of the four medical advances in the texts (put the most important first).

8b Now think of two more medical inventions that you think are very important (e.g. the thermometer, the scalpel).

8c Join another pair and justify your choices.

SPEAKING

9 Work in small groups and discuss the questions about medicine and the medical profession.
1 Should people have to pay for healthcare?
2 Do you think nurses and midwives are paid enough in your country? Why?/Why not?
3 Soon, medical advances will allow people to live to a very old age. Is this desirable? Why?/Why not?
4 Should new drugs be tested on both animals and humans before being prescribed by doctors?

ASPIRIN

Aspirin is one of the most effective painkillers in the world. Hippocrates, a Greek physician, wrote in the 5th century about a powder made from the willow tree, which could help aches and pains and reduce fever. However, it was not until 1897 that Felix Hoffmann, a German chemist, synthesised the ingredient acetylsalicylic acid to treat his father's arthritis. This was the first synthetic drug, which means it was a copy of something already existing in nature. Aspirin was patented on 6 March 1899. It was marketed alongside another of Hoffmann's products, a synthetic of morphine, called heroin, which he invented eleven days after aspirin. To start with, heroin was the more successful of the two painkillers and was thought to be healthier than aspirin. However, aspirin took over and has become the world's best-selling drug. In 1969, it even went to the Moon with Neil Armstrong. Today, it is still one of the most effective painkillers, despite having a number of side effects. Aspirin is also effective against many serious diseases such as heart disease, diabetes and arthritis.

ANAESTHESIA

Anaesthesia is a way of preventing patients from feeling pain during surgery. Crawford Williamson Long was the first person to use ether as an anaesthetic during operations in 1842. Then on 30 September 1846, in Boston, Massachusetts, William Morton, an American dentist, performed a painless tooth extraction after giving ether to a patient. He also gave the first public demonstration of the use of ether to anaesthetise a patient on 16 October 1846. Following the demonstration, Morton tried to hide the identity of the substance as he planned to patent it and profit from its use. However, it was quickly shown to be ether, and it was soon being used in both the USA and Europe. It was then discovered that ether could catch fire easily, so in England it was replaced with chloroform. Nevertheless, Morton's achievement was the key factor in the development of modern surgery.

LISTENING

1 Which illnesses are the biggest killers in your country, and in the world? Do you know what scientists are doing to try to prevent these illnesses?

2 [4.3] Listen to a talk by Professor John Dodge, honorary Professor of Child Health at the University of Wales, Swansea. Which of these does he mention?

- **Diseases:** high blood pressure, asthma, polio, diabetes, dengue fever, malaria
- **People who pay for drugs:** insurance companies, major hospitals, state health services
- **International agencies:** the World Health Organisation, the World Bank, the United Nations, the European Union

3a Listen again and take notes.

3b Work with a partner. Take turns to summarise the main points in thirty seconds.

4 Reacting to the topic Work in small groups and discuss the questions.

1 Who should pay for medicines in poor countries?
2 Which disease/diseases do you think deserves the most research money spent on it? Why?

READING

5 Is malaria a problem in your country? What do you know about malaria and ways of fighting it?

6 Scan the texts to find the following.

1 two universities
2 two famous people who were killed by malaria
3 three continents where malaria is common
4 the leader of the study in the journal
5 the name of the parasite that spreads malaria
6 the name of a scientific journal
7 the date of Africa Malaria Day
8 the language that the word *malaria* originates from

7 Read the texts again. Are these statements true, false or not given?

1 It is not possible to recover from malaria.
2 Genetically modified mosquitoes could reduce mosquitoes which spread wild dengue fever.
3 Many scientists are trying to modify bacteria that live in mosquitoes.
4 Currently malaria is prevented by bed nets.
5 Professor Crisanti thinks it would be possible to introduce genes which will make mosquitoes target animals rather than humans.
6 The number of deaths from malaria is rising.
7 The study has had success in getting the genetic modification to spread effectively in large mosquito populations.

8 Work with a partner to discuss the questions.

1 Which do you think are the three most interesting facts about malaria, and why?
2 Are there any ethical issues around using genetically modified technology?

Facts about malaria

- The word *malaria* comes from the Latin for 'bad air'.
- Malaria is spread by the single-celled parasite plasmodium and it is endemic in parts of Asia, Africa and Central and South America.
- Symptoms of malaria include neck stiffness, fits, abnormal breathing and fever.
- Malaria kills over 600,000 people a year – more people than any infection apart from HIV/Aids.
- Pregnant women and children are at high risk of dying from the complications of severe malaria.
- 90 percent of malaria deaths occur among young children in sub-Saharan Africa.
- Every minute a child dies from malaria.
- Alexander the Great, Oliver Cromwell, Dante, Tutankhamen and Genghis Khan died of malaria.
- John F. Kennedy, Mother Theresa, Dr David Livingstone, Abraham Lincoln and Mahatma Gandhi contracted malaria but recovered.
- Celebrities who have had malaria include Didier Drogba, Cheryl Cole, Michael Caine and George Clooney.
- Malaria killed more people in Italy during World War II than bombs and bullets put together.
- There is currently no effective vaccine against malaria.
- Malaria mortality rates have fallen by more than 25 percent globally since 2000.
- Early diagnosis and prompt treatment of malaria helps prevent death.
- Sleeping under insecticide-treated nets protects against malaria.
- Africa Malaria Day takes place on 25 April every year.

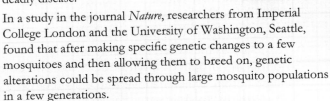

Genetically Modified Mosquitoes Could Dramatically Reduce Spread Of Malaria

Scientists working on malaria have found a way of genetically manipulating large populations of mosquitoes that could eventually dramatically reduce the spread of the deadly disease.

In a study in the journal *Nature*, researchers from Imperial College London and the University of Washington, Seattle, found that after making specific genetic changes to a few mosquitoes and then allowing them to breed on, genetic alterations could be spread through large mosquito populations in a few generations.

This is the first successful proof-of-principle experiment of its kind, they said, and suggests the method may in future be used to spread genetic changes in wild mosquito populations to make them less able to transmit malaria.

'This is an exciting technological development, one which I hope will pave the way for solutions to many global health problems,' said Andrea Crisanti of Imperial's Life Sciences department, who led the study. But the success of a genetic approach depends on getting the genetic modification to spread effectively in large mosquito populations.

VOCABULARY
ILLNESS AND MEDICINE

9 Match words in *Facts about malaria* to their meanings 1–8.

1 a disease in part of your body caused by bacteria or a virus
2 a plant or animal that lives on or in another plant or animal and gets food from it
3 something that shows you have an illness
4 a symptom of illness in which you have a very high body temperature
5 to get a serious illness
6 a substance used to protect people against a disease, which contains a weak form of the virus that causes the disease
7 when a doctor says what illness someone has
8 another illness that happens when someone is already ill

GRAMMAR
FUTURE CONTINUOUS, *GOING TO*, PRESENT CONTINUOUS

10a **4.4** Listen to three people talking about a project to raise money using celebrities. The project plans to deliver mosquito nets to Western Uganda to help prevent malaria. Complete the extracts with the appropriate future form of the verbs in the box.

distribute	film	fly (x2)	meet	raise
spend	wait	work		

1 All the support team ¹_____ out to Kampala at 5 p.m. on Friday. We ²_____ from Heathrow. We ³_____ all ⁴_____ at check-in at 3 p.m. Everyone has been emailed and all the arrangements have been made.
2 The Ugandan team ⁵_____ for the celebrities in the hotel reception on Monday morning at 9 a.m. when the celebrity bus arrives.
3 Then we ⁶_____ the celebrity interviews for the fundraising appeal all Monday morning and then we ⁷_____ the first batch of mosquito nets with the celebrities on Monday afternoon. Tom and I ⁸_____ in Uganda all next month.
4 Some of the celebrities ⁹_____ a few days sightseeing, but no arrangements have been made yet.
5 Well, everything's looking good … and based on the money we've raised so far and the support we've had, I think we ¹⁰_____ a lot more money than last year.

10b Which future form is used in the extracts in Exercise 10a?

a Extract 1
b Extracts 2 and 3
c Extracts 4 and 5

10c Match the future forms in Exercise 10b with meanings 1–5.

1 to talk about a planned action in progress over a certain period of time in the future
2 to talk about intentions
3 to talk about a longer action in the future that will be interrupted by a shorter action in the future
4 to refer to the future when arrangements have been made (e.g. tickets bought, bookings made) and someone is expecting us to do something or be somewhere at a particular time
5 to make a prediction based on present or past evidence

➡ Language reference and extra practice, pages 126–149

11 Choose the correct form. (In some cases, both are possible.)

1 *I'm going to study / I'm studying* medicine, but I don't know where yet.
2 *Will you be passing / Are you passing* the doctor's when you're out? I need my prescription.
3 I can't see you next Monday as *I'm going to start / I'll be starting* my new job that day.
4 *I'm seeing / I'm going to see* the doctor next week.
5 Don't contact me between 2 and 3 p.m. as *I'll be operating / I'm going to operate* on a patient then.
6 We can't deliver the nets because I think *it's going to rain / it'll be raining.*
7 In a few minutes, *we are landing / we will be landing* in Lusaka.
8 I'm having an operation on Monday. *I'll be recovering / I'm recovering* next week and will miss the monthly meeting.
9 *We will be waiting / We are waiting* in the café opposite the station when the train arrives.

SPEAKING

12a Work in small groups. You are going to plan a fundraising day at your college/place of work to help support a malaria charity. Plan the day using the prompts below and your own ideas.

- how you are going to raise money
- how much money you will charge for tickets (adults, students, small children)
- sponsorship
- which celebrities to invite
- how to advertise the day and what publicity you want
- what events and activities you will have on the day (e.g. sports, music, dance, choirs, bands)
- the timetable for the day
- food and drinks

12b Form a new group with people from other groups and summarise your plan.

LISTENING

1 **What medical developments do you think will happen in the next 100 years?**

2 `4.5` **Listen to six doctors and medical researchers predicting what medical developments will take place. Tick the topics which are mentioned.**

1	radiation	4	blindness
2	heart attacks	5	obesity
3	knee injuries	6	cancer

3 **Listen again. Match statements a–i with extracts 1–6. There are three extra statements.**

a People will wear airbag suits to avoid injury to their knees.

b Cancer is probably not going to be a problem.

c We will have developed the ability to diagnose at birth all known genetic diseases.

d Scientists will have created miniature robots capable of performing microsurgery.

e X-rays and radiation will still be around.

f We probably won't be able to grow a baby completely outside a woman's body.

g We will probably find a genetic way to cure the main cause of blindness.

h Most medical education will be done at a distance.

i We will be able to help people exposed to radiation through research in space.

4 **Work with a partner. Which of the developments do you think will be the most useful?**

VOCABULARY
DEPENDENT PREPOSITIONS

5a **Write the prepositions that follow these verbs. Then look at Audio script 4.5 on page 172 to check. Look at Extracts 1, 3, 4 and 6.**

1	focus	5	worry
2	succeed	6	agree
3	suffer	7	protect
4	recover	8	care

5b **Complete the sentences with verbs and prepositions from Exercise 5a.**

1 Has he _____ his illness yet?

2 I feel very lonely and I _____ depression.

3 He spent five years _____ his aged mother.

4 This net should _____ you _____ mosquitoes.

5 Parents are often anxious and _____ their children.

6 The doctor _____ me that while she's sick, she needs a little extra care.

7 You need to concentrate and _____ your exams.

8 You have to work hard if you want to do well and _____ medicine.

6a **Complete the questions with the prepositions in the box.**

about	for	in	on	with

1 What do you complain _____ the most?

2 Who is the most difficult person you have to deal _____ ?

3 What courses have you applied _____ recently?

4 What subject have you / would you like to specialise _____ ?

5 Who can you rely _____ the most?

6b **Work with a partner and ask and answer the questions.**

GRAMMAR
FUTURE PERFECT SIMPLE, FUTURE SIMPLE

7a **Look at these examples of the future perfect simple and choose the correct alternative in the explanation.**

1 By 2120, engineers **will have developed** a 'smart suit'.

2 In 100 years **we will have developed** a way to protect astronauts from radiation.

> **GRAMMAR TIP**
>
> We use the future perfect simple for an action *completed before a point in time in the future / in progress at a time in the future*.

7b **Now complete this rule for the formation of the future perfect simple.**

The future perfect simple = _____/won't + _____ + past participle (e.g. *developed*)

➥ Language reference and extra practice, pages 126–149

8 **Look at Audio script 4.5 on page 172 and underline examples of the following. Do the adverbs come before or after *will* and *won't*?**

1 the future perfect simple

2 the future simple

3 adverbs of certainty (e.g. *certainly, possibly*)

9 **Complete this company announcement using the correct form of the verbs in brackets.**

Anderson Bio-Sciences announces its takeover next week of the Essex-based company HGP. Together, ABS and HGP ¹_____ (form) the largest genetic engineering company in the UK, and by 2025, we ²_____ (expand) to employ over 1,000 people. In addition, by 2025, the company ³_____ (become) the largest employer of medical researchers in the country. HGP has made exciting discoveries about the human chromosome set and we ⁴_____ (publish) that knowledge on the internet. This ⁵_____ (revolutionise) biology and medicine and ⁶_____ (give) researchers huge potential to develop new drugs. In 2025, medical records ⁷_____ (include) people's complete genomes and this ⁸_____ (permit) doctors to treat people as genetic individuals. By 2025, the company ⁹_____ (make) substantial progress towards true 'cloning' of certain organs.

10 **Write five sentences about yourself using the future simple or the future perfect simple. Use time references as well.**

READING

11 Work in small groups to discuss the questions.

1 What do you think are the most exciting recent or current medical breakthroughs?

2 What would you most like to see, smell, taste, hear or touch, if you could only have that sense for one more day?

3 Which of the following do you think are the most important: bionic eyes, bionic arms, bionic hands, bionic legs, bionic nose, bionic tongue?

4 How do some animals sense the world differently to humans?

12 Read the online article about a current medical breakthrough quickly and note down who or what the following are.

1 Dianne Ashworth
2 The Royal Victorian
3 Bionic Vision Australia
4 Penny Allen

13 Read the article again and decide which three of the following could be subheadings (to attract online readers to read the article).

1 Australian woman was first to receive radical implant.
2 Scientists make blind mice see with radical new implant.
3 Dianne Ashworth has spoken for first time of the 'little flash' that signalled the return of her vision.
4 Breakthrough is one of several projects around the world that could restore vision for millions.
5 Researchers hope blind people will be able to move independently.

14a Make notes on the key points in the article. Make sure you cover the following main topics.

- what has just happened
- what the bionic eye is, how it works, who designed it
- future developments and hopes

14b *Retelling a story* Work with a partner and retell the story in your own words.

SPEAKING

15 Work in groups. What do you hope for your country, in terms of health and society? Discuss your hopes for the next fifty years.

I hope my country will have eradicated polio in the next few years and I also hope my country will have improved opportunities for women.

▶ MEET THE EXPERT

Watch an interview with Dr Tina Chowdhury, a lecturer in Musculoskeletal Science, about medical bionics.
Turn to page 151 for video activities.

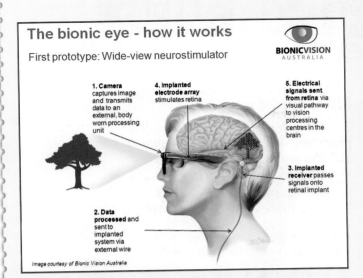

The bionic eye - how it works
First prototype: Wide-view neurostimulator

BIONICVISION
AUSTRALIA

1. **Camera** captures image and transmits data to an external, body worn processing unit

4. **Implanted electrode array** stimulates retina

5. **Electrical signals sent from retina** via visual pathway to vision processing centres in the brain

3. **Implanted receiver** passes signals onto retinal implant

2. **Data processed** and sent to implanted system via external wire

Image courtesy of Bionic Vision Australia

Vision of the future: The bionic eye that could help millions of blind to see again after woman had some sight restored in pioneering tests

Scientists have taken an important step towards helping visually impaired people lead independent lives after a bionic eye gave a blind Australian woman some sight.

Dianne Ashworth, who has severe vision loss due to the inherited condition retinitis pigmentosa, was fitted with a prototype bionic eye in May at the Royal Victorian Eye and Ear Hospital. It was switched on a month later, and today researchers revealed the results.

'It was really funny when it switched on. I was waiting, waiting,' she said. 'I had these goggles on and I didn't know what to expect, and I don't know if anyone did know what I was going to see. Then, all of a sudden, I went "yep" – I could see a little flash and it was like a little, I suppose, a splinter. There were different shapes and dark black, lines of dark black and white lines together. Then that turned into splotches of black with white around them and cloud-like images. I can remember when the first bigger image came I just went "Wow", because I just didn't expect it at all, but it was amazing.'

The bionic eye, designed, built and tested by Bionic Vision Australia, a group of researchers supported by the Australian government, is equipped with twenty-four electrodes with a small wire that extends from the back of the eye to a receptor attached behind the ear. It is inserted into the space next to the retina within the eye.

'The device electrically stimulates the retina,' said Dr Penny Allen, a specialist surgeon who implanted the prototype. Electrical impulses are passed through the device, which then stimulate the retina. Those impulses then pass back to the brain, creating the image. The device restores mild vision, where patients are able to pick up major differences and edges, such as light and dark objects. Researchers hope to develop it so blind patients can walk independently.

'Di is the first patient of three with this prototype device, the next step is analysing the visual information that we are getting from the stimulation,' Allen said.

The operation itself was made simple so it can be readily taught to eye surgeons worldwide. 'We didn't want to have a device that was too complex in a surgical approach that was very difficult to learn,' said Allen.

According to the World Health Organization, 39 million people around the world are blind and 246 million have low vision. ■

SCENARIO
MEDICAL DILEMMAS

SITUATION

1a Work with a partner. Read about the pharmaceutical company RXZ and discuss the questions.

1 In your opinion, was the doctor's mistake very serious, quite serious, or not very serious? Give reasons.
2 What do you think is the best way for RXZ to deal with the problem?

RXZ is an international company with its Head Office in a European country. Like all pharmaceutical firms, it has to deal with problems concerning confidential medical data about the drugs it is developing, and also with ethical issues that arise from time to time.

The Human Resources Department (HRD) is currently dealing with the following problem.

The company often asks doctors to trial new drugs. One of the doctors who frequently does this kind of work for the company didn't tell his patient that he was trialling a new drug. He was doing research for RXZ, but without the permission of the patient. The patient has found out what the doctor was doing and is now threatening to take legal action against RXZ.

1b Work with other pairs and compare your answers.

KEY LANGUAGE
DISCUSSING IMPLICATIONS

2 4.6 Two members of the HRD, Sandra and Hans, are talking about the problem. Which possible solutions do they mention?

1 Emphasise the good qualities of the doctor to gain the patient's cooperation.
2 Advise the patient to continue using the drug and persuade her to take no further action.
3 Offer her money to stop her taking legal action against the company.
4 Explain that the doctor was trying to give the patient the best treatment currently available.
5 Say that there is an effective alternative drug that can replace the drug she is taking.

3a Listen again. The implications of the possible actions are jumbled. Number them in the order you hear them.

a   If we support him too strongly, the press may get hold of the story.
b   It would have a huge impact on our profits.
c   We need to look at the implications of doing it.
d   It could be really bad for our reputation.
e   But it's a risky option.
f   It would also result in other patients coming forward with complaints.
g   That could be a big problem for us.
h   One consequence could be that she'll start negotiating with us.
i   It has a serious disadvantage.

3b Work with a partner. You are senior managers at a hospital. Read the situation, decide what action to take and consider its implications.

A young, inexperienced nurse at your hospital has given the wrong dose of a drug to a patient. Her mistake could have resulted in the patient's death.

TASK
MAKING DIFFICULT DECISIONS

4a Work in small groups. You are members of the Human Resources Department at RXZ. Each person chooses a different problem or issue on page 165. Make notes about the problem/issue so that you can summarise it for the other members of your group.

4b Summarise your problem or issue for your group. Then discuss how to solve or deal with it. Consider the implications of each option that you discuss.

4c Discuss the questions with the class.

1   Which was the most interesting problem/issue?
2   Which decisions from the other groups do you agree or disagree with?
3   Which decision was the most difficult to make?

STUDY SKILLS
EVALUATING RESOURCES ON THE INTERNET

1 Work in small groups. People use the internet for different purposes. Discuss the questions about how you use the internet.

1 What was the most recent thing you looked up on the internet for your studies or work?
2 How many clicks did you take before you found the information you were looking for?
3 For what purposes do you use the internet in your studies or work?
4 How do you use the internet to make new contacts in your field of studies or work?
5 Do you use social networks in your studies or work? If so, how do you use them?
6 Which blogs or forums do you read, follow or contribute to?

2 **4.7** Listen to Jeffrey Davis, a business consultant, talking about how he uses the internet for his work. What three uses of the internet does he mention?

3a Listen again and make notes about these topics.

1 how he deals with the great amount of material on the internet
2 how he finds out about new articles or publications
3 the kind of networking he does
4 the difficulty of keeping up to date with trends and business issues
5 how to make a lot of money in the future from the internet

3b With a partner, compare the way Jeffrey uses the internet with your own use of internet resources. In what ways is your use similar or different? Do you have the same problems he mentions?

3c What did you find most interesting about his talk?

4 When evaluating websites for research purposes, useful information can be found by looking at the domain suffix at the end of the website address. Complete the sentences with the domain suffixes in the box.

.ac	.co	.com	.edu	.gov	.net	.org

1 The domain suffix for companies and businesses is either _____ or _____.
2 Another popular website suffix is _____. It is used by non profit-making organisations.
3 Internet-based companies, such as network providers, frequently use the _____ suffix but it is also used by all kinds of businesses.
4 Educational organisations, such as schools and universities, usually use either the _____ suffix, or the _____ one.
5 The _____ suffix indicates that it is a government website.

5 Work in small teams. You are going to have a competition to test your knowledge of country domain suffixes (e.g. .uk at the end of a website means that it is a United Kingdom-based website). In your teams, try to identify as many of the country websites below in two minutes.

.ru	.de	.tr	.us	.cz	.fr	.ch	.cn	.dk	.uz
.in	.jp	.ar	.br	.ua	.sg	.th	.vn	.it	.hu

6a Work in small groups. Read the suggestions for evaluating websites used for research and choose the six suggestions that you consider to be most useful.

1 You should always find out who runs the website.
2 You need to consider the purpose of the website.
3 It is important to know how old the website is.
4 It is not possible to know in which country a website is based.
5 Websites run by governments are usually fairly reliable.
6 Commercial websites give reliable, accurate information.
7 Professional associations (e.g. scientific societies) are probably a good source of information.
8 A reputable website will not give you links to other websites.
9 A website will be a useful source of information only if it is updated regularly.
10 A website is usually reliable if it contains facts and opinions, and the names of experts.
11 Social networks are the best source for finding new contacts in your field.
12 A good website will often invite responses.
13 Reliable websites will usually give you links to other websites.
14 You need to consider if the writer of the website is objective or biased.
15 It is helpful if the website invites responses and you can see who to respond to.

6b Join another group and compare your choices. Try to agree on the top six choices.

7 **4.8** Listen to a lecturer giving a presentation on evaluating internet resources. Note down her six key points. Then compare her tips with the ones you chose in Exercise 6b. Are they the same or different?

8 Imagine you are going to write a report on hypnotherapy for a serious magazine called *Science Today*. Look up the topic online and choose the three best websites to get information for your article. Compare your choice with other students.

WRITING SKILLS
A SHORT REPORT

9 The government's Health Department plans to provide information about alternative therapies on its internet site. It has asked a consumer research agency, GRS, to write a report on a very popular alternative therapy, homeopathy. Read the report. Are these statements true, false or not given?

1 Mr J. Simmons, Health Department, is the writer of the report.
2 The purpose of the report is to highlight the dangers of homeopathy.
3 Homeopathy was invented by a German scientist.
4 Homeopathy products do not use large amounts of natural materials.
5 Medical experts believe that homeopathy products are effective in treating illnesses.
6 The writer believes that all homeopaths should be registered.
7 The writer advises people not to buy homeopathic products on the internet.

10 Read the report again. Put the topics in order.

a the writer's advice to readers of the report
b what the writer discovered in her investigation
c the subject of the report
d the person who asked for the report
e the writer's opinion of the facts

11 Making recommendations **Report recommendations are usually written in an impersonal style to make it clear that they are based on fact, not just the opinion of the writer. They are often written using a structure which makes the information clear and gives it impact. What impersonal phrase is used to introduce each recommendation?**

12 Rewrite five recommendations using the alternative grammatical structures below.

- *must* + active or passive verb
- *It is advisable to …*
- *It is vital that …*
- *should/might/could* + active/passive verb
- *It is a good idea to …*

Patients must understand that symptoms can get worse before they get better.

13 Choose one of the following tasks. (You work for GRS and both reports have been requested by Mr J. Simmons, Health Department.)

1 Write a report on herbal remedies (i.e. plant-based treatments to improve health). Use the notes on page 166.
2 Write a report on hypnotherapy, using your research from Exercise 8.

14 Work with a partner. Look at each other's reports and try to improve them.

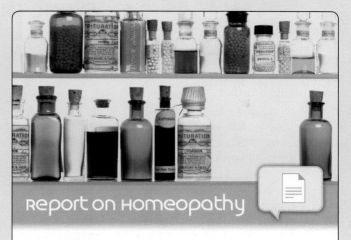

report on Homeopathy

Introduction

This report was requested by Mr J. Simmons, Health Department. It investigates homeopathy and considers whether the therapy is effective and safe. The report was to be submitted by 10 May.

Facts and findings

1 Homeopathy was developed in Germany in the late 1700s. Illnesses are treated with very small samples of natural materials such as plants, minerals and some animal products.

2 Homeopathic prescriptions are tailored to each patient. Two patients may have the same symptoms, but be given different remedies.

3 Homeopathy is considered safe by most users and experts because the ingredients are used in small quantities and are diluted.

4 Some leading medical journals say that the therapy does not have any real benefits. However, some studies have found that homeopathic remedies are 'equivalent to conventional medicines' in treating certain illnesses.

Conclusion

Scientific experts and users of the therapy are divided about its benefits. However, homeopathy is considered to be safe.

Recommendations

It is recommended that patients:
- consult their doctor before using homeopathic remedies.
- get advice from a registered homeopath before taking a remedy.
- understand that symptoms can get worse before they get better.
- read the instructions on homeopathic products carefully before using them.
- buy products from an established outlet, for example a reputable healthcare store.
- think carefully before using products advertised on the internet as they may not be of good quality.

Aileen McGuire
Director, GPS

5 Transport

5.1 GETTING FROM A TO B

Everywhere is walking distance if you have the time. Steven Wright, 1955–, US comedian

LISTENING AND VOCABULARY
TRANSPORT

1 What methods of transport do you use most often?

2a Work with a partner. Add some of your own ideas to the word web.

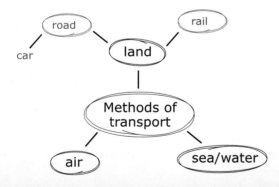

2b What are the advantages and disadvantages of the different methods of transport?

3 **5.1** Listen to four people talking about transport and answer the questions.

1   Which method of transport is each person talking about? Which words helped you decide?
2   How do they feel about the method of transport in general?

4a Match the words and phrases in the box with the methods of transport mentioned in the listening.

fogbound runway	lane closure	low tide
platform alteration	engineering work	lost baggage
delayed sailing	rough weather	signalling problems
long tailback	turbulence	congestion charge

4b Listen again and check your answers.

5 What is your own experience of the transport mentioned in Exercise 3, both in general and the last time you used these methods? (Think about punctuality, convenience, comfort, cost, speed and efficiency.)

READING

6 Work in small groups and discuss the questions.

1 Do you drive? Do you enjoy it? Why?/Why not?
2 If you don't drive, would you like to? Why?/Why not?
3 How do you feel about the quality of driving in your country? What about other countries you have visited?

7a Which of the following do you think are the most important as causes of crashes on the road today? Choose your top three. Then, explain your choices and reasons to a partner.

1 the age of drivers
2 speed
3 the number of cars on the road
4 the weather
5 mechanical problems
6 the sex of drivers
7 the psychology of drivers
8 the quality of roads

7b Read the article below quickly and decide which the writer feels is the most important cause.

8 Read the article again. Which methods below of making roads safer are mentioned? Support your choices with examples.

1 restricting the speed at which people can drive
2 introducing technological innovations to make people slow down
3 educating drivers
4 improving safety features in cars
5 having tough penalties for drivers who break the law
6 introducing an upper age limit for drivers
7 assessing drivers' abilities and issuing of documents
8 introducing street lighting to improve visibility

9 Analysing arguments Read the article again and answer the questions. Then compare your answers with a partner.

1 What are the main points made by the writer?
2 How well do you think the writer supports these points?
3 Which arguments in the text do you find convincing/unconvincing. Why?

VOCABULARY
SAFETY FEATURES

10a Without looking back at the article, complete these safety features.

1 speed _____
2 one-way _____
3 traffic _____
4 _____ cameras
5 seat _____
6 traction _____
7 anti-lock _____
8 air _____

10b Discuss the questions with a partner.

1 Which three of the safety features do you think are the most important, and why?
2 Which do you think are the least popular with drivers in your country?
3 Is there another safety feature you would like to see made compulsory in all cars, e.g. on-board cameras?

SPEAKING AND WRITING

11a Work in groups of three. You are going to have a discussion about the best ways of making the roads safer.

Student A: look at page 155.
Student B: look at page 157.
Student C: look at page 161.

11b Discuss the ways of improving road safety. Decide together which method you think would be the most effective.

11c Report your decisions to the class.

11d As a class, reach a decision as to the best course of action on this issue.

12 Write your recommendations for a report on road safety.

The dangers of safety

Travelling by road is widely accepted as being the most dangerous way to travel, with far more deaths per kilometre than rail, sea or air. In fact, while road traffic injuries represent about 25 percent of worldwide injury-related deaths, fatalities on the road in the UK have been decreasing for some time, with the most recent figure standing at 1,901. We take a look at why the number is decreasing, but why it seems impossible to eradicate fatalities completely.

Over the years, different methods of reducing the number of crashes have been tried. The Locomotive and Highways Act of 1865 introduced the idea of speed limits to the motoring world. Since then, more and more ways of controlling the behaviour of drivers have been introduced, such as one-way streets and traffic signals, as well as compulsory driver testing and licensing. These days, there are many more methods of enforcement, including speed cameras and fines for breaking motoring laws.

Another solution has been to make cars themselves safer in case of an accident. This has resulted in a focus on passive safety or crash survival rather than active safety or avoiding crashes. There are many innovations by motor manufacturers which have made cars safer, such as seat belts, traction control, anti-lock brakes and airbags. At the same time, a lot of attention has also been paid to car interiors. This means cars have got quieter, more comfortable and more luxurious. Taken together, these improvements have tended to make the driver feel more in control and insulated him/her from the fast-moving and dangerous environment outside the car. Given that cars are now safer as these improvements have been made, it is surprising that the number of pile-ups is not decreasing.

Actually, it is wrong to talk about safe and dangerous cars in this way. The key to this problem is not actually the car, but the driver. In fact, making drivers feel safer is not the solution to the problem, it is the cause of the problem. As drivers feel safer, it encourages them to drive aggressively and to ignore other road users and therefore increases the number of crashes. The problem of car safety is not an engineering problem but a psychological one. Ironically, if we want the roads and driving to be safer, we need to make cars more dangerous!

Enforcement cameras

40

LISTENING

1a You are going to hear a news report. Look at the two pictures. What do you think the report will be about?

1b `5.2` Listen and check your predictions.

2 Listen again. Are these statements true, false or not given?

1 The two new ideas involve conventional rocket ships.
2 The space train involves a train carriage in a vacuum tube.
3 One of the inventors of the space train also invented superconducting Maglev.
4 Estimates suggest that building an Orbital Maglev space train that could carry passengers would take 20 years.
5 The space-elevator base station would be located near the equator.
6 A Tokyo-based construction company hopes to have a space elevator operational by 2030.
7 Both ideas would be cheaper than using conventional rocket ships.

3 What other transport developments do you think will take place in the next 50 years? Why will these happen?

READING

4 Read this introduction to an article quickly. Find six reasons why transport will change over the next fifty years. Are they the same as your reasons in Exercise 3?

During the next fifty years, there will be great changes in our means of transport. Some of the new developments will come from our need to depend less on fossil fuels as a source of power. Other developments are likely to respond to the ever-faster pace of society by aiming to increase the speed of different means of transport, and others may pander to the thrill-seeking sections of society by introducing newer and more exciting methods of transport. Looking specifically at traffic on our roads, some developments will reflect our need to reduce traffic congestion. Others will focus on our need to reduce traffic accidents. Finally, some developments will focus on saving wasted commute time.

5 Work with a partner. Read your part of the article. Which two of the reasons given in Exercise 4 does your text describe?

Student A: read Text A.   **Student B:** read Text B on page 158.

A A Chinese company has made a significant contribution to reducing traffic congestion, while making use of existing infrastructure. Cars will be able to drive underneath a giant bus which runs on wheeled 'legs'.

The enormous bus is as wide as two road lanes and carries more than 300 passengers per bus. Preliminary findings suggest the bus network could carry as many as 1,400 passengers at once. The bus will travel at a speed of up to 60 km per hour. Passengers will get on and off at elevated stops and in the event of emergencies, passengers would escape from the bus using an inflatable slide, like on a passenger aircraft. The bus will need to have the roads it runs on redesigned with rails for the bus to run on, or white lines that an automated system can use as guides.

In the future, we will all have to travel in a more carbon-efficient way and it is hoped that each bus could reduce fuel use by 860 tonnes per year, bringing carbon emissions down by 2,640 tonnes. Its designers say it might reduce traffic congestion in China's crowded cities by as much as 30 percent. Traffic jams in rush hour may soon be a thing of the past.

6a Read your text again and make notes on the main points. Include the following.

- what your project is
- which country your project originates in
- what the advantages of your project are

6b Tell your partner about the main points in thirty seconds, using your notes. Do not look back at your text.

7 Evaluating projects Work in small groups and discuss the questions.

1 Which of the four projects (two in the listening, two in the reading) do you find the most convincing?
2 Which would you most like to invest in?
3 Which has the most advantages and solves the most problems?
4 Which has the most potential problems?
5 Which would be most suitable for your country?

VOCABULARY
COLLOCATIONS

8a What word often comes before these nouns?

1	contribution	6	hour
2	congestion	7	advances
3	findings	8	future
4	system	9	impact
5	emissions	10	error

8b Look at the texts again and check your answers.

8c Complete the text with collocations from Exercise 8a.

¹_____ of a study currently being carried out by the Departments of Transport and Health have shown that reducing transport activity by 30 percent will reduce ²_____ and will have a ³_____ on health conditions in the not too ⁴_____. Reducing ⁵_____, especially at peak times like ⁶_____, will improve traffic flow. This will also reduce stress. ⁷_____ in the use of sensors in driverless cars may eliminate ⁸_____ and reduce traffic accidents.

GRAMMAR
MODAL VERBS: ABILITY, POSSIBILITY AND OBLIGATION (FUTURE)

9 Work with a partner. Look at the texts and find ways of expressing future ability, possibility and obligation. Complete the table.

	Ability	Possibility	Obligation
Text A			
Text B			

➡ Language reference and extra practice, pages 126–149

10 Work with a partner. There are grammatical errors in six of these sentences. Correct the errors and discuss what is wrong in each case.

1 Security will must improve in airports in the next twenty years.
2 Astronauts will never be able to travel to the sun.
3 We might work faster than that if we want to meet the deadline.
4 In fifty years' time, we will all have to travel in space because space travel will become much cheaper.
5 In twenty years' time, many of us can travel on magnetic trains.
6 He's had an accident so I'll be able to drive him to hospital.
7 We will need find feasible renewable energy sources in the near future.
8 We will have to apply for our travel visas before the end of the month.

11 Complete the sentences and discuss them with a partner.

1 In five years' time, I'll be able to / I'll have to / I might …
2 In ten years' time, I'll be able to / I'll need to …
3 In twenty years' time, I won't be able to / I won't have to / I might not …

SPEAKING

12 Work with a partner and make predictions about the future to complete the sentences.

1 Governments _____ within the next 20 years.
2 Airline companies _____ in the near future.
3 City councils _____ in the next ten years.
4 Space travel companies _____ in the next 30 years.
5 Flying cars _____ in the near future.

READING AND VOCABULARY
WORDS FROM THE TEXT

1a Look at the photos and guess where these rail journeys are.

1b Read the article quickly and check your predictions.

2 Scan the article and find the following.

1 eight countries
2 two authors
3 a Russian ruler
4 the largest freshwater lake in the world
5 the most luxurious railway in the world
6 the longest railway (and its length)
7 the highest railway (and its height)
8 the highest tunnel (and its height)

3 Read the article again and answer the questions.

1 Why was the toilet water heated on the Quinghai–Tibet line?
2 What did the writer like looking at most on the Quinghai–Tibet line and on the Trans-Siberian?
3 What sort of people travelled on the Orient Express?
4 What does the article say about the luxury of the Orient Express?

4 Find the words in the box in the article. Then complete the sentences.

era	nostalgia	gruelling	altitude	icon
impeccable	nomads	opulence		

1 She was tired after the long and _____ journey.
2 We were impressed by the _____ manners of the smartly dressed porters.
3 The age of the railway brought an _____ of prosperity.
4 He was struck by the _____ of the Blue Train, with its elaborate furnishings and en-suite bathrooms.
5 Breathing becomes more difficult at high _____.
6 The _____ travelled far looking for grass for their animals.
7 The historic _____, Mallard, is the holder of the world speed record for steam locomotives.
8 He had always felt a certain amount of _____ for his life on the railways.

5 Identifying attitude What is the writer's attitude to these journeys? Underline words and phrases which convey his attitude.

6 Which of the railway journeys in the article would you most like to go on? Why?

The golden era of the great express trains conjures up feelings of nostalgia, romance and beautiful views. Last year, my publishers sent me and a photographer on ten amazing journeys as research for a *Great Railways* travel guide. Here are my top three.

In the past, if you wanted to go from Beijing (the capital of China) to Lhasa, the journey was long and difficult, including a gruelling 48-hour bus journey. Now, you can travel from Beijing to Lhasa on the Quinghai–Tibet line, as we did. It still isn't easy, however, and we couldn't get tickets at first because of the bureaucracy – we had to get a special permit to travel through Tibet. The line includes the Tangula Pass – at 5,072 metres above sea level, it's the world's highest rail track. It also includes the 1,338-metre-long Fenghuosha Tunnel, which, at 4,905 metres above sea level, is the highest rail tunnel in the world. On our journey, extra oxygen was pumped into our carriages to counter the high altitude. Even the water in the toilets had to be heated to prevent freezing. The views of the Himalayas were absolutely breathtaking and this is a journey that will live long in my memory.

All train enthusiasts want to travel on the longest and most famous railway of all – the Trans-Siberian Express. It runs from Russia's capital, Moscow, to Vladivostok, on the western shore of the Sea of Japan. It is 9,198 kilometres long, spans eight time zones, and it takes about seven days to complete its journey. We took a more leisurely 14-day journey that included several stops. We succeeded in getting first-class tickets: our sleeping carriages were stylish and luxurious and we had impeccable service and cuisine.

For me, the highlight was skirting the scenic Lake Baikal, the largest freshwater lake in the world. We then travelled via Ulaanbaatar, the capital of Mongolia, and were able to eat in a yurt, the round felt-covered tent traditionally used by Mongolian nomads. It is amazing to think that in 1891, Tsar Alexander III had said, 'Let the railway be built.' And here I was on it. My memories of frosted plains and snowy steppes will always stay with me, but our best memory was making good friends with a wonderful Russian couple, and although they didn't speak much English and we certainly didn't speak any Russian, we managed to communicate very well.

In the past, only the wealthiest could afford the level of luxury offered by the Orient Express. The Express attracted the rich and the famous, including royalty, and was made a household name by writers such as Agatha Christie and Graham Greene. Our journey to London – via Italy, Austria, Switzerland and France – on the Orient Express, with its unmatched comfort, was 31 hours of railway heaven. We boarded in Venice and immediately entered a world of stylish travel. Stepping up on the brass plates to board felt like we were being transported back to the 1920s. We made our way past the restaurant and saloon cars with ladies' drawing rooms, to our cabin in carriage H and enjoyed some of Europe's finest window seats. Everything was done for us – we didn't need to lift a finger. It is an icon of passenger rail. Extravagantly elegant, it has everything – opulence, romance, and the food we were served was out of this world.

GRAMMAR
ABILITY, POSSIBILITY AND OBLIGATION (PAST)

7a Look at the article and underline different ways of talking about ability, possibility and obligation in the past.

We were able to eat in a yurt.

7b Which of the verbs in Exercise 7a are full modals? (Full modals do not change in the third person and are followed by the infinitive.)

7c Choose the correct verb forms.

1 We use *can / was able to / could* to talk about general abilities in the past.
2 We use *must / had to* to talk about obligation in the past.
3 We use *managed to / could* to suggest that we had difficulty in achieving the action.
4 The verb *manage to* is similar to *must / succeed in*.
5 We use the *-ing* form of the verb after *manage to / succeed in*.

➡ Language reference and extra practice, pages 126–149

8 Choose the most appropriate alternative in the text. Sometimes both alternatives are correct.

When we read a fantastic review about the Quinghai–Tibet line, we knew we [1]*weren't able to / had to* go on it. We were so busy before we left London that we didn't [2]*manage to / succeed in* organise the train journey. Once we were in China, we didn't have much access to the internet and [3]*weren't able to / didn't have to* get much information. Still, we found a good travel agency and [4]*could / managed to* get tickets. We travelled first to Golmud and stopped there for only one day, but we [5]*managed to / were able to* pack a lot into it.

The train journey from Golmud to Lhasa takes a day. Although most of it is really high, we didn't have any altitude problems and we [6]*were able to / had to* enjoy the fabulous scenery. It's so high, they have to heat the water in the toilets to stop it from freezing, but we [7]*didn't need to / had to* use them anyway. Our train attendant was very helpful. Her English was not great, but she still [8]*had to / succeeded in* getting her message across and pointing out interesting sights to us, such as herds of wild Tibetan antelopes.

In the past, you [9]*could / were able to* travel to Lhasa from Golmud, but you [10]*couldn't / didn't have to* get there in comfort – you [11]*could / had to* take a slow, uncomfortable bus.

SPEAKING

9a Think of a memorable journey you have been on. Make notes on how you prepared and planned it, and any difficulties you had during the journey.

9b Work with a partner. Tell your partner about the journey.

SCENARIO
BEAUCIEL

SITUATION

1 What kind of transport problems are there in your town/city? What about other major cities in your country?

2 Read the information about Beauciel and look at the map. What kind of transport problems might the city have?

Beauciel, a city in the south of France, is experiencing severe transport problems which are affecting all sections of the community. If the city council can solve the problems, it will improve the lives of everyone who lives and works there. Members of the Planning Department of the city council are studying the problems and looking for ways to provide a better transport system.

3 5.3 Listen to an English-language broadcast for tourists travelling in Europe. Tick the problems that the newsreader refers to. Then write the percentage of residents who mentioned each problem.

Problems relating to transport in Beauciel

- traffic jams
- open-air markets
- air pollution
- on-street parking
- too many cars
- not enough car parks
- too much noise
- unreliable bus services

4 Work with a partner to discuss the questions.

1 How does your city, or a city you know well, deal with the problems in Exercise 3?

2 What solutions can you think of for three of the above problems? Note down your ideas so that you can talk about them at a forthcoming council meeting.

KEY LANGUAGE
THE LANGUAGE OF MEETINGS – SUMMARISING

5 `5.4` Listen to three international consultants, Françoise, Daniel and Kirsten. They are talking about one of the transport problems which particularly worries them. Answer the questions.

1   What is the problem that concerns them most?
2   What solutions do they discuss?
3   What do they finally decide to do?

6a Listen to the conversation again. Tick the phrases for summarising that Françoise uses.

1   OK, let me summarise our discussion.
2   Let me recap, please.
3   So, just to confirm.
4   Right, what have we covered so far?
5   OK, do we essentially have agreement?
6   Right, I'll now sum up.
7   Everyone happy with my summary?

6b Check your answers by looking at Audio script 5.4 on page 174.

TASK
EVALUATING PROPOSALS

7a Work in small groups. You are members of the Planning Department of the city council. Read the proposals below for solving the problems and add any ideas from Exercise 4.

7b Discuss the advantages and disadvantages of each proposal. Choose five of the best ideas for further study and decide whether they can be achieved in the short, medium or long term.

7c Consider the cost of the five proposals you have chosen. How might the city raise the money to pay for them?

7d Join other groups. Discuss and comment on each other's ideas for solving the city's transport problems.

Proposals for solving the traffic problems

1   Introduce a 'congestion charge'. Drivers coming into the city during the day would pay a certain amount of money to the city council each time (e.g. 15 euros for each visit).
2   Increase parking fines by 50 percent – use the money to finance wider roads.
3   Build a new subway system in the city or a ring road round the city.
4   Rebuild the old tram system, using old lines as far as possible.
5   Have free bus transport in the city, with more bus lanes. Introduce big fines for drivers of private cars who use the bus lanes.
6   Put a 'park and ride' scheme into place: drivers leave their cars in car parks outside the city centre, then they catch a special bus into the centre.
7   Build a huge underground car park under the city centre.
8   Increase the road tax on motorcycles by 50 percent to reduce noise.
9   Create more cycle lanes.
10 Have exclusive lanes on busy bus routes for taxis.

STUDY SKILLS
USING GRAPHS, CHARTS AND TABLES

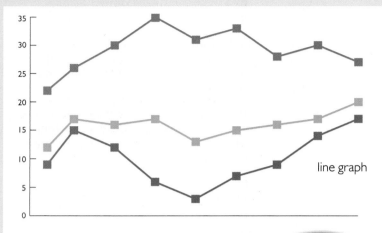

line graph

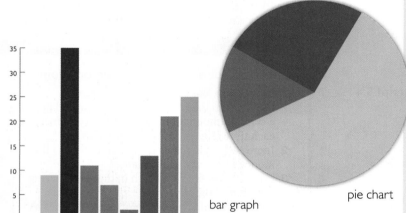

bar graph

pie chart

Euro NCAP ratings for medium family cars			
Vehicle	Adult (%)	Child (%)	Pedestrian (%)
Volvo V40	98	75	88
Audi A3	95	87	74
Seat Leon	94	92	70
Volkswagen Golf	94	89	65
Honda Civic	94	83	69
Seat Toledo	94	80	69
Skoda Rapid	94	80	69

table

1 Graphs, charts and tables are ways of presenting information in a form that is easy to understand. Match each type shown above with one of the descriptions.

1 A _____ shows the different parts of a total amount. For example, it could show the percentage of money that a student spends on entertainment, study materials, clothes, accommodation and food.
2 A _____ is useful for comparing things and showing amounts or quantities at specific times. For example, the percentage of people who own certain products (cars, televisions, etc.) in three different periods.
3 A _____ contains a list of numbers or facts arranged in rows and columns. It could, for example, be a list of results for football league tables.
4 A _____ is useful for showing how things change over time, and for showing two or more sets of measurements which are related to each other. For example, it might show how the number of passengers of an airline has changed from month to month.

2 What would you use to illustrate this information? Give reasons.

1 the amount of rainfall falling in an area each month during a 12-month period
2 the results of a survey of 100 students giving information about the subject they chose to study in their first year
3 the increase in the sales of iPads compared with two other similar tablet computers not made by Apple
4 a comparison of the changes in population in four world regions (Africa, Europe, South America and North America) during three periods: 1900, 1950, 2000

3a Read this internal report for the staff at FlyAway Travel Agency. Create a table to illustrate the information.

FlyAway
NEWSLETTER · SUMMER

Last year, Spain and Italy were the most popular destinations for our customers: 44 percent (Spain 20 percent, Italy 24 percent) chose those countries for their holiday. This compares with 35 percent (Spain 17 percent, Italy 18 percent) the previous year. Similarly, the United States was an extremely popular destination: approximately 22 percent chose to go there whereas only 11 percent of our customers visited the US the previous year. Fewer people, just 12 percent, chose North Africa this year. The figure last year was 15 percent.

Germany and France showed little change over the period. Germany attracted 4 percent of our customers last year compared to 5 percent the year before. However, the number of customers visiting France rose from 5 to 7 percent.

On the other hand, results were very disappointing in the Netherlands, which was visited by only 2 percent of our customers, in contrast to 9 percent the previous year. Although our performance in the Netherlands was below expectations, this was offset by an increase in the number of customers visiting Denmark and Sweden. Six percent chose this destination, which was significantly more than 2 percent the previous year. We see considerable potential in these countries for increasing sales, so we will be spending more on advertising in the area in the future.

Other destinations accounted for only 5 percent of our customers last year, while the figure for the previous year was 16 percent.

3b Now draw a pie chart to show last year's figures only.

3c Compare your table and chart with a partner.

WRITING SKILLS
DESCRIBING INFORMATION IN A TABLE

4a Underline the words/phrases used in the text in Exercise 3a to express comparison and contrast.

4b Comparison and contrast Complete the sentences with appropriate words or phrases from the box. Sometimes more than one answer is possible.

in comparison (to/with)   on the other hand   however   while   whereas   in contrast (to)   by (way of) contrast   far more/fewer   significantly more/fewer   slightly more/less

1   Twenty-four percent of our customers visited Italy, _____ only four percent visited Germany.
2   _____ the United States, our performance in the Netherlands was disappointing.
3   Sales in Denmark and Sweden were _____ than in the previous year.
4   _____ people visited Spain and Italy this year.
5   France was not a good market for us last year. _____, the United States was an excellent one.
6   _____ customers went to Spain and Italy than to France and Germany.

4c Write four more sentences comparing the holiday destinations, using words and phrases from the box.

5 Look at the table below, which shows some of the world's busiest airports by passenger traffic.

Which airport(s):

1   increased the total number of passengers the most?
2   increased the total number of passengers the least?
3   was the highest-ranking European airport?
4   fell to a lower place in the ranking?
5   was the third biggest in handling passengers?
6   had the second highest increase in passengers?

6 Read the summary of the 2012 statistics for passenger traffic. Compare it with the information in the table. Correct the six mistakes in the summary.

The 2012 statistics for passenger traffic at international airports make interesting reading.

Hartsfield-Jackson Atlanta International Airport maintained its ranking between 2011 and 2012. Based in Jackson, USA, it transported just over 95 million passengers, an increase of 3.3 percent compared with the previous year. Beijing Capital International Airport also maintained its ranking in second place. However, the percentage change in the number of its passengers was slightly less than Hartsfield-Jackson Atlanta Airport.

Dubai International Airport had a significant increase in the number of its passengers – 13.2 percent was an impressive performance. Its ranking also rose by three places. Frankfurt had a similar boost in passengers, but its ranking fell by two places.

Hong Kong Airport fell two places in the ranking. On the other hand, it increased its passengers by slightly more than 5 percent. This was a good performance in view of the difficult economic conditions worldwide.

One of the fastest-rising airports was Atatürk International Airport, based in Ismir, Turkey. Its ranking rose by 10 places and the number of passenger by a remarkable 20.6 percent. It handled almost 45 million passengers. Likewise, Shanghai Pudong International Airport increased its ranking and the total number of its passengers.

Overall, the changes in ranking and total passengers were less than in previous years. What is most significant in the 2012 statistics is the increasing passenger traffic at Dubai International Airport, Suvarnabhumi Airport (Thailand) and especially at Atatürk International Airport in Turkey. The Turkish airport has also increased its ranking significantly compared to the other airports in the list.

7 The table on page 135 contains selected rankings of the world's busiest airports by cargo traffic. Write a short description summarising the information in the table. Try to use some expressions of comparison and contrast.

Passenger Traffic at International Airports 2012: 50 airports are included in the ranking.					
Rank	Airport	Location	Total passengers	Rank change	% change
1	Hartsfield-Jackson Atlanta International	Atlanta, Georgia, USA	95,462,867	–	▲ 3.3%
2	Beijing Capital International	Chaoyang, Beijing, China	81,929,359	–	▲ 4.1%
3	London Heathrow	Hillingdon, London, UK	70,037,417	–	▲ 0.9%
4	Tokyo International	Ōta, Tokyo, Japan	66,795,178	▲ 1	▲ 6.7%
10	Dubai International	Garhoud, Dubai, UAE	57,684,550	▲ 3	▲ 13.2%
11	Frankfurt	Frankfurt, Hesse, Germany	57,520,001	▼ 2	▲ 1.9%
12	Hong Kong International	Chek Lap Kok, Hong Kong, China	56,057,751	▼ 2	▲ 5.1%
14	Suvarnabhumi	Bang Phli, Samut Prakan, Thailand	53,002,328	▲ 2	▲ 10%
20	Atatürk International	Istanbul, Turkey	45,124,831	▲ 10	▲ 20.6%
21	Shanghai Pudong International	Pudong, Shanghai, China	44,880,164	–	▲ 8.3%

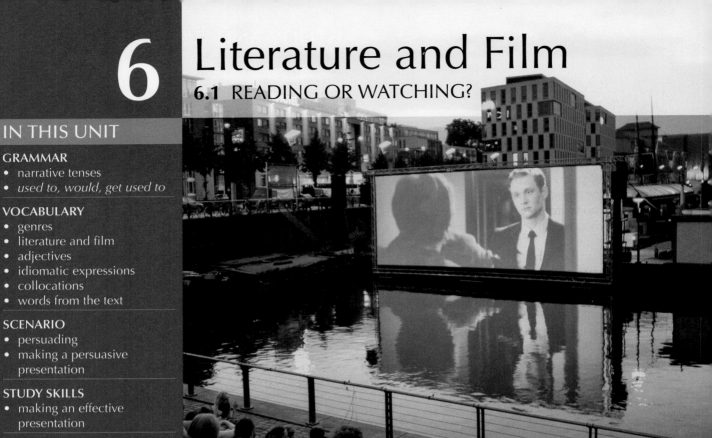

6 Literature and Film

6.1 READING OR WATCHING?

IN THIS UNIT

GRAMMAR
- narrative tenses
- *used to, would, get used to*

VOCABULARY
- genres
- literature and film
- adjectives
- idiomatic expressions
- collocations
- words from the text

SCENARIO
- persuading
- making a persuasive presentation

STUDY SKILLS
- making an effective presentation

WRITING SKILLS
- an online review

I took a speed reading course and read 'War and Peace' in twenty minutes. It involves Russia. Woody Allen, 1935–, US film-maker

VOCABULARY AND READING
GENRES

1 Look at the words and phrases in the box and answer the questions.

1 Which ones describe films, books or both?
2 Which are fiction and which are non-fiction?

autobiography	biography	crime	biopic
costume drama	romcom	novel	horror
play	science fiction (sci-fi)		psycho drama
poetry	short story	thriller	travel writing

2 Work with a partner to discuss the questions.

1 Do you prefer reading books or watching films? What sort of books/films do you like? Why?
2 Can you think of any books you have read and then watched the film afterwards? What was your reaction?
3 Have you ever seen a film which has made you want to read the book afterwards? How did they compare?
4 For what reasons do you think people may find a film of a book disappointing?

3 Read the article on page 57 and compare your discussion in Exercise 2 with the author's ideas.

4 Inferring opinion **Based on the opinions in the article, which of these could the author have said, do you think? Find evidence to support your answers.**

1 'Good books don't often don't make good films.'
2 'Films of books can be well scripted or beautiful to look at, but often boring.'
3 'Writers of the book need to be involved in the film version.'
4 'Children's books made into films can never be considered serious works of art.'
5 'Great movies should make you think, not just entertain you.'
6 'Actors should be believable in their roles.'
7 'You should be able to watch a great movie many times.'
8 'New adaptations can give new life to classic books.'
9 'It's best to avoid film versions of your favourite book.'

5 Work with a partner. Discuss the opinions in Exercise 4. Which do you agree/disagree with? Why?

VOCABULARY
LITERATURE AND FILM

6 Match words in the article with their meanings 1–10.

1 a writer
2 a writer of fiction
3 books about someone's life
4 a writer of books for other people
5 a person who writes films
6 a person whose job is to give their opinion of books, plays, etc.
7 the story of a film or book
8 the words spoken in a book or film
9 a new version of a film
10 all the people who perform in a film, play, etc.

7 Work in small groups to discuss the questions.

1 What book should be made into a film?
2 Which actors do you think would be good in it?
3 Is there a film which you think should be remade because the original was not very successful?

LISTENING AND SPEAKING

8a [6.1] Listen to four members of a discussion group (Michael, Jenny, Paul and Erika) talking about the book and film of *The Da Vinci Code*. Who liked/disliked it? Why?

8b Listen again. Which adjectives did they use?

awful · brilliant · disturbing · dreadful · dull · gripping · interesting · lightweight · moving · overrated · riveting · shocking · tedious · tense · thought-provoking

9 Complete the following expressions used by the members of the group. Check your answers in Audio script 6.1 on page 174. Which express a positive and which a negative opinion?

1 It's a real _page turner_
2 It's not my _sort_ of thing. _kind_
3 I couldn't _put_ it down.
4 The ending was a real _let. down_
5 I just couldn't get _into_ it.
6 It's _light_ and _easy_ to read.
7 It was very _hard_ _____ at the beginning.
8 It certainly _lived_ up to all the _hype_

10 Work in small groups. Talk about a book or film you really enjoyed and one you really didn't like. Use language from Exercises 8b and 9.

From page to screen

In the first of a new series, our arts correspondent James Hope takes a look at the sometimes uneasy relationship between the printed word and the silver screen.

Reading a book and watching a film are two very different experiences, but expectations can be high when a film of a favourite book is made. There are very many times I have been disappointed by a film of a book I love. Although highly regarded books do not always make good films, it is safe to say that great movies may be made from not particularly good books. (*The Godfather* immediately springs to mind.)

The source material may be anything from classic novels, short stories, comic books and stage plays, as well as non-fiction such as biography and autobiography, even those written by ghostwriters. All can work well, but why do many adaptations and indeed remakes fail with both cinema audiences and critics?

A key question is obviously how close to the original the film is. Since a typical film is only around two hours long, it becomes a question of what to leave out, and how to script the dialogue. Sometimes there may be changes to the plot, additions, and even different endings to please producers, directors and test audiences. I, like many people, have often left the cinema feeling 'the film is not like the book.'

Another problem area is the cast. Finding actors acceptable to film audiences can mean the difference between success and failure. Readers of the book use their imaginations to visualise characters and have very definite ideas about how characters look and sound. This is where I think many film adaptations fall down.

Some books are just too difficult to film for technical reasons, although movies like *The Life of Pi* are changing this perception. The impact of CGI technology has had a huge impact on the movie industry and allowed the previously unfilmable to become a reality.

Sometimes authors are very involved in the process and may even be the screenwriter. This can actually be a bad thing because they may be too close to the material and find it difficult to adapt. At other times they are not, and there are instances where writers have been very unhappy with the film versions of their work. Roald Dahl and Stephen King are examples of this. Even more extreme was reclusive novelist J. D. Salinger who made sure no film versions of his popular novel *A Catcher in the Rye* could ever be made. In this situation it is clear viewers will not be disappointed! For me, anyway, it is always a bad idea to watch a film of a book you love.

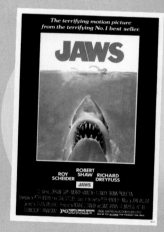

Despite the challenges, there have been some highly successful films made from popular books. For me *Jaws, Harry Potter, Lord of the Rings* and *Twilight* all fit this category. And possibly the best example is the James Bond series, the majority of which has been derived from the 007 novels of Ian Fleming. Perhaps strangely, audiences seem to accept the change of actors who have played James Bond, although everyone seems to have their favourite. I know I do.

The result of all this is that a film adaptation can introduce a new audience to a book and author, or it may put them off forever!

Next week: *Do Androids Dream of Electric Sheep?* … and how a change of title can make all the difference!

SPEAKING AND LISTENING

1 **Which films, books, or characters have had an impact on you? Why?**

2 6.2 **Listen to four people discussing the question in Exercise 1 and answer these questions for each person.**
1 What is the film or book?
2 Who are the main characters or actors?
3 Does the speaker say if the film is based on a book?
4 What does the speaker say about preferring the book or the film?

3 **Listen again. Take notes on why the speakers like the films, books or characters. Compare your notes with a partner.**

4 6.3 **Listen to another person describing a book.**
1 What three reasons does the speaker give for liking the book?
2 Why do you think Gatsby invites Nick to his party?
3 Why did the book have a great impact when it was first published?

5 **Listen again and match the pairs of words.**
1 favourite   **a** parties
2 upper-class   **b** people
3 extremely   **c** smile
4 evocative   **d** plot
5 charming   **e** well-written
6 lavish   **f** language
7 fascinating   **g** characters
8 richly-drawn   **h** novel

READING

6 **Read the extract from *The Great Gatsby* and answer the questions.**
1 Who tells the story?
2 Which characters appear?
3 Where do you think the extract is set?
4 What does Gatsby look like?
5 What happens at the end of the extract?

7 Referencing **What do the words highlighted in the extract refer to?**
1 we   5 it
2 it   6 himself
3 she   7 he
4 his   8 us

8 **What other stories do you know which talk about regrets that people have about the past or lost opportunities?**

GRAMMAR
NARRATIVE TENSES

9a **Underline the tenses. Which tenses are they?**
1 We were sitting at a table with a man …
2 … the man looked at me and smiled …
3 Some time before he introduced himself I'd got a strong impression that he was picking his words with care.
4 A butler hurried toward him with the information that Chicago was calling …

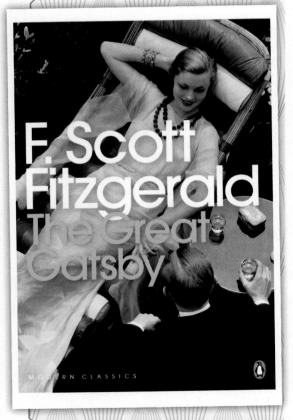

I was still with Jordan Baker. We were sitting at a table with a man of about my age and a rowdy little girl, who gave way upon the slightest provocation to uncontrollable laughter. I was enjoying myself now. I had taken two finger-bowls of champagne, and the scene had changed before my eyes into something significant, elemental, and profound.

At a lull in the entertainment the man looked at me and smiled.

"Your face is familiar," he said, politely. "Weren't you in the Third Division during the war?"

"Why, yes. I was in the Ninth Machine-gun Battalion."

"I was in the Seventh Infantry until June nineteen-eighteen. I knew I'd seen you somewhere before."

We talked for a moment about some wet, gray little villages in France. Evidently he lived in this vicinity, for he told me that he had just bought a hydroplane, and was going to try it out in the morning.

"Want to go with me, old sport? Just near the shore along the Sound."

"What time?"

"Any time that suits you best."

It was on the tip of my tongue to ask his name when Jordan looked around and smiled.

"Having a gay time now?" she inquired.

"Much better." I turned again to my new acquaintance. "This is an unusual party for me. I haven't even seen the host. I live over there ———"
I waved my hand at the invisible hedge in the distance, "and this man

9b Match the tenses in Exercise 9a with functions a–d.

a describing events which took place one after the other in the story and are seen as complete actions

b describing events which set the scene and provide the background against which a story happens

c describing an event that was already in progress, and which was interrupted by another event

d describing an event which took place in the past, before another event in the past

10 Choose the correct verb forms.

1 All children, except one, grow up. They soon know that they will grow up, and the way Wendy knew was this. One day when she was two years old she *played / was playing* in a garden, and she plucked another flower and *had run / ran* with it to her mother. (J. M. Barrie, *Peter Pan*)

2 Having no near relations or friends, I *had tried / was trying* to make up my mind what to do, when I ran across John Cavendish. I *had seen / was seeing* very little of him for some years. (Agatha Christie, *The Mysterious Affair at Styles*)

3 The last minutes of the day *had been ticking / were ticking* away, and Martin Turner *could not / had not been able to* wait to be set free. The minutes dragged on as Mr Lincoln, the form tutor, lectured the class ... (Benjamin Zephaniah, *Face*)

Gatsby sent over his chauffeur with an invitation." For a moment he looked at me as if he failed to understand.

"I'm Gatsby," he said suddenly.

"What!" I exclaimed. "Oh, I beg your pardon."

"I thought you knew, old sport. I'm afraid I'm not a very good host."

He smiled understandingly — much more than understandingly. It was one of those rare smiles with a quality of eternal reassurance in it, that you may come across four or five times in life. It faced — or seemed to face — the whole external world for an instant, and then concentrated on you with an irresistible prejudice in your favor. It understood you just so far as you wanted to be understood, believed in you as you would like to believe in yourself, and assured you that it had precisely the impression of you that, at your best, you hoped to convey. Precisely at that point it vanished — and I was looking at an elegant young rough-neck, a year or two over thirty, whose elaborate formality of speech just missed being absurd. Some time before he introduced himself I'd got a strong impression that he was picking his words with care.

Almost at the moment when Mr. Gatsby identified himself, a butler hurried toward him with the information that Chicago was calling him on the wire. He excused himself with a small bow that included each of us in turn.

11a Look at the example of the past perfect continuous from the same scene in *The Great Gatsby* and choose the correct option in the rule.

> Tom Buchanan, who had been hovering restlessly about the room, stopped and rested his hand on my shoulder.

The past perfect continuous is used to emphasise that an activity which happened *before/after* another activity or time in the past went on for some time.

11b Complete the rule to show the three parts of the past perfect continuous.

_____ + _____ + _____ form of the verb

11c Look again at the sentences in Exercise 9a and the extract in 11a. Are these statements true or false?

1 The past perfect is the most common tense for telling stories.

2 Writers use other tenses to add variety and add interest by being able to refer to different times in the past.

3 We use the past continuous and the past perfect continuous to talk about an activity in progress and to set the scene.

4 We use the past simple to introduce events further back in time that help explain the story.

➥ Language reference and extra practice, pages 126–149

12 Complete this story with the correct form of the verbs in brackets.

The clock struck ten. Lucien ¹_____ (sit) alone in the kitchen and he ²_____ (shake) uncontrollably. After he ³_____ (wait) for over an hour, he ⁴_____ (hear) a key in the front door.

His parents ⁵_____ (come) in. He ⁶_____ (tell) them what ⁷_____ (happen) earlier that evening. He ⁸_____ (borrow) their car without asking, and ⁹_____ (crash) into a lamp post because he ¹⁰_____ (drive) too fast. Then the door bell ¹¹_____ (ring). It ¹²_____ (be) the police.

SPEAKING

13 Work in small groups to discuss the following.

Which books or films do you know have had an impact in these ways?

- socially
- culturally
- politically
- personally
- visually

I think 'Things Fall Apart' had a huge cultural impact. The novel was written by Chinua Achebe in 1958 and is still widely read and studied as an example of the damage of colonialism. We are invited into the lives of the Ibo tribe in Nigeria and learn their customs and beliefs.

SPEAKING

1a Put the topics in order (1 is the most important reason).

I read because:

- it's fun.
- it's a skill for life.
- it helps me find what I want.
- it helps me understand the world.
- it gives me a break.
- it teaches me how other people live.
- it will help me get a job.
- it helps me understand myself.
- I have to.

1b Work with a partner and compare your answers.

2 With your partner, answer the questionnaire on reading habits. Take it in turns to ask and answer the questions.

1	What do you like reading?
2	How often do you read?
3	Where do you like reading?
4	Have you read an entire book in the last three months?
5	Who taught you to read?
6	What sort of fiction do you like reading?
7	Have you ever pretended that you had read a book when you hadn't?
8	What is the last book that you read?
9	How often do you go to a library?

READING

3 **Look at these short summaries of a report. Read the report and choose the best summary.**

1 Girls read with greater enjoyment than boys because they read more fiction and boys prefer newspapers and comics. Boys will read better if they are encouraged to read more literature.

2 Girls and boys have different reading habits. Girls read more fiction while boys like magazines and comic books. Boys need to read more novels to improve their reading skills.

3 Girls read better than boys because they enjoy reading more. The best way to improve boys' reading ability is to focus on reading materials they really enjoy such as newspapers.

4 **Decide who reads more for enjoyment.**

1 Japanese boys or Japanese girls
2 Japanese boys or Austrian boys
3 Austrian boys or Thai boys
4 Indonesian girls or Japanese girls

5 Identifying facts and opinions **Find three opinions and three facts in the text.**

6 **Do you think the situation described in the report is similar in your country? What do you think are the causes of these findings?**

PISA   Programme for International Student Assessment

PISA Reports at a glance
Do boys and girls have different reading habits?

What it means

The fact that girls outperform boys in reading is associated with girls' greater enjoyment of reading. Policymakers in countries where this gap is particularly pronounced should consider incorporating measures to improve students' engagement in reading into all strategies that are used to raise reading proficiency levels. With PISA results showing that boys have different reading habits to girls, policymakers should take into account boys' preference for reading different types of material when trying to raise their interest in and enjoyment of reading.

Findings

In every country except Korea, girls reported reading for enjoyment more than boys. On average across OECD countries, just over half of boys (52 percent), but nearly three-quarters of girls (73 percent) said that they read for enjoyment.

The gender gap in the proportion of girls and boys who read for enjoyment is greatest in Estonia, the Netherlands and in the partner countries Latvia and Lithuania, where it is at least 30 percentage points.

In 14 countries, only a minority of boys said that they read for enjoyment. In Austria, Luxembourg, the Netherlands and the partner country Liechtenstein, fewer than 40 percent said that they read for enjoyment.

In some of the countries that show small gender differences in enjoyment of reading, both boys and girls are relatively unlikely to report that they enjoy reading. In Japan, for example, only 54 percent of boys and 58 percent of girls reported that they enjoy reading. However, in other countries where there is a narrow gender gap, a high percentage of boys and girls report that they enjoy reading. For example, in the partner countries and Albania, Indonesia, Kazakhstan, Kyrgyzstan, Shanghai in China and Thailand, at least 80 percent of boys and 90 percent of girls said that they read for enjoyment.

Other data from PISA show that girls and boys typically enjoy different kinds of reading. Girls are twice as likely to read fiction for enjoyment, and are more likely than boys to read magazines; boys more commonly read newspapers and comic books. This pattern applies across virtually every country in the case of boys preferring comic books and newspapers.

The fact that two in three boys on average in OECD countries reported that they read newspapers for pleasure, compared to only one in five who said they read fiction for enjoyment, shows that there could be far more potential for strengthening boys' reading skills by encouraging other types of reading in addition to literature.

OECD: Organisation for Economic Co-operation and Development

VOCABULARY
WORDS FROM THE TEXT

7a Match the highlighted words and phrases in the report with the meanings 1–9.

1 a part of an amount or group
2 when someone likes something more than something else
3 connected
4 almost
5 the difference between male and female
6 what usually happens
7 do something better than other people or things
8 quite, when compared with other things
9 very noticeable

7b Complete the text using the words and phrases from Exercise 7a.

PISA assesses the extent to which students have acquired some of the skills that are important for full participation in modern society. Data shows that girls ¹_____ boys in most reading tests and a higher ²_____ of girls do better than boys in key literacy tests in elementary school. The data also shows that the most ³_____ difference is in attitudes to reading. For many boys, reading is ⁴_____ with being a 'nerd', but that is true for only a ⁵_____ small number of girls. Girls show a ⁶_____ for reading fiction, but there is ⁷_____ no difference between boys and girls for reading non-fiction books. The ⁸_____ in reading starts in elementary school. However, for mathematics, gender differences ⁹_____ do not emerge until high school.

LISTENING

8 `6.4` Listen to five people talking about their reading habits.

Which speaker or speakers:

1 reads less now than they used to?
2 reads more now than they used to?
3 used to read a lot, then hardly read at all, but now reads again?
4 mentions an author?
5 talks about where they used to read as a child?
6 talks about where they like to read now?

9 `6.5` Listen to the first speaker again and complete the text, using a maximum of three words for each gap.

When I was in elementary school, I ¹_____ a devoted reader and a good student. I ²_____ in bed for an hour every night before I ³_____ asleep. And at school, I ⁴_____ to the library every afternoon. I ⁵_____ reading. Then, my dad ⁶_____ his job and we kept moving schools. As soon as I ⁷_____ the new school and new friends, I would have to leave. And finally, I ⁸_____ up in a school where reading was not cool, certainly not for boys. My grades ⁹_____ worse and I ¹⁰_____ only read one or two books a year. When I left school, I ¹¹_____ a band and started composing songs. I ¹²_____ reading again because reading ¹³_____ me understand the world and understand myself, and helped me find ideas for my songs.

GRAMMAR
USED TO, WOULD, GET USED TO

10a Look again at the text in Exercise 9. Are these statements true or false?

1 *Used to* is the most common verb form used.
2 We use *used to* and *would* as alternatives to the past simple when describing habits and repeated actions which took place over a period of time.
3 Once we have used either *used to* or *would* we stick to that choice and do not use the past simple.
4 *Would* cannot be used to talk about past states but *used to* can.
5 If you *get used to* something, you become accustomed to it (it was strange, now it's not so strange).

10b Look at these examples. How does the form of *used to* change in the negative and question forms?

I didn't use to read books when I was young.

Did you use to read a lot when you were young?

➥ Language reference and extra practice, pages 126–149

11 Find the mistakes of form or use in each sentence and correct them.

1 Women of Jane Austen's time would to write anonymously.
2 Vlad the Impaler was used to sign himself Dracula.
3 George Orwell is used to work in a bookshop.
4 I used to read a lot of short stories at the moment.
5 He didn't used to read a lot as a child.
6 I was uncomfortable at first, but I used to speaking in public.
7 The Brontë sisters all would suffer from bad health.
8 Did you used to read comics when you were a child?

12 What is wrong with this short text?

I used to like reading. I also used to like watching television and I used to play football in the park. I used to read in bed at night and I used to read two or three books a week.

13 Write a short text about your reading habits in the past. Try to vary *used to* and *would* with the past simple.

PRONUNCIATION

14 `6.6` *used to* Listen to a sentence from the listening said in two ways. Which is correct? Repeat the correct version.

15 Work with a partner. Discuss things you used to or didn't use to do, think or believe when you were a child.

I used to watch a lot of television as a child.

SITUATION

1 Read the situation and the email. Work with a partner to discuss the questions.

1 What film genres can you think of (e.g. horror, romcoms)?
2 What genre would you choose if you were entering the competition? Why?

Starlight, a film production company in Los Angeles, California, is looking for ideas for a new film project and has asked its own staff to pitch their ideas. The Executive Producer has written to all staff, inviting them to work in pairs on a film project and to present their ideas to the management team in a five-minute presentation. The pair with the best idea for a film will receive a cash prize.

To:	all staff
From:	Don Jameson, Executive Producer

Subject: Film presentation – ideas

We are looking for ideas for a new film project. We invite members of staff to work in teams of two, develop their ideas for a film and make a five-minute presentation of their concept to the management team.

We hope to receive a wide range of ideas and styles for different film genres. There is a medium-sized budget for the film of up to $50 million.

The winners of the competition will receive a substantial cash prize, the amount to be announced shortly.

KEY LANGUAGE
PERSUADING

2 **6.7** A member of staff, Jerry, has an idea for a film. He is enthusiastic about it and tries to persuade his partner, Francesca, that they should work on the idea to win the prize. Listen to their conversation and answer the questions.

1 What is the genre of Jerry's film idea?
2 Who are the main characters?
3 What audience is the film aiming at?

3a Listen again. Tick the statements you hear. Put a cross next to the statements you don't hear.

1 I'm sure it'll be a winner.
2 I'm confident you'll like my idea.
3 I think you'll agree, it's a really interesting and creative idea.
4 They'd be perfect.
5 They're bound to appeal to the audience.
6 They'll love our concept.
7 It will attract a wide range of filmgoers.
8 We think it's got tremendous potential.
9 We think our concept is great and hope we've been able to persuade you, too.

3b Look at Audio script 6.7 on page 175. Underline the expressions Jerry used which are similar in meaning to the statements you put a cross against.

TASK
MAKING A PERSUASIVE PRESENTATION

4a Work with a partner. Choose one of the storylines in the list or choose a genre and invent your own storyline.

4b Prepare a five-minute presentation of your ideas for a film project. Use the following structure and phrases from the Key language and the Useful phrases below. Decide how you will divide the presentation between you.

- storyline summary – include some details of the plot and how the film ends
- target audience
- setting – where the action will be located
- special features – what is different and exciting about your concept
- description of one key scene
- main characters – which actors will play them? Explain your choices.
- why will the film be successful?
- how will the film be distributed? In art houses? By a major distributor?

OTHER USEFUL PHRASES

Good morning/afternoon everyone.
I'll start with …
Let me start by telling you about …
Turning now to …
Moving on to …
Who is our target market?
What's special about our concept?
To summarise …
Let me sum up …
Thanks for listening to our presentation.

5a Make your presentation to your class and answer any questions they may have.

When you are not making your own presentation, listen to the presentations of your colleagues and give each one a score out of 10. Use the following scoring system and base your scores on the content and effectiveness of the film presentation.

10	Brilliant
8–9	Very good
6–8	Good
3–5	Average

5b Add up the scores for each pair. The pair with the highest score wins the cash prize.

FILM CONCEPTS – BASIC STORYLINES

1 The Danger of Too Much Curiosity
An American youngster finds out he is adopted. He goes to meet his real family and discovers that they belong to a crazy, violent cult. The members of the cult stop at nothing to make him stay with them. (Horror)

2 Surprise Meeting
A woman is having a drink with friends in a bar. A man passes in front of her. Ten years ago, she had a short but passionate relationship with him. However, one day he disappeared from her life with no explanation. (Romantic drama)

3 A Shocking Image
A woman, on holiday abroad, is sitting in a café. She looks up at the television and sees a picture of herself on the screen. (Mystery/Thriller)

4 A Good Match?
A young woman from a wealthy family falls in love with a man from a poor family. They meet strong opposition from the woman's parents who do everything they can to break up the couple. (Musical)

5 A Scheming Husband
A husband is married to a woman who is psychologically fragile. The husband wants to get control of his wife's money, so he plays tricks on her to make her go mad. (Thriller)

6 The Trap
A politician visits a woman he has met on the internet. He goes to her house and she offers him a drink. She goes to the kitchen to fetch the drink. After ten minutes, he becomes anxious when she doesn't return. He goes to the kitchen and finds her on the floor covered in blood. She is dead. (Political drama)

7 Underwater Adventure
A man living in a very old house discovers a map which seems to show the location of a shipwreck which occurred two centuries ago. He gets together a team to search for the wreck which was apparently carrying a load of gold bullion. They discover the wreck, but that's when their problems begin. (Adventure)

8 An Unlikely Hero
People in a village find out that they are about to be attacked by a group of hostile zombies who intend to destroy their village and everyone in it. They disagree about how to defend themselves but one person becomes their leader and saves them. (Horror)

STUDY SKILLS
MAKING AN EFFECTIVE PRESENTATION

1 **6.8** **Listen to five people talking about a memorable presentation they have heard. Match each speaker to the reason why the presentation was effective.**

a   The presenter delivered his message in a clear voice.
b   The presenter used some effective techniques to express his idea.
c   The presenter used memorable images in her slide presentation.
d   The presenter quoted from a poem.
e   The presenter told a story at the beginning of his talk.

2 **Can you recall a particularly effective presentation? If so, why was it so impressive?**

3a **Rhetorical techniques Presentations can be persuasive or informative. If they are persuasive, presenters often use rhetorical techniques to make their presentations more effective. Look at the definition of a rhetorical device. Can you think of an example of one?**

A rhetorical device is a technique which uses language to increase the persuasiveness of a piece of writing or speaking. It is often used to emphasise a point or to produce an emotional response in the reader or listener.

3b **Match rhetorical techniques 1–11 with examples a–k. Sometimes there is more than one possible answer.**

1   Rhetorical questions (asking a question but not expecting an answer)
2   Quotation
3   Alliteration (repeating sounds at the beginning of words)
4   Contrast
5   Repetition
6   Simile
7   Tripling (listing or chunking points in sets of three)
8   Imagery (metaphor)
9   Hyperbole (using exaggerated language for effect)
10   Anecdote (a short story based on your personal experience)
11   A surprising fact, statistic or opinion

a   The film *Heaven's Gate* was one of the biggest failures in history but some critics consider it a masterpiece.
b   In *Sleepless in Miami*, he was like a man in a coma for most of the film.
c   Why would anyone want to see the film when they can't relate to the characters?
d   '*In the House* is a clever psychological comedy. It is François Ozon's best work to date.' Film critic.
e   His performance was intelligent, intuitive and intense.
f   Alfred Hitchcock's film *Rear Window* is undoubtedly the greatest film ever made.
g   On the one hand, the film held your interest. On the other hand, the ending was disappointing.
h   She had the smile of an angel, but the soul of the devil.
i   It was a long film. It was a boring film. It was a film that shouldn't have been made.
j   When I was in Paris, I met the director of the film in a café on the Left Bank. He told me …
k   He was the son of a millionaire. She was from a shanty town.

4 **Work with a partner. You are going to watch a presentation on *The Girl with the Dragon Tattoo* at a university film society. Read this description of the film, then discuss the questions.**

The niece of a powerful businessman disappeared forty years ago. A journalist, Mikael Blomkvist and his assistant, an anti-social young woman, Lisbeth Salander, are hired by the uncle to carry out an investigation.

1   If you haven't seen the film, do you think you'd like to see it?
2   If you have seen the film, did you enjoy it? Why?/Why not?

5 **6** **Watch the presentation and answer the questions.**

1   What are Mikael and Lisbeth trying to find out in their investigation?
2   Who is the more interesting character, Mikael or Lisbeth? Why?
3   Why has the film been so successful?

6a **Watch the presentation again and note some of the rhetorical techniques used by the presenter.**

6b **Check your answers by looking at Video script 6 on page 176.**

7 **Choose a film you know well. Make notes on it, then make a five-minute presentation of the film to your group. Try to use rhetorical techniques from Exercise 3b.**

BOOKS | MUSIC | **FILMS** | PC AND VIDEO GAMES | TOYS AND GAMES
SOFTWARE | ELECTRONICS AND PHOTO

CUSTOMER REVIEWS SKYFALL

Bond is back (again)
Matthew Drake (London)

A I was surprised to learn that *Skyfall* is the 23rd James Bond film, and Daniel Craig is the 6th actor to play 007. This new adventure came out on the 50th anniversary of the first film. It is an original screenplay and not adapted from one of the James Bond books by Ian Fleming. In the film we learn a bit about James Bond's past, and his relationship with his parents. There are also many clever references to past Bond films. Directed by Oscar winner Sam Mendes (*American Beauty*, *Revolutionary Road*), he has made a film which is boring in parts, but exciting in others.

B The writers have created a script which is interesting and also funny in places. Of course, as you would expect with any James Bond film, the action sequences are **generally** exciting and well done, and it's good to see there are no **completely** stupid special effects like in some previous Bond films. The opening chase is **particularly** exciting. As always with Bond, there are a variety of nice locations such as Istanbul, Shanghai, Macau and Scotland, although much of the action takes place in London.

C The **really** good thing about the film, though, is once again Daniel Craig as Bond. He is **definitely** the best since Sean Connery. His acting is always good and in some scenes he is very funny. His co-stars, especially Javier Badem as the baddy, are also good. The title song by Adele is very powerful, as is the rest of the music. The film is very long, at over two and a half hours, and some scenes are quite boring, **especially** the last 30 minutes when the action moves to Scotland.

D The worst thing about the film was the product placement which was **truly** bad. I don't want to see brand names everywhere when I watch a film. This is a shame as other Bond films are **usually** good in this respect. The last part of the film was for me **totally** uninspiring. The ending of the film was too over the top even for the usual exciting Bond-style conclusion. Overall, however, it is great cinema and I would **certainly** recommend this to any Bond fan or film lover.

WRITING SKILLS
AN ONLINE REVIEW

8 Work with a partner to discuss the questions.
1   What sort of films do you like to watch at home?
2   What films have you watched recently?
3   Do you read online reviews before you buy/see movies. Why?/Why not?

9 Which of the following do you think it is a good idea to have in an online review?
• information about the story
• information about the acting
• how much it costs to buy
• the genre
• whether it is a good idea to watch it or not
• the special effects
• names of the actors/director
• the music
• what happens at the end

10 Read the customer review. Is it positive or negative?

11 Read the review again. Match the following aspects of a film with the correct paragraph A–D.
1   the cast
2   the director
3   the background
4   the music
5   the writing
6   the plot
7   the setting
8   the recommendation

12 Adjectives Change the highlighted adjectives in the review to make the review more interesting and improve the writing. (Look back through the unit or use a thesaurus to help you.)

boring → *dull/tedious*
exciting → *thrilling/dramatic*

13a Adverbs Look at the ten adverbs in bold in the review. Put them in pairs of adverbs with a similar meaning.

completely – totally

13b Match the pairs of adverbs with meanings 1–5.
1   in every way
2   without doubt
3   in most cases
4   more than usual
5   extremely

14 Write a review of a film/DVD you have seen. Use the *Skyfall* review as a model. Use some of the adjectives and adverbs you have learnt.

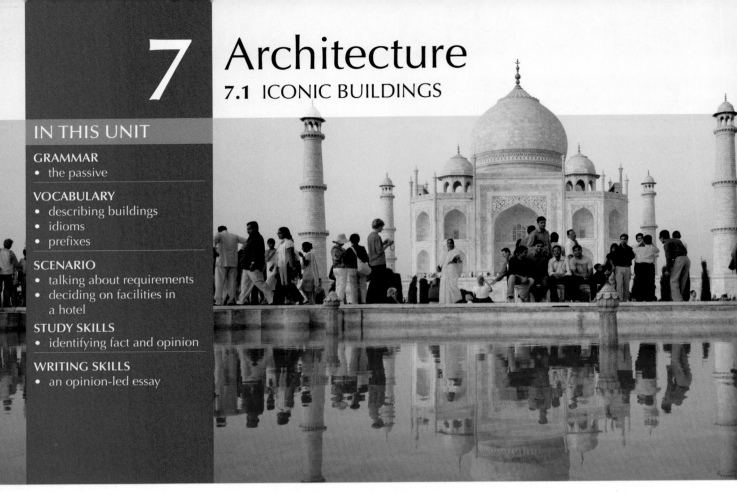

7 Architecture

7.1 ICONIC BUILDINGS

A house is a machine for living in. Le Corbusier (Charles-Edouard Jeanneret-Gris), 1887–1965, Swiss architect

VOCABULARY
DESCRIBING BUILDINGS

1 What is your favourite building? Why do you like it?

2a Are these adjectives for describing buildings positive, negative or neutral?

ancient	classical	contemporary	derelict
dilapidated	elegant	graceful	imposing
impressive	innovative	magnificent	ornate
run-down	stylish	traditional	ugly

2b Decide which adjectives in Exercise 2a can describe a building which is:

1 not in good condition
2 not modern
3 unattractive
4 new and different
5 attractive
6 decorative
7 modern
8 important-looking

PRONUNCIATION

3 7.1 Word stress Underline the stress on the adjectives in Exercise 2a. Put them in groups of words with first- and second-syllable stress. Compare your ideas with a partner, then listen and check.

A | THE COLOSSEUM

I always visit the Colosseum when I'm in Rome; it's magnificent. I suppose it's what many people think of when you say classical architecture. It's an incredibly impressive building, and to me represents the power of the Roman Empire. It was constructed way back in AD 80. It's a vast amphitheatre and big crowds used to go there to watch gladiators and fights between wild animals. It's made of stone and concrete, and although it was damaged by earthquakes in the 15th century, the main structure has survived for almost 2,000 years. It used to look rather run-down, but recently it has been renovated and partly restored.

4 Look at the photos on these pages. Describe each building. Which do you like most? Why?

5a Match verbs 1–8 with their meanings a–h.

1	damage	a	repair to put in original condition
2	rebuild	b	keep in good condition
3	construct	c	build
4	demolish	d	ask someone to build
5	maintain	e	erect again
6	restore	f	plan
7	commission	g	harm
8	design	h	knock down

5b Put the verbs in order to show the stages in the life of a building.

READING

6a Read the statements. Are they true or false? Guess the answers from your knowledge. Compare your ideas with a partner.

The Colosseum
1 was built in the 15th century.
2 was a place where people watched fights.
3 is older than the other two structures.
4 is currently in very bad condition.

The Taj Mahal
5 was built as a palace for an emperor.
6 was constructed over 500 years ago.
7 is in danger.

The Eiffel Tower
8 has always been popular.
9 was the world's tallest building.
10 was never intended to be permanent.

6b Read the website texts and check your answers.

7 Match words in the texts with their meanings 1–10.
1 a circular building with seats arranged on a slope (text A)
2 continued to exist in difficult conditions (text A)
3 repair a building so it is in good condition (text A)
4 a place for a dead person (text B)
5 a round roof on a building (text B)
6 the outside (text B)
7 the inside (text B)
8 a building which is easily noticed (text C)
9 not lasting or needed for very long (text C)
10 something ugly or very unpleasant to look at (text C)

SPEAKING AND WRITING

8 Work with a partner. Describe a building in your country or a country you know well. Talk about these topics.
- where it is
- why you like it
- what is special about it
- why you would recommend a visitor to see it

9 Interpreting ideas Discuss the questions with your partner.
1 What do you think is the most iconic building in your country?
2 Do you think it is a good representation of your architectural culture? Why?/Why not?
3 What buildings in other countries do you consider to be iconic?

10 Write a paragraph about the building you discussed in Exercise 8 or 9.

▶ MEET THE EXPERT

Watch an interview with Laura Mark, an architectural journalist, about innovative designs.
Turn to page 152 for video activities.

B THE TAJ MAHAL

I love the Taj Mahal in Agra, India. Seeing it for the first time was a breathtaking moment. It was built by Emperor Shah Jahan in memory of his wife, who died in childbirth. Although it looks like a palace, it is a tomb. It's strange that something so beautiful was built for such a sad reason. It looks very traditional with the huge dome, but actually the design also feels very contemporary, even though it was finished in 1653. The white marble exterior and its carvings look amazing in the sun. The interior decoration is also very detailed and ornate. It was built using materials from all around India and Asia, and using over 1,000 elephants. I read that in the 19th century it was looking quite dilapidated, but was then restored. It seems environmental pollution is the biggest threat today as it is making the marble yellow.

C THE EIFFEL TOWER

My favourite building, or structure, I suppose, is the Eiffel Tower in Paris. It's one of the world's best-known landmarks and it captures the atmosphere of Paris for me. It looks so elegant and graceful rising above the city. It was commissioned and designed as a temporary structure for the 1889 Universal Exhibition, but has never been taken down, although apparently at the time there was a lot of opposition from the public to it, with many people calling it an eyesore. It's massive. I think it's about 300 metres tall – and it was the world's tallest structure until about 1930. When it was built, it was a very innovative design, but it takes a lot to maintain – each part of it is repainted every seven years!

SPEAKING AND READING

1 Work with a partner to discuss the questions.

1 Where do most people live in your country? In houses or apartments?
2 How large is the average house/apartment? Is limited space a common problem?
3 Do young people tend to live with their parents or live alone? Why?

2a Look at the photos and describe them. Which looks the most interesting building, and why?

2b Read the article and match the photos with parts 1–4.

3 Read the article again and complete the table.

	1	2	3	4
Who designed it?				
Where is the building?				
What materials are used?				
How big is the building?				
Why is the building special?				

4 Evaluating Work in small groups to discuss the questions.

1 What are the advantages and disadvantages of living in each house?
2 Which house would you most like to live in, and why?
3 Which of the following do you think are the most important problems facing architects in your country?
   • insulation (maintaining heat in cold climates)
   • keeping cool in hot climates
   • efficient use of space
   • being environmentally friendly
   • fitting in with the local surroundings
   • being visually attractive

5 Match words in the article with their meanings 1–6.

1 excellent and unusual (part 1)
2 extremely clever (part 1)
3 many (part 2)
4 not having enough space (part 3)
5 the shape or arrangement of the parts of something (part 3)
6 tiny (part 4)

GRAMMAR
THE PASSIVE (1)

6a Look at the three highlighted examples of the passive in the article. Match them with statements a and b.

a We use the passive if the agent is unimportant, obvious or unknown.
b If the agent is specified, this comes at the end of the clause and follows *by*.

6b Match the highlighted examples with the tenses.

• present simple
• present continuous
• future simple

6c How are the passives formed?

➥ Language reference and extra practice, pages 126–149

7 Complete the sentences with the correct passive form of the verb (present simple, present continuous or future simple). Sometimes there is more than one possible answer.

1 At present, several space-saving houses _____ (manufacture) by our firm.
2 Triangular floating schools _____ (build) in Nigeria in the near future.
3 The house _____ (make) mainly of glass.
4 New apartments _____ (build) across the street.
5 Next year, the disused garages _____ (convert) into affordable homes.
6 Research _____ (carry out) by the R&D team into the living needs of young adults.
7 The project _____ (not finish) on time if we don't get the information we need.

LISTENING

8a 7.2 Marta Gattarosa, an architect, is answering questions from students of architecture. Listen and write the three questions they ask.

8b Listen again and take notes on her answers.

8c Compare your notes with a partner.

SPEAKING

9 Work in small groups. Why do young people increasingly live with their parents till later in life? Think about these questions and discuss.

• Is it more expensive for young people these days (college loans, expensive car insurance)?
• What percentage of their income do people spend on rent/mortgage?
• Is there a lack of affordable housing?
• Are there other reasons why young people might choose to stay at home?
• Are people getting married and having families when they are older?

Who wants to live in a house like this?

From the 'Sliding House' to Poland's narrowest house, Sachiko Kimura chooses her favourite homes that solve space problems or deal with the challenge of the climate.

1 The Sliding House

This remarkable building was built in Suffolk, UK, by architects dRMM. They were asked by the owners to prioritise three things: light, space and a connection with the outdoors. The architects came up with a space that changes, using a huge, 20-tonne sliding glass cover on railway tracks. The cover protects the building and also transforms it. The building lives and breathes and is an ingenious solution. But most of all, I think it is fun and makes people smile when they see it. At present, several sliding houses are being manufactured by dRMM.

2 Reflection of the Mineral

I have always loved Japanese space-saving architecture and especially the brilliant capsule hotels. This 146m² house, built in Nagano, Tokyo, is proof that 'less is more'. It was designed by Yasuhiro Yamashita and I like the successful use of modern architectural ideas combined with clever use of space as well as structural design. It really has made use of every inch of space available. Even the furniture and appliances have been constructed keeping the contours of this extraordinary building in mind. The house has won numerous architectural awards and experts think it will soon be recognised as a landmark in its own right.

3 Domestic Transformer

Hong Kong is one of the world's most densely populated cities. Architect Gary Chang grew up there in a tiny flat with six others. Chang has come up with an innovative answer to the increasingly cramped lives of many urban dwellers. I think he has transformed his cramped apartment into something really special. The tiny 32m² rectangular apartment has polished chrome walls that can change into 24 different configurations, each serving a specific need. The space available can change into a home theatre, spa, kitchen, bedroom or a chill-out room with a hammock, depending on what Chang needs at any moment. Chang hopes his dwelling offers a viable life-enhancing alternative for people in Hong Kong who can't afford anything bigger.

4 Keret's House

I was intrigued by Poland's narrowest house. The tiny house measures just 91cm across at the narrowest point and is wedged into the gap between two buildings in Warsaw. It is clearly not designed with family life in mind and is only just big enough for one person to inch their way from the single bed through the miniscule kitchen and into the tiny toilet. The building started life as an art installation designed by film maker Etgar Keret, who then decided to use the property as a workplace when he was in Poland. There is only a total floor space of 46 square feet in the two-floor structure which is made of iron.

READING

1 Do you recognise the bridges in the photos? What is the most impressive bridge in your country?

2 Read the introduction to the article. Which of these reasons account for the importance of bridges?

1 They are essential for transporting goods and trade.
2 They have military significance.
3 They bring beauty into our lives.
4 They symbolise people or places.
5 They give people more belief in their ability to achieve things.

3 Read the rest of the article and answer the questions.

1 Which bridge was made with soft stone?
2 Which was built to resist disasters?
3 Which changes its dimensions according to the temperature?
4 Which looks like a musical instrument?

4 Comparing features Read the article again and make notes. Compare the bridges in terms of age, length, appearance and use.

VOCABULARY
IDIOMS, PREFIXES

5 Read the introduction again. Complete the sentences with the correct form of the idioms in the article.

1 I'm not leaving this job till I've got something to go to. I don't want to _____.
2 We don't need to look at the problem of falling sales yet. Let's _____.
3 Don't worry about it anymore. It's _____.
4 I've had a few arguments with colleagues. If I want to get promoted, I need to _____.

6a Look at the words in the box. Underline the prefixes, then match them with meanings 1–4.

indisputable   misplaced   overcome   revitalise
unusual

1 again
2 not (x2 prefixes)
3 wrongly
4 be too strong / too much

6b Add prefixes to the words to change the meaning.

1 important
2 understand
3 crowded
4 significant
5 define
6 sensitive

Alamillo Bridge

Akashi Kaikyo Bridge

BRIDGING THE GAP

Measured by the effect they have on our spirits and imagination, bridges are the highest form of architecture. They stand as metaphors for so much in life. 'Let's cross that bridge when we come to it,' I remark, when I want to put off thinking about some nasty dilemma. If I quit a secure job, I am 'burning my bridges'. If I make friends with strangers, I am 'building bridges'. If I argue with someone, but want to forget it and be friends again, I say, 'It's all water under the bridge.'

Why do we hold bridges in such regard? One reason is surely that, because of their strategic importance, they are often scenes of fierce battles and thrilling heroics. Another is that a bridge can often embody the spirit of a city, even an entire nation, as the Sydney Harbour or Brooklyn Bridges do, or the Stari Most did until it was destroyed in the Bosnian conflict. (Fortunately, it has since been rebuilt and is now listed as a World Heritage Site.)

But perhaps the chief reason is that a bridge is a leap of daring: a symbol of mankind's belief in its ability to overcome any natural obstacle, no matter how wide, deep or windswept. That belief has occasionally been tragically misplaced, for example the collapse of the Hintze-Ribeiro bridge in Portugal killing fifty-nine people, but it has never been shattered.

What's indisputable is that our own age has seen one of the most innovative bursts of bridge-building ever.

Charles Bridge

Golden Gate Bridge

- Built for Expo 92, the Alamillo Bridge across the River Guadalquivir in Seville demonstrates how a striking new bridge can revitalise an old city. The bridge, which was designed by Santiago Calatrava, is supported by a pylon and cables which form the graceful shape of a harp. It has a span of 200 metres and was painted in Calatrava's trade mark bright white.

- The Akashi Kaikyo Bridge in Japan is the longest, tallest and costliest suspension bridge ever constructed. It took around ten years to be completed. Connecting Kobe with Awaji-Shima Island, this bridge has been built to withstand hurricanes, tidal waves and earthquakes. In 1995, an earthquake added a metre to the bridge's length while it was still being built. It has a total length of 3,910 metres.

- The famous Charles Bridge (Karlov Most) was built in the 14th century and named after the king. It is unusual because it is made of sandstone, not hard granite, which required some maintenance work in the 15th century after a flood. Street vendors, street artists and tourists can always be seen along its 500-metre length.

- The Golden Gate Bridge spans the mile-wide mouth of San Francisco Bay. The total length of the bridge is 2,739 metres. The bridge expands on hot days and contracts when it is cold. On hot days, the heat lengthens the cable. As a result, the bridge becomes 4.9 metres lower and 1.8 metres longer. The bridge was opened on 21 May 1937 with a 'pedestrians' day', during which 200,000 people walked across the bridge. On the morning of the following day it was opened to traffic.

GRAMMAR
THE PASSIVE (2)

7a Look again at the article and underline examples of the past simple passive and the present perfect simple passive. How are they formed?

7b Look at sentences 1 and 2 from the article. Match them with forms a and b.

1 An earthquake added a metre to the bridge's length while it was still being built.
2 It took around ten years to be completed.

a passive infinitive
b past continuous passive

➥ Language reference and extra practice, pages 126–149

8 Correct the mistakes in bold in the report.

Complaints [1]**have received** about the recent construction of the Sheridan Hotel. It [2]**was completing** in November last year. While it [3]**was constructing**, many residents and business people of the town suffered great inconvenience. Building materials [4]**were delivering** at all hours of the day and night, and the noise level was unbearable. When the foundations [5]**were digging**, the air became polluted and the streets were very dusty. Complaints [6]**were making** daily to the Council, but nothing [7]**was doing**. As a result, several shops [8]**have been closed** for some weeks during the worst period and now several claims for compensation [9]**have received** by the Council. The hotel [10]**has now built** and the Council is meeting next week to discuss the complaints and what [11]**is be done** about compensation. We expect the conclusions [12]**to publish** by the end of the month.

9a Look at examples 1 and 2 of the passive. Match them with uses a and b.

1 The 'Gherkin' is an impressive example of modern architecture. It was designed by Lord Foster and Ken Shuttleworth.
2 Many tourists have been impressed by the strange-shaped building in the City of London.

a It is more natural to put subjects which consist of a long expression at the end of a sentence.
b We prefer to start a new sentence with a familiar subject (something already mentioned).

9b Look at the highlighted passives in the article. Which use from Exercise 9a does each one illustrate?

SPEAKING AND WRITING

10 Work with a partner. You have a photo of one bridge and information about two. Share your information, then write a paragraph about your bridge.

Student A: look at page 155.
Student B: look at page 158.

SITUATION

1 Work with a partner. Discuss what facilities you would expect to find in a top-class hotel and conference centre.

2 Read the 'Invitation to Tender' document. What facilities are mentioned?

3a Read the document again and answer the questions.

1 What sort of reputation does HHCC have?
2 What will the ground floor look like?
3 What will the main purpose of the hotel be?
4 How will HHCC decide which architectural firm to choose for the design of the building?

3b Why do you think HHCC has chosen to build the hotel and conference centre in Rio de Janeiro?

INVITATION TO TENDER

Contract for the design of a luxury hotel and conference centre in Rio de Janeiro

Horizon Hotel & Conference Centre – 5 stars
www.hotelhorizon.br | 320 rooms

Candidates are asked to submit their letter of intent before 24 June.

Horizon Hotels and Conference Centres (HHCC) invites the architectural firms listed below to present a plan for designing a Hotel and Conference Centre in Rio de Janeiro.

HHCC is an international chain of high-class hotels and conference centres. It is famous for providing luxury accommodation and outstanding service. We intend the hotel to be used for conferences and congresses by groups from all over the world.

Selected architectural firms are asked to submit a plan for the ground floor of the building, which will be L-shaped. Details of the project are as follows.

The hotel will have seven floors:
Basement – equipment and storage
Ground floor – facilities to be decided
First floor – a large conference room, three meeting rooms and a seminar room
Second floor – office accommodation
Third–fifth floors – bedrooms
Sixth floor – a large restaurant, available for guests and the general public

The contract to design the hotel and conference centre will be awarded to the architectural firm which produces the best plan for the ground floor.

KEY LANGUAGE
TALKING ABOUT REQUIREMENTS

4 7.3 **Listen to three architects talking about designing the ground floor of a hotel. Answer the questions.**

1 What four suggestions do the architects make to meet the needs of health-conscious guests?
2 What do the architects finally decide to do?

5a Listen again and tick the phrases you hear.

Talking about <u>essential</u> requirements
1 We really must have ...
2 It's vital we have ...
3 It's absolutely essential to offer ...
4 It's a priority ...
5 We've got to offer ...
6 We certainly need ...

Talking about <u>desirable</u> requirements
7 It'd be very popular with ...
8 We should offer them ...

Talking about <u>possible</u> requirements
9 It might be a good idea to ...
10 We could also consider ...
11 Another possibility would be to ...

5b Listen again and complete the phrases you have ticked with information from the conversation. Then check your answers by looking at Audio script 7.3 on page 176.

5c Practise saying the phrases. Pay attention to stress and intonation.

TASK
DECIDING ON FACILITIES IN A HOTEL

6a Two architectural firms are going to submit a plan for the ground floor. Work in three groups.

Groups A (Lindsay Associates) and B (Jackson and Li Consultants): You are the architectural firms. In your groups, discuss and decide what six facilities should be put on the ground floor and where each facility should be located. Study the diagram and draw a rough plan of the ground floor, with all its facilities.

Group C (Representatives of Horizon Hotels and Conference Centres): Discuss what six facilities should be on the ground floor. Think about where you might locate each facility.

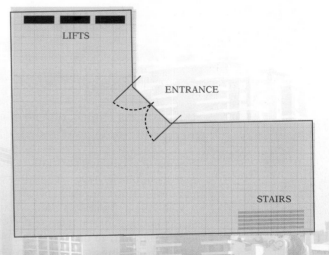

LIFTS

ENTRANCE

STAIRS

6b The two firms (Groups A and B) present their plans for the ground floor to the HHCC representatives (Group C) and answer any questions.

6c HHCC representatives decide which architectural firm should be given the contract to design the ground floor, explaining the reasons for their choice.

STUDY SKILLS
IDENTIFYING FACT AND OPINION

1a Work in small groups. Read the definition of a 'high-rise apartment block'. Then discuss the essay question and give your opinions.

A high-rise apartment block can be defined as a building which has a large number of storeys and is equipped with elevators. It is generally 35 metres or greater in height.

1b Skim the essay. Does the writer agree with your opinions?

2 Look again at the essay question. Which of the statements is the best description of this kind of essay?

In an opinion-led essay, the writer:

a   presents the arguments objectively for and against a controversial issue.

b   discusses and evaluates the opinions of other writers on the essay topic.

c   states his/her opinions on the topic and supports them with evidence.

'If they had a choice, few people would live in high-rise apartments.'
Discuss the statement and give your opinion.

Because of expanding populations and the lack of space for building new houses, high-rise apartment blocks have become increasingly common in most of the world's major cities
5   and towns. However, some people say that residents in multi-storey buildings do not really enjoy living in them. It is claimed that they feel isolated, are often lonely and live in such blocks not by choice but out of necessity. This is a misconception. There are, in fact, many benefits of living in this type of accommodation and few disadvantages. Most people enjoy this style of living and do not crave for a house or low-level apartment.

10   The most significant advantage of choosing to live in a high-rise building is that the residents are close to most things they need for their everyday living. High-rise apartments tend to be in desirable, urban locations, near to the downtown area. As a result, residents have quick and easy access to shopping, nightlife, cultural institutions, transport facilities and often their place of work. However, there are also high-rise apartments situated in beautiful,
15   natural surroundings, such as parks, gardens and beach areas. These are generally outside the city centre and they will be chosen by people looking for an alternative to city life.

Another major advantage of high-rise accommodation is that it offers a wide range of shared amenities such as: doormen, controlled entry, fitness centres, swimming pools, recreation areas, morning coffee sessions and hosted events aimed at bringing residents together. These
20   provide opportunities for residents to get to know each other better. They develop a sense of community, which helps residents to avoid feelings of isolation and loneliness. The residents look out for each other, so that a sense of safety and security is fostered.

Critics of high-rise apartments point out that there are limited opportunities for gardening in such buildings. This is not entirely true since many residents have
25   balconies and they can use these to grow vegetables, plants and flowers. More importantly, there is a tendency nowadays for architects to design high-rise buildings which include 'green' spaces for trees, plants and shrubs. A high-rise building in Milan, Italy, 'BoscoVerticale' is typical of this trend. It will provide hundreds of new homes and bring a hectare of forest into the city's central business district. The building will
30   be a perfect model for architects designing tower blocks in the future.

To sum up, there are unquestionably many advantages of living in high-rise apartment buildings. Rather than creating feelings of isolation and loneliness, these buildings develop a sense of community and for many people they offer an ideal lifestyle. Such apartments will undoubtedly increase in the future because of the population growth
35   and lack of space in many countries.

3 Read the essay again. In which paragraph(s) of the essay can you find the following?

a   the writer's strongest argument to support his/her opinion
b   a counter-argument which is challenged by the writer
c   a strong opinion linking with the opening paragraph
d   the opinion(s) of the writer on the topic
e   additional arguments to support the writer's opinion

4 Fact and opinion What is the difference between a fact and an opinion? Complete the text with the words in the box.

| belief | emotions | evaluation | proved |
| scientific | subjective | | |

A fact is true and based on [1]_____ testing or practical experience, not on ideas. It can be supported by objective evidence. An opinion is a [2]_____ that may or may not be true. It is normally [3]_____. It can be based on a person's perspective, [4]_____ or understanding of something. The essential difference between a fact and an opinion is that a fact can be [5]_____ by study, research, [6]_____ or previous knowledge.

5 Work in small groups. Are the statements from the essay facts (F) or opinions (O)? Give reasons.

1   Most people enjoy this style of living. (paragraph 1)
2   High-rise apartments tend to be in desirable, urban locations. (paragraph 2)
3   There are also high-rise apartments situated in beautiful, natural surroundings. (paragraph 2)
4   These provide opportunities for residents to get to know each other better. (paragraph 3)
5   There are limited opportunities for gardening in such buildings. (paragraph 4)
6   There is a tendency nowadays for architects to design high-rise buildings which include 'green spaces'. (paragraph 4)
7   The building will be a perfect model for architects designing tower blocks in the future. (paragraph 4)
8   Living in such apartments will undoubtedly increase in the future. (paragraph 5)

6 Find the phrases 1–6 in the essay. What can you infer about the writer's intention?

1   It is claimed that they feel isolated … (paragraph 1)

You can infer from the phrase 'It is claimed …' that the writer may not agree with this opinion.

2   This is a misconception. (paragraph 1)
3   This is not entirely true … (paragraph 4)
4   More importantly, … (paragraph 4)
5   Unquestionably … (paragraph 5)
6   Undoubtedly … (paragraph 5)

WRITING SKILLS
AN OPINION-LED ESSAY

7a Avoiding repetition – nouns Most texts contain pronouns. These are used instead of a noun or noun phrase. Complete the lists with other pronouns that you know.

Personal pronouns: *I, she, him* …
Possessive pronouns: *mine, hers,* …
Demonstrative pronouns: *that,* …
Relative pronouns: *who,* …
Other pronouns: *one,* …

7b Look at the essay again. What do the highlighted pronouns refer to?

them (line 6) = high-rise apartments

1   This (line 7)   5   which (line 21)
2   their (line 14)   6   This (line 24)
3   These (line 15)   7   these (line 25)
4   These (line 19)

8a Avoiding repetition – nouns/noun phrases It is common to avoid repeating nouns and noun phrases by using phrases with similar meanings. Find three alternative phrases in paragraph 1 which avoid repeating *high-rise apartment blocks* and one alternative in paragraph 4 for *tendency*.

8b Avoiding repetition – verbs and adverbs Find the following in the essay.

• two verbs in paragraph 3 which avoid repeating *offers*.
• an adverb in paragraph 5 which avoids repeating *unquestionably*.

9 Improve this paragraph about high-rise apartments by avoiding repeating nouns phrases, verbs, verb phrases and adverbs.

Another great advantage of high-rise apartments is that they are generally cheaper to buy than a house. They are also cheaper for living and maintenance. Buying an apartment typically costs from $200,000–300,000, but buying a house will cost a lot more. Maintenance costs are undoubtedly cheaper for high-rise apartments because the surface area of high-rise apartments is smaller than the surface area of houses. Also, living and maintaining a house is generally a lot more time-consuming. A great argument, too, is that living above the ground in an apartment is more peaceful and less noisy than living in a house.

10 Write an opinion-led essay on one of these questions.

• Too much money is spent on maintaining and repairing old buildings rather than on building new, modern, space-saving ones.
• It is more important for a building to serve its purpose than to be a work of art.
• In old towns, new buildings should always be in the traditional style.
• Modern architecture is ugly compared with classical styles.

In the emerging global economy, everything is mobile. Bill Clinton, 1946–, former US president

SPEAKING AND VOCABULARY
GLOBALISATION

1 What do you understand by the term *globalisation*?

2 Complete the description with the words in the box.

| communications | experience | improvements |
| life | world | |

Globalisation is a term used to describe the way in which the ¹_____ is developing a single economy and culture. This is as a result of ²_____ in technology and ³_____, and the influence of large multinational companies. Globalisation is changing people's ⁴_____ of everyday ⁵_____ all over the world.

3 Work with a partner. Which of the following causes/ results of globalisation are the most important? Why? Can you think of any others?

- cheap air travel
- availability of global brands and products (e.g. Sony, Adidas, Nestlé, Nokia, McDonald's)
- entertainment (e.g. music, TV, films, shows from other countries)
- communication advances
- world events (e.g. the Olympic Games, the World Cup)
- opportunities to work or study abroad
- international organisations (e.g. the United Nations, the World Health Organisation, the World Bank)

4a Complete the sentences with the nouns in the box.

companies	competition	cultures	environment
gap	manufacturing	poverty	standards
understanding	workers		

Globalisation:
1. exploits _____ in sweatshops in poorer countries.
2. widens the _gap_ between rich and poor.
3. reduces _poverty_ and increases wealth.
4. promotes global _culture_ and tolerance.
5. destroys local _____ and traditions.
6. damages the natural _environment_
7. improves the quality of _manufacturing_, leading to more jobs and better pay.
8. creates _____ and increases the choice of goods and services.
9. encourages better _____ for the environment, literacy, health, working conditions.
10. gives multinational _companies_ too much power.

4b Work in small groups. Discuss the sentences about globalisation in Exercise 4a. Which do you agree/ disagree with?

READING AND LISTENING

5 *Viewpoint* is a weekly current affairs programme. Read the opinions on the *Viewpoint* message board and complete the table for messages 1–4.

	For or against globalisation?	Reasons
1 Marco		
2 Cindy		
3 Anna		
4 David		
5 Michel		
6 Mike		
7 Astrid		
8 John		
9 Maria		

MESSAGE BOARDS > VIEWPOINT

Is globalisation a good thing?

1 Globalisation is definitely about progress. It leads to better products, which are more cost effective to produce and therefore cheaper for everyone. It's about consumer choice. Globalisation also connects people by means of communication and offers them new opportunities for travel, work and education. It means a faster rate of development for the whole world. Many poorer countries have benefited from investment as a result of globalisation. *Marco, Italy*

2 The global economy simply means sweatshops in poor countries so that rich countries can have cheap goods. There is a lot of inequality involved in globalisation and the desire for cheaper products. It also leads to the destruction of natural resources. Globalisation benefits the rich nations, who control prices, who influence the economies of poor countries and cause populations to migrate in order to try and improve their lives. *Cindy, China*

3 Globalisation has been a force for change in so many ways for so many people. It has given them access to information and improved their lives, and has given global mobility to skilled workers. Fair trade has the ability to lift people out of poverty. It creates a level playing field and allows countries across the world to share their best products, goods and services. Many workers in developing countries now have employment because of globalisation. Globalisation benefits all nations by increasing competitiveness and efficiency. *Anna, Brazil*

4 Globalisation's only good for those who are already economically strong. It's the big multinational companies who really benefit, and it worries me that sometimes they seem to have more power and influence over our lives than elected governments. Some of them are actually richer than whole countries, which must be a bad thing. *David, Nigeria*

6 8.1 Now listen to some other views from the podcast of last week's show and complete the table.

7 Choose two of the messages and summarise each person's view point in one or two sentences.

VOCABULARY
COLLOCATIONS

8a Complete the collocations with the words in the box.

change   choice   greed   rights   trade

1 consumer ___choice___
2 climate ___change___
3 corporate ___greed___
4 fair ___trade___
5 human ___rights___

child   free   global   multinational   natural

6 ___natural___ resources
7 ___global___ warming
8 ___multi___ companies
9 ___child___ labour
10 ___free___ markets

8b Now check your answers to Exercise 8a in Audio script 8.1 on page 177.

8c Choose three or four collocations and write sentences about your own country.

SPEAKING AND WRITING

9 Assessing results and consequences **Work in groups to discuss the questions.**

1 Discuss the impact of globalisation up to now on your own life and your country.
2 Are you optimistic or pessimistic about the future? Why?
3 Thinking about the issues involved in globalisation, and having looked at some of the arguments in this lesson, do you think it is a force for good, for bad or a mixture of both?

10 **Summarise your argument in a short paragraph for the** *Viewpoint* **message board.**

 ▶ MEET THE EXPERT

Watch an interview with Richard Cook, a consultant and coach, about working in a global workplace.
Turn to page 152–153 for video activities.

LISTENING AND VOCABULARY
ABSTRACT NOUNS

1 **Work with a partner to discuss the questions.**

1 Would you like to work for an international company that employs people in many different countries?
2 Would you like to work or travel abroad? Why?/Why not?
3 What problems could arise when people from different countries have to work together in a global team?
4 What skills do you think you need to work in a global team?

2a **Match words 1–5 with their meanings a–e.**

1 adaptability
2 curiosity
3 consensus
4 sensitivity
5 intuition

a the desire to know about something
b the ability to change and be successful in different situations
c agreement between everyone in a group
d the feeling that you know something is correct or true even if you don't know why
e thinking about how other people will feel about something

2b **Complete the sentences with words from Exercise 2a.**

1 My _____ told me not to trust him.
2 He definitely has _____ – he could live in any country.
3 All team members need to have a _____ about the country they are going to.
4 The team leader's rude comments show a lack of _____.
5 The team failed to reach a _____ on the issue.

3 **8.2** **Listen to four international managers giving advice to young people who want to work for global companies. Decide which speaker does the following.**

a gives an example of how to adjust to someone with a different communication style
b talks about a number of skills needed to work globally
c talks about cultures with different ideas about the individual and the team
d talks about what employers want

4 **Listen again and complete the notes using one word in each gap.**

My notes

Global employers want people who:
- are willing to work with people from different ¹_____ and ²_____
- take an active ³_____ in the world around them
- have a global ⁴_____
- treat people as ⁵_____ and don't ⁶_____ them

When dealing with someone who has a more indirect communication style to you, you should:
- pay more attention to how you ⁷_____ things
- make sure ⁸_____ and information don't come across too directly
- speak to them in ⁹_____

Individual-focused cultures:
- value an individual's contributions and ¹⁰_____
- like focused, ¹¹_____ only meetings

Team-focused cultures:
- think deciding something ¹²_____ is a vital step in decision-making
- like to make the person look ¹³_____

READING

5 **Scan the texts quickly. Which countries or continents are mentioned in each one?**

A A group of exchange students from Europe were attending a lecture by Professor Lee at a university in Hong Kong. After a while, one of the exchange students put up her hand. Professor Lee didn't seem to notice her at first and the local students looked a bit awkward. After a few minutes, Professor Lee noticed her and she asked him to clarify something. Then other exchange students started asking more questions and the professor appeared to be uneasy. He hadn't encountered so many questions before.
Then some of the exchange students started to challenge the professor's point of view. The atmosphere was quite strange. The local students preferred to be more reserved and wanted everyone to show more respect towards the professor.

B A group of clinical researchers for an international pharmaceutical company were meeting in Moscow to discuss the studies they were running all over the world. Most of the researchers were Chinese and Russian but the group leader was American. Some of the researchers were unhappy because the group leader called everyone by their first names and forgot to use their titles. Although he tried to be friendly, he was not polite and had a very relaxed tone and stance and dressed very casually. In fact, some of the group said they would never forget seeing him attend one meeting wearing shorts. He seemed to think that what was said was more important than how it was said and he never seemed to pay attention to body language.

6 Read the texts again. Which texts, if any, refer to the following topics?

1 building relationships
2 dressing conservatively
3 indirect and direct communication styles
4 avoiding stereotypes
5 showing respect for authority
6 understanding handshakes
7 using titles and correct forms of address
8 exchanging business cards
9 punctuality and deadlines
10 space issues between people

7 Work with a partner. Describe the problems in each text. What advice would you give the people in the three situations?

8 Drawing conclusions With your partner, look again at the listening and reading sections. What are the three most important skills you need when working in a global team?

GRAMMAR
VERB PATTERNS

9 Look at the highlighted sentences in the texts and match verbs 1–5 with patterns a–e.

1 appear
2 ask
3 dislike
4 forget
5 start

a followed by the infinitive with *to*
b followed by either the infinitive with *to* or the *-ing* form with a different meaning
c followed by an object and the infinitive with *to*
d followed by the *-ing* form
e followed by either the infinitive with *to* or the *-ing* form with no change in meaning

C Team members from Mexico, India, China, Germany and the USA were having a series of business meetings in Mexico when some problems arose with regard to punctuality and deadlines. Team members from Mexico, India and China were sometimes late for meetings, giving the reason that they had been getting to know their colleagues from other countries over coffee in the staff canteen. However, the team members from Germany and the USA disliked waiting for team members who turned up late and had become frustrated. For the Germans and Americans if someone said 'the deadline is tomorrow', then that meant tomorrow. However, the Mexicans, Indians and Chinese argued that getting to know each other was more important to the success of the project than a deadline, because only by building trust together could they work as a team. They also found that the Americans and Germans didn't seem to value tact and diplomacy enough. For example, sometimes the Americans said things without considering the feelings of the people they were talking to.

10 Work with a partner. Look at the pairs of sentences 1–5 and discuss the differences between the verb patterns.

1 a I **remember watching** the first TV reports of the tsunami.
  b **Remember to lock** the door when you go out.
2 a I'll never **forget meeting** Brad Pitt when I went to Hollywood.
  b I won't **forget to switch off** the lights when I go.
3 a I **stopped driving** after three hours at the wheel.
  b I **stopped to have** a break for a few minutes.
4 a I **tried sending** her flowers, but it had no effect.
  b I **tried to persuade** her to listen to me, but she wouldn't.
5 a I **regret to inform** you that you did not get the job.
  b I don't **regret changing** jobs.

GRAMMAR TIP
After *remember, forget, stop, regret* and *go on*, we choose infinitives to look forward and *-ing* forms to look at the present or past.
I must remember to download a map of the city. (I'm going there next week.)
I remember meeting him at a conference in Seoul. (The conference was two years ago.)

→ Language reference and extra practice, pages 126–149

11 Complete the sentences with the infinitive or *-ing* form of the verbs in brackets. In some sentences both may be possible.

1 I'm sorry I forgot _____ (respond) to your email.
2 I tried _____ (talk) to the team leader, but he didn't really listen.
3 I'll never forget _____ (attend) the Forbes Global CEO conference in September.
4 Don't forget _____ (go) to the meeting.
5 I remember _____ (hear) something about how popular the book was in China.
6 I stopped _____ (buy) global brands like Adidas and Nike.
7 She remembered _____ (bring) her video camera to the conference, so we've got a great film of it.

12 Work with a partner and discuss topics from this list.

- someone you'll never forget meeting
- something you stopped doing recently
- something different you should try doing next year
- something you'll never forget seeing
- something you shouldn't forget to do before going to an interview
- something you remember doing on one of your birthdays

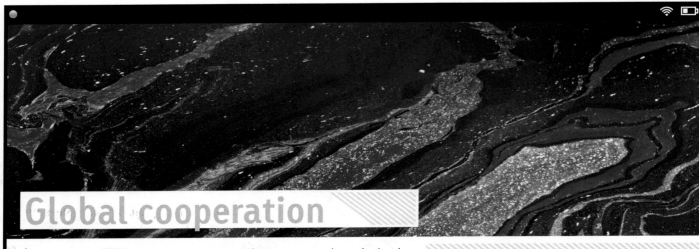

Global cooperation

1 _____ Now, in the 21st century, we've seen a new dynamic that is pushing the boundaries of invention and innovation – global cooperation. Scientific and technical research and development is now so complicated and sophisticated that no one scientist, however brilliant, can know it all. So, increasingly, innovation is coming from the combining of cutting edge expertise from diverse scientific fields. Scientists at CERN, for example, have come together from all over the world to seek answers to questions such as what is the universe made of and how did it start. In this article we will look at two more examples of this new global phenomenon that is quietly revolutionising our world.

2 _____ There are now over 8,000 scientific journals worldwide and it is impossible to be an expert in all areas. Professor Bob Langer at Massachusetts Institute of Technology (MIT) has made significant breakthroughs in the field of biomedical engineering and cancer treatment. But he hasn't done it on his own. His skill has been in bringing together truly interdisciplinary teams. He has invited experts from around the world in polymer science, medicine, pharmaceuticals, radiology, neurosurgery, molecular biology and engineering to form a global team to design new polymers* which can go inside the body, deliver medicines and then dissolve. Professor Langer is constantly looking for new global collaborators and experts in different fields.

3 _____ When Cesar Harada heard about the effects of the oil spill in the Gulf of Mexico in 2010, he quit his dream job as project leader at MIT and tried to develop a more efficient way to soak up the oil. But rather than prioritising profit, he decided to 'open-source' the design. He shared his own ideas on the web for free and then got experts from all around the world to contribute ideas and even donations. He then invited scientists and engineers to join him in New Orleans, and together they designed a highly manoeuvrable, flexible boat capable of cleaning large tracts of oil quickly. This free, not-for-profit way of sharing ideas, and releasing intellectual property on the internet, meant that innovation happened very quickly. All they had to do was credit all the inventors who cooperated. Harada's 'open-source' reciprocity is a new economic model with global cooperation at its core.

4 _____ Drawing people together from all over the world and creating synergy is a powerful way of driving innovation. Global teams with a united purpose building on everyone's expertise can collectively do far more than one brilliant individual. The inventor today is a global collaborator, a sharer, and not a protector of ideas. With 2.3 billion people online, collaboration and global cooperation can happen really quickly and it is possible to connect in a more profound way than ever before.

*polymers = a chemical compound formed from long chains of the same molecule group

READING

1 You are going to read an article about global cooperation. Work in small groups. How many examples of global cooperation can you think of for the areas below? How did the global cooperation occur?

- scientific breakthroughs
- humanitarian crises
- natural disasters
- environmental disasters

Scientists from all over the world worked on the Higgs Boson project in Switzerland.

2 Read the article quickly and choose the best title.

1 Global cooperation is on the increase.
2 Is innovation dependent on globalisation?
3 Global cooperation is needed more than ever before.

3 Complete gaps 1–4 in the article with sentences a–d.

a International cooperation based on sharing information freely has produced innovative approaches to solving problems.
b In a highly specialised world, scientists, medics and engineers have to collaborate in order to innovate.
c It appears that the days of brilliant individual inventors working in garages on their own is over.
d We live in a world which has benefited from huge advances in technology, medicine and science made during the last century.

4 Summarising Summarise these topics in one or two sentences.

1 What is happening with innovation in this century
2 Langer's approach to teams
3 Harada's innovative approach to problem solving

VOCABULARY
WORDS FROM THE TEXT

5a Match words or phrases in the article with their meanings 1–7.

1 the force that controls the relationships people or things have with each other (paragraph 1)
2 to challenge the limit of what is thought to be possible (paragraph 1)
3 the newest way of doing something (paragraph 1)
4 an event or situation that can be seen (paragraph 1)
5 to work together (paragraph 2)
6 the combined power of a group of things when they are working together (paragraph 4)
7 serious (paragraph 4)

5b Complete the text with words from Exercise 5a.

All our scientists have ¹_____ with scientists throughout the world leading to ²_____ research which will have ³_____ impacts in the field of space exploration. Working together has led to great ⁴_____ and we will only be able to push the ⁵_____ of scientific knowledge through further collaboration.

GRAMMAR
CAUSATIVES

6a [8.3] Listen to three people from a global charity discussing their latest campaign and answer the questions.

1 What was successful?
2 Did Jane fix her own computer?
3 Who updated the website?
4 Who approved the figures?
5 What was a shame?
6 Who will sign off the plan?

6b Look at Audio script 8.3 on page 177 and underline examples of structures 1–3.

1 *have* + object + past participle to describe something which is done for the subject by someone else (i.e. the subject arranges or pays for somebody else to do something for them)
2 *get* + object + past participle to describe something which is done for the subject by someone else (i.e. the subject arranges or pays for somebody else to do something for them)
3 *have* + object + past participle to describe something unexpected or unpleasant which happens to the subject

GRAMMAR TIP

In this structure, *get* is usually more informal than *have* and we tend to use it in spoken English. *We must get the house decorated soon.*

➡ Language reference and extra practice, pages 126–149

7 Put the words in order to make correct sentences.

1 removed / the / protesters / had / the / authorities
2 we / have / will / new phone lines / three / installed / next month
3 at the airport / the photographers / searched / had / bags / their
4 is having / she / her new book / into Japanese / translated
5 you / do / your / done / hair / get / at / Alleycatz?
6 had / their / taken / fingerprints / the police / by / the demonstrators
7 he / is / to / have / going / tested / his eyes / tomorrow
8 of / I / to / you / have / had / a copy / the report / sent
9 passport / last year / my brother / his / stolen / had
10 my / friend / slashed / his / tyres / got / by / some hooligans

SPEAKING

8a Work with a partner. Read notes about two examples of global cooperation.

Student A: look at page 156.
Student B: look at page 158.

8b Share your information and discuss what else you know about these topics.

SITUATION

1 **Read the extract from a TV guide and discuss the questions with a partner.**

1 Do you prefer shopping in a supermarket or smaller stores? Why?
2 What do you expect to be able to buy in a supermarket? Discuss your ideas with a partner.
3 Do you think supermarkets are generally good or bad for the communities they serve?

English language channel

Thursday 10 p.m.

VISTA Live debate

This week the panel discusses the plans of Smithsons, the international supermarket giant, to open branches in towns and cities all over the country. Opinions on the company and its activities are sharply divided so this will definitely be one to watch.

[handwritten: In]

---

2 **Now read the newspaper report and answer the questions.**

1 When was Smithsons founded? *[handwritten: was]*
2 What does it sell?
3 Where does it sell?
4 What sort of stores does it have?
5 What is happening in the near future?

Supermarket plans further expansion

SMITHSONS, THE SUPERMARKET giant, is on the move again, as it looks at entry into a number of new markets around the world.

From its small beginnings as a market stall over eighty-five years ago, Smithsons has become one of the world's biggest companies and employers. Growing out of its bases in the USA and UK, it now has around 5,000 stores around the world. From out-of-town superstores to small city-centre convenience shops, it claims to offer something for everyone.

Today it sells a vast range of goods and has seen huge growth since it entered the non-food area. It now sells everything from clothing, household items and electrical goods to financial services, fuel and insurance. The larger stores can now organise weddings and funerals. The company's slogan, 'Smithsons – for everything in life', is, it seems, becoming a reality.

3a 8.4 **Bob Craven, the Chief Executive of Smithsons, is on the hard-hitting radio programme *In the Hot Seat*. Listen and tick the topics that are mentioned.**

1 environmental damage
2 staff unions
3 consumer choice
4 competition
5 fair trade *[handwritten: How much they will pay to worker]*
6 treatment of staff

3b **Listen again and take notes on the topics in Exercise 3a.**

SUPERMARKET SUPERPOWER

KEY LANGUAGE
CLARIFYING

4a Correct the mistakes in the extracts. Look at Audio script 8.4 on page 177 to check your answers.

1 ... what do you think by good value?
2 Basically, what I'm meaning is the customer is ...
3 Sorry, I don't catch what you mean.
4 What I really try to say is ...
5 Or to give it another way, ...
6 Could you expand that in more detail, please?
7 Could you be more clear?
8 Let me research that.
9 Could you explain me an example?
10 To be more clear ... we really appeal to ...

4b Put the phrases in Exercise 4a into two groups.

a for making your meaning clearer   **b** asking for clarification

TASK
TAKING PART IN A DEBATE

5a Work in groups. Smithsons is planning to come to your country. You will be taking part in an edition of *Vista*, the live TV debate programme.

Student A (Chairperson): look at page 156 and study your role card.
Student B (Labour relations expert): look at page 158 and study your role card.
Student C (Government representative): look at page 161 and study your role card.
Student D (Opposition party representative): look at page 163 and study your role card.
Student E (Consumer group representative): look at page 163 and study your role card.

5b Work in pairs of the same roles (two As, Bs, etc.). Discuss what you believe, and think about the arguments you can use in the debate.

5c Hold the debate in groups of Students A–E.

OTHER USEFUL PHRASES
Chairing I'd like to ask (name) for his/her views (on this). Thank you, (name). You've had your say. Let the others give their views now, please. I'd like to move on now to …
Interrupting I'd just like to say … Can I just come in here? If I can interrupt you at this point …
Dealing with interruptions If you could just let me finish. Hold on a minute, please. If I can just finish what I'm trying to say …
Getting your point across The main issue here is … The really important thing is … Surely, the point is that …

STUDY SKILLS
SUMMARISING

1a Work with a partner and discuss the questions.

1   When do you need to summarise things in your life?
2   Are your summaries generally formal or informal? Written or spoken?

1b Discuss what you think makes a good summary.

2a Are these statements true or false, do you think? Give reasons.

1   A summary is a short version of the original text.
2   To write a good summary, you must understand every word in the original text.
3   A summary is generally about one-third of the length of the original text.
4   You should use your own words when summarising.
5   You must not change the order of the ideas in the text.
6   You should never use words from the original text.
7   You must not include any quotations from the original text.
8   A summary should not include your own opinions.
9   It is difficult to do a summary if you cannot paraphrase well.
10 It is helpful to find synonyms for words when summarising.

2b Which of the ideas that are true did you think of in Exercise 1b?

3 Put the stages of writing a summary below in order.
a   Highlight the key points in the original text.
b   Make notes of the key points. Paraphrase the points, do not copy them.
c   Check the summary to make sure it is accurate and complete.
d   Read the original text carefully and check the meaning of unknown words.
e   Write the summary from your notes.

4 Work with a partner. What do you understand by the terms *paraphrasing* and *topic sentences*? Read the text below to check.

When you summarise a text, you need to select the key point in each paragraph. The main point is usually in the topic sentence. This is generally the first sentence of the paragraph, though it may appear in other places, including at the end. You also need to paraphrase the important points. This means that you express them in a shorter, different way, using your own words if possible.

5 Topic sentences Look at paragraphs 1–3 of the article on page 80. Underline the topic sentence in each paragraph, and identify one important idea that supports it.

Paragraph 1

Topic sentence: Now, in the 21ˢᵗ century, we've seen a new dynamic that is pushing the boundaries of invention and innovation – global cooperation.

Supporting idea: Scientific and technical research and development is now so complicated and sophisticated that no one scientist, however brilliant, can know it all.

6 Paraphrasing Read paragraph 1 of the article again and say which paraphrase below is better. Give your reasons.

Paraphrase A
In this century, new ways of dealing with the world's problems are the result of experts from different fields working together rather than from achievements by individuals. For example, at CERN, scientists from different countries have joined together to find solutions to complex problems. (44 words)

Paraphrase B
Global cooperation can result in invention and innovation. This depends on advances in different fields. One individual cannot find new ways of solving problems. New solutions need cooperation. Scientists at CERN are studying the problems of the universe. These can only be solved by experts from diverse fields. (47 words)

7 Work with a partner. Read paragraph 2 of the article. It contains 129 words. Discuss the summary below. Give reasons why it is *not* a good one.

Scientists have to collaborate to innovate. There are now over 8,000 scientific journals in the world. One person cannot be an expert in all the areas of research. Professor Langer at MIT has made breakthroughs in the medical field. He has done this by forming teams from different disciplines to find new polymers for treating a medical condition. He is always trying to find new global collaborators. (67 words)

WRITING SKILLS
A SUMMARY

8 Read techniques a–c about paraphrasing. Then paraphrase sentences 1–6.

a Using synonyms
Some people believe/say/argue/claim that innovation/ creativity is driven/stimulated by competition.

b Changing the word class
innovation – innovate or innovative; competition – compete or competitive; collaboration – collaborate

c Changing the word order
Drawing people together from all over the world and creating synergy is a powerful way of driving innovation.

One of the most effective ways of encouraging innovation is to form an international team to work on a project.

1 So, increasingly, innovation is coming from the combining of cutting edge expertise from diverse scientific fields. (paragraph 1)
2 In a highly specialised world, scientists, medics and engineers have to collaborate in order to innovate. (paragraph 2)
3 His skill has been in bringing together truly interdisciplinary teams. (paragraph 2)
4 But rather than prioritising profit, he decided to 'open source' the design. (paragraph 3)
5 It appears that the days of brilliant individual inventors working in garages on their own is over. (paragraph 4)
6 The inventor today is a global collaborator, a sharer, and not a protector of ideas. (paragraph 4)

9 You are going to summarise an article about a new trend in manufacturing in the USA. Before writing the summary, do the following.

1 Underline the topic sentence in each paragraph.
2 Try to paraphrase each of the sentences.

10 Write your summary in approximately 120 words. Use this structure. (To ensure that the summary is cohesive, use linking words such as *however, in addition, finally*.)

- what the new trend is
- how American firms used to manufacture
- reasons why some American firms are changing their way of manufacturing
- examples of firms that are changing their method of manufacturing
- the situation in Europe

Early next month, local officials will gather for a ribbon-cutting ceremony at a facility in Whitsett, North Carolina. A new production line will start to roll and the seemingly impossible will happen: America will start making personal computers again. Mass-market computer production had been slowly disappearing for the past thirty years, and the vast majority of laptops have always been made in Asia. Dell shut two big American factories in 2008 and 2010 in a big move to China, and HP now makes only a small number of business desktops at home. The new manufacturing facility is being built not by an American company but by Lenovo, a highly successful Chinese technology group.

The original ideas behind offshoring was that Western firms with high labour costs could make huge savings by sending work to countries where wages were much lower. Offshoring means moving work and jobs outside the country where a company is based. For several decades, that strategy worked, often brilliantly. But now companies are rethinking their global footprints.

The first and most important reason relates to labour costs. Wages in China and India have been going up by 10–20 percent a year for the past decade, whereas manufacturing pay in America and Europe has hardly changed. Other countries, including Vietnam, Indonesia and the Philippines, still offer low wages, but not China's scale, efficiency and supply chains. Lenovo's labour costs will still be higher than in its factories in China and Mexico, but the gap has narrowed a great deal.

Second, many American firms now realise that they went too far in sending work abroad and need to bring some of it home again. Well-known companies such as Google, General Electric and the Ford Motor Company are bringing some of their production back to America and adding new capacity there. Michael Porter, Harvard Business School's guru on competitive strategy, says that a lot of chief executives offshored too quickly, and too much.

In Europe, there was never as much enthusiasm for offshoring as in America, and the small number of companies that did it are in no rush to return.

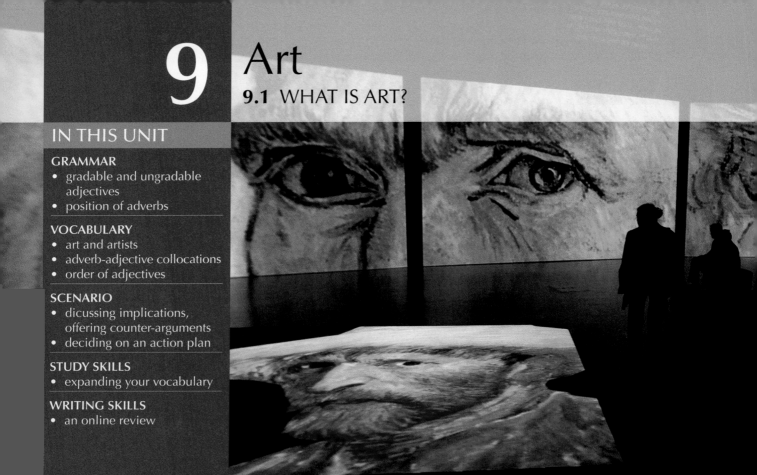

9 Art

9.1 WHAT IS ART?

IN THIS UNIT

GRAMMAR
- gradable and ungradable adjectives
- position of adverbs

VOCABULARY
- art and artists
- adverb-adjective collocations
- order of adjectives

SCENARIO
- dicussing implications, offering counter-arguments
- deciding on an action plan

STUDY SKILLS
- expanding your vocabulary

WRITING SKILLS
- an online review

I paint objects as I think them, not as I see them. Pablo Picasso, 1881–1973, Spanish artist

SPEAKING AND READING

1 Work in small groups and discuss the questions.

1 Did you study Art at school? Did you enjoy it? Why?/Why not?
2 How often do you visit museums and art galleries?
3 Do you think art is important in people's lives? Why?/Why not?

2 Read the debate on the webpage and match the people to the opinions below.

1 Art is about someone's feelings.
2 Art is to show the craftsmanship of the artist.
3 Art is a waste of time.
4 The purpose of art is to represent the natural environment.
5 The purpose of art is to make viewers think about their own ideas.
6 The purpose of art is for financial gain.

3 Which people do you agree/disagree with? Who makes the best point, in your opinion?

4 How would you describe the views of each person? Select from the following adjectives and find reasons in the article to support your answers. Can you add any other adjectives?

conservative	critical	dismissive	intellectual
passionate	radical	respectful	undecided

5 Justifying opinions **Work in small groups. Which of the following do you consider to be art? Explain your reasons.**

- some graffiti on a wall
- a tattoo on someone's body
- a holiday photograph
- a pile of bricks in an exhibition
- a screensaver on a mobile phone
- a comic book
- a painting of a bowl of fruit
- an advert for a product
- a firework display

ART OPINION HAVE A SAY

Following the provocative and hard–hitting article by Louise Trench *Do you believe in Art?*, we thought you should have your say. So this week's question is …

WHAT IS THE PURPOSE OF ART?

Dan
For me, it is all about the skill of the artists. I can't draw or paint, so I like to see how they can recreate reality just by using shapes and colour. It's a real skill. I tried at school, but I just had no talent for it. It's amazing what they can do. I just like naturalistic art, I suppose. I think it's called realism.

Karen
I feel art should be thought-provoking and get people to question things, you know, the world around them, and their views on it. It can also be used for political purposes – to criticise governments or challenge authority – just as Banksy does today with his murals. Art should be controversial and get people talking, you know, stimulate debate. It may also be shocking. Maybe I'm idealistic, but I believe art can help change the world.

Kylie
I'm really not sure. I mean, I've read books about art, but at the end of the day, I think it's about your emotional reaction to a piece of art. Some art you respond to and like – other art you don't. Some people like more traditional art, like portrait painting, or sculpture. Other people prefer more modern and contemporary art, which can be very unusual. Some people feel this is not art and they just can't stand it.

Taco
It's just a business really, isn't it? Some of these so-called masterpieces – they can fetch millions. It seems criminal when people are starving in the world. Museums make too much money, particularly from these big retrospectives of famous artists. They've usually all been dead for years, so what's the point of looking at their work? I don't go to art galleries or museums for that reason. Anyway, I don't think they want people like me there who don't understand art.

Rina
The purpose of art, for me, is to represent the world – to show things around us. Paintings can show the natural beauty of the world. Even those really early cave paintings show the world of the people who painted them. I love landscape painting. I'm not interested in groundbreaking modern and contemporary art, or all that abstract art which people like. I'm not interested in what critics and collectors say. I don't want to think about what it means. I just want it to look nice and to make me feel good.

Matt F
There's no point to art at all. It's ridiculous. I mean, it's a stupid question. The fact that you need to ask means that it doesn't have a point. You don't need to ask what the purpose of engineering or science is, do you? Art is rubbish – there's nothing useful about it at all. And being an artist isn't a real job anyway. I think a lot of so-called art is a con. You know when 'artists' put a pile of leaves in a corner of an art gallery and claim it's a work of art? Well, it's not. Any fool can do that.

VOCABULARY
ART AND ARTISTS

6 Find nouns or adjectives in the article which mean the following.

1 causing people to think
2 art which is done on a wall
3 causing a lot of disagreement
4 a very good piece of art
5 involving new methods or ideas
6 a show of the past work of an artist

7 List all the types of art and artworks mentioned in the article.

painting, naturalistic art, …

LISTENING

8 [9.1] Listen to three people talking about art. Make notes on each person's attitude.

9 Match the three speakers to the types of art they like from the box below.

landscape   portraits   sculpture   ceramics
video art   performance art   abstract art   classical art
contemporary art   modern art

10a Listen again and complete the expressions.
1 I'm really _____ of thing.
2 It was so impressive – _____ of _____.
3 It really took _____.
4 It really _____ my expectations.
5 It was _____ and the cost.
6 This was a _____-_____-_____-_____ opportunity.

10b Choose three of the expressions from Exercise 10a and write sentences which are true for you.

SPEAKING

11 Describe a well-known painting or piece of art you have seen or know about. Talk about the following topics.
- what it looks like
- what is interesting about it
- why it is well-known
- if you like or dislike it, and why

1 Do you take photos? When? Why? Do you prefer colour or black and white photos?

2 Read the article and choose the best title.

1 What makes a good photo?
2 The best photo in the world.
3 Is photography an art form?

3 Identifying arguments Find arguments in the article that support the idea that photography is an art form.

4 Work with a partner and discuss the questions.

1 What does the article say about the difference between photography and paintings?
2 What reasons are given in the article for photography not being an art form?
3 Do you think photography is an art form?

Paintings are almost always considered an art form, but what about photography? The Frenchman Henri Cartier-Bresson, possibly the most famous photographer of the 20th century, emphasised the difference between painting as art and photography as art. In 1957, he told *The Washington Post* that 'There is a creative fraction of a second when you are taking a picture. Your eye must see a composition or an expression that life itself offers you, and you must know with intuition when to click the camera. That is the moment the photographer is creative.' He is, of course, referring to the immediacy of photography – the absolutely unique moment, never to be repeated, when the exposure is taken.

A further characteristic of photography, unlike painting, is that more can be captured in a photograph than was intended by the photographer. Fine details, entirely unexpected and often invisible to the naked eye, can be revealed. The photograph 'does not lie' because it has not passed through the brain of the photographer. This is completely different from the brain processes of the painter, who decides what he is going to paint, how he will make the subject interesting and how he is going to paint it.

Some critics of photography claim that modern cameras reduce photo-taking to an automatic process. They say, 'Just point and shoot. The camera does the rest. You will get a good photo.'

However, those who see photography as an art form say that the critics are completely wrong. They argue that the camera cannot decide between an ordinary, functional, regular photo and a really excellent, cleverly composed photo, consciously constructed. Rather, it is the photographer who has the skill to pick out the essential qualities of the subject at a particular moment and brings creativity to the process.

Not all photographers are primarily interested in producing photos that are art – some take photos to record the world for scientific purposes or to capture a news story. But occasionally, these types of photos can become iconic works of art because they are so stunning. Examples of this are the very unusual photographs taken by explorers in the Antarctic for geographical purposes, which often reveal the wonders of nature by showing contrasts between ice and water. They can also become iconic because they come to represent an important moment in time. A classic instance of this is the picture taken by Robert Capa during the Spanish Civil War of a soldier at the moment of being shot, falling backwards. This photograph is both deeply moving and historically extremely important. A more recent example of a photo representing an important moment in time is the Pulitzer prize-winning photo taken by Kevin Carter of a vulture waiting for a child to die during the 1994 Sudan famine.

VOCABULARY
ADVERB-ADJECTIVE COLLOCATIONS

5 Find the following adjectives in the article. Note the adverbs that go with them.

different   moving   unexpected   wrong

6 Complete each sentence below using an adverb-adjective collocation from the boxes.

heavily   highly   painfully   totally

criticised   praised   qualified   shy
unbelievable   unjustified

1   Cartier-Bresson was _____ for his excellent coverage of Gandhi's funeral in India in 1948.
2   Mario Testino was _____ in many fields before he moved to London to train as a photographer.
3   The plot of the film was _____ and the war scenes were fake.
4   *One Hour Photo* is a film starring Robin Williams about a quiet and _____ photo technician.
5   A top university was _____ for spending £1.4m on art works when its main building needed repair.
6   The banning of photographers from the area was _____ as there was no obvious danger to people.

GRAMMAR
GRADABLE AND UNGRADABLE ADJECTIVES

7a Look at these adjectives from the article. Put them into pairs with similar meanings.

essential   excellent   good   important
unique   unusual

7b Now put the following adjectives into pairs with similar meanings.

angry   bad   big   cold   devastated
enormous   exhausted   fascinating   freezing
furious   hungry   interesting   small
starving   terrible   tiny   tired   upset

Adjectives can be gradable or ungradable. For example, *cold* is gradable (there are degrees of 'coldness'), but *freezing* is ungradable – it is at the end of the scale of 'coldness'.

Some ungradable adjectives express extreme qualities (e.g. *terrified, furious, starving*) and others express absolute qualities (e.g. *alive, correct, dead, male, human*).

8 Which of the adjectives in Exercise 7 are gradable and which are ungradable?

Gradable	Ungradable
angry	*furious*

9a Find the adjectives from Exercise 7a in the article and note the words before them. Then choose the correct option in the statements below.
1   *Gradable/Ungradable* adjectives can be made stronger or weaker with words like *very, a bit, extremely,*_____, _____ and _____.
2   We often use *absolutely*, _____ and _____ with *gradable/ungradable* adjectives.

9b Now complete the statements above with the words in the box.

a little   completely   pretty   slightly   totally

> **GRAMMAR TIP**
>
> We can use *really* with both gradable and ungradable adjectives:
> *The film was really interesting.*
> *The exhibition was really fascinating.*
> *Really, awfully* and *terribly* are more common in informal spoken English.

→ Language reference and extra practice, pages 126–149

10 Correct the adverbs if they are wrong.
1   I thought it was a very excellent photograph.
2   We were a bit tired after our visit to the Louvre.
3   I was very devastated when they said the exhibition was closed.
4   The photographs were extremely terrible.
5   When we had finished going round the photo exhibition, we were absolutely exhausted.

11 Identify the adverb-adjective combinations in the text below. Are there any combinations that don't go together? Why?

> The National Gallery of Ireland has a very excellent collection of European fine arts. It opened in 1854 and now has over 2,500 paintings. Admission is very cheap. It has a wonderful Irish collection, including works by Jack B. Yeats, and the Flemish and Dutch collection is very enormous. There is even a Vermeer. There are also works by Caravaggio, Picasso and Monet. We were absolutely hungry at the end of our visit, and luckily the café has great food. The shop is located in the new wing, which is itself an extremely fascinating piece of architecture. For such a small country, this collection is absolutely interesting and most visitors have a really wonderful day.

SPEAKING

12 Work in small groups. Find a favourite photo on your phone or think of one you have taken that you like. Describe the photo and say why it is one of your favourites.

READING

1 Work with a partner. Do you know of any sculptures in your country, or in the rest of the world?

2 Read the profiles of three artists quickly, and say what artistic disciplines each has worked in.

3 Read the profiles again and answer the questions.

According to the texts, which artist:
1 still lives in his/her country of birth?
2 did not complete his/her education?
3 had a husband/wife who was more famous than he/she was?
4 is influenced strongly by his/her country of birth?
5 has received criticism of his/her talent?
6 uses him/herself as a model?
7 has recently combined two artistic disciplines in his work?

4 Which of the works of art in the photos do you like the most? Would you like to go to the artists' exhibitions? Why?/Why not?

VOCABULARY
ORDER OF ADJECTIVES

5a Look at the highlighted phrases in the profiles. List the adjectives under some of these headings.

age, material, colour/pattern, opinion, nationality, size, shape, most other qualities

5b Add the adjectives from the following examples under the headings in Exercise 5a. Try to work out the order of adjectives before a noun (i.e. opinion is first). Check your answers in the table on page 166.

beautiful, antique, colourful, Japanese silk paintings
a huge, well-known, dark bronze sculpture

6 Complete the sentences below, putting the adjectives in brackets in the correct order.
1 Michael Ayrton made _____ sculptures. (bronze, fabulous, large)
2 Rothko's paintings often consist of a number of _____ boxes. (coloured, large, rectangular)
3 These _____ figures date back 2,000 years. (antique, wonderful, Javanese)
4 The artist created a _____ sculpture. (fantastic, stainless steel, shiny)
5 Lacquer is a _____ varnish. (hard, coloured, heat-resistant)
6 Wall paintings are used to brighten up some _____ environments. (dreary, urban, modern)
7 The bird was made with a piece of _____ paper. (square, Japanese, origami)

Anish Kapoor

Anish Kapoor was born in Mumbai, India, in 1954 and moved to England **in 1972**. He studied at two famous art schools in London, before starting out as a sculptor. Kapoor soon became well-known because of his particular style, which, in his early works, involved the clever use of monochrome and brightly-coloured pigments surrounding the sculpture.

Although he is **mainly** resident in London, he often visits India, and Western and Eastern styles influence his work. His use of colour is **strongly** influenced by the heaps of coloured spices and powders found in Indian markets.

Kapoor's later works are **often** very large. In fact, his 110-ton Cloud Gate sculpture in Chicago is amongst the largest in the world. This sculpture is forged from a series of highly-polished stainless steel 'plates' that create an arched, highly-reflective work with Chicago's skyline and Millennium Park in the background.

Kapoor has also worked on subway design in Italy and his work is increasingly becoming a mixture of art and architecture. In 2012, he completed 'Orbit' for the 2012 London Olympic Games. At 115 metres tall, Orbit is the tallest sculpture in the UK.

Yoko Ono

Yoko Ono, who once said 'Everybody's an artist', was born in 1933 in Tokyo, Japan. In 1945, at the end of World War II, she had to hide with her family when Tokyo was fire-bombed. Although she came from a rich, aristocratic family, she had to pawn her mother's property to obtain rice when Japan surrendered and everyone was poor. She moved with her family **to New York** when she was eighteen. She went to college, but dropped out after two years.

Antony Gormley

Antony Gormley was born in 1950 **in Hampstead, England**, and, like Kapoor, is famous for his large-scale sculptures. He studied at Cambridge from 1968 to 1971 before travelling to India and Sri Lanka to study Buddhism **until 1974.** On his return, he studied in a number of colleges in London.

His work **mainly** focuses on the human body and he uses his own body **creatively** to form metal casts for his sculptures. One of his best-known sculptures is 'The Angel of the North', an enormous metal figure, now completely rusted to a brown colour, with huge, fully-extended wings. Motorists travelling on the A1 road to the North of England and Scotland see the Angel rising above them **dramatically** as they drive closer to it.

Another striking sculpture is 'Asian Field', installed in Sydney in 2006. It has 180,000 small brown clay figurines crafted by 350 Chinese villagers in five days from 100 tons of red clay. The installation is reminiscent of the terracotta warriors of Xian, China.

His spectacular public art installation 'Event Horizon' premiered in London in 2007, before being displayed in a number of major world cities, including New York, Sao Paolo and Rio de Janeiro.

She is **primarily** known for her sculpture and installation art, but she has also worked in film, poetry and music. She is **probably** most famous for her marriage to John Lennon of The Beatles. Lennon once described her as 'the world's most famous unknown artist: everybody knows her name, but nobody knows what she does.'

Her artistic work has **frequently** been criticised. Indeed, Brian Sewell, a traditional art critic, said, 'She's shaped nothing, she's contributed nothing, she's simply been a reflection of the times ...'. There is **certainly** disagreement with Sewell's views in the art world. In 2009, she received a Golden Lion for Lifetime Achievement from the Venice Biennale, and in 2013 the largest retrospective of her work opened in Frankfurt, coinciding with her 80th birthday.

GRAMMAR
POSITION OF ADVERBS

7a Look at the adverbs/adverb phrases in bold in the profiles. Add them to the list below.
1 Time: *then, in May,* ...
2 Place: *there, at home,* ...
3 Manner: *quickly, carefully,* ...
4 Frequency: *sometimes, never,* ...
5 Certainty: *definitely, perhaps,* ...
6 Degree: *a lot, mostly,* ...

7b Look at the clauses these adverbs/adverb phrases appear in and answer the questions below.
1 Do groups 1–3 come at the beginning, middle or end of the clause?
2 Where do groups 4–6 come in the clause?
3 Where do the adverbs in 4–6 go in relation to the verb they modify?
4 Is this the same with all verbs? (Look at *mainly*.)

GRAMMAR TIP

We can emphasis adverb phrases of time and place by putting them at the beginning of the clause.
In 2012, Yoko Ono received a lifetime achievement award.

➤ Language reference and extra practice, pages 126–149

8 Put the adverbs in brackets in the correct place in the sentences.
1 Rahmi Pehlivanli, the famous Turkish painter, painted portraits. (often)
2 Many artists have been influenced by Picasso. (strongly)
3 Leonardo da Vinci sketched technical designs. (very skilfully)
4 The French post-impressionist Paul Gauguin died alone. (in Tahiti)
5 Katushika Hokusai is the most famous Japanese artist ever. (probably)
6 The batik effect is produced by machines rather than being hand made. (nowadays)

SPEAKING

9a Developing arguments **Work with a partner and think of three arguments that support the following statement and three arguments against it.**
Public works of art are a waste of money.

9b Work with a new partner and discuss the statement using the arguments you have developed.

▶ MEET THE EXPERT

Watch an interview with Yulia Podolska, a sculptor, about her work and influences.

Turn to page 153 for video activities.

SCENARIO
THE RUSSELL DRAKE GALLERY

SITUATION

The Russell Drake Gallery sells contemporary art in Chelsea, New York. Chelsea, with its 300 galleries, is the centre of modern art in the city and there is strong competition to try and satisfy existing customers as well as attract new ones. Location is not enough. Galleries need to stand out from the crowd and offer something different to collectors and the general public. The Russell Drake Gallery represents about thirty-five artists, whose works are priced from $5,000–200,000. The gallery's aim is to sell between eight and ten pieces each month.

Recently, the gallery has not been meeting its sales targets. As a result, its owners, Russell and Vanessa Drake, realise that they must make changes to increase sales and attract more customers to their gallery. They have a meeting planned with Dennis Paul, an art consultant, about how to increase their profits.

1 Read the situation and answer the questions.

1 What is the Chelsea area of New York famous for?
2 What do galleries need to do in order to be successful?
3 How many works of art would the Russell Drake Gallery like to sell each month?
4 What problem is the gallery currently facing?

2a Work with a partner. Read the reviews from the gallery's website and decide which are the three most serious criticisms.

2b Compare your opinions with other pairs.

The Russell Drake Gallery | Reviews

I've visited the gallery several times. Usually disappointed. The range of art is too great. I'm not interested in photography, sculpture and video art, and I can't get excited about modern African art (last week's exhibition). You need to focus more on what you're offering.

I didn't enjoy my visit. The artists were boring. Most of the paintings were landscapes and portraits. Middle-of-the-road stuff that you can see in plenty of galleries. There was nothing to talk about.

I liked the artists on show, and the naturalistic art was really impressive. The exhibition 'Realism in the arts' was the highlight of my visit. But I got really tired after a while and wanted to sit down. Unfortunately, there weren't enough seats. What about having a café to relax in at the end of a visit?

Your prices are far too high for what you're offering. Only collectors can afford that sort of money. By the way, parking's really difficult in your area. I had to walk miles to get to you. It's not easy to find your gallery, either. You're right on the edge of the district, I found out.

Your staff were friendly, but there weren't enough signs to show what was going on in some of the rooms. I wanted to see more works by New York artists, I'm not really interested in Asian art.

You need to be more innovative in your choice of artists. I like naturalistic art, not abstract art and splash paintings. I'd love to buy some paintings by young, emerging artists.

I like the high ceilings in the gallery, but there isn't enough light, so I didn't enjoy my visit. It's about time you repainted the walls, isn't it? That'd make the rooms lighter.

You must improve your website. It's not enough to show just one painting from a collection you're going to feature in your gallery. Also, the site's difficult to navigate. I couldn't find any map showing where you are located.

3 Look at the visitor ratings below. What do they show, in your opinion? Do they indicate that customer satisfaction of the gallery is: a) high, b) fairly high, c) acceptable, d) too low or e) totally unacceptable?

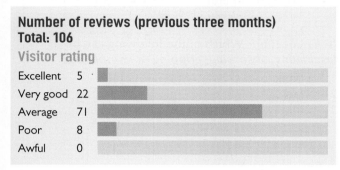

Number of reviews (previous three months)
Total: 106

Visitor rating

Excellent	5	
Very good	22	
Average	71	
Poor	8	
Awful	0	

KEY LANGUAGE
DISCUSSING IMPLICATIONS, OFFERING COUNTER-ARGUMENTS

4 **9.2** Russell and Vanessa Drake and Dennis Paul are discussing the commission that the gallery charges artists to exhibit their work. Listen and choose the arguments that Dennis Paul uses to oppose lowering the commission rate.

1 The artists do not object to the present commission system.
2 Other galleries might start lowering their commission.
3 Russell Drake's commission is already fairly low.
4 The artists do not like changes in commission rates.
5 The best customers would be unhappy about variable rates.
6 A lower commission rate will have an impact on the gallery's profitability.

5a Listen again and number the phrases below in the order you hear them.

a But think of the consequences. (Dennis)
b I think there's a strong argument for doing it. (Vanessa)
c But it wouldn't if we charged variable commission rates. (Russell)
d You need to take into account the reactions of the other gallery owners. (D)
e There are plenty of things you could do ... (D)
f Maybe, but consider the implications. (D)
g We do need to have more young artists on our books. (V)
h If you lower your commission, other galleries might start doing the same thing. (D)
i That may be true, but our situation's getting pretty desperate. (V)
j We've got to do something if we want to survive. (V)
k the problem with that is that it could really upset your best customers ... (D)
l It'll affect your profits if you lower your commission rate. (D)

5b Decide whether each phrase is 'discussing implications' (I) or 'offering a counter-argument' (C).

TASK
DECIDING ON AN ACTION PLAN

6 Work in small groups. You are members of a team of art consultants headed by Dennis Paul. Do the following tasks together.

1 Consider the implications of each of Dennis Paul's ideas below. Then choose the best five ideas for further study. Make notes of your reasons for not choosing the other ideas.
2 Discuss the cost of the ideas you've chosen. Which ones will be:
  a inexpensive   b quite expensive
  c very expensive   d easy to implement
  e more suitable as a long-term project?
3 Think of any other ideas that could make money for the gallery. Make notes.
4 Work out an action plan for the next year.

MEETING AGENDA

Ideas

1 Change the gallery's strategy. Focus on exhibiting exclusively young emerging artists based in New York.

2 Sponsor a young, promising artist, perhaps someone already exhibiting on the internet.

3 Sponsor a competition of modern art in New York's major art colleges.

4 Exhibit at one major art fair in New York rather than at several smaller fairs, as the gallery does at the moment.

5 Hire an expert to improve the gallery's website. Aim to attract more foreign visitors by advertising in specialist art magazines.

6 Redecorate the gallery and enlarge the windows.

7 Move to a new location where the rents are much cheaper.

8 Vary the commission rate, charging 50 percent to established artists and a lower commission rate for young artists.

9 Set up a café in the gallery offering high-quality snacks and lunches.

10 Invite famous modern artists to give lectures on their work at the gallery.

---

7 Compare your action plan with the plans of other groups. Explain your reasons for not choosing some of Dennis Paul's ideas.

8 As one group, take a vote to decide which is the best action plan.

STUDY SKILLS
EXPANDING YOUR VOCABULARY

1 Look at these phrases. What do you think the word *nice* means? Does it mean the same in each phrase?

1 Have a **nice** day.
2 **Nice** to meet you.
3 She's really **nice**.
4 That's a **nice** haircut.
5 Let's have a **nice** cup of tea.
6 It's a **nice** place to live.

2 Read this extract from a book about expressing yourself accurately. Is this the same as in your language?

It pays to increase your word power

Expanding your vocabulary is a sure way of improving your English and the way you express yourself in English. However, spoken and written English are often quite different.

Take a simple example – the word *nice* is very common in spoken English. It is a very general adjective, which is rather vague in meaning, as in the following examples: *Have a nice day, Nice to meet you, She's really nice, That's a nice haircut*. In this spoken context, *nice* is very useful – often we don't need to be very precise because a lot of meaning is carried by our intonation and facial expression. Also, the listener and speaker can clarify what exactly is meant. In written English, these clues are absent so we need to be more precise in order to convey what we really mean.

In addition, it is good to expand your vocabulary for stylistic reasons. Your writing will be much more interesting if you avoid repeating the same words.

3 What does the word *nice* really mean in phrases 1–6? Choose two words from the box for each phrase.

beautiful	charming	delicious	friendly
picturesque	productive	relaxing	restful
stylish	tasty	trendy	useful

1 a nice view
2 a nice meal
3 a nice holiday
4 a nice jacket
5 a nice person
6 a nice meeting

4 Look at these other common, basic adjectives 1–8. Add three more precise adjectives from the box below to each one.

1 good: *excellent*
2 bad: *terrible*
3 interesting: *fascinating*
4 sad: *upsetting*
5 boring: *dull*
6 funny: *humorous*
7 exciting: *dramatic*
8 stupid: *crazy*

absorbing	absurd	amusing	appalling	awful
brilliant	compelling	dreadful	exhilarating	
gripping	heartbreaking	hilarious	laughable	
monotonous	moving	nailbiting	outstanding	
repetitive	ridiculous	tedious	terrific	
thrilling	touching	witty		

GRAMMAR TIP

Adjective-noun collocations are also important. A good thesaurus will help you to recognise collocations and find better words to express what you mean. Look up the basic idea of what you want to say and you can find alternatives.

5 Collocations Which of the following can be *fascinating, absorbing, gripping* or *compelling*?

1 a book
2 a fact
3 a film

WRITING SKILLS
AN ONLINE REVIEW

6 Look at the different ways you can use to research a holiday. What are the advantages and disadvantages of each? Which would you use to get information?

- visit a travel agent
- check the websites of travel agencies
- look at some travel blogs
- consult a guidebook
- get advice from friends or colleagues

7 9.3 Listen to an extract from a talk on 'How to improve your writing skills'. Denise Couture, a lecturer in Communications, is talking about travel blogs. Work with a partner and discuss the questions.

1 What advantages of writing a travel blog does she mention in her talk?
2 Which do you think is the most important advantage?
3 Does she mention the same advantages you thought of in Exercise 6?

8 Read the travel blog about Nice, a city in the southern region of France known as the Côte d'Azur, and answer the questions.

1 Which tourist sites did Alessandra and her friend visit during the day?
2 What was their general impression of each site?
3 What did Chagall and Matisse have in common? In what ways were they different?

9 Vocabulary competition Work in small teams. Note down as many words as you can that are similar in meaning to the ones in bold in the blog. The time limit is five minutes and you may use a dictionary. At the end, count your words. The team with the most wins.

10 Write a travel blog of a trip you have made, either in your country or abroad. Mention any unusual or interesting experiences you had and describe one or two sites. Try to use some of the new vocabulary that you have learnt.

Alessandra.com

NICE BLOG

A DAY IN NICE: CHAGALL AND MATISSE MUSEUMS

Nice is a great city to stroll around. In the morning, we decided to visit Cours Saleya, the market square. It's a historic area, surrounded by 500-year-old buildings. It's also a **trendy** place. There are always lots of tourists who go to enjoy the atmosphere, sample the range of foods and admire the flowers on display. A lot of residents go there on Sundays to buy their supplies of meat, cheese, spices and fruit for the week. We had a **nice** meal at a restaurant. The salad was really good and the waiter was **charming** and helpful. It was a really relaxing time for both of us.

It wasn't just the food that was **great**. There were several street performers in the square playing various musical instruments, but the highlight for us was a group of Brazilian dancers and acrobats. They were all men and incredibly athletic. Their performance was really **exhilarating**. They jumped incredibly high and did somersaults on the hard ground, accompanied by Brazilian music. One of them was very **funny**. He made jokes in French and English to the crowd and managed to persuade a young child to climb up the human pyramid formed by the other acrobats. There was a **thrilling** end to the performance when the most athletic performer jumped over a wooden bar which had been raised to an incredible height. It was really dangerous to do it, but exciting for the crowd.

In the afternoon, we hired bicycles and visited the Chagall and Matisse Museums. We had to ride up a long, steep hill to get there. It was exhausting. At one point, we were passed by a group of young, fit cyclists who seemed to find our efforts hilarious! We really suffered and felt **dreadful** when we got there, but it was worth it. Both museums were **outstanding**: the Chagall Museum had lovely gardens and a p**eaceful** café, while the Matisse Museum was in a beautiful park. Once you got to the museum, you had a **fantastic** view of Nice.

Chagall (1887–1985) and Matisse (1869–1954) lived in Nice at the same time. They were inspired by the sunlight and bright colours of the landscape. Matisse once said, 'When I realised that every morning I would see this light, I couldn't believe my luck.'

Although they were in Nice at the same time, their artistic styles are different. Chagall, born in Russia, was greatly influenced by East European Jewish folk culture. He developed a surrealistic style and many of his paintings have dream-like figures in them. Matisse was born in Northern France. His paintings show a wider range of styles from Impressionism to Neo-classicism and abstract art. Apparently, some people find it confusing when they visit the Matisse museum.

We thought both museums were **brilliant**. You really must visit them if you are an art lover, or even if you're not, the museums are well worth a visit because the paintings are so colourful and full of light.

Comments

Frank said ...
Great blog, A. Art brings immense joy to my life. **Terrific** photos.
JUNE 29, 2014 15.00

Kylie said ...
Thanks Alessandra. I'm inspired to visit the museums and see the paintings!
JUNE 28, 2014 11.45

10 Psychology

10.1 GROUP PSYCHOLOGY

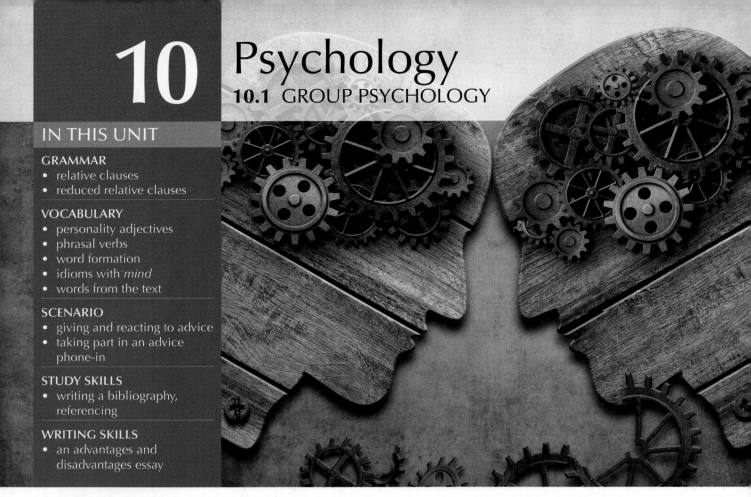

IN THIS UNIT

GRAMMAR
- relative clauses
- reduced relative clauses

VOCABULARY
- personality adjectives
- phrasal verbs
- word formation
- idioms with *mind*
- words from the text

SCENARIO
- giving and reacting to advice
- taking part in an advice phone-in

STUDY SKILLS
- writing a bibliography, referencing

WRITING SKILLS
- an advantages and disadvantages essay

I am a deeply superficial person. Andy Warhol, 1928–1987, American pop artist

READING AND VOCABULARY
PERSONALITY ADJECTIVES

1 Work in small groups and discuss the questions.

1 What teams have you been in (e.g. playing sports, at work)?
2 Describe some of the personalities in one of the teams.
3 Was it a successful team? Why?/Why not?
4 What do you think makes an effective team? What sort of people do you need?

2 Look at the adjectives in the box. Did you use any in your answer to question 2 in Exercise 1? Which do you think are the most important qualities for people in a team?

ambitious	authoritative	conscientious	
creative	diplomatic	energetic	knowledgeable
objective	practical	resourceful	

3 What are the nouns which are formed from the adjectives above? Use a dictionary to find the nouns related to these adjectives and write adjective-noun pairs.

PRONUNCIATION

4 `10.1` Stress patterns Mark the stress on each word in Exercise 3. Does the stress pattern change between the adjective and noun in any of them? Listen and check, then practise the pronunciation.

READING

5a Read the webpage about the Belbin model (an analysis of roles within a team). Which role(s) do you think you would be good at? Which ones wouldn't you be good at?

5b Now work with a partner. Tell each other about your choices and explain your reasons.

6 Look at the second column (*Strengths*) again and match the adjectives in Exercise 2 with the correct team role. Underline the words and phrases which help you decide. There is one extra adjective.

plant = creative (comes up with ideas)

LISTENING

7a You are going to listen to part of a lecture on group dynamics. Before you listen, look at the stages in the life of a group and decide on the order they happen in.

a members become more familiar with each other and start to develop confidence in each other
b the group comes together and members seem to have a friendly relationship
c members' real personalities come out and they may argue with each other as they try to begin work
d the group separates and members go their own ways
e members work together well and produce good results

Belbin model

How understanding team roles can improve team performance.

Dr Meredith Belbin is an expert on teams. During his research, he identified nine key roles in management teams, which are given in the table. One of his most important findings was that effective teams have members covering all the roles. However, he also noted that people may have more than one role. A team does not need to be made up of nine people, but should be at least three or four.

Role	Strengths	Weaknesses
Plant	Creative, imaginative, free-thinking. Generates ideas and solves difficult problems.	Ignores incidentals. Too preoccupied to communicate effectively.
Resource investigator	Outgoing, enthusiastic, communicative. Explores opportunities and develops contacts.	Over-optimistic. Loses interest once the initial enthusiasm has passed.
Coordinator	Mature, confident, identifies talent. Clarifies goals. Delegates effectively.	Can be seen as manipulative. Offloads own share of the work.
Shaper	Challenging, dynamic, thrives on pressure. Has the drive and courage to overcome obstacles.	Prone to provocation. Offends people's feelings.
Monitor-evaluator	Sober, strategic and discerning. Sees all options and judges accurately.	Lacks drive and ability to inspire others.
Teamworker	Co-operative, perceptive and diplomatic. Listens and averts friction.	Indecisive in crunch situations. Avoids confrontation.
Implementer	Practical, reliable, efficient. Turns ideas into actions and organises the work that needs to be done.	Somewhat inflexible. Slow to respond to new possibilities.
Completer-finisher	Painstaking, conscientious, anxious. Searches out errors. Polishes and perfects.	Inclined to worry unduly. Reluctant to delegate.
Specialist	Single-minded, self-starting, dedicated. Provides knowledge and skills in rare supply.	Contributes only on a narrow front. Dwells on technicalities.

7b `10.2` Look at the names of the stages in the box and match them with their meanings in Exercise 7a. Listen to check your answers.

---

adjourning   forming   norming   performing   storming

---

8 Listen again and answer the questions.

1 In which decades were: a) Lewin and b) Tuckman working?
2 What does the expression *honeymoon period* mean?
3 What three practical examples of group dynamics in use does the expert give?

9 Evaluating ideas Work in small groups and discuss the questions.

1 How useful do you think the ideas of: a) Lewin and Tuckman, and b) Belbin and his model are for understanding teams and group dynamics today?
2 Do you think they can fit all team/group situations? Why?/Why not?
3 Do any of your experiences of teams match with what you have heard and read about?
4 Do you think teams and groups always need a (strong) leader to perform well?

VOCABULARY
PHRASAL VERBS

10a Match the verbs from the lecture with their meanings.

1 get on (with)   a start work
2 fall out (with)   b tolerate
3 get used to (+ -*ing*)   c become comfortable with
4 get down to   d separate
5 break up   e argue
6 put up (with)   f have a friendly relationship

10b Complete these sentences so they are true for you.

1 I get on well with people who …
2 It sometimes takes me ages to get used to …
3 I find it difficult to get down to …
4 I tend to fall out with people who ...
5 A team I was in broke up because …
6 I can't put up with people who …

SPEAKING

11a Work in groups of four. You are going to do a task together that makes use of the Belbin model, then work on a project to launch a new community/student newspaper. Do the following tasks.

1 Look at this list of things you will need to do, then add two more tasks to the list.

   • research the competition
   • come up with a brand, title and design concept
   • think of a USP (unique selling point)
   • decide the structure of the newspaper
   • decide on the budget
   • find a sponsor
   • co-ordinate the project

2 Discuss what roles (or multiple roles) from the Belbin model you have in your team and what roles you lack.
3 Discuss who will perform each task you have listed.

11b Join another group and compare your action plans.

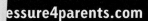

...essure4parents.com

Parentline 020 5320 4444
Kids helpline 020 5320 1111

1 What is peer pressure and why does it happen?

We all want to be part of a group and feel like we belong in our community. Peer pressure can happen when we are influenced to do something we would not usually do because we want to be accepted by our peers (i.e. groups of friends who are about the same age and share the same interests).

Children and young adults especially feel social pressure to conform to the peer group with which they socialise. Conformity, which is the most common form of social influence, is usually defined as the tendency to think or act like other members of a group.

2 How does peer pressure affect people?

Peer pressure can influence how people dress, how they talk, what music they listen to, what attitudes they adopt and how they behave. Teenagers want to belong and it is hard to belong if you are always going against the grain. They want to be liked, to fit in and to be accepted, which means peer pressure can be powerful and hard to resist. People never want to be looked down upon or made fun of. This means that people who are low on confidence and unsure of themselves may be more likely to seek their peers' approval by going along with risky suggestions. Peer pressure can lead people to do things they would not normally do on their own. In one study, a student who knew the correct answer to a question actually gave the wrong answer because all the others in the class gave the wrong answer and he didn't want to be different.

3 Can peer pressure lead to bullying?

Peer pressure definitely plays a role in bullying. If a teenager is generally seen as weak or different by the majority of their peers, they can become a safe target for bullies. Bullies pick easy targets, people that the group are unlikely to defend or get upset over. Bullies can also threaten and tease other teenagers anonymously over the internet. This is called cyber-bullying. Unfortunately, some bullies are popular and liked by many of their peers, which means others are less likely to call the behaviour bullying. These popular bullies can act appropriately towards teachers and adults so the problem often goes unnoticed. Many victims of bullies feel very lonely, have low self-esteem and become depressed. Understandably, parents are often deeply worried when their children are being bullied.

4 What can parents do about it?

To achieve peace of mind, parents need to know with whom their children are associating. They need to encourage children to stay out of situations in which they know they would be pressurised and uncomfortable. Children should learn to feel comfortable saying 'no', to choose their friends wisely, to talk to someone they trust, to think about the consequences of their actions and be true to themselves.

More information
You may want to check out the links at the bottom of the page for more information:

Bullying • Differences and values • Finding help

READING AND VOCABULARY
WORD FORMATION

1 What do you understand by the phrase *peer pressure*? Can you give an example of it?

2 Read the webpage quickly, then briefly answer the four questions in the webpage from memory.

3 Read the webpage again and match the comments from people who have phoned the kids helpline or the parentline with the paragraphs they most closely link to in topic.

a 'I had no idea who my son was hanging out with. And now he spends all his time with a really bad group who get in trouble all the time.'

b 'I know one girl who the teachers love because she's always polite to them, but she is really cruel to some students who can't stand up for themselves.'

c 'I pretend to like the same heavy metal music as my friends, but actually I prefer classical music.'

d 'I'm in a friendship group at school and we do the same things and have similar hobbies. I wouldn't do anything to upset the group.'

4a Look at the verbs in the box and find their nouns in the webpage.

approve	behave	conform	suggest

4b Form the noun for the verbs in the box using the suffixes from Exercise 4a.

associate	continue	define	disable	propose
refuse	save	secure		

5 Evaluating effectiveness Work with a partner and discuss the questions.

1 What is the purpose of the webpage?
2 How successful do you think it is?
3 What other questions would you add?

6 Which of the following forms of bullying do you think is the worst, and why? Physical, verbal or cyber-bullying?

VOCABULARY
IDIOMS WITH *MIND*

7a Match the idioms 1–5 with their meanings a–e.

1 peace of mind
2 keep an open mind
3 make up (your) mind
4 out of (your) mind
5 in two minds

a unable to decide what to do
b a feeling of calm and not being worried
c decide
d deliberately not form a definite opinion
e crazy, insane

7b Complete the sentences with the idioms.

1 I can't _____ about what to do with the money.
2 Having insurance often gives you _____.
3 It is important to _____ when you are on a jury.
4 You must be _____ to give up such a good job.
5 I was _____ about applying for the job.

GRAMMAR
RELATIVE CLAUSES

8 Read the webpage again. Underline all the examples of relative clauses that you can find.

9a Look at the clauses you have underlined. Identify which are defining and which are non-defining clauses, then choose the correct options below.

1 *Defining / Non-defining* relative clauses give us extra information which can be left out without affecting the main meaning of the sentence.
2 *Defining / Non-defining* relative clauses are necessary in order to complete the meaning of a sentence or identify someone or something.

9b Now complete the rules about relative clauses with words from the box.

after	before	defining	non-defining	that
which	who	whom		

1 _____ relative clauses have commas around them.
2 We use _____ instead of *who* after prepositions.
3 We use _____ (not *that*) after prepositions.
4 Prepositions come _____ the relative clause in formal English.
5 We often omit the relative pronoun _____ (or *who/which*) when it is the object of the clause.

GRAMMAR TIP

In informal English, the preposition comes at the end of the sentence.
Just don't do it unless it's something that you feel comfortable with.

➥ Language reference and extra practice, pages 126–149

10a Look at the highlighted sentence in the leaflet and choose the correct answer.

What does the relative clause here refer to?
1 teenagers
2 the fact that teenagers want to be liked

10b This kind of relative clause adds a 'comment' to the main clause. Find another example of this in paragraph 3.

11 Match the main clauses with relative clauses below. Rewrite them as one sentence. The relative clause refers to the bold part of the main clause.

1f We are seeking a counsellor to whom we can refer special cases.

1 We are seeking **a counsellor**.
2 **Even the bullies were crying**.
3 **Kurt Lewin** fled to the USA from Germany.
4 Teenagers like to turn for advice **to other young people**.
5 **People** will follow someone else's lead first.
6 **The type of peer pressure** is never good
7 Peers are **the individuals**
8 **We took all the teenagers to the seaside**.
9 **The bullying problem** has now been solved.

a about which we had a lot of discussion
b which made a good break for them
c that leaves you feeling confused or hurt
d who are easily influenced
e which was surprising
f to whom we can refer special cases
g with whom a child or adolescent identifies most
h who they sympathise with
i who many see as the father of social psychology

12a Work with a partner. Ask your partner questions to find out things you don't already know about them. Ask extra questions to get more information and make some notes.

Where were you born? Where's that? What's it like?

12b Write a short profile of your partner and use relative clauses to add information.

Hiroshi was born in Sapporo, which is …

SPEAKING

13 Work in small groups and discuss the questions.

1 Is peer pressure and bullying common in your society?
2 How do peer pressure and bullying appear in your society?
3 Compare your society to other societies you know.
4 Is pressure on teenagers greater now than when you were teenagers?

READING AND VOCABULARY
WORDS FROM THE TEXT

1a Look at the following profile. In groups, brainstorm what crime the person could have committed, then check your ideas on page 167.

> Caring, well-respected but arrogant doctor with trusting patients. Middle one of three children, devoted to his mother, stable marriage, successful children. Helped organise charity collections and served on local committees.

1b Why are we surprised when doctors commit crimes?

2 Read the article quickly and answer the questions.

1　What is a criminal profiler?
2　What do they do?

3 Read the article again. Which paragraph or paragraphs contain the following information? Underline the relevant phrases in the article.

1　how profilers work
2　a phrase for 'where people live'
3　terms for criminals who have killed lots of people
4　mention of a famous profiler
5　mention of looking at all the small pieces of information at the scene of a crime
6　types of criminals/crimes that profiling is used for
7　another name for psychological profiling
8　the disadvantages of profiling

PSYCHOLOGICAL PROFILING

A This investigative technique, also referred to as criminal profiling, has recently risen in popularity both in police work and media portrayals. A quick visit to any bookstore will reveal the popularity of the true crime section, and there has been a recent flood of novels with a likeable lead detective profiling the offender.

B The origins of profiling can be traced back to the second half of the 19th century and it has become very common, especially in America, since the 1950s. It deals with methods used to detect criminals such as serial killers, and to prevent crimes such as aeroplane hijacking. Other criminals for whom psychological profiling has been used are suicide bombers and mass murderers.

C Without doubt, one of the best-known profiles of the last century was that of 'The Mad Bomber of New York' who was profiled by James Brussels, a New York psychiatrist in 1956. Brussels was called on to help police in their search as the bomber had left about thirty-two explosive packages across the city over approximately eight years. Reviewing the huge case file, the photographs, and a number of letters mailed by the suspect over a sixteen-year period, Brussels suggested the police were looking for '... a heavy man. Middle-aged. Foreign born. Roman Catholic. Single. Lives with a brother or sister.' He also added '... when you find him, chances are he will be wearing a double-breasted suit. Buttoned.' He also deduced that the man was paranoid, hated his father, was obsessively loved by his mother and lived in the state of Connecticut. When police officers finally arrested the Mad Bomber, they were amazed by how close Brussels was in his assessment, even down to the double-breasted suit that was buttoned.

D What exactly is psychological profiling? Essentially, it involves investigating an offender's behaviour, motives and background to provide specific information about the type of person who commits a certain crime. This makes it possible to draw up a profile of actual or potential offenders. The investigation covers such areas as the criminal's age, sex, employment, place of residence and distinctive personality characteristics. Profilers note and evaluate minute details of the crime scene, enabling them to describe the specific methods of operation of the criminal, e.g. how he kills, where he kills, and what type of victim he selects. Profiling tries to identify potential serious offenders early; for example, in their teens they often commit petty crimes, defying authority, until they begin killing in their mid- to late twenties.

E Some experts say that psychological profiling is at best useless and at worst harmful. They argue that the profiling of killers has no real-world value, wastes police time and risks bringing the profession into disrepute. Incorrect information from profiling can lead to serious mistakes. Police may find a suspect who appears to fit an incorrect profile and stop investigating other leads. This happened in the case of Richard Jewell and the Olympic Park bombing in Atlanta. Jewell was wrongly investigated because he fitted the criminal profile, delaying the identification of the real culprit, Eric Rudolph.

4 Work with a partner and discuss your reaction to the final paragraph.

5 Complete the sentences with the words in the box.

| assessments | case file | deduce | motive |
| profile | psychiatrist | | |

1 At first, it was difficult to find a _____ for Shipman's murders.
2 People who have memory gaps tend to fill in the gaps or _____ what has happened.
3 Two experts, a _____ and a psychologist, recommended that he should receive treatment.
4 I read a short _____ of the doctor in the local newspaper.
5 'She is also very depressed,' psychiatrists noted in her _____.
6 Psychological _____ frequently use intelligence and personality tests alongside interviews.

GRAMMAR
REDUCED RELATIVE CLAUSES

6a Look at the following relative clauses. Underline two clauses in the article that mean the same.
1 ... a number of letters **which were mailed by the suspect** ...
2 ... the crime scene, **which enables them to describe the specific methods of operation** ...

6b What are the differences between the clauses above and the clauses in the article?

7 Look at the article again and underline four more reduced relative clauses.
1 Which of the underlined sentences use an -ing form, and which use a past participle?
2 Which type of clause is active and which is passive?

➥ Language reference and extra practice, pages 126–149

8 In each pair of sentences below, write the same verb, once in the -ing form and once as a past participle.
1a She took a course in psychotherapy, _developing_ her skills as a counsellor.
b Psychoanalytical theory, _developed_ by Freud, has been the subject of much controversy.
2a Psychology magazines _____ out of the library must be returned within one week.
b There were photographers everywhere, _____ photographs and blocking the court entrance.
3a The people _____ the real decisions are not the profilers.
b The decision to arrest, _____ by the senior detective and profiler, was correct.
4a A serial killer was at large, _____ panic in the city.
b The jury believed that the death was an accident _____ by the illness of the driver.

9 In this article, cross out the pronoun and auxiliary verbs and use just the present or past participle where possible.

> *focusing*
> There are several films ~~which focus~~ on profilers who are investigating criminal cases such as *Seven* with Morgan Freeman and Brad Pitt and *The Bone Collector* with Denzel Washington and Angelina Jolie. The classic one has to be *The Silence of the Lambs*. This is a film which is directed by Jonathan Demme. In it, Clarice Starling, who is played by Jodie Foster, questions a brilliant forensic psychologist and serial killer, who is named Hannibal Lecter. Lecter, who is currently serving nine life sentences in a mental institution, is charming and polite to Starling, and eventually offers her a psychological profile of the murderer Starling is trying to find. The performance of Lecter, who is played by Anthony Hopkins, is the shortest Oscar-winning performance ever by a leading actor. The most famous book series on profiling is probably the Kay Scarpetta series, which is written by Patricia Cornwell. These novels feature Benson Wesley, a criminal profiler who works for the FBI.

SPEAKING

10 Work in small groups and discuss the following topics.
- books you have read or films you have seen that involve profiling or serial killers
- famous criminals or crimes from your country

WRITING

11 Summarising Underline the key points in the article and write a short summary (between 150 and 180 words) about psychological profiling.

▶ MEET THE EXPERT

Watch an interview with Dr Jack Lewis, a neuroscientist, about the field of neuroscience.
Turn to page 154 for video activities.

Professor Tamara Bright is a well-known psychologist. She is the presenter of a weekly radio phone-in programme called *What's on your mind*. She invites readers to phone or email her about their personal or professional problems and offers practical advice to deal with them.

1 Work with a partner. Read the situation and discuss the questions.

1 Do you ever listen to radio phone-in programmes? Why?/Why not?
2 Professor Bright advises people of all ages. What problems do you think each age group below might wish to discuss with her?
   a people under twenty
   b people aged twenty-forty
   c people aged forty+
3 Why are radio phone-ins and advice columns in magazines so popular?
4 Do you think phone-ins and advice columns help people to lead happier lives?
5 What experience and personal qualities do you think Professor Bright should have to do her job well?

2 10.3 **Listen to Professor Bright talking to a caller. Read the three summaries of the problem. Which one is the best summary? Give reasons for your choice.**

Summary A
Michelle loves her husband, but is worried because he spends too much. Early in their marriage, they were very happy and they had a lot of money. But now she is planning to divorce him.

Summary B
Michelle's husband has always been a big spender. He has so many debts that they may have to sell their house. At times, Michelle has considered leaving her husband, even though she loves him.

Summary C
Michelle's husband owes a lot of money because he has many gambling debts, which worries his wife. Earlier in the marriage they were happy, but now Michelle wants to leave him.

3 Work with a partner and discuss the problem. What advice would you give Michelle if you were Professor Bright?

4 10.4 **Listen to the advice that Professor Bright gives to Michelle. Which of her ideas did you think of?**

KEY LANGUAGE
GIVING AND REACTING TO ADVICE

5a Listen again to the second part of the phone-in when Professor Bright gives Michelle several pieces of advice and she reacts to them. Complete the sentences below.

1 OK, first of all, you _____ to someone about the debts you have.
2 Yes, that _____.
3 Now, you _____ your local Citizens Advice Centre …
4 Well, I like the idea, but I don't think _____.
5 Well, you know, it _____ to have a separate bank account.
6 I don't think so. What's _____ that?
7 There's _____ he'd agree to it.
8 Well, if _____ , I'd look at some of the sites offering help.
9 Also, it _____ a finance company.
10 That _____ a good idea to me.
11 Well, it's _____ do something about his overspending, Michelle.
12 I've got one final bit of advice. You _____ getting some counselling yourself.

5b Check your answers in Audio script 10.4 on page 179.

5c Look at the phrases in the box and decide whether each phrase is strong, neutral or tentative (not very strong).

GIVING ADVICE

I'd advise you to …
I think you need to …
Why don't you … ?
You could also …
You might consider …
If I were you, I'd …
It's vital that …
It's essential that …
It might be a good idea to …
It'd be advisable to …
It might be worth …

REACTING TO ADVICE

Yes, that could be helpful.
OK, it's worth trying.
I like the idea, but I don't think it'd work.
I'm not sure, I could try it.
What's the point of doing that?
That sounds like a good idea to me.
That's really good advice.
Yes, I like that idea.

6a Choose four sentences from Exercise 5a that give advice. Use different phrases from the box to give the same advice.

6b Work with a partner. Listen to each other's sentences and comment on the language and intonation.

TASK
AN ADVICE PHONE-IN

7a You are going to do a role-play between Professor Bright and a caller who first writes to her, then phones her show.

Student A: choose one of the problems below. Make notes on your problem so you are ready to talk about it.

Student B: choose one of the problems on page 159. Make notes on your problem so you are ready to talk about it.

7b Role-play the situation.

Student A: you are the caller. Describe your problem to Professor Bright, and respond to the professor's advice.

Student B: you are Professor Bright. Listen to your caller's problem and give him/her advice.

Now change roles and Student B describes his/her problem.

8 Now work in groups. Discuss which problem was the most interesting and which was the most difficult to solve.

To: Professor Bright

Subject: Favouritism

Dear Professor Bright,
I'm 20, my brother Paul's 22. My problem is my mother. Since I was very young, she's always preferred Paul to me. In her eyes, Paul can do no wrong. As I grew up, I got tired of hearing her say, 'Why can't you be more like your brother?'

OK, Paul's practical, thoughtful – the perfect son in many ways. He's very good at repairing things around the house. That really impresses my mother. I'm different. I'm a bit of a dreamer. I know I probably misbehaved a lot when I was younger to get my mother's attention. But can you blame me? Nowadays, I get annoyed that she doesn't treat us equally. For example, Paul can borrow my mother's car whenever he likes, but if I ask, she generally says 'no'. I could give you a lot of other examples like that.

My mother's favouritism has had a very bad effect on me. I've no self-confidence at all. At times, I feel I'm a loser, and that I'll never get anywhere in life. Lucy, my younger sister, says I'm imagining things, but she's my only sister and gets plenty of attention from my mother. Lucy simply doesn't understand. What advice can you give me?

To: Professor Bright

Subject: Unhappy student

Dear Professor Bright,
My name's Adam. I'm a university student studying Oriental languages. For about six months now, I've had a girlfriend, May. She's Asian, studying for a Masters in Engineering. I love her a lot and I think she loves me. Actually I'm sure she loves me. But she's tried to end our relationship twice before, and yesterday she sent me a note saying it's all over.

I feel so upset. I can't do anything at the moment. I can't study, I can't sleep. Sometimes, I think I'm going crazy. It's all because of her parents. They're far away, and they don't want her to have a boyfriend, and certainly not an Englishman. They're proud of her being at university and want her to do really well. They don't want any distractions! But also I think they're afraid that she might end up marrying an Englishman, and then they won't see her very often.

May loves her parents. She respects them and doesn't want to upset them. They have a strong influence on her. Her family is very important to her. I'm certain they've told her to stay away from me and focus on her studies. What can I do?

STUDY SKILLS
WRITING A BIBLIOGRAPHY, REFERENCING

1 Why do you need to provide references when writing academic essays or articles?

2 Work with a partner. Discuss whether you think each statement is correct or incorrect.

1 Facts which are common knowledge do not need to be referenced.
2 An idea of your own based on reading different sources must be referenced.
3 Primary data, for example, information gathered from interviews or questionnaires, does not have to be referenced.
4 Written work looks more professional if you provide references.
5 Ideas which have been very loosely paraphrased need no reference.
6 References enable readers to know which are your ideas and which come from other sources.
7 Ideas that have been adapted do not need a reference to the original author.
8 Readers are more likely to accept your ideas if you reference the source.
9 A graph or chart taken from an internet source does not need a reference.
10 Quotations from a book or journal must have quotation marks and references.

3 Read about the Harvard System of Referencing, and look at the extracts from a bibliography below. Find the four entries which are incorrect, and give your reasons.

1 Adler, A. (1964) *Problems of Neurosis*, New York: Harper and Row.
2 Belmont, M. & Marolla, F. A. (1973) Birth order, family size, and intelligence, *Science* , vol. 182, pp. 1096–1101.
3 Zajonc, R. B. & Mullally, P. R. 1997 Birth order: Reconciling conflicting effects, *American Psychologist*, vol. 52(7), pp. 685–699.
4 Zajonc, R. B. (2001) Birth order debate resolved?, American Psychologist, vol. 56(6–7), pp. 522–523.
5 Harris, J. R. (2006) *No Two Alike: Human Nature and Human Individuality*, New York: W.W. Norton.
6 Leman, K. (1985) The Birth Order Book: Why You Are the Way You Are, [Online], Available at: www.drleman.com, [14 April 2008].
7 Michalski, R. L. & Shackelford, T.K. (2002) Personality and Individual Differences, [Online], Available at: www.sciencedirect.com.
8 Eysenck, M. & Keane, M. (2010). 6th edition, *Cognitive Psychology*, Psychology Press.
9 Prinz, J. (2012) *Beyond Human Nature: How Culture and Experience Shape our Lives*, London: Allen Lane.

●●● Providing References using the Harvard System
Bibliographies

A list of references must be presented in alphabetical order by surname of the author(s), or by title, if there is no author. Harvard has no one true style of punctuation so the most important thing is to choose one style of punctuation and use it consistently throughout your work.

For a book, the order is:
Author's surname, initial(s). (date of publication in brackets) title in italics, edition, place of publication: publisher.

For a first edition:
  Moody, S.A. (2007) *Principles of Developmental Genetics*, New York: Elsevier Academic Press.

For a 4th edition:
  Desmond, P.W. (2005) *The Child-centred Approach*, 4th edition, Cambridge: Independent Publications.

For a paper in a journal, the order is:
Author's surname, initial(s), (year in brackets), title of the paper, full title of the journal in italics, volume and issue numbers, pages of journal.

  MacKay, T. (2000) Educational psychology and the future of special education needs' legislation, *Education and Child Psychology*, vol. 17, pp. 27–35.

For a book, article or any document on the web:
The same rules as the above, but the web address and the date the page was accessed are given.
  Jones, P. (2008) *Peer Pressure*, [Online], Available at: www.psychology/dossier/gov.html, [7 February 2012].

Citing references within a text

When making references to an author's work in your text, their name is followed by the year of publication of their work.
  Firstborn children tend to have higher IQs because they receive more attention from their parents. This view is supported in the work of Marzollo (1990).

When you are mentioning a particular part of a work, and making direct reference to this, a page reference should be included.
  Harrigan (1992, p. 54) argues that 'firstborn children tend to be perfectionist'.

Web-based references
Electronic sources such as www pages, electronic databases and electronic journals are cited in the text in much the same way as traditional print sources, with the exception of page numbers. The author's name is followed by a publication date, but no page numbers are listed. If no publication date is available, and this might be the case for www pages, then where the date should go, insert (n.d.) which stands for 'no date'.

WRITING SKILLS
AN ADVANTAGES AND DISADVANTAGES ESSAY

4 Complete the description of different types of essay with the words in the box.

---
formal   issue   objectively   paragraph   sides   unbiased

There are two main types of discursive essay: evidence-led and opinion-led. Evidence-led essay types include 'For and Against' and 'Advantages and Disadvantages'. In an evidence-led essay, you discuss a problem, controversy or ¹_____ in an ²_____ way. You present all ³_____ of the question ⁴_____. The style of the essay is usually ⁵_____ rather than informal. If you are asked to give an opinion, you do so at the end of the essay. In an opinion-led essay, you indicate your opinion of the topic in the first ⁶_____ and restate it in the last one.

5a Read the essay title below. Work with a partner and think of three advantages of being an only child and three disadvantages. Note them down.

'It is a big advantage in life to be an only child in a family.' To what extent do you agree with this statement?

5b Compare your ideas with other pairs.

6 Read the first paragraph of the essay. Why, in the writer's opinion, is this topic worth writing about?

In many parts of the world, it is becoming more common for parents to have only one child. An obvious reason for this is that people are tending to marry at a later age than they did some years ago. This is an important area of discussion because some people think that being an only child is a big disadvantage in life. Others take a different view. This essay discusses the arguments and considers whether, on balance, it is truly an advantage to be the only child in a family.

7 Read the rest of the essay. Compare your ideas from Exercise 5a with the writer's opinions.

A major advantage of being an only child is that the child gets more attention and financial support from his or her parents. They will help the child with his or her homework, so that the child achieves above-average results at school. In addition, because the only child is the sole focus of the parents' love, he or she develops more confidence and becomes more mature at an early age. Another advantage of being an only child is that they are on their own a lot more. As a result, they learn how to occupy themselves and to become more independent than other children. They are also more able to cope with feelings of loneliness.

On the other hand, some people argue that only children miss out on brother and sister relationships as they do not have siblings to share their joys and sorrows. It is said that children who have siblings are less selfish and learn at an early age how to get on with other people – an important life skill. Even though this is probably true, it is a fact that brothers and sisters often quarrel a lot. Only children may well have quieter and more peaceful childhoods.

A recent study of China's one-child policy supports the view that there are disadvantages to being an only child. The study was published in *Science* by Professor Lisa Cameron and colleagues from Australian universities. It investigated the impact of one-child families in China. The researchers compared the behaviour of Chinese people born before and after the one-child policy was adopted. Their results showed that children born after the one-child policy, in other words 'only children', had certain characteristics. They were less willing to take risks, less conscientious, less trustworthy and more pessimistic. According to Professor Cameron, the amount of contact that subjects had with other children, such as their peers, did not affect the results of the study. While this research seems to confirm that only children in China are at a disadvantage, this may not be the case in other countries. The results, therefore, are not conclusive.

8a **Complex sentences** Complex sentences contain conjunctions (e.g. *and*, *but*, *because*, *in spite of*) or relative pronouns (e.g. *that*, *who* or *which*). Which of the following sentences are complex sentences?

1 Others take a different view. (paragraph 1)
2 They are also more able to cope with feelings of loneliness. (paragraph 2)
3 This will help a child with his or her homework, so that the child achieves above-average results. (paragraph 2)
4 It is said that children who have siblings are less selfish. (paragraph 3)
5 Even though this is probably true, it is a fact that brothers and sisters often quarrel a lot. (paragraph 3)
6 Only children may well have quieter and more peaceful childhoods. (paragraph 3)
7 While this research seems to confirm that only children in China have an advantage, this may not be the case in other countries. (paragraph 6)
8 On the whole, the evidence seems to suggest that it is an advantage to be an only child. (paragraph 7)

8b Find three other examples in the essay of each type of complex sentence (with a conjunction or a relative pronoun) and underline them. Check your answers on page 167.

9 Write four complex sentences containing a conjunction or a relative pronoun expressing opinions about the advantages and disadvantages of being an only child.

10 **Conclusions** Read the conclusion of the essay below. Which of the following does it contain?

1 a restatement of the points in the introduction
2 a summary of the main ideas in the essay
3 new evidence or ideas about the topic
4 the writer's opinion

On the whole, in spite of the research on only children in China, evidence seems to suggest that it is an advantage to be an only child. However, the key point, surely, is that a child has the love and support of his or her parents. This is the most important influence which will determine a child's development, happiness and future success in life.

11a Choose one of the essay topics and discuss it in pairs. To what extent do you agree with the writer's point of view?

- Women have the primary responsibility for bringing up children.
- Children have too much freedom nowadays.
- Today's world is not a safe place to bring up children.
- 'The desire to be accepted by their peers is perhaps the strongest motivating force during adolescence.' (Bruce A. Epstein)

11b Write a short essay on one of the topics, using the internet to look up some articles or ideas. Include some references in the text and a short bibliography.

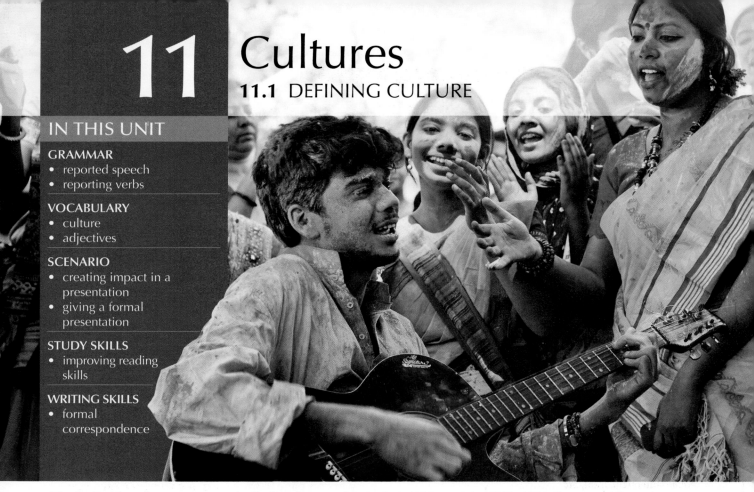

11 Cultures
11.1 DEFINING CULTURE

The limits of my language mean the limits of my world.   Ludwig Wittgenstein, 1889–1951, German philosopher

READING AND VOCABULARY
CULTURE

1 What do you understand by *a culture*? What comes into your mind?

2 Read the webpage on page 107 quickly and choose an appropriate heading for each section from the box.

Architecture	Climate	Cuisine	Values
Customs/Traditions	Geography		Religion
Historical events	Institutions		The arts
Language	Life rituals	Rules of behaviour	

3a Look at these meanings for words and phrases from the webpage. Which section (1–13) do you think you might find each of the words in?

a   a kind of food eaten every day
b   a particular linguistic form (often spoken)
c   ways of behaving politely
d   a belief that some things are lucky/unlucky
e   a particular type of land
f   a ceremony which makes you remember and respect someone or something from the past
g   a small group with particular beliefs and practices

3b Find the words or phrases in the webpage which match the definitions in Exercise 3a.

4 Work with a partner. Select three or four of the words from Exercise 3b to discuss. Give an example from your country, or another country you know well.

5 Reflecting on the topic Work in small groups and discuss the questions.

1   Which three of the thirteen factors listed on the webpage do you think are the most useful for defining cultures? Why?
2   What do you think are the typical features of your own national culture? What do you imagine people from other cultures would say?
3   The heritage of a society is those aspects or things from the past that are considered important to its culture today. What parts of your heritage are you most proud of?
4   Which factors do you think make your culture different from those of other countries? (Think about countries which are far away and those that are near neighbours.)
5   Are there aspects of any other cultures which you admire? What? Why?

WHAT IS CULTURE?

Module 1 (weeks 1 and 2)

The word 'culture' has a number of meanings, but in its widest sense it refers to everything that makes up the identity of a particular group of people, society or nation.

1 _____ – the general terrain and physical features such as mountains, rivers, proximity to the sea, whether there is a coastline

2 _____ – weather conditions in different seasons, length of seasons, average temperatures and types of extreme weather if appropriate, e.g. hurricanes, typhoons, droughts

3 _____ – written and spoken means of communication used by a particular group of people; this may include particular dialects, and characteristics of grammar, vocabulary and pronunciation

4 _____ – a particular style of cooking; this will include specialities, unusual dishes and staple diet of a particular area (e.g. rice, potatoes, pasta)

5 _____ – things which are considered important to people and tend to guide their lives (e.g. attitudes to family, money, honesty, superstitions, nature, animals)

6 _____ – characteristic styles of music, theatre, film, painting, opera, literature, etc. and their relative importance and status

7 _____ – particular faith/belief systems, e.g. Islam, Christianity, Buddhism, Judaism, including sects within a particular tradition

8 _____ – unspoken/unwritten ways of doing things, e.g. rules of etiquette and manners regarding how to eat, socialise, dress, drive, greet and address each other; punctuality, tipping, the way people treat each other (male/female/adults/children), etc.

9 _____ – particular national/public holidays, feast days, festivals (e.g. carnivals), commemorations, anniversaries and activities associated with and performed on these occasions

10 _____ – (civil) wars, invasions, revolutions, famines, natural disasters, etc.

11 _____ – birth, marriage, maturity, employment, retirement, death, and how these are treated

12 _____ – the political system and type of government and/or monarchy, the legal system, education, financial system

13 _____ – characteristic style of buildings and interior design; also common building materials used, ratio of old/new buildings, the built environment in general and its appearance

Professor Mancini, Institute of Cultural Studies (ICS)

LISTENING

6 What do/would you miss about your culture when you are abroad?

7 11.1 Listen to six people answering the question in Exercise 6. What does each person miss about their culture?

8 Listen again and answer the questions. What does:

1 Ayla say about Turkish hospitality?
2 Ingrid say about supermarkets in Germany?
3 Anna say about Russian friendship?
4 Danielle say about the food in Cameroon?
5 Alessandra say about hearing her dialect of Italian?
6 Nancy say about making arrangements in Argentina?

9 Work in small groups. Think back to Exercise 6. Were any of the speakers' opinions like yours? Have the speakers made you think of anything else which you miss? Compare your ideas. Do you have any things in common which you would miss?

SPEAKING

A time capsule is a sealed container filled with objects. It is then buried in the ground and not opened until some time in the future. The idea behind this is to communicate to people in the future about what life is like now.

10a Work in small groups and agree on twelve items to be placed in a time capsule which will be opened in 200 years' time. Choose the items which you think best represent your culture as it is today. (The time capsule is the size of a piece of luggage for a two-week holiday.)

10b Join another group and explain the content of your time capsule and the reasons for your choices.

107

READING AND SPEAKING

1 Work with a partner and discuss the questions.

1 What is culture shock?
2 Who gets culture shock?
3 What does it include?

2 Read the first paragraph of an article which gives advice to foreign students and check your answers to the questions in Exercise 1.

3 Read the five stages of culture shock and match the statements from five people with the stage they are likely to be in.

a 'Actually, I think I appreciate all the cultural differences and feel very comfortable living here now. I also appreciate my own culture and enjoy going home on holiday.'
b 'I think I'm getting used to living here now and I don't worry anymore.'
c 'I love all the different tastes, the spices in the food, the smells, the sights and the sounds.'
d 'I don't like the way people stare at me all the time and how they just rush onto the trains without waiting for people to get off.'
e 'I feel a little bit lonely at the moment and I miss having my sisters to talk to.'

4 Work in small groups and discuss the questions.

1 Have you lived in another culture, or do you know someone who has? What have been your/their experiences with culture shock?
2 What countries have a similar culture to your own?
3 Do you agree with the following quote? *A fish only discovers its need for water when it is no longer in it. Our own culture is like water to a fish. It sustains us. We live and breathe through it.* (Dr F. Trompenaars)

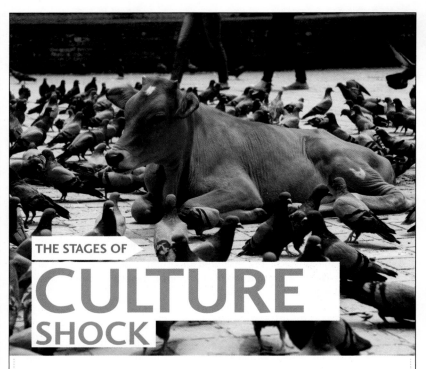

THE STAGES OF

CULTURE
SHOCK

Culture shock describes the impact of moving from a familiar culture to one which is unfamiliar. It is an experience described by people who have travelled abroad to work, live or study; it can be felt to a certain extent even when abroad on holiday. It can affect anyone, including international students. It includes the shock of a new environment, meeting lots of new people and learning the ways of a different country. It also includes the shock of being separated from the important people in your life, maybe family, friends, colleagues, teachers: people you would normally talk to at times of uncertainty, people who give you support and guidance. When familiar sights, sounds, smells or tastes are no longer there, you can miss them very much.

The process (of culture shock) can be broken down into five stages:

1 The 'honeymoon' stage
When you first arrive in a new culture, differences are intriguing and you may feel excited, stimulated and curious. At this stage you are still protected by the close memory of your home culture.

2 The 'distress' stage
A little later, differences create an impact and you may feel confused, isolated or inadequate as cultural differences intrude and familiar supports (e.g. family or friends) are not immediately available.

3 The 're-integration' stage
Next, you may reject the differences you encounter. You may feel angry or frustrated, or hostile to the new culture. At this stage, you may be conscious mainly of how much you dislike it compared to home. Don't worry, as this is quite a healthy reaction. You are reconnecting with what you value about yourself and your own culture.

4 The 'autonomy' stage
Differences and similarities are accepted. You may feel relaxed, confident, more like an old hand, as you become more familiar with situations and feel well able to cope with new situations based on your growing experience.

5 The 'independence' stage
Differences and similarities are valued and important. You may feel full of potential and able to trust yourself in all kinds of situations. Most situations become enjoyable and you are able to make choices according to your preferences and values.

VOCABULARY
ADJECTIVES

5a Look at the following adjectives from the article. Which are positive and which are negative?

frustrated	hostile	inadequate	intriguing
isolated	stimulated		

5b Match the adjectives in Exercise 5a with the closest synonym in the box.

disappointed	excited	interesting	insufficient
lonely	unfriendly		

5c Complete the sentences with the adjectives in Exercise 5a.

1 It was such an _____ story, so unusual and mysterious.
2 They hope the students will feel _____ by the talk.
3 She's quite angry at the moment and feels _____ towards British culture.
4 The old people felt so lonely and _____.
5 The teacher made us feel _____ and stupid if we made mistakes.
6 I often get _____ and impatient with my computer.

LISTENING

6a 11.2 Listen to three young people talking about their experience of culture shock in Japan. Make notes to complete the table below.

	Lars	Hugo	Sofia
1 Where live?			
2 Study? Job?			
3 How long in Japan?			
4 Enjoying Japan?			

6b Listen again. Which of the five stages of culture shock are they in? (They may be between two stages.)

6c Justifying answers Work with a partner and compare and justify your answers to Exercise 6b.

GRAMMAR
REPORTED SPEECH

7a Look at these reported statements. Underline the actual words used in Audio script 11.2 on page 180.

1 She said she had arrived there the previous month.
2 She said that she had met up with people for language exchange.
3 He said the winter landscapes are stunning and the people in Hokkaido are wonderful.
4 He said that when he went out into the countryside, children would stare at him.
5 He said he is just not fitting in at the moment.
6 The interviewer asked if it was safe.

7b Look at sentences 1 and 2 in Exercise 7a. What changes do we make when we report speech?

7c What is different about sentences 3–5 in Exercise 7a?

7d Here are three reasons for not changing the direct speech verb in reported speech. Match the reasons with sentences 3–5 in Exercise 7a.

a The action or situation in the indirect speech is still happening/true.
b The reported verb expresses a fact or situation that cannot or is unlikely to change.
c The verb comes immediately after a time conjunction (e.g. *when*, *after*).

7e Look at sentence 6 in Exercise 7a. What happens to word order in reported questions?

➥ Language reference and extra practice, pages 126–149

8 Susan has recently returned to England from Japan. Report the following things she said. Change the tense of the verb only if necessary.

1 I studied the language before I went.
2 I lived in a tiny studio flat while I was there.
3 The trains were crowded, but were always on time.
4 I gave chocolates to my boss once and he was really surprised.
5 I really miss Japan and would love to go back.
6 I often go to Japanese restaurants to eat Japanese food.
7 Yesterday, I bought a ticket for a holiday in Japan.
8 I can't wait to get back there!

SPEAKING AND WRITING

9a Think of a person you know who lives in your country, but comes from somewhere else. Describe and comment on this person in terms of where they are in the five stages of culture shock. Think about the following questions and make notes.

- How long has the person been in your country?
- Did they choose to come themselves?
- How much do they fit into your country's culture?
- Are they happy living in your country?

9b Work with a partner. Tell each other about the person you thought of in Exercise 9a.

> **GRAMMAR TIP**
>
> If we want to report the general topic of a conversation rather than what was said in detail, we can use 'topic' or 'summarising' verbs such as *discuss* or *talk about*:
> *I saw my best friend last night. We talked about the problems she's having at work.*

9c Write a summary of what your partner said.

LISTENING

1 You are going to listen to two people talking about mistakes they made while visiting Spain and Turkey. What do you know about the culture and people of these two countries?

2  Listen to the two people talking. What mistakes did they make?

3 Listen again and complete the sentences.

1 My wife _____ there by *dolmus*.
2 I _____ the money and _____ it to him.
3 He _____ not to get on his bus again. I _____ by *dolmus* …
4 I'd _____ the orientation programme because I'd been to Malaga …
5 … my hosts had _____ me up at nine o'clock and that I'd _____ them …
6 They _____ lots of different dishes.
7 They nearly fell off their chairs laughing and _____ forget about eating any more food.

4 Work with a partner and discuss the questions.

1 Have you ever made any cultural mistakes? What were they?
2 What mistakes do visitors to your country sometimes make?

GRAMMAR
REPORTING VERBS

5 Look at the verbs you wrote in Exercise 3 and add them to the table.

verb + *to* + infinitive	*offer, promise*
verb + object + *to* + infinitive	*invite, advise*
verb + *-ing* form	*consider, deny*
verb + preposition + *-ing* form	*talk about, agree on*

➡ Language reference and extra practice, pages 126–149

6 We often use verbs like the ones in the table to report speech. Report the bold parts of the sentences, using some of the verbs from the table.

1 She encouraged me to study my heritage.

1 '**You should study your heritage.**'
2 'Yes, I think **I did sound a bit rude.**'
3 '**We really must treat everyone equally.** It's really important.'
4 '**You really should think about it for a few more days.**' 'OK, I will.'
5 '**Don't come into my shop again!** I'll phone the police next time!'
6 '**I shouldn't have left university early.** It was a stupid move.'
7 'I haven't done anything wrong. **I'm not going to resign.**'
8 '**I'm sorry I was so late.**'

7a In groups of three, look at your prompts and make sentences.
Student A: turn to page 156.
Student B: turn to page 159.
Student C: turn to page 162.

7b Now say and report your sentences. Student A reads a sentence to Student B, who reports it to Student C. Then change roles.

A: *I'll take notes and photocopy them for you.*
B: *Henri offered to take notes and photocopy them for me.*

A

CULTURAL DIFFERENCES

A knowledge of differences between cultures, in an ever-shrinking globalised world, is becoming one of the essential key skills that modern 'citizens of the world' need to possess in order to work and learn effectively. At a superficial level, this involves knowing about food or body taboos. For example, some cultures don't eat meat, cows can be sacred, the head must not be touched. But while it is important to know about these things, if this is where your intercultural knowledge stops, you will still end up offending people or being misunderstood.

More important than superficial behaviour is the value system of a culture. In the same way that a good doctor needs to understand underlying causes rather than just treat symptoms, the culturally aware individual needs to have not only a knowledge of publicly visible behaviours and stated beliefs, but also an awareness of the underlying value systems of cultures that shape those behaviours and stated beliefs.

Of course, these belief systems can be very different from one's own, and it is very easy to label other people's behaviours and beliefs as strange. It is more difficult to accept that one's own ways of behaving, which seem perfectly normal, can be seen as strange and even rude in another culture. But unless one tries to observe one's own culture objectively and have an understanding of why other cultures do things differently, it is inevitable that cultural mistakes will be made.

Culturestoyou.com

B

Don't believe the people who say that we must be 'culturally aware', that we should always think about where people come from so we don't offend them. That's nonsense! You know what it does? It makes people concentrate on tiny, small things, like where you put the soles of your feet when you're sitting down in case you give offence. Or how close you get to somebody on a bus or train – invading their physical space it's called. It's all trivial and really unimportant. No, what everybody really needs is loads of politeness and patience. Once you get that, you don't have to worry about other people's culture.

The other thing people say is that we reject other people because they threaten us – our culture. I think that's so true. We don't like to feel threatened – to worry about our kids, our jobs, and so on. The important thing is that your kids can get a decent education, you can get work and your family feel safe. If those three things are OK, cultural differences aren't really important and you won't find anything about cultural problems in the newspapers. Multiculturalism with all cultures mucking in together works fine then. But, and it's a big but, if any of these three things goes wrong or missing, you're in trouble, big trouble. That's when the little things between people of different cultures start to matter and can become big, troublesome issues.

READING

8 What other cultures are you aware of in your country?

9 Read texts A and B and choose the most appropriate answer.

1   Text A argues for the following
  a   Doctors should treat symptoms of illness.
  b   We should all understand the causes of illness.
  c   We should all be culturally aware.
2   Text A argues that
  a   thinking about other people's behaviours and beliefs is strange.
  b   it is very easy to describe what other people believe and how they behave as strange.
  c   our own ways of behaving are perfectly normal.
3   Text B states that
  a   small differences don't get into the newspapers.
  b   it is important to know how close you should get to someone on public transport.
  c   small cultural differences are unimportant.
4   Text B states that
  a   multiculturalism can work in certain circumstances.
  b   multicultural communities should be easy to establish.
  c   your kids' education is more important than being able to find a job.

10 Read texts A and B again. What are the main differences between the opinions of the two writers?

11a Which of the words below suggest a style closer to text A? Which words are closer to text B? You may choose more than one word to describe each text.

blog	chatty	distant	email	essay
formal	informal	textbook		

11b Recognising features of register What examples of differences in style can you find between the two texts? Think about the following.
* the pronouns that are used
* the formality of the vocabulary and grammar
* questions in the text

12 Look at the text extracts on page 167 and say whether each is closer in style to text A or text B, and why.

SPEAKING

13 Work in groups of four. Choose one of the following statements to discuss. Two of you should argue in favour of the statement and two of you should argue against it.
* People are basically the same all over the world. It is not essential to be aware of other people's cultures.
* Cultural differences are becoming less important.

▶ MEET THE EXPERT

Watch an interview with Anna Colquhoun, a culinary anthropologist, about the cultural importance of food. Turn to page 154 for video activities.

SITUATION

1 Work with a partner and discuss the questions.

1 What foreign country would you like to visit?
2 Why does it interest you?
3 If you visited the country, what kinds of things would you do to learn about its culture (e.g. visit a museum, do an official tour)?

2 Read the newspaper article and the advert and answer the questions.

1 What is the purpose of Kaleidoscope World?
2 Where does it get its money from?
3 What do you think are the benefits mentioned in the text?
4 What change is taking place?

28 | NEWS

EXPANDING WORLD

Kaleidoscope World, the cultural exchange organisation, is expanding its network of destinations. Founded back in the 1960s, it has been operating cultural exchange programmes to over thirty countries for the past fifty years. These give people aged 18–25 the opportunity to experience a completely different culture from their own for a short time. The visits have been highly praised for their benefits by academics and writers. Funding comes partly from government grants and partly from donations. A spokesman explained, 'In these troubled times, Kaleidoscope World has decided to increase its activities and reach out to young people all across the world.'

CALLING ALL TOURIST BOARDS

- Are you proud of your culture and heritage?
- Do you think people in other countries misunderstand your way of life?
- Do you want to improve your country's image around the world?

If you answered YES to any of the above, read on.

KALEIDOSCOPE WORLD

invites presentations in English from tourist boards around the world wishing to become destinations for our popular and successful cultural exchange programmes.

For further details go to:
www.kaleidoscopeworld.com

3 `11.4` Listen to the first part of a presentation made by a representative of the Toronto tourist board to the Kaleidoscope World organisation. Answer the questions.

1 How many sections are there in the presentation?
2 What does the presenter say about questions?
3 Which of the following are mentioned in the first part of the presentation?

   a population
   b climate
   c location
   d type of city

4 `11.5` Listen to the second part and answer the question: what three sights are recommended? Why?

5 `11.6` Listen to the third part and answer the question: What three activities are suggested for visitors to try and do?

KEY LANGUAGE
CREATING IMPACT IN A PRESENTATION

6a `11.7` Listen to an extract of the presentation again. Complete the examples of the techniques.

Tripling (saying things in threes)

1 … it's an important industrial, _____ and _____ centre.
2 … they help to create the _____, friendly, _____ atmosphere the city is famous for.

Repetition

3 Toronto's getting _____ and _____ these days, as _____ and _____ people come from all over the world …

Rhetorical questions
(These help to create anticipation in the minds of the audience.)

4 So, _____ are the main _____ of the city?
5 OK, _____ is the CN Tower _____ seeing?

6b Now look at Audio scripts 11.4–7 on page 181 and find other examples of the techniques described in Exercise 6a.

TASK
GIVING A FORMAL PRESENTATION

7a You work for the tourist board of your home town (or city/region). You are going to prepare and deliver a five-minute presentation to Kaleidoscope World. Use the notes below to prepare your presentation.

- The purpose of the presentation is to persuade the Kaleidoscope World agents to include your town/city/region in their list of destinations for cultural visits.
- The presentation should have an introduction and conclusion.
- The main body of the presentation should be structured in the following way.
  A – three key pieces of background information, e.g. location, climate, population, history
  B – three places to visit/main sights
  C – three other things a visitor should try/do, e.g. special food, sporting events, customs, traditions, festivals
- Try to use some of the techniques for creating impact in your presentation.

7b Work with different groups and take turns to give your presentations. Choose the best one(s).

OTHER USEFUL PHRASES

Starting
Good morning, everyone. I'd like to talk to you today about …

Signalling structure
The presentation is organised into three sections.
I'll begin with … Next, … and lastly, …

Moving on
Turning to the next part, …
Let's now look at …

Summarising
In conclusion, I would just like to say …
To summarise …

Inviting questions
Now if there are any questions, I'll be happy to try and answer them.
Please feel free to ask any questions and I'll do my best to answer them.

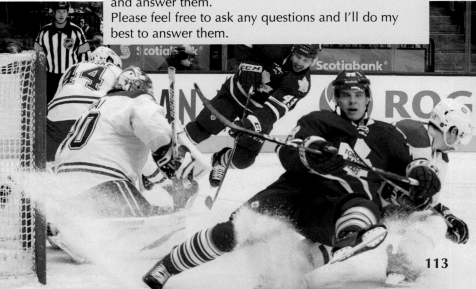

STUDY SKILLS
IMPROVING READING SKILLS

1a Think about when you read in English. Which of the following techniques do you use and in what situations?

Do you:
1 focus on headings and subheadings?
2 only look at summaries and conclusions?
3 read every word very carefully?
4 predict what comes next?
5 ask yourself questions about what you are reading?
6 use your finger to help you follow what you read?
7 have questions to which you want to know the answers before you read?
8 read aloud?
9 focus on the unknown vocabulary?

1b Compare your ideas with a partner.

2 **11.8** Listen to part of a radio programme on the subject of reading and answer the questions.
1 Who is the guest and what has she written?
2 What does she say about the benefits of reading?
3 What advice does she give?

3 Listen again. Which techniques in Exercise 1a does the guest mention?
There are different techniques for improving reading speed and ability. Do Exercises 4–6 to try them out.

4 Reading and chunking If you want to improve reading speed, it's important to look at groups of words rather than individual words. You can read the sentence below one word at a time.

All | cultures | develop | from | a | range | of | diverse | influences.

However it is better to 'chunk' groups of words as below:

All cultures | develop from | a range of | diverse influences. The cosmopolitan atmosphere | of many world cities | is a result of | centuries of immigration.

How are the sentences above chunked? Do you notice any patterns? Divide the sentences below into appropriate chunks.
1 He wrote a brief history of Western culture.
2 Many people argue that American culture will soon take over the world.
3 Cultural Studies is becoming an increasingly popular university course.

5a Guessing unknown words The context will help with the meaning of vocabulary items because of the following.
• the position of the word in the sentence
• the part of speech (e.g. noun, verb, adjective, etc.)
• the use of prefixes and suffixes

Match the prefixes below with their meanings.
1	**pre**date	a	after
2	**inter**national	b	before
3	**post**war	c	between
4	**multi**cultural	d	many
5	**sub**culture	e	opposite
6	**mis**understanding	f	bad or wrong
7	**anti**social	g	against
8	**counter**culture	h	under

5b Identify the suffixes in the words below. Decide if they are noun or adjective suffixes.
1	sociology	5	responsible
2	sexism	6	development
3	timeless	7	communication
4	valuable		

5c Add some more words with the same suffixes.

5d Look back at the texts on page 111 and identify as many prefixes and suffixes as you can (look for verbs, nouns and adjectives).

6 Reading linkers Focusing on linking expressions will help you to understand how the ideas in a text are connected. Match the common formal linking expressions 1–8 with their functions a–h.
1 alternatively
2 on the contrary
3 provided that
4 in addition
5 similarly
6 nevertheless
7 in order to
8 therefore

a adds something
b introduces a result
c gives the purpose of something
d introduces a surprising piece of information
e introduces another choice
f suggests a condition
g makes a comparison
h makes a contrast

7a Work with a partner. You will each read a different text, then summarise it orally for your partner. What ideas are similar in both texts?

Student A: turn to page 156.
Student B: turn to page 159.

7b Identify the prefixes, suffixes and linking phrases in your text. How did you chunk the text as you read? Discuss your ideas with your partner.

WRITING SKILLS
FORMAL CORRESPONDENCE

8 Work with a partner and answer the questions.

1 What sort of formal correspondence (letters/emails) do you write or receive?
2 What is the usual purpose of the correspondence (e.g. asking for information, applying for something, complaining)?
3 What form does the correspondence generally take?
   a an email
   b a letter sent in the post
   c a letter attached to an email

9a Letter layout Match items 1–12 with A–L on the diagram of a formal letter.

1 greeting (*Dear Sir/Madam* or *Dear Mr/Mrs/Miss/Ms* + name)
2 main message of the correspondence
3 writer's address
4 subject heading (where appropriate)
5 date
6 writer's name and position
7 ending (*Yours faithfully* or *Yours sincerely*)
8 signature
9 reference to previous contact or reason for contact
10 address of recipient
11 reference to future contact
12 closing remarks

9b Compare the letter layout in Exercise 9a with the layout of an email. Which of the items 1–12 would be in the same place and which would be different? If different, where would you find them in an email?

10a Formulaic language The language of formal correspondence is very formulaic (i.e. we tend to use the same expressions again and again). Complete the expressions below with words from the box.

assistance	contacted	enclosed/attached	forward
require	contacting	information	question	additional
reference	request	contact	future	hestitate	writing

1 I look _____ to hearing from you in the near _____.
2 I am _____ with _____ to (your advertisement).
3 If I can be of any further _____, please do not _____ to contact me.
4 Please find _____ a copy of my (CV) for your _____.
5 Regarding the _____ of (the conference dates), I think …
6 I can be _____ on the above phone number at any time.
7 Should you _____ any _____ information, please feel free to _____ me.
8 I am _____ you in relation to your _____ for …

10b Match the sentences in Exercise 10a with their functions a–f.

a reason for contact
b how to get in touch
c including something with your letter
d reference to the future
e closing remark
f reference to an issue

11 Work in small groups. Read the advertisement and discuss the questions in it.

UNICORN Television

Unicorn Television is commissioning a series on the history and influence of youth cultures around the world, to be called 'Street Styles'.

We would like to hear from people all over the world who would be willing to be interviewed on any of the following points:
1 Do youth cultures give young people a sense of identity?
2 Are youth cultures a problem for parents?
3 What are your personal experiences of youth cultures?
4 Are youth cultures a normal part of growing up?
5 What are the main youth cultures in your country?
6 Are youth cultures simply a way for business to exploit the young?
7 Do youth cultures pose a danger to society?

Please write to the following address stating your age, availability, and include a recent photograph.

The Commissioning Editor
CE@ut.co.uk
Unicorn Television | Forest Lane | London W1
All replies will be acknowledged.

12 Write a piece of formal correspondence in reply to the advertisement. In your correspondence, you should do the following.

• refer to the advertisement
• give the topic you would be willing to answer questions on
• briefly state your views/experience of youth cultures
• say when you will be available
• make a closing remark
• refer to the future

12 Technology

12.1 DEVICES AND GADGETS

IN THIS UNIT

GRAMMAR
- conditionals: first and second
- conditionals: third and mixed

VOCABULARY
- technology
- opposites (prefixes)
- words from the text

SCENARIO
- persuading, making a case for something
- conducting a problem-solving meeting

STUDY SKILLS
- plagiarism – what it is and how to avoid it

WRITING SKILLS
- an opinion article

Computers are stupid. They can only give you answers. Pablo Picasso, 1881–1973, Spanish artist

VOCABULARY
TECHNOLOGY

1 Work with a partner and discuss the questions.

1 What are the three items of technology you use most often?
2 Are you technologically minded or are you a technophobe?
3 How important is technology in your life?

2a Look at the words in the box. Are they countable or uncountable?

apparatus	appliance	device	engine
equipment	gadget	machine	

2b Complete the questions with the words in Exercise 2a.

1 How many household _____ can you name?
2 How often should you upgrade your computer _____?
3 How often do you use a cash _____ to get money?
4 What do you think is the most useful labour-saving _____?
5 What clever _____ can you think of (e.g. satellite navigation system, can opener)?
6 What is the name of the breathing _____ which divers use so they can stay underwater?
7 Is the internal combustion _____ the greatest piece of 20th-century technology?

2c Work with a partner and ask and answer the questions in Exercise 2b.

3a Match two adjectives in the box to each of these concepts.

1 non-polluting	4	simple to operate
2 very new	5	long-lasting
3 old-fashioned	6	useful

cutting edge	durable	easy to use	state-of-the-art
environmentally friendly	out-of-date	handy	
hard-wearing	obsolete	green	practical	user-friendly

3b Look at the objects below. Use some of the adjectives to describe them.

3c Think about some items of technology you own. Which of the qualities listed in Exercise 3a does each one have?

LISTENING

4 ▮12.1▮ **Listen to three people describing technological equipment and answer the questions.**

1   What piece(s) of technology is mentioned by each speaker?
2   What do they like/dislike about the technology they mention?
3   What adjectives do they use to describe the technology they talk about?

5 Discuss a piece of technology you like and one piece you dislike, giving your reasons.

READING

6 What inventions do you associate these names with?

Alexander Graham Bell	W.H. Hoover	Frank Whittle
John Shepherd Barron	Steven Sasson	Laszlo Biro
King Camp Gillette	Norman Joseph Woodland	
Orville and Wilbur Wright	John Boyd Dunlop	

7 Work in groups of three. Read the introduction of the article and summarise it to each other.

8 Now read one text each and answer the questions.
Student A: read the text on this page.
Student B: turn to page 160.
Student C: turn to page 162.

1   Who is the text about?
2   What did the person do?
3   When did they do it?
4   Why did they fail?
5   What recent developments have there been?

9 Exchange information about your texts in your groups. What are the similarities and differences between the three people?

10 Reflecting on the topic **Discuss these questions in your groups.**

1   What is your view of the people mentioned in the texts?
2   Do you think it is common that pioneers do not benefit from their work and are not recognised?
3   Is it OK to copy the ideas of others if they are not protected? What about if they are protected?
4   How do you feel about the following:
    • downloading movies/music/games from the internet without paying?
    • buying copies of products (e.g. designer goods)?
5   Are some ideas and inventions too important to be 'owned' by one person?

SPEAKING AND WRITING

11 Work in small groups to discuss the following statements. Think of arguments for and against each one.

1   People rely on technology too much these days.
2   Inventors of new technology should share ideas, not protect them.
3   The amount of technology in developed countries is a bad thing.
4   Technology can solve all the world's problems.
5   Technology often leads to social and environmental problems.
6   Today's technology does not make people's lives better.

12 Write a short text (100–150 words) giving your opinion (for or against) of one of the statements from Exercise 11.

The Nearly men

Technological advance is not a smooth process. Often the pioneers don't get the credit they deserve, or they pay the price for being first. Sometimes they fail to protect their ideas by taking out a patent. In this article we celebrate three of these unsung heroes responsible for some of the most important pieces of communication technology.

Up in the air

PERCY PILCHER was an English engineer and pioneer aviator. In the 1890s, he built and flew a glider called 'the Hawk'. However, Pilcher's dream was to achieve powered flight. He built another 'soaring machine', this time with an engine. In September 1899, he was ready to make his first test flight. Unfortunately, the engine broke, and not wanting to disappoint the audience, he decided to fly his 'Hawk' glider instead. Tragically, he crashed and died of his injuries two days later. As there was no one to carry on his work, his designs were lost. The American Wright brothers were to achieve the first powered flight four years later on 17 December 1903. In 2003, at the time of the centenary of powered flight, a replica of Pilcher's plane was built and flown, achieving a controlled flight of one minute and 26 seconds, significantly longer than the Wright brothers' first flight of 59 seconds.

Lancaster County, Pennsylvania

Amish FAQs • Amish-made furniture • Amish quilts • Amish faith • History of the Amish • Amish videos

Amish: Frequently Asked Questions

A _____

People say they are different because of their plain style of dress, limited use of technology, such as cars and electricity, and their simple way of life. If you visit an Amish area, you'll see women in long dresses and people travelling in buggies drawn by horses. And if you pass an Amish farm, you'll notice farm equipment being pulled by horses. You're unlikely to get to know any of the Amish, but if you were invited into an Amish home, you'd find no televisions, no telephones and no kitchen appliances run by electricity. The Amish are different and wish to separate themselves from mainstream society. They do not join the military, pay social security or accept financial assistance from the government.

B _____

The Amish value simplicity and self-sufficiency. They are not inefficient. They just do not wish to depend on the outside world or on modern technology. The conveniences that we take for granted, such as electricity, television, cars and tractors are thought to create inequality and to lead the Amish away from their close-knit community. They are considered inappropriate and are not encouraged or accepted. The Amish believe in equality and they are not attracted by material comforts. They live in a separate world, with its own values, the most important of which is a mistrust of anything modern, especially modern technology.

C _____

The Amish do compromise with the modern world, as long as it is strictly necessary. They dislike telephones and don't use them unless it's an absolute emergency, as they interfere with their separation from the world. It brings the outside world into their home and is an intrusion into their privacy. But, supposing that an Amish had to make an important telephone call, they would go to a small outbuilding usually located at an inconvenient distance from their home. And, to answer the second part of the question, if they had to go to hospital, they would be able to ride in cars and travel in planes. One final example: the Amish will even allow the use of modern farm equipment, provided that it is pulled by teams of horses and not tractors.

D _____

There are a number of other websites dedicated to presenting the Amish way of life. There are also a number of films and documentaries you could look out for. The film *Witness*, starring Harrison Ford, is now quite old (1985), but many think the film portrayed the Amish fairly accurately, although it showed a limited segment of their lifestyle. A lot of Amish had reservations about the film because it was filmed in the geographical area of the Amish, but not on a real Amish farm, and obviously the actors were not Amish. There is also *Amish: out of order*, a documentary reality series made by the National Geographic Channel in 2012 that follows the lives of former Amish who have left the community. Finally, the 2013 TV series *Banshee* is set in a fictional small town in Amish Country, Lancaster, Pennsylvania and features Amish people.

READING

1 Look at the photos on these pages which were taken recently. What is unusual about them?

2 Look at these questions from a website about the Amish community in North America. Read the webpage and match the questions with the answers.

1   I'm going to Pennsylvania next month and may meet some Amish. Why do people say they are so different?
2   Is there any way I can find out more about them?
3   Do they ever use modern technology? I mean, imagine one of them had to go to hospital for an operation – would that be OK?
4   Why do they live in such an old-fashioned way?

3 Read paragraph B again. Do the Amish value or reject the following ideas?

simplicity   self-sufficiency   modern technology
close-knit community   material comforts
independence from the outside world   equality

4a Summarising Read the webpage again and summarise each paragraph in one sentence.

4b Work with a partner and compare your sentences.

5 What do you think of the Amish's attitude to modern technology?

VOCABULARY
OPPOSITES (PREFIXES)

6a Find the opposites in the webpage of the words in the box.

appropriate   convenient   efficient   equality
like   likely   trust

6b What other opposites can you think of beginning with *in-*, *dis-*, *mis-* or *un-*?

7 Complete the text using the opposites of the words in the box.

able   accurate   effective   efficient   equality
necessary   sensitive   understanding

There has been a great deal of ¹ _____ about the Amish. You often hear that the Amish are ² _____ because they do not use modern technology. For them, modern devices are ³ _____ and do not add any fulfilment to life. There have recently been a number of TV programmes which have been ⁴ _____ to the Amish who don't have a public relations arm to defend their reputation. One programme attacked them for not using vaccinations, which they believe to be ⁵ _____. There have also been a number of ⁶ _____ newspaper reports about ⁷ _____ between men and women in the community. Although the man is the head of the household, this does not mean that women are not respected or are ⁸ _____ to make decisions.

GRAMMAR
CONDITIONALS: FIRST AND SECOND

8a Complete the sentences, then check in the text.
1   If you visit an Amish area, you _____ women in long dresses …
2   If you _____ invited into an Amish home, you _____ no televisions …

8b Which sentence in Exercise 8a is a first conditional? Which is a second conditional? Find other examples of these two conditionals in the text.

8c Which conditional describes an unlikely situation? Which describes a real possibility?

➥ Language reference and extra practice, pages 126–149

9 Put the verbs into the correct conditional form according to the likelihood of the condition.
1   He's always late. If he _____ (be) late again this week, I _____ (fire) him.
2   If you _____ (wait) a moment, I _____ (call) the technician. He'll come immediately.
3   If I _____ (have) enough money, I _____ (buy) a Ferrari – what a dream!
4   Look, if you _____ (buy) this computer now, I _____ (give) you a free pair of headphones.
5   Are you around later? If I _____ (have) enough time, I _____ (call) you.
6   If I _____ (know) the answer, I _____ (tell) you, but I don't.

10a Find the following conjunctions in paragraph C of the website (including the question). Which have a similar meaning to *if* and which have a similar meaning to *if not*?

as long as   imagine   provided that
supposing that   unless

10b Which two of the conjunctions introduce a strict condition (*only if X happens …*)? Which two introduce imaginary situations?

11 Correct the sentences. (Some can be corrected in two ways.)
1   I'd buy you a new tablet as long as you agree to study harder.
2   Would you be interested in investing in more technology, if you have the chance?
3   If I start this technology course again, I think I'd do it differently.
4   Imagine you had no access to the internet, what will you do?
5   Supposing that the computer crashed, who will you phone?
6   You can borrow my iPad provided that you would bring it back tomorrow.

12 Work with a partner and write sentences based on the prompts below. Think about whether the situation is possible or unlikely.
If scientists find a cure for cancer, people will live longer.
1   ice cap melt / next twenty years
2   people / live longer
3   government / not invest in medicine
4   computer games / ban
5   fewer people / drive
6   Earth / in danger

SPEAKING

13 Work in small groups and discuss how you would manage without technology. What would you miss? What would you find most difficult?

READING AND VOCABULARY
WORDS FROM THE TEXT

1 **Work with a partner. Are these statements true or false?**

Genetically Modified (GM) Quiz

1   GM food is food from crops whose genes have been scientifically changed.
2   93 percent of the world's cotton is GM.
3   Sri Lanka has a ban on GM foods.
4   GM foods have been proved to be safe to eat.
5   GM foods reduce the need to use pesticides and herbicides.
6   The sweetener aspartame, used in many diet drinks, is not a GM product.
7   Apples are currently non-GM.
8   Up to 75 percent of food items on US supermarket shelves contain GM ingredients.
9   Popcorn, baby formula, canned soups and frozen pizza may all contain GM ingredients.

2 **Read the text quickly and decide which paragraph mentions the following topics.**

a   how golden rice was developed
b   the first country to plant golden rice
c   other Asian countries interested in golden rice
d   opponents of golden rice
e   how much money companies developing golden rice will make
f   the amount of golden rice needed to get enough vitamin A
g   problems caused by a lack of vitamin A
h   how the opinion of someone who was originally against GM food has changed

3 **Read the text again and say who the following people are.**

1   Adrian Dubock
2   Bill and Melinda Gates
3   Mark Lynas
4   Peter Beyer
5   Ingo Potrykus

4   Identifying arguments **Read paragraphs 4–7 again and find two arguments against golden rice. Then find two points that challenge those arguments.**

5 **Look at the text again and find words and phrases which match the definitions below.**

1   a phrase that means 'the system in your body that protects it against illness' (paragraph 3)
2   a word that means 'large amount or large number' (paragraph 4)
3   a phrase that means 'fight against very strongly' (paragraph 5)
4   a phrase that means 'say you will not do something that someone has asked you to do in a firm and sometimes impolite way' (paragraph 5)
5   a phrase that means 'working with someone or something else' (paragraph 6)

6 **What is your opinion of genetically modified food?**

1   Scientists say they have seen the future of genetically modified foods and have concluded that it is orange or, more precisely, golden. Next year, golden rice – normal rice that has been genetically modified to provide vitamin A to prevent blindness and other diseases in children in the developing world – could be given to farmers in the Philippines for planting in paddy fields.

2   Thirty years after scientists first revealed they had created the world's first GM crop, they hope that they will finally be able to reduce global malnutrition problems. Bangladesh and Indonesia have indicated they are ready to accept golden rice and other nations, including India, have also said that they are considering planting it.

3   'Vitamin A deficiency is deadly,' said Adrian Dubock, a member of the Golden Rice project. 'It affects children's immune systems and kills around two million every year in developing countries. It is also a major cause of blindness in the third world. Boosting levels of vitamin A in rice provides a simple, straightforward way to put that right.'

4   Recent tests have revealed that a substantial amount of vitamin A can be obtained by eating only 60g of cooked golden rice. 'This has enormous potential,' said Dubock.

5   But scientists' satisfaction over the Golden Rice project has been lessened by the fact that it has taken an extraordinarily long time for the GM crop to be approved. Golden rice was first developed in 1999, but its development and cultivation has been opposed vehemently by campaigners who have flatly refused to accept that it could deliver enough vitamin A, and who have also argued that the crop's introduction in the developing world would make farmers increasingly dependent on western industry. The crop has become the cause célèbre of the anti-GM movement, which sees golden rice as a tool of global capitalism.

6   This view is rejected by the scientists involved. 'We have developed this in conjunction with organisations such as the Bill and Melinda Gates Foundation as a way of alleviating a real health problem in the developing world,' says Dubock. 'No one is going to make money out of it. The companies involved in developing some of the technologies have waived their licences just to get this off the ground.'

7   This view is shared by Mark Lynas, an environmental campaigner and one of the founders of the anti-GM crop movement. He has publicly apologised for opposing the planting of GM crops in Britain. 'The first generation of GM crops were suspect, I believed then, but the case for continued opposition to new generations – which provide life-saving vitamins for starving people – is no longer justifiable. You cannot call yourself a humanitarian and be opposed to GM crops today.'

8   Golden rice was created by Peter Beyer, Professor for cell biology at Freiburg University in Germany, and Ingo Potrykus of the Institute of Plant Sciences in Switzerland, in the late 1990s. They inserted genes for a chemical known as beta-carotene into the DNA of normal rice. In this way they modified the rice genes so that the plants started to make beta-carotene, a rich orange-coloured pigment that is also a key chemical used by the body to make vitamin A.

GRAMMAR
CONDITIONALS: THIRD AND MIXED

7 [12.2] **Listen to two students talking about golden rice and answer the questions.**

1 Did Edward Jenner discover vaccines?
2 Did the authorities block the introduction of golden rice?
3 Did they save many from blindness?
4 Does wheat grow in the desert?

8 Listen again and complete the sentences with up to four words in each gap.

1 If Edward Jenner _____ vaccines, there _____ far more fatalities every year than there actually are.
2 If the authorities _____ the introduction of golden rice, we _____ many from blindness.
3 If wheat _____ in the desert, we _____ to develop GM crops.

9 Use the clauses in Exercise 8 to complete the examples in the table.

We use the third conditional to speculate about past events and about how things that happened or didn't happen might have affected other things.	
If- clause	Main clause
If + past perfect	*would/could*, etc. + *have* + past participle
_____	_____

There are also mixed conditionals to describe:	
1 things that happened in the past which may have present consequences	
If- clause (3rd conditional)	Main clause (2nd conditional)
_____	_____

2 past events which may be the result of timeless or present facts	
If- clause (2nd conditional)	Main clause (3rd conditional)
_____	_____

➡ Language reference and extra practice, pages 126–149

10 Match the beginnings of conditional sentences 1–9 with their endings a–i. Some are third conditional, some are mixed (both types).

1 If Sir Alexander Fleming hadn't discovered penicillin in 1928,
2 If we didn't like the professor,
3 If he didn't believe in his research proposal,
4 If I had studied harder,
5 If we'd bought a GPS system for the car,
6 If I'd wanted to,
7 If Sir Tim Berners-Lee hadn't invented the internet,
8 If she hadn't wasted so much money,
9 If I weren't so busy,

a we would know where we are now.
b he wouldn't have started his doctorate.
c we'd find it difficult to treat infections.
d I could have gone to university to study technology.
e I might have passed the technology exam.
f we would find it much more difficult to get information.
g we wouldn't have invited him to lecture here.
h I could have gone to the conference on GM foods last week.
i we'd be able to afford a better laboratory.

11 Complete the prompts, in more than one way if possible. Then discuss them with a partner.

1 If I had won the lottery last week, …
2 If I'd told my friend the truth, …
3 If we hadn't gone to live abroad, …
4 If we wanted to have solar panels, …
5 If we had had more money when we were growing up, …
6 If we didn't take life so seriously, …
7 If I weren't so busy, …

SPEAKING

12 Hold a class debate on the motion: *The rapid rate of technological development has improved our lives.* **First, discuss the motion in two groups.**

Group A: you are **for** the motion; turn to page 160.
Group B: you are **against** the motion; turn to page 160.

SITUATION

Apparel Unlimited is a clothing manufacturing company based in downtown Los Angeles, California. It makes a wide range of basic clothing products for men and women aged 18–40. The management try to create a family atmosphere for the 2,500 workers in the company, and emphasise in all their literature that their staff are their greatest asset. Up to now, the management have had good relations with the union representatives. In the last three years, their profits have fallen because of cheap foreign imports of clothing and the general depressed state of the economy. They are looking at ways of reducing their costs and increasing workers' productivity. They are planning to invest heavily in state-of-the-art cutting and sewing machines which will increase the production staff's efficiency and ability to produce more goods, more quickly while maintaining their quality.

The management have not yet told staff about their plan and are thinking about the best way to break the news to them. The new machines will affect about 1,800 staff, mainly those in the cutting and sewing areas, but also in product design. Over 60 percent of the workforce have been in the company for more than ten years.

1 Read the situation about Apparel Unlimited and answer the questions.

1 What are the basic facts about Apparel Unlimited? What do they make? Where? How big is the workforce?
2 How does the management get on with the unions?
3 What do Apparel Unlimited plan to do in the near future?
4 Why are they planning the change?
5 Which departments will be affected by the company's plan?

2 Work in small groups. Rumours are already circulating in the company that the management are going to make cuts in the workforce. How do you think the workers will react when they learn about the plan to introduce state-of-the-art sewing and cutting machines?

3a `12.3` Listen to two workers, Jessie and Carol, talking about the rumour and take notes on the key points.

3b Work with a partner. One of you summarises the conversation. The other listens and checks the summary for accuracy.

4a Work in small groups. Because of the rumours, the management realises they must inform staff that they are considering new technology to modernise the production process. Discuss the options they have for communicating their plan. Consider the advantages and disadvantages and decide which method is best.

1 an email message sent by the CEO (Chief Executive Officer) to all members of staff
2 an announcement by each head of department to their staff
3 an announcement by the CEO at a public meeting with staff most likely to be affected by the new technology
4 an article by the CEO in the weekly staff newspaper informing everyone of the plans

4b Compare your decision with the decisions of other groups. Try to persuade them that your decision is the right one.

CONDUCTING A PROBLEM-SOLVING MEETING

KEY LANGUAGE
PERSUADING, MAKING A CASE FOR SOMETHING

5a `12.4` **Listen to two managers, Don and Stephanie, talking about the plan to modernise the production process. Don thinks it is a good idea to introduce the new technology. Note down some of the arguments he uses to make his case.**

5b **Work with a partner and compare notes. Do you have the same points or different ones?**

6 **Listen again. Complete the sentences that Don uses to persuade Stephanie with information from the conversation. Use a maximum of three words to complete each sentence.**

1 Let's face it, the economy's not …
2 We don't want to be …
3 It's true what you say, Stephanie, but we do need to modernise …
4 That's a very strong argument for spending some money on …
5 Another reason is that the new machines will enable operators to produce a wider …
6 I would argue that we'll be using our resources …
7 That's a fair point, Stephanie, but look at …
8 I'm sure you'll agree with me, it's our job …
9 I've heard about the objections. My answer …
10 Look, I think you'll agree, we've got some of the best and …
11 That's the way …
12 We don't have any …

TASK
CONDUCTING A PROBLEM-SOLVING MEETING

The workers in the company are very worried about how the new machines will affect their lives. They are also not clear why the management wishes to introduce the machines. To address these problems, a meeting has been set up between the CEO and Production Manager and two representatives of the biggest unions. The meeting will be organised as follows:

1 an informal presentation by the management of the case for introducing the machines
2 an informal presentation by the union representatives of the workers' concerns
3 discussion and decisions about how to deal with the workers' concerns

7a **Work in groups of four. Choose one of the following roles. One of you must take the role of CEO.**

Union representative A: turn to page 156.
Union representative B: turn to page 160.
Chief Executive Officer (CEO): turn to page 162.
Production manager: turn to page 162.

7b **Hold the meeting outlined above. Make your presentations and discuss how to deal with the workers' concerns. Note any decisions that have been taken.**

STUDY SKILLS
PLAGIARISM – WHAT IT IS AND HOW TO AVOID IT

1 Work with a partner and discuss the questions.

1 What is plagiarism?
2 Can you give an example of plagiarism?

2 ▶ 12.1 You are going to see a video of four postgraduate students. They are taking part in a panel discussion on plagiarism which has been organised by the Student Union. Watch the first part of the video and make notes on George's definition of plagiarism. Then compare it with your definition from Exercise 1.

3 Watch the first part again. Choose the reasons mentioned by the panel to describe why plagiarising is serious.

1 It is unfair and deceives people.
2 It shows a lack of respect to writers.
3 It is not a correct way of behaving.
4 Students should present their own ideas.
5 It enables students to get high grades.

4 ▶ 12.2 Watch the second part of the discussion. Match each example below with the correct speaker (S = Sophia, L = Li, I = Ismet, G = George).

1 copying, with no quotation marks or references
2 giving in a piece of writing that someone else has produced
3 using too many words from the original text
4 using other writers' ideas without acknowledging the source

5 Watch the second part again. Work with a partner and discuss the questions.

1 Who thinks that their example of plagiarism is the most serious?
2 How would you rank the above examples in order of seriousness? (1 = least serious, 4 = most serious)

6 ▶ 12.3 Watch the third part and make notes on the four reasons for plagiarising that the panel give. Compare your notes with a partner.

7 Work with a partner. Do you think that the software available, such as Turnitin, will stop plagiarism? Why?/Why not?

8 Work in small groups and decide which of the following are examples of plagiarism.

1 Quoting from a text without mentioning the name of the author.
2 Cutting and pasting a paragraph from a website without acknowledging the source.
3 Rewriting a sentence from another text in your own words.
4 Copying material from another student for an essay or report.
5 Taking a graph or a chart from a book, giving the source.
6 Rephrasing an idea from another source without acknowledgment.
7 Using information that you consider to be general knowledge.
8 Quoting from another source, but misspelling the author's name.
9 Discussing an essay with your colleagues and using some of their ideas in your writing.
10 Using the results of your own research, e.g. from questionnaires, without giving the source.

9 These examples show the difference between acceptable paraphrasing and plagiarism. Work with a partner and discuss whether each version is an example of plagiarism.

Original	
	Developing countries have significant unmet food needs, and GMO food crops are positioned to help. In Asia, poor consumers who currently don't get enough vitamin A from their rice-only diets could be better protected against blindness if their farmers had permission to plant so-called Golden Rice, which has been genetically engineered with high beta-carotene content. Paarlberg, R. (2013) *The World Needs Genetically Modified Foods*, [Online], *The Wall Street Journal*, European edition, Available at: http://online.wsj.com/article/SB100014241278873241052045 78380872639718046.html#articleTabs%3Darticl), [22 August 2013].
Version A	GMO crops could provide more food for developing countries. If farmers were allowed to grow Golden Rice containing vitamin A, many people in Asia could be prevented from going blind.
Version B	Developing countries have a significant need for food and GMO food crops could help. Poor consumers in Asia don't get enough vitamin A from their rice-only diets. If farmers had permission to plant Golden Rice, which has high beta-carotene content, consumers would be better protected from blindness.
Version C	Paarlberg (2013) points out that GMO food crops could help to provide more food for developing countries. Poor people in Asia don't get enough vitamin A. He argues that many of these people could be prevented from going blind if farmers were allowed to produce Golden Rice.
Version D	Developing countries have food needs. GMO crops could help. In Asia, poor people don't get enough vitamin A. They could be protected against blindness if farmers could plant Golden Rice. This has high beta-carotene content.

Technology:

Modern technology is changing the way our brains work, says neurologist.

By Susan Greenfield

1   Human identity, the idea that defines each and every one of us, could be facing a crisis. It is a crisis that would threaten our ideas of who we are, what we do and how we behave. It goes right to the heart – or the head – of us all. This crisis could change how we interact with each other, alter what makes us happy, and modify our capacity for reaching our full potential as individuals. It's caused by one simple fact: the human brain. This most sensitive of organs is under threat from the modern world.

2   Of course, there are benefits from technical progress – but there are great dangers as well, and I believe that we are seeing some of those today. One vital fact I have learnt is that the brain is not the unchanging organ that we might imagine. It not only goes on developing, changing, and in some tragic cases, eventually deteriorating with age, it is also substantially shaped by what we do to it, and by the experience of daily life.

3   The pace of change in the outside environment and in the development of new technologies has increased dramatically. This will affect our brains over the next 100 years in ways we might never have imagined. Our brains are being influenced by the ever-expanding world of new technology: multichannel television, video games, MP3 players, the internet, wireless networks, Bluetooth links – the list goes on and on.

4   Electronic devices and pharmaceutical drugs all have an impact on the structure and biochemistry of the brain. And that, in turn, affects our personality, our behaviour and our characteristics. In short, the modern world could well be altering our human identity.

5   With our brains now under such a widespread attack from the modern world, there's a danger that our sense of self could be decreased or even lost. For example, it's pretty clear that the screen-based, two-dimensional world that so many teenagers – and a growing number of adults – inhabit is producing changes in behaviour. Attention spans are shorter, personal communication skills are reduced and there's a decrease in the ability to think abstractly.

6   But we mustn't be too unhappy about the future. It may sound frightening, but there may be some potential advantages to be gained from our growing understanding of the human brain's tremendous flexibility. What if we could create an environment that would allow the brain to develop in a way that was of universal benefit?

7   I do see potential in one particular direction. I think it is possible that we might one day be able to use outside stimuli in such a way that creativity – surely the best expression of individuality – is actually increased rather than diminished.

8   I am optimistic and excited about what future research will reveal into the working of the human brain. However, I'm also concerned that we seem so unaware of the dangers that are already upon us.

WRITING SKILLS
AN OPINION ARTICLE

10 Work with a partner and read the title of the article. In what ways do you think our brain is changing because of new technologies?

11 Read the article, then choose the statements which are an accurate paraphrase of Susan Greenfield's ideas.

1   New technology will affect the way we think and behave.
2   Our brain changes in good and bad ways over time.
3   We will not be able to achieve our goals in the modern world.
4   We will probably be very surprised at the changes in our brain in the future.
5   Technology will have no physical effect on our brains.
6   There is no evidence that the modern world is changing human behaviour.
7   In the future, our sense of identity will be lost.
8   There could be advantages for us because the brain is so flexible.
9   The writer looks forward to more discoveries about the human brain.
10 She is worried that we are not taking seriously the effects of technology on our brain.

12a Stylistic features Opinion articles that appear in newspapers and magazines often have a number of stylistic features. Work with a partner and find examples of the following in the article by Susan Greenfield.

1   Strong vocabulary: strong nouns, adjectives and adverbs *crisis, vital*
2   Use of the personal pronoun *I*
3   Use of the dash – for punctuation
4   Use of informal language (e.g. abbreviations)
5   Compounds (noun adjective, adverb adjective) *ever-expanding*
6   Use of imagery *It goes to the heart – or the head – of us all.*

12b Compare your examples with other pairs.

13 Write an opinion article on the topic below. It should be 300–350 words. Try to use some of the above techniques in your article.

The increased use of mobile technology, social networks and gaming is changing the way people think and behave.

GRAMMAR

G1 THE CONTINUOUS ASPECT

Use the continuous aspect to talk about:
- an action which is in progress.
  Answer the door! I'**m watching** something.
- an unfinished action.
  She **was working** on a new novel when she died.
- a temporary action.
  I'**m using** Jo's laptop while mine is being repaired.
- a trend, changing action or situation.
  Scientists say the weather **is getting** hotter.

Compare the present simple and continuous:
I **live** in a small flat. (permanent situation)
I'**m living** with a host family for six weeks. (temporary situation)

We can also use the present continuous for repeated actions which are happening around now.
  I'**m watching** the new series of *Breaking Bad*. It's fantastic. (I watch it every Thursday evening.)

We often use the past continuous and the past simple to talk about a longer background action in the past when a shorter action happens during it or interrupts it.
  I was washing the car **when the phone rang**.

We can also use the present continuous to describe future arrangements.
  We're collecting our new car **at the weekend**.

G2 STATE VERBS

Some verbs describe something passive or a state. Examples of these verbs are: *agree, believe, belong, depend, hate, hear, know, like, love, prefer, see, understand, want*.

We rarely use state verbs in the continuous:
  I'm not understanding this word. ✗
  I don't understand this word. ✓

G3 THE PERFECT ASPECT

Use the perfect aspect to look back from one time to another.

PRESENT PERFECT

The present perfect looks back from now to a time before now. There are four main uses.
- a state that started in the past and is still continuing
  I'**ve lived** here all my life.
- a completed action in the past which has some relevance to the present (e.g. a present result)
  There **has been** a severe storm and the airport is now closed.
- finished actions in a period of time that is still continuing
  I'**ve been** there once already today.
- actions in the past which may happen again
  Deborah Tannen **has written** several books on communication. (She could write more books.)

❗ Use the past simple, not the present perfect, when talking about a definite time in the past.
  Our lesson has finished at four o'clock. ✗
  Our lesson finished at four o'clock. ✓

PAST PERFECT

The past perfect looks back from a time in the past to another time before that.
  She'**d applied** for ten jobs before she got this one.

We can use the past perfect to describe a sequence of events. The past perfect describes the first action.
  When we arrived, the train **had left**. (First the train left, and then we arrived.)

We can use *just* or *already* to show that the first action happened recently or earlier than expected.
  We arrived at six, but the train **had just left**.
  When they arrived, the film **had already started**.

We can use the past perfect for repeated earlier actions.
  By 2006, Deborah Tannen **had written** twenty books.

KEY LANGUAGE

KL OUTLINING PROBLEMS AND OFFERING SOLUTIONS

OUTLINING PROBLEMS
The problem is …
The trouble is …
It's a tricky situation because …
It's a vicious circle.

OFFERING SOLUTIONS
One way of dealing with this could be …
Well, there's an obvious solution.
We could talk to …
The best way to deal with it is to …

REACTING TO SUGGESTIONS
That might well solve the problem.
That seems the best way to deal with it.

VOCABULARY

V1 PHRASAL VERBS
bump into, catch up with, get in touch with, keep track of, lose touch with, stay in touch with, track down

V2 SCIENTIFIC STUDY
concept, experiment, method, random, research, results, sample, theory
analyse (v), confirm (v), prove (v), test (v)

V3 IDIOMS
actions speak louder than words, be on the same wavelength, get a word in edgeways, get straight to the point, have a quick word with someone, hear it on the grapevine, think before you speak

V4 COLLOCATIONS
display similarities, establish connections, establish rapport, exhibit knowledge, impart information, maintain status, negotiate relationships, negotiate status

G1 **1 Choose the best explanation for each sentence.**

1 We were quite poor when I was growing up.
  a I'm an adult now.
  b I'm still a child.
2 She's on a diet so she isn't eating any ice cream.
  a She ate ice cream in the past.
  b She never eats ice cream.
3 By the end of the day we were feeling quite tired.
  a We got more tired as the day went on.
  b We felt tired all day.
4 I was checking my emails when my computer stopped working.
  a I managed to check all my emails.
  b I only managed to check some of my emails.
5 Michael's doing a project on wind farms.
  a Michael has finished the project.
  b Michael has not finished the project yet.
6 The family was living in a caravan at that time.
  a The family lived there for a temporary period.
  b The family always lived there.

G2 **2 Make questions from the prompts. Use a continuous form if possible.**

1 you / prefer / chicken or fish ?
2 you / read / anything interesting at the moment ?
3 this mobile phone / belong / to you ?
4 your course / get / more difficult ?
5 anyone / know / the answer to this question ?
6 you / agree / with him ?
7 the students / learn / about / pollution this week ?
8 your parents / know / how to send emails ?

G3 **3 Complete the text with the correct form of the verb in brackets.**

John Gray is a famous US psychologist and author. His best-known work is *Men Are from Mars, Women Are from Venus,* which he [1]_____ (write) in 1992. By 2007, the book [2]_____ (sell) over six million copies. For over twenty years he [3]_____ (lead) seminars and courses on relationships and communication, and he [4]_____ (appear) frequently on television shows, including *Oprah* and *The Today Show.*
Gray was born in Houston, Texas, in 1951. He [5]_____ (attend) high school and the University of Texas, but instead of completing his degree he [6]_____ (decide) to move to Switzerland. After he [7]_____ (be) in Switzerland for nine years, Gray decided to return to the USA, where he [8]_____ (complete) a doctorate in Psychology at Columbia Pacific University. The research for his PhD formed the basis of *Men Are from Mars, Women Are from Venus.*
Following the success of that book, Gray [9]_____ (write) several more best-selling guides to relationships and communication. He now [10]_____ (live) in California with his wife and three children.

KL **4 Complete the dialogue with one word in each gap.**

A: What's the problem?
B: Well, it's a [1]_____ situation because my boss keeps asking me to work late. And the more I do, the more she expects – it's a [2]_____ circle.
A: Well, there's an [3]_____ solution. Why don't you just say 'no'?
B: The [4]_____ is that she'll think I'm lazy and I might lose my job …
A: One way of [5]_____ with this could be to explain your situation to her. I'm sure she'll understand.
B: I'm not sure. It's a very tricky [6]_____.
A: Well, maybe the best way to [7]_____ with it is to talk to the area manager. He's very helpful.
B: OK. That might well [8]_____ the problem.

V1,2 **5 Replace the words in italics with words from V1 or V2 with a similar meaning.**

1 It was great to *meet* my old boss *by accident* at the conference.
2 It's important to *maintain a relationship with* your customers.
3 Can you help me *find* last year's sales figures, please?
4 We need *to know for sure* how many people to cater for.
5 I'd like to tell you about the *idea* behind our new design.
6 We can't just say our product is the best – we need to *provide the facts to demonstrate* it.

V3 **6 Choose a–e to continue the sentences.**

1 Carol and Jim always have very different ideas.
2 I can't get a word in edgeways.
3 They spend ages talking about irrelevant things.
4 Can I have a quick word with the manager?
5 It's important to see what they've actually done.

a After all, actions speak louder than words.
b They're just not on the same wavelength.
c They should get straight to the point.
d They never stop talking.
e It won't take very long.

V3 **7 Choose a–g to continue the sentences.**

1 Although we want our products to look different, they need to have
2 A big part of attending conferences is establishing new
3 Face-to-face meetings are the best way to establish a
4 He didn't get the job because he didn't exhibit enough
5 The more information you can
6 We have been working hard to maintain our

a status as the world leaders in mobile technology.
b connections with potential business partners.
c good rapport with your employees.
d knowledge of the construction industry.
e some similarities to create a common identity.
f impart, the more your employees will trust you.

GRAMMAR

G1 PRESENT PERFECT SIMPLE AND CONTINUOUS

Form the present perfect continuous with *has/have + been + -ing*.

John's **been telling** us about climate change.
Have you been watching that new series on global warming?

Use the present perfect continuous to talk about an ongoing situation or action that started in the past and is still continuing.

Sea levels **have been rising**.
The climate **has been getting warmer**.

Compare this use of the present perfect continuous with the present perfect simple:

We've **been painting** the house. (continuing action)
We've **painted** the house. (completed action)

We also use the present perfect continuous to talk about the reason for something in the present. We are more interested in the activity than the result.

'Why are you wet?' 'Because I've **been washing** the car.'
(This is the reason I'm wet.)

With the present perfect simple the focus is on the result, not the activity.

'Is the car ready?'
'Yes, I've **washed** it.' (So now it is ready.)

❗ To describe repeated actions we use the present perfect simple, not the present perfect continuous.
I've watched that film ten times. ✓
I've been watching that film ten times. ✗

SINCE, FOR AND OTHER TIME EXPRESSIONS

We often use *since* or *for* and expressions such as *recently, over the last …*, etc. with the present perfect continuous to talk about an ongoing situation or action that started in the past and is still continuing.

We've been studying climate change **since the 1980s**.
Recently, I've been thinking about changing jobs.
With *since* and *for* and some verbs that describe continuous actions or states (e.g. *live, stay, work, study, teach*) we can use the present perfect simple or continuous with little difference in meaning.

I've **waited** for ages. / I've **been waiting** for ages.
He's **worked** there since 1995. / He's **been working** there since 1995.

G2 INDIRECT QUESTIONS

An indirect question is a question inside another question or statement.

What is the answer? + Do you know …?
→ Do you know what the answer is?

There are a number of introductory phrases that can be used to begin an indirect question. For example:

I'd like to know …   Do you know …?
Can/Could you tell me …?   I wonder …

Use indirect questions in formal situations or to be tentative.

Could you tell me if it's OK to use mobiles here?
I wonder if she likes me.

❗ In indirect questions use statement word order (subject before the auxiliary), not question word order (subject after the auxiliary).
Do you know where the post office is? ✓
Do you know where is the post office? ✗

But with an indirect subject question (when we use *who, what* or *which* to ask about the subject of a sentence), do not change the word order.

Who knows him? (I wonder **who knows him**.)
What made it go wrong? (Do you know **what made it go wrong**?)

We use *if* or *whether* to introduce *yes/no* questions.

Are they expensive? (I wonder if/whether they are expensive.

❗ We only use question marks if the introductory phrase itself is a question.
I'd like to know how much it costs. (not a question)
Do you **know** how much it costs? (a question)

KEY LANGUAGE

KL BEING POLITE

ASKING POLITE QUESTIONS
I'd like to know …
I'm interested in knowing …

AGREEING
You're absolutely right, because …
That's very true, because …
I'd go along with you there, because …

BEING DIPLOMATIC
That's one way of looking at it, but …
You have a point, but don't you think … ?

VOCABULARY

V1 TYPES OF AREAS
coastal, inner-city, long-established, recently developed, residential, rural, smart, suburban, traditional, up-and-coming, urban

V2 LOCAL ENVIRONMENT COLLOCATIONS
abandoned cars, apartment block, cosmopolitan atmosphere, crime rate, cultural activities, desirable area, detached house, environmental issue, friendly neighbourhood, mindless vandalism, natural environment, noise pollution, open spaces, recycling points, renewable energy, rush hour, traffic congestion, transport connections, urban environment, wind farm

V3 THE ENVIRONMENT
deforestation, drought, ecosystem, emissions, extinction, famine, fossil fuels, glaciers, habitat, species

V4 ADVERBS WITH SIMILAR MEANINGS
comparatively – relatively, generally – normally, intentionally – deliberately, mostly – mainly, possibly – perhaps, thoughtfully – slowly and carefully

G1 **1 Choose the best answer to complete the dialogues.**

1 Why are you so out of breath?
   a I've run.
   b I've been running.
2 Are the exam results ready?
   a Yes, our teacher's put them on the wall.
   b Yes, our teacher's been putting them on the wall.
3 Did my mother contact you?
   a Yes, she's phoned three times.
   b Yes, she's been phoning three times.
4 Is the computer working now?
   a Yes, I've just repaired it.
   b Yes, I've been repairing it.
5 What a mess!
   a I know, we've cleared out the cupboards.
   b I know, we've been clearing out the cupboards.

2 Complete the email extracts with either the present perfect simple or continuous form of the verbs in brackets. Use at least one form of the present perfect continuous in each extract.

I ¹_____ (look at) the website you recommended, but I didn't really understand the information. I ²_____ (read) the chapters in our coursebook, but I still don't really understand them. I ³_____ (worry) about it all day.

Although I ⁴_____ (live) here for three years, I still can't get used to the climate. Right now we're in the middle of the monsoon. It ⁵_____ (rain) for days! I ⁶_____ (buy) a new air conditioner, but it doesn't seem to be very effective.

G1 **3 Choose the correct answer.**

1 I wonder where *he works / does he work*?
2 Can you tell me *if are they / if they are* for sale?
3 Do you know how much *is it / it is*?
4 Could you tell us where *we can get / can we get* application forms?
5 Do you know whether *it is / is it* expensive?
6 I'd like to know what *does she do / she does* for a living.

4 Put the words in the correct order to make indirect questions.

1 it / me / could / how much / you / costs / tell / ?
2 I'd / starts / the film / like / when / to know
3 coming / you / know / she's / whether / to the / party / do / ?
4 this model / can / if / you / me / is available / tell / ?
5 put / I / where / the keys / wonder / they
6 what / earthquakes / to know / like / I'd / causes

KL **5 The residents of an apartment block are discussing the budget for roof repairs. Complete the dialogue with five of the phrases below.**

A: OK. Any more questions before we vote?
B: Yes. I'm ¹_____ knowing how much this is going to cost.
A: Well, I think that depends on the damage.
C: That's ²_____ because we don't know how much work is needed yet.
B: OK. You ³_____, but we can't just sign a blank cheque. We need to get an estimate of costs.
D: You ⁴_____ right, because we only have a limited budget for next year.
C: Yes. I'd ⁵_____ you there.

a very true
b one way of
c are absolutely
d don't you think
e interested in
f have a point
g go along with

V1,2 **6 Complete the text with words from V1 and 2.**

Are you fed up with life in the ¹_____ city? Do you want to escape from mindless ²_____ and the rising ³_____ rate? Come to Lensford Green, the new town just outside Birmingham. We have a range of affordable properties available, from spacious ⁴_____ houses to flats in smart apartment ⁵_____. There are plenty of ⁶_____ spaces for children to play in. And with our excellent transport ⁷_____ you can be in Birmingham in twenty minutes. Who wants to look at ⁸_____ cars and busy streets when they can have stunning views of unspoilt countryside?

V3 **7 In each sentence two words are in the wrong order. Put them in the correct order.**

1 The government has promised to halve emissions carbon by 2020.
2 The burning of fuels fossil is one of the biggest causes of global warming.
3 We must try to protect species endangered.
4 Deforestation is destroying the habitat natural of many animals.
5 Due to the destruction of its ecosystem, the polar bear extinction faces.
6 The melting glaciers of is causing sea levels to rise.

V4 **8 Choose the correct adverb.**

1 Mobiles are *pensively / relatively* cheap these days.
2 I think the factory owner started the fire *deliberately / thoughtfully*.
3 There are plenty of car parks in the city centre, but elsewhere there are *possibly / comparatively* few.
4 Poisonous insects are *mainly / relatively* found in tropical countries.
5 The professor nodded *generally / pensively* and told us she would think about it.
6 The weather is *normally / intentionally* warmer at this time of year.

GRAMMAR

G1 QUANTIFIERS

Use quantifiers to describe the quantity of something. We use different quantifiers with plural countable nouns and uncountable nouns.

+ plural countable noun	+ uncountable noun	+ countable or uncountable noun
few, (too) many, several	little, (too) much	hardly any, a lot of, some, all

To talk about things in general, use quantifier + noun.
Many people prefer football.

To talk about something specific use quantifier + *of* + *the* / *my* / *our* / *these*, etc. + noun.
Some of the people in the survey prefer golf.

LITTLE / FEW / A LITTLE / A FEW
Little and *few* have a negative meaning similar to 'not much / not many / almost none'.
There's **little** food in the house. We'll have to do some shopping.

But *a little* and *a few* have a positive meaning similar to 'a small quantity / some'.
There's **a little** food in the fridge if you're hungry.

SOME/ANY
We usually use *some* in positive statements and *any* in questions and negatives.
We are playing **some** games next month, but there aren't **any** at the weekend.

G2 DEFINITE AND ZERO ARTICLES

Use the definite article (*the*):
* when referring to something that is already known to the listener because it has been mentioned before.
So I showed **the** photos to the police. (I've mentioned these photos before.)
* when referring to something that is already known to the listener because it is obvious from the context.
I forgot to give **the** cat her supper. (It is obvious I'm talking about *my* cat.)
* when something is unique (including superlatives and *first*, *last*, *next*, *only*.)
She is **the** greatest sportswoman.
* when a defining or prepositional phrase makes the noun specific.
It's **the** house at the top of the street.
* before the names of some geographical features, buildings and places.
I live in **the** countryside, not **the** town.

Use the zero article (no article):
* before abstract nouns.
You can't stop **time**.
* before general plural nouns.
Computers are very powerful now.

❗ But if the abstract or plural noun is made specific by a defining phrase, we use an article.
The computers we've just bought are fantastic.

* before people's names and the names of most companies, materials, countries, mountains and lakes.
Alexandra lives in **Italy**. She lives near **Lake Como**. She works for **Deutsche Bank**.

* before the names of types of institutions, for example *school*, *hospital*, *university*.
My brother is about to start **school**.

❗ But if we are referring to a particular building, we use the definite article.
Excuse me. Is **the school** near here?

KEY LANGUAGE

KL EMPHASIS AND COMPARISON

EMPHASISING ADJECTIVES
an *outstanding* achievement
exceptional qualities
an *astonishing* performance
extraordinary technical skills

EMPHASISING ADVERBS
a *truly* remarkable sportswoman
She *undoubtedly* is a superstar …

EMPHASISING EXPRESSIONS
… and *above all* her admirable personal qualities
What's *also extraordinary* about her is …
There seems to be no end to Yuna Kim's remarkable talents

VOCABULARY

V1 IDIOMS

a level playing field, score an own goal, a whole new ball game, start the ball rolling, be on the ball, take your eye off the ball, move the goalposts

V2 *SELF-*

self-confidence, self-control, self-defence, self-development, self-discipline, self-respect

V3 ABSTRACT NOUNS (FROM ADJECTIVES)

agility, (agile), calm, (calm), coordination, (coordinated), courtesy, (courteous), flexibility, (flexible), tolerance, (tolerant)

V4 AMBITION

determination, extremes, intensity, make sacrifices, obsessive, set apart

G1 **1** Choose the correct word or phrase.

1 Borrow one of my pens – there are *few / a few* in the cupboard.
2 Hardly any *students / of students* passed the test.
3 There's *few / hardly any* music on my MP3 player.
4 Almost *none / none of* our photos came out well.
5 *Several / Several of* my friends are at university.
6 I need *a few / a little* help with my homework.
7 There's *a little / little* furniture in the flat so we'll have to buy some.
8 You should invest your money with my bank. *Few / A few* other banks offer such good interest rates.
9 There's far too *much / many* rubbish on the streets.

G2 **2** Read the text and add six definite articles.

Quidditch is a fictional sport invented by the author J.K. Rowling for best-selling Harry Potter books. It is a ball game in which players try to score goals. There are four balls and two teams of seven players. Usually players are wizards and witches and play game by flying on their broomsticks. The goals are ring-shaped and are above the ground. The object of game is to score more goals than opposing team.

3 Complete the sentences with either the definite article or a blank space if no article is needed.

1 How far is it from _____ capital city?
2 Did you see _____ last episode of *Heroes*?
3 I've bought a new phone. _____ phone's got a fantastic camera.
4 Who is _____ best singer at the moment?
5 All children should do _____ sports when they are at _____ school.
6 Is that _____ house where you grew up?

KL **4** Two managers are discussing job applicants they have just interviewed. Complete the dialogue with the words and phrases below.

A: So who do you prefer, Caroline or Toby?
B: Well Toby [1]_____ has the right technical skills, but [2]_____ his drive and determination really impressed me.
A: Yes, but there seems to be [3]_____ to Caroline's achievements. And what's [4]_____ about her is her range of experience – her CV is [5]_____ remarkable.
B: That's true, and she has [6]_____ personal qualities – she'd get on really well with the rest of the team.

a truly
b undoubtedly
c outstanding
d no end
e also extraordinary
f above all

V1 **5** Read the summary of a business meeting and use the information to complete the sentences below with the names in italics.

Once everyone had sat down, *David* started the meeting by making some suggestions and asking everyone for their ideas. *Steve* made sure everybody had a chance to speak. *Lucy* said she wanted to talk about the marketing campaign, but then she realised she had left her notes behind, which made her look foolish. But of course *Walter* remembered that he had a summary of the campaign on his laptop, so he was able to help her with the details. We then asked *Miranda* to give a summary of the situation, but she hadn't been listening so she couldn't say much. Then *Caroline* said she wanted to discuss everybody's opinions on the new US office, but then suddenly decided she wanted us all to write our opinions in a report, which was rather annoying.

1 _____ tried to create a level playing field.
2 _____ moved the goalposts.
3 _____ scored an own goal.
4 _____ started the ball rolling.
5 _____ took her eyes off the ball.
6 _____ was really on the ball.

V2 **6** Match the sentences.

1 I'm always nervous at interviews.
2 I never lose my temper.
3 I want to improve my skills and understanding.
4 I find it difficult to make myself work hard.
5 I'm not really happy with my personality and behaviour.

a I lack self-discipline.
b I have a lot of self-control.
c I don't have much self-respect.
d I don't have any self-confidence.
e I'm interested in self-development.

V3,4 **7** Choose the correct word.

1 The aim of the game is not to hurt your opponent, but to demonstrate your skill and physical *agility / agile*.
2 Success in the game depends on *coordination / coordinated* between all parts of the body.
3 The gymnasts are extremely *flexibility / flexible* to make all the moves they do.
4 The coach wasn't very *tolerance / tolerant* when the team made mistakes.
5 She showed great *determination / determined* throughout the difficult race.
6 It is said you have to *make / have* sacrifices to get to the top in sport.
7 He is slightly *obsession / obsessive* when it comes to his training – he doesn't know when to stop!
8 His talent set him *apart / upon* from the rest of the team.

GRAMMAR

G1 FUTURE CONTINUOUS, *GOING TO*, PRESENT CONTINUOUS

FUTURE CONTINUOUS

Form the future continuous with *will/won't + be + -ing* form of the verb.

> I **will be working** from home tomorrow, so I **won't be meeting** any clients.

Use the future continuous to talk about a temporary action in progress at a particular time in the future.

> They**'ll be opening** the new hospital next Tuesday.
> I **won't be working** on Wednesday. It's my day off.

We can also use the future continuous to ask tentative questions about people's plans, especially if we want them to do something.

> **Will** you **be coming** to the party? (I want you to come.)
> **Will** you **be using** your car this evening? (I'd like to borrow it.)

We can also use this form to give reasons for refusing something.

> I'm afraid I can't come to the party – I**'ll be working**.

GOING TO

Use *going to* to talk about intentions (things you plan to do).

> I'm **going to get** a new computer. (I want to get one, but I haven't ordered it yet.)
> We're **going to work** much harder next term. (We want to do this, but we may not.)

PRESENT CONTINUOUS

Use the present continuous for fixed arrangements (things that have already been planned and organised).

> I**'m getting** a new computer tomorrow. (I've already ordered it.)
> Jane**'s working** at the supermarket next week. (It's organised.)

We normally use a time reference (or the speakers know what time is being referred to) with the present continuous for fixed arrangements.

> I'm starting my degree course **this September**.

G2 FUTURE PERFECT SIMPLE, FUTURE SIMPLE

FUTURE PERFECT SIMPLE

Form the future perfect simple with *will/won't + have +* past participle.

> He **will have arrived** home by the time you phone.
> We **won't have done** the work in time for the meeting.

Use the future perfect to talk about an action you expect to be completed by a time in the future.

> By this time next year I **will have finished** all my exams. (My exams will finish before this time next year.)

We usually use a time expression (*soon, by then, by +* date, *in +* date).

> Don't worry – we'll have finished the project **by then**.
> They will have completed the stadium **in time for the Olympics.**

FUTURE SIMPLE

We use the future simple (*will* + infinitive) to make predictions about the future.

> They **will** lose the next election.

Use adverbs of certainty (*probably, possibly, definitely, certainly*) to make the predictions more or less certain. In affirmative sentences, the adverbs come after *will*, before the main verb.

> The old hospital will **probably** close down in the next few years.
> He'll **definitely** call you if he's interested in coming.

In negative sentences, the adverbs come before *will not*.

> I **probably** won't come to the lecture tomorrow.

KEY LANGUAGE

KL DISCUSSING IMPLICATIONS

We need to look at the implications of doing it.
If we support him too strongly, the press may get hold of the story.
It could be really bad for our reputation.
But it's a risky option.
One consequence could be she'll start negotiating with us.
It has a serious disadvantage.
That could be a big problem for us.
It would have a huge impact on our profits.
It would also result in other patients coming forward with complaints.

VOCABULARY

V1 MEDICAL TERMS

Alzheimer's, anaesthetist, antibiotic, arthritis, cancer, chest infection, diabetes, heart disease, injection, midwife, morphine, patient, painkiller, pharmacist, physiotherapy, psychiatrist, radiologist, surgeon, transplant

V2 ADJECTIVES

authoritative, calm, efficient, knowledgeable, objective, open-minded, patient, reassuring, sensitive, sociable, sympathetic

V3 ILLNESS AND MEDICINE

complication, contract (v), diagnosis, fever, infection, parasite, symptom, vaccine

V4 DEPENDENT PREPOSITIONS

agree with, apply for, care for, complain about, deal with, focus on, protect from, recover from, rely on, specialise in, succeed in, suffer from, worry about

G1 **1** Match sentences 1 and 2 with the explanations/continuations a or b.

1   1   We're seeing *Swan Lake* tonight.
    2   We're going to see a ballet soon.
    a   We haven't bought the tickets.
    b   We've bought the tickets.

2   1   I'm going to do some exercise.
    2   I'll be doing lots of exercise.
    a   I'm spending two weeks at a health spa next month.
    b   I'd like to get fit.

3   1   I'll be speaking to the manager.
    2   I'm going to speak to the manager.
    a   We always have a meeting on Wednesday.
    b   I want to make a complaint.

4   1   I'm going to do a yoga course.
    2   I'll be doing a yoga class on Tuesday.
    a   I enrolled for it last week.
    b   I think there's one at my local gym.

5   1   We'll be repainting the house.
    2   We're going to repaint the house.
    a   We haven't decided when to do it yet.
    b   We've arranged to take a week off work to do it.

G2 **2** Read the itinerary for a day trip to the Tower of London. Complete the sentences to talk about what the tour group will or will not have done by certain times in the day. Use the future perfect.

8:30	Collection from your hotel
9:15	Arrive at main gate
9:30–11:00	Lecture on history of the Tower
11:00–11:20	Coffee
11:40–12:25	Visit to the White Tower
12:30–13:30	Lunch
13:45–14:45	Visit the Crown Jewels
15:00–15:40	Tour of Traitor's Gate
16:00	Depart from main gate
16:45	Arrive at your hotel

1   We _____ (see) the Crown Jewels before lunch.
2   By 2 p.m. we _____ (have) lunch.
3   We _____ (finish) seeing Traitor's Gate by 3.30 p.m.
4   By 9.30 a.m. we _____ (arrive) at the main gate.
5   We _____ (leave) the Tower by 3 p.m.
6   By 5 p.m. we _____ (return) to our hotel.
7   We _____ (listen) to a lecture before having coffee.
8   By the time we leave we _____ (spend) over six hours in the Tower.

3 Complete the dialogue with the phrases below. There are two extra phrases.

A: Sorry, I can't meet you on Monday. I'm still working on my project and I ¹_____ it by then.
B: OK. Well what about Tuesday?
A: I'm not sure. I ²_____ most of the work by Tuesday evening. What are your plans?
B: I ³_____ Sara then, but it depends on her.
A: ⁴_____ your car with you?
B: No, it's being serviced and the garage ⁵_____ it by Tuesday.
A: That's a pity. Well, look, I ⁶_____ you on Tuesday afternoon and we can talk then.

a   will have had   e   'll definitely phone
b   'll probably visit   f   'll have done
c   won't have finished   g   won't have returned
d   'll phone certainly   h   Will you have

KL **4** There is one word missing in these sentences. Complete them with words or phrases from the box. There are two extra words or phrases.

could   consequence   disadvantages   impact
implications   option   problem   serious

1   It sounds a good idea, but we'll need to look at the of doing it.
2   It has a disadvantage. It's going to cost quite a lot of money.
3   We'll have to think about that; it's a risky.
4   If the press get hold of the story, it be really bad for our reputation.
5   It could result in more patients coming forward with complaints. That could be a big for us.
6   We need to be careful. That would have a huge on our sales.

V1–3 **5** Complete the sentences with an appropriate word.

1   It took the doctors a long time to come up with the correct _____ .
2   Everyone does what she says because she has such an _____ manner.
3   The surgeon was very _____ and I calmed down immediately.
4   I can't sit in the sun for very long because my skin is so _____ .
5   Extreme tiredness is a _____ of diabetes.
6   She has read a great deal and is clearly very _____ .
7   He died of a _____ following the operation.
8   She's very _____ and goes out all the time.

V4 **6** Match the sentence halves.

1   My friend had to give up work to care
2   Many people complain
3   I asked my physiotherapist to focus
4   Many children are vaccinated to protect them
5   When I qualify as a doctor, I want to specialize
6   You will only succeed
7   I think she spends too much time worrying
8   Do you think I should apply

a   from serious diseases.
b   about things which are out of her control.
c   on my neck muscles at our last appointment.
d   in radiology.
e   for the job, despite my lack of experience?
f   for her mother full-time.
g   about health problems as they get older.
h   in business if you work hard.

GRAMMAR

G1 MODAL VERBS: ABILITY, POSSIBILITY AND OBLIGATION (FUTURE)

Use *will/won't be able to* to talk about future ability.

> After I pass my driving test I**'ll be able to** drive a car on my own.
> She's going on holiday so she **won't be able to** see you next week.

! Don't use *can* for future ability. Use *will be able to* instead.

> ~~Can~~ I type by the end of the course? ✗
> **Will** I **be able to** type by the end of the course? ✓

! Use *may, might* or *could* to describe future possibilities.

> In the future cars **might** contain high pressure hydrogen tanks.
> We **could** go to Greece next summer.
> They **may** be able to help you with your problem.

! To describe a negative possibility in the future, we use *might not*; we don't use *could not*.

> The weather forecast is good so we **might not** need our umbrellas tomorrow. ✓
> The weather forecast is good so we ~~could not~~ need our umbrellas tomorrow. ✗

Use *will have to* or *will need to* to describe future obligation.

> There's an admission charge so we**'ll have to** take some money with us.

Use *will not have to* and *will not need to* to describe a lack of obligation in the future.

> They're going to give us lunch so we **won't need to** take any food.

Use *can't* to talk about a prohibition (a negative obligation) in the future.

> We should eat something now. You **can't** take food into the theatre.

G2 MODAL VERBS: ABILITY, POSSIBILITY AND OBLIGATION (PAST)

Use *could* or *was/were able to* to talk about a general ability/possibility in the past.

> When I was young I **could** run for miles without getting tired.
> Years ago people **were able to** drive without taking a test.

! But to talk about a single action in the past we only use *was able to*, not *could*.

> There was a bus strike, but I ~~could~~ get a lift with a colleague. ✗
> There was a bus strike, but I **was able to** get a lift with a colleague. ✓

Use *manage to* or *succeed in* to talk about something you did that was difficult. Use the *-ing* form of the verb after *succeed in*.

> Our flight was cancelled, but we **managed to** get seats on the next one.
> After several phone calls we **succeeded in** speak**ing** to the manager.

Use *couldn't* or *wasn't/weren't able to* for a negative possibility in the past.

> I lost my key and I **couldn't** find it.
> When I was young I **wasn't able to** stay out late.

Use *had to* to talk about obligation in the past.

> I **had to** get a visa when I went to the USA last summer.

Use *didn't have to* to talk about a lack of obligation in the past.

> At my old school we **didn't have to** wear a uniform.

Use *couldn't* to talk about a negative obligation (a prohibition) in the past.

> We **couldn't** use calculators in class when I was at school.

KEY LANGUAGE

KL THE LANGUAGE OF MEETINGS

SUMMARISING
OK, let me summarise our discussion.
Let me recap, please.
So, just to confirm …
Right, what have we covered so far?
OK, do we essentially have agreement?
Right, I'll now sum up.
Everyone happy with my summary?

VOCABULARY

V1 TRANSPORT PROBLEMS
congestion charge, delayed sailing, engineering work, fogbound runway, lane closure, lost baggage, low tide, platform alteration, puncture, rough weather, signalling problems, (long) tailback, turbulence

V2 SAFETY FEATURES
airbag, anti-lock brakes, one-way street, seat belt, speed cameras, speed limit, traction control, traffic signals

V3 COLLOCATIONS
air pollution, automated system, carbon emissions, construction company, distant future, human error, inflatable slide, preliminary findings, rush hour, significant contribution, significant impact, space elevator, technological advances, traffic congestion, traffic jam, transport infrastructure, transport system

V4 WORDS CONNECTED WITH (ICONIC) TRAVEL
altitude, era, gruelling, icon, impeccable, nomads, nostalgia, opulence

G1 **1 Match the sentence halves.**

1 We'll have to go by train
2 We could go by train
3 We won't be able to go by train
4 We might not go by train
5 We won't need to go by train

a because Uncle Jim's going to give us a lift.
b if the bus fare is a lot cheaper.
c as it's more relaxing than flying.
d because my car isn't working.
e because there's going to be a rail strike.

G1 **2 Choose the correct word.**

1 A: Did you fix the car?
  B: Yes, I *could / managed* to repair it.
2 A: Did you get lots of homework last term?
  B: No, we *mustn't / didn't have to* do much.
3 A: Was the Maths test very difficult?
  B: Yes. We *couldn't / didn't able to* use calculators.
4 A: Did you speak to the manager?
  B: Yes. We succeeded *in getting / to get* a refund.
5 A: Did you pay for the meal by credit card?
  B: No, we *didn't able to / couldn't* use it.
6 A: I thought you lost your front door key.
  B: Yes, but we managed *finding / to find* it.
7 A: What did you do about that broken camera?
  B: I *could / was able to* get a replacement.
8 A: Were your parents strict when you were small?
  B: No, we *didn't have to / could* do whatever we liked.

3 Complete the second sentence so that it has a similar meaning to the first, using a form of *could, able to, have to, manage* or *succeed*.

1 It wasn't possible to repair your computer.
  I _____ repair your computer.
2 I had the ability to sing well when I was a child.
  I _____ sing well when I was a child.
3 It wasn't necessary for Juan to wear a suit.
  Juan _____ wear a suit.
4 We had no problem getting tickets for the show.
  We _____ get tickets for the show.
5 It was necessary for me to pay a €20 fine.
  I _____ pay a €20 fine.
6 It was possible for me to borrow the money from the bank, although it was extremely hard.
  I _____ in borrowing money from the bank.

KL **4 Complete the sentences with the words in the box.**

summarise	recap	confirm	covered
agreement	sum	summary	

1 OK, I'd like to move on. But first, let me _____, please.
2 Right, I'll now _____ up.
3 So, just to _____, you won't support the proposal if it goes to a vote.
4 OK, let me _____ our discussion.
5 Everyone happy with my _____?
6 OK, do we essentially have _____, then?
7 Right, what have we _____ so far?

V1 **5 Choose the correct word or phrase.**

1 The flight was delayed because of a *tailback / fogbound runway*.
2 The only time I hate flying is when you are going through *turbulence / signalling problems*.
3 The *low tide / rough weather* made us seasick.
4 Can you repair a *lane closure / puncture*?
5 It took us hours to get here; there was a massive *tailback / turbulence* on the motorway.
6 There's been a *platform alteration / lane closure* so we'll have to cross to the other side of the station.

V2 **6 Complete the table with words from V2.**

something inside or part of a car	something on the road	a law

V3 **7 Complete the sentences with words from V3.**

1 The government's budget cuts have had a significant _____ on schools and hospitals.
2 More and more companies are replacing people with _____ telephone systems.
3 The _____ findings of the report are extremely worrying.
4 The court ruled that the plane crash was due to _____ error.
5 Fossil fuels will run out in the not-too-_____ future.
6 Due to technological _____, cars' carbon emissions are much lower than twenty years ago.

V4 **8 Match words 1–6 with descriptions a–f.**

1 impeccable
2 nostalgia
3 icon
4 era
5 opulence
6 gruelling

a a feeling that a time in the past was good
b a period of time in history, known for a particular event or reason
c beauty, expense and luxuriousness
d without any faults and impossible to criticise
e very difficult and tiring
f someone or something which is famous and admired or important

GRAMMAR

G1 NARRATIVE TENSES

PAST SIMPLE

Use the past simple for single finished actions. We also use it for a sequence of single actions (to say that one action was followed by another one).

> I **opened** the door and **walked** into the room.

PAST CONTINUOUS

Use the past continuous for an ongoing action which sets the scene or background for a story.

> The rain **was falling** as we left the house.

Use the past continuous to contrast an ongoing action with a single shorter (past simple) event which occurs during or interrupts the ongoing event.

> I **was washing** the car when the phone **rang**.

PAST PERFECT

The past perfect looks back from a time in the past to another time before that, so we can use it to describe an earlier action in a sequence of events.

> It was dark. Someone **had turned off** the light.
> When we arrived, the train **had left**. (First the train left, then we arrived.)

PAST PERFECT CONTINUOUS

Form the past perfect continuous with *had + been + -ing* form of the verb.

> A lady **had been sitting** in the chair.

Use the past perfect continuous to describe an ongoing action which continued up to or finished just before another action or time in the past.

> Karl realised he**'d been waiting** for over an hour.

We often use the past perfect continuous to explain a past result.

> I was angry because I**'d been waiting** so long.

We often use the past perfect continuous with *before, after* and *when*.

> Carol **had been working** there for a year before they gave her a pay rise.

G2 *USED TO, WOULD, GET USED TO*

USED TO

Use *used to* + infinitive without *to* to talk about states that existed in the past, but no longer exist, and for actions that were repeated in the past, but don't happen now.

> We **used to live** in the suburbs. (past state)
> I **used to read** a lot, but I don't have enough time now. (past repeated action)

> **!** Note the spelling changes for statements, questions and negatives.
> I **used to** be a student. Did you **use to** be a student? We didn't **use to** be students.

WOULD

Use *would* + infinitive without *to* to talk about things that happened regularly in the past.

> When I was a child, we **would spend** every summer by the seaside.

> **!** We never use *would* to talk about states in the past.
> Summers ~~would~~ be cooler here in the past. ✗
> Summers **used to** be cooler here in the past. ✓

GET USED TO

Use *get used to* + gerund to talk about situations you weren't accustomed to doing / found strange in the past but are beginning to find less strange.

> I **didn't used to** read electronic books but I**'m getting used to reading** them now.

KEY LANGUAGE

KL PERSUADING, MAKING A PERSUASIVE PRESENTATION

PERSUADING

I'm sure it'll be a winner.
I'm confident you'll like my idea.
I think you'll agree, it's a really interesting and creative idea.
They'd be perfect.
They're bound to appeal to the audience.
They love our concepts.
It will attract a wide range of filmgoers.
We think it's got tremendous potential.
We think our concept is great and hope we've been able to persuade you, too.

MAKING A PERSUASIVE PRESENTATION

I'll start with …
Turning now to …
Who is our target audience?
To summarise …

VOCABULARY

V1 GENRES

autobiography, biography, biopic, blog, crime (story), costume drama, horror, novel, play, poetry, psycho drama, romcom, science fiction (sci-fi), short story romance, thriller, travel writing

V2 PEOPLE IN LITERATURE

author, autobiographer, biographer, critic, dramatist, ghostwriter, novelist, poet, screenwriter

V3 ADJECTIVES (FOR LITERATURE/FILM/PLOT REVIEWS)

awful, brilliant, classic, disturbing, dreadful, dull, gripping, interesting, lightweight, moving, overrated, riveting, shocking, tedious, tense, thought-provoking

V4 COLLOCATIONS AND IDIOMS

a charming read, a child's perspective, a moral tale, a remake of a film, (dynamic) dialogue, evocative language, extremely well-written, key character, incredibly heart-warming, (realistic) plot
I (just) couldn't get into it. I couldn't put it down. It's a real page turner. It's light and easy to read. It (certainly) lived up to all the hype. It's (not) my kind of thing. It was (very) hard going at the beginning. The ending was a real letdown.

V5 REPORT (READING HABITS)

associated, outperform, preference, pronounced, proportion, relatively, the gender gap, typically, virtually

G1 1 Read the sentences and choose the best explanation.

1 We were cooking dinner when there was a power cut.
   a We finished cooking dinner.
   b We didn't finish cooking dinner.
2 Darlene stood up, walked to the window and put on her glasses.
   a She walked to the window before putting on her glasses.
   b She put on her glasses and walked to the window at the same time.
3 When we arrived, we realised it had been raining.
   a It stopped raining before we arrived.
   b It was still raining when we arrived.
4 Although I knew his name, I'd never actually met him before.
   a I met him.
   b I didn't meet him.

2 Complete the text with the words in the box.

brought	had brought	looked	was looking
sat	was sitting	had been sitting	had
hadn't had	was	went	had been working

Joe ¹_____ on the balcony when he suddenly felt his arms burning. He ²_____ down and noticed his skin was red and felt hot. It wasn't surprising as he ³_____ in the sun all day. He knew he ⁴_____ some after-sun cream, but he wasn't sure where it ⁵_____ – he ⁶_____ so hard in the few days before leaving home that he ⁷_____ time to pack everything properly. Firstly, he ⁸_____ into the bathroom, but it wasn't there. He ⁹_____ his bag into the bedroom and ¹⁰_____ at the desk, trying to think. He ¹¹_____ through the bag again when he remembered that he ¹²_____ a tube of shaving cream – it was probably just as good!

G2 3 There are two mistakes in each extract. Correct them.

A
When I was a child, I use to read lots of adventure stories at night. I would lie in bed and pull the sheets over my head. Then I would to read by the light of a torch.

B
Years ago, I would live in a house by the sea. Every day we would go down to the beach and spend hours swimming. It would be such good fun.

C
Don't I know you? Didn't you used to live in Dorking Street? Do you remember me? I would live in number 16 – the house with the blue front door.

D
He took a long time to get used to live in the city. At first, the crowds and the constant noise were very scary. He would thought of quiet places to help him sleep.

KL 4 There is a mistake in some of the sentences below. Add or delete a word to correct them.

1 I'm sure it'll be winner.
2 I think you agree, it's a really interesting and creative idea.
3 They're bound to appeal the audience.
4 We think it's tremendous potential.
5 We think our concept is great and hope we've been able to persuade to you, too.
6 Who is our target market?

V1 5 Complete the word puzzle with the eight different writing genres.

1			B		O					
2				P	O					
3			B		O					
4			S		O					
5	P				O					
6		A			O					
7				R	O					
8			N	O						

V2 6 Which person in V2 is described in each sentence?

critic	novelist	autobiographer	biographer
poet	dramatist		

1 Jeremy has decided to start writing his life story.
2 Cindy has just published a book of poems.
3 Has Joe completed his book on Nelson Mandela?
4 They're putting on Debbie's play at a local theatre.
5 I've just read Henry's review of the play.
6 Janet has just published her second novel.

V3,4 7 Find the following words in V3 and V4.

1 two adjectives that mean bad: _____, _____
2 two adjectives that mean boring: _____, _____
3 a phrase that means words which make you remember or feel something: _____, _____
4 an adjective that means you feel happy because other people are happy: _____-_____
5 a noun that means point of view: _____

GRAMMAR

G1 THE PASSIVE: PRESENT SIMPLE AND CONTINUOUS, FUTURE SIMPLE AND -ING FORMS

Form the present simple passive with *am/is/are* + past participle.

> The castle **is protected** by high walls.

Form the present continuous passive with *am/is/are being* + past participle.

> We'**re being watched**.

❗ Form the future simple passive with *will be* + past participle.

> The new bridge **will be opened** next year.

❗ The form of *be* agrees with the subject of the passive verb.

> A bag **was** stolen.
> Ten bags **were** stolen.

❗ Form the passive of *-ing* forms with *being* + past participle, for example after prepositions.

> The children **insisted on being taken** to the zoo.
> I don't like **being watched**.

Intransitive verbs (verbs which don't have an object) cannot be made passive.

> The train ~~was arrived~~ on time. ✗

We often use the passive when:
- the agent is obvious from the context.
  > The man **was arrested** yesterday. (obviously by the police)
  > I'**m going to be given** a promotion. (obviously by my boss)
- the agent is unknown or isn't important.
  > My watch **has been stolen**.
  > The house **has been demolished**.

G2 THE PASSIVE: PAST SIMPLE AND CONTINUOUS, PRESENT PERFECT, INFINITIVES

Form the past simple passive with *was/were* + past participle.

> The building **was demolished** in 2005.

Form the past continuous passive with *was/were being* + past participle.

> The rooms **were being decorated** so we couldn't go in.

Form the present perfect passive with *has/have been* + past participle.

> The factory **has been designed** by a Spanish architect.

Form the past perfect passive with *had been* + past participle.

> The flight **had been cancelled** because of fog.

Form the passive of infinitives with *to be* + past participle.

> The builders are scheduled **to complete** the work within two years. (The work is scheduled **to be completed** within two years.)
> I wanted somebody **to help** me. (I wanted **to be helped**.)

G3 USE OF THE PASSIVE

In English we prefer to start a new sentence with a familiar subject (something that has already been mentioned). The passive can help us do this.

> **The house** is in Illinois. **It** was designed by Frank Lloyd Wright. ✓
> **The house** is in Illinois. Frank Lloyd Wright designed **it**. ✗

We usually prefer to put short subjects at the beginning of a sentence and longer expressions at the end. The passive helps us do this.

> The new bridge was designed by an engineer who had previously worked on a bridge in Spain. ✓
> An engineer who had previously worked on a bridge in Spain designed the new bridge. ✗

KEY LANGUAGE

KL TALKING ABOUT REQUIREMENTS

ESSENTIAL REQUIREMENTS
We really must have …
… it's vital we have …
It's absolutely essential to offer …
It's a priority …
We've got to offer them …
We certainly need …

DESIRABLE REQUIREMENTS
It'd be very popular with …
We should offer them (something) …

POSSIBLE REQUIREMENTS
It might be a good idea to have …
We could also consider …
Another possibility would be to …

VOCABULARY

V1 DESCRIBING BUILDINGS

ancient, classical, contemporary, cramped, derelict, dilapidated, elegant, graceful, imposing, impressive, ingeneous, innovative, magnificent, miniscule, numerous, ornate, remarkable, run-down, stylish, temporary, traditional, vast, ugly
amphitheatre (n), configuration (n), dome (n), exterior (n), eyesore (n), interior (n), landmark (n)

V2 VERBS USED WITH BUILDINGS

commission, construct, damage, demolish, design, maintain, rebuild, restore, renovate, survive

V3 IDIOMS

build bridges, burn one's bridges, cross a/that bridge when we come to it, water under the bridge

V4 PREFIXES IN-, MIS-, OVER-, RE-, UN-

indisputable, insensitive, insignificant, insoluble, misplaced, misunderstand, overcome, overcrowded, redefine, revitalise, uncrowded, unimportant, unusual

G1,2 1 Complete the second sentence so that it has a similar meaning to the first. Do not include the agent (the person or thing that does the action).

1 Someone has stolen my dictionary.
My dictionary _____.
2 A security guard was watching the building.
The building _____.
3 Something is keeping me awake at night.
I _____.
4 They gave my father a watch when he retired.
My father _____ when he retired.
5 We require a large deposit.
A large deposit _____.
6 We can't explain it.
It _____.

2 Complete the text with a passive form of the words in brackets.

The Parthenon was commissioned while democracy
[1]_____ (establish) in Athens in the 5th century BC. Many of the old buildings in Athens had been burnt down by the Persians and Phidias, a sculptor, [2]_____ (give) the task of rebuilding them. The Parthenon [3]_____ (build) to house the statue of Athena. Phidias insisted on [4]_____ (allow) to use only the most expensive and beautiful materials. Ever since ancient times architects, all over the world
[5]_____ (influence) by the Parthenon. Over the years a number of exact copies [6]_____ (construct) in different parts of the world. Even the Capitol building in Washington DC [7]_____ (inspire) by it.
At the moment, the Parthenon [8]_____ (damage) by pollution, but it is expected [9]_____ (restore) to its former glory in the years to come.

G3 3 Choose the best way to follow the sentences.

1 Jane's lived in that house by the river all her life.
  a It was built by Don Baum, who was a famous architect.
  b Don Baum, who was a famous architect, built it.
2 The bridge only lasted twenty years.
  a The terrible earthquake that damaged much of the city destroyed it.
  b It was destroyed by the terrible earthquake that damaged much of the city.
3 I've always enjoyed talking to my grandmother.
  a Great stories about her life are told to me by her.
  b She tells me great stories about her life.
4 The film has received five Oscar nominations.
  a It was directed by James Cameron, who also directed *Titanic*.
  b James Cameron, who also directed *Titanic*, directed it.

KL 4 Complete the sentences with the words in the box.

| absolutely | find | need | got | offer | vital |
| idea | through | | | | |

1 We've _____ to offer good value for money.
2 But we need to think all the problems _____.
3 It's _____ we have plenty of time to discuss this.
4 It's _____ essential to offer leisure facilities.
5 It might be a good _____ to have a sauna.
6 It might be a good idea to _____ out how many rooms we need.
7 We should _____ them something, that's for sure.
8 We certainly _____ parking spaces.

V1 5 Circle the odd one out in each group.
1 derelict / dilapidated / ornate / run-down
2 elegant / innovative / graceful / stylish
3 ancient / imposing / impressive / magnificent
4 classical / ugly / contemporary / traditional

V2 6 Replace the phrase in italics with the correct form of a verb from V2.
1 After the fire many buildings had to be *made again*.
2 The earthquake *harmed* large areas of the country.
3 We decided to *ask* a German construction company to build our new company headquarters.
4 They plan to *knock down* the dangerous building.
5 Who *planned* the Sydney Opera House?
6 This building is hard to *keep in good condition*.
7 We'd like to *repair* all the original decoration.
8 They plan to *build* a new library here.

V3 7 Match the sentence halves.
1 We should forgive that past mistake. It's
2 You don't need to deal with that now – you can
3 If you do that, you'll never be able to work there again, so don't
4 After their past disagreements, they all need to
a cross that bridge when you come to it.
b build bridges.
c burn your bridges.
d water under the bridge.

V3 8 Choose the correct word.
1 We'll never know the answer to that question – it's *misplaced / insoluble*.
2 Some of the old houses in the city are terribly *insensitive / overcrowded*.
3 Investment in industry has *revitalised / misplaced* the town.
4 I'm sorry – I obviously *misunderstood / overcame* what you said.
5 Don't worry about that – it's *indisputable / unimportant* right now.

GRAMMAR

G1 VERB PATTERNS: VERB + -*ING*/INFINITIVE

When one verb follows another, it may appear in the infinitive or -*ing* form. The form depends on the first verb, and the following structures are possible:

* verb + infinitive, e.g. *appear, attempt, decide, manage, need, offer, promise, seem, want.*
  Globalisation **appears to be** a serious political issue these days.
* verb + object + infinitive, e.g. *advise, allow, encourage, invite, persuade, remind, request, tell.*
  The internet **allows people to communicate**.
* verb + -*ing* form, e.g. *consider, deny, dislike, enjoy, feel like, finish, practise, suggest.*
  Would you **consider giving** us a refund?
* verb + -*ing* or infinitive with different meanings:

REMEMBER

Remember to bring the tickets. We need them for our flight. (+ infinitive: thinking about a future action)
I **remember watching** the Olympics in 2004. (+ -*ing* form: thinking about an earlier action)

FORGET

Don't **forget to bring** your passport. (+ infinitive: thinking about a future action)
I won't **forget eating** my first Thai curry. (+ -*ing* form: thinking about an earlier action)

STOP

I **stopped to have** a break. (+ infinitive: stop one action in order to do something else)
They **stopped making** them in 2002. (+ -*ing* form: finish an action)

TRY

Carla's **trying to lose** weight. (+ infinitive: make an effort to do something difficult)
Why don't you **try cooking** it in olive oil? It might taste better. (+ -*ing* form: do something as an experiment – you don't know if it will work or not)

G2 CAUSATIVES: *HAVE/GET SOMETHING DONE*

Use this form when an action is done for you by somebody else.
I **had my suit cleaned**. (The shop did it.)
He **had his mobile phone repaired**. (An engineer did it.)

Use a form of *have* + object + past participle:
* present simple
  Claire **has her hair cut** every month.
* present continuous
  Dave and Bill **are having their hair cut**.
* past simple
  Claire **had her hair cut** last week.
* present perfect
  Claire **has had her hair cut**.

! Do not confuse this form with the past perfect.
We **had a new computer system installed.**
The technician **had installed a new computer system.** (past perfect)

We can make questions and negatives.
Are you **having your car serviced** this week?
I **haven't had the windows cleaned** for ages.

In spoken or informal English, we can also use *get* + object + past participle.
I **got my eyes checked** last week because I've been having headaches.

We also use this form to talk about something that happens to us that we have no control over.
In this street we **have our rubbish collected** once a week.

We often use the form for unexpected or unpleasant things that happen to us.
To our great surprise, we **had our money refunded**.
He **had his mobile phone stolen**.

KEY LANGUAGE

KL CLARIFICATION

ASKING FOR CLARIFICATION
Sorry, I don't know what you mean.
What do you mean by … ?
Could you explain that in more detail, please?
Could you be more specific?
Could you give me a specific example?
Sorry, I don't follow you.
I'm sorry, I don't see what you mean by …

CLARIFYING (MAKING YOUR MEANING CLEARER)
Basically what I'm saying is … the customer is …
What I really want to say is …
Or to put it another way, …
Let me rephrase that.
To be more precise, … we really appeal to …

VOCABULARY

V1 GLOBALISATION
creates competition, damage the natural environment, destroy local culture(s), encourages better standards, exploit workers, increase wealth, improves the quality of manufacturing, promote global understanding, reduce poverty, widen the gap

V2 COLLOCATIONS (GLOBALISATION)
child labour, climate change, consumer choice, corporate greed, fair trade, free markets, global warming, human rights, multinational companies, natural resources, single economy, working conditions

V3 ABSTRACT NOUNS
adaptability, curiosity, consensus, intuition, sensitivity

V4 GLOBAL COOPERATION
collaborate, cutting edge, dynamic, phenomenon, profound, push the boundaries, synergy

G1 **1 There is a missing or incorrect word in each sentence. Find the mistakes and correct them.**

1 Our teacher allowed us use calculators.
2 We stopped the car look at the beautiful view.
3 Would you consider give us a larger room?
4 I'm afraid I forgot locking the door before I left.
5 The door seems be locked. Do you have the key?
6 There's no answer. I'll try send him a text message.
7 Did you remember turning off the lights?
8 I always try stay in touch with my old friends.

2 Complete the gaps with the appropriate phrase, a or b.

1 1 They _____ sugar in those drinks years ago.
  2 We _____ some petrol in the car.
  a stopped to put   b stopped putting
2 1 Don't _____ eggs when you go shopping!
  2 I'll never _____ only 10 percent in my final university exam. It was so embarrassing!
  a forget to get   b forget getting
3 1 I _____ my first girlfriend to meet my parents.
  2 I must _____ some warm clothes with me.
  a remember to bring   b remember bringing
4 1 I _____ the door, but it was stuck.
  2 She _____ a shop, but it never made a profit.
  a tried to open   b tried opening

G2 **3 Complete the second sentence so that it has a similar meaning to the first, using a form of *have something done*.**

1 The police have searched the suspect's house.
  The suspect _____.
2 The children are washing my car.
  I _____.
3 The jeweller repaired Uncle David's watch.
  Uncle David _____ by the jeweller.
4 Janice cuts my hair once a month.
  I _____ by Janice.
5 The company has cancelled Danielle's contract.
  Danielle _____ by the company.
6 They searched our bags when we arrived.
  We _____ when we arrived.

KL **4 Match the sentence halves.**

1 Could you explain that   a to say is …
2 Could you be more   b rephrase that.
3 What I really want   c what you mean.
4 What do you   d in more detail, please?
5 Let me   e another way …
6 Could you give me   f specific?
7 Or to put it   g a specific example?
8 Sorry, I don't know   h mean by globalisation?

V1–3 **5 Complete the crossword using the clues.**

Clues Across
1 The annual conference is a great _____ opportunity.
3 There's a complicated _____ in this organisation which you should be aware of.
5 _____ is a valuable attribute, especially if you are a scientist or a researcher.
7 Our new advertising campaign shows great _____ and inventiveness.
8 Disagreements between employees need to be treated with _____.
9 As a multinational company, we need to promote _____ on an international scale.

Clues Down
2 A good leader needs business _____ as well as business knowledge.
4 _____ is an important attribute to have if you work in a dynamic, ever-changing industry.
5 The general _____ is that the workers aren't happy.
6 Old, traditional company structures are changing due to the _____ of young technology companies.

V4 **6 Complete the text with words in the box.**

collaborate   cutting edge   dynamic   phenomenon
profound   push the boundaries   synergy

The internet is a ¹_____ which has had a ²_____ effect on our lives. In the beginning, features that we take for granted now such as email were considered to be ³_____ technology.
Nowadays, computer companies and IT enthusiasts alike are constantly ⁴_____ of what is possible online. From ⁵_____ games to social networks, we can now share experiences with our friends and ⁶_____ with our colleagues, regardless of the distance between us; the ⁷_____ the internet creates is mind-blowing.

141

GRAMMAR

G1 GRADABLE AND UNGRADABLE ADJECTIVES

Adjectives describe a quality that something possesses. To describe, for example, variations in temperature, we can use *hot* or *cold*, which are gradable adjectives. But to describe the limits (the maximum or minimum level) of temperature, we use *boiling* or *freezing*, which are ungradable adjectives.

ungradable	gradable	← →	gradable	ungradable
tiny	small	size	big	enormous
excellent	good	good/bad	bad	terrible
boiling	warm/hot	temperature	cold	freezing

Some other common gradable and ungradable forms are:
tired → exhausted, angry → furious, hungry → starving, interesting → fascinating, upset → devastated, unusual → unique and important → essential.

Adverbs make adjectives stronger or weaker. Some adverbs can only be used with gradable or ungradable adjectives.

+ gradable adjectives	+ ungradable adjectives	+ gradable / ungradable adjectives
very, extremely, a bit, slightly	absolutely, completely, totally	really

The weather was **very** cold and I was **extremely** hungry. I was also **really** exhausted.

> ! Don't use comparative or superlative forms of ungradable adjectives. Use gradable adjectives instead.
> ~~This water is more freezing than the water in the sea.~~ ✗
> This water is colder than the water in the sea. ✓

With some adjectives, we don't use *very*, *absolutely*, etc., but instead we use other adverbs, e.g. *highly qualified, completely wrong*.

G2 ORDER OF ADVERBS/ADVERB PHRASES

ADVERBS/ADVERB PHRASES OF TIME, PLACE AND MANNER
We usually put adverbs of time and manner at the end of a clause.
> The last invasion of England took place **in 1066**.
> When did you live **there**?

We can emphasise adverbs of time and place by putting them at the beginning of the clause:
> **In 2009**, I decided to give up my job and go back to college.

ADVERBS OF FREQUENCY, CERTAINTY AND DEGREE
We usually put adverbs of frequency, certainty and degree in the middle of a clause, between the subject and the verb.
> **We often take** the train to college.
> **You probably left** your mobile phone in the taxi.
> **His work mainly focuses** on the human body.

With the verb *to be*, we put the adverb after the verb.
> She **is probably** the best person for the job.
> His later works **are often** very large.

With auxiliary verbs, we put the adverb between the auxiliary and the main verb.
> We **have often laughed** at his jokes.
> She **was definitely staying** in the big hotel.

KEY LANGUAGE

KL DISCUSSING IMPLICATIONS; OFFERING COUNTER-ARGUMENTS

DISCUSSING IMPLICATIONS
Maybe, but consider the implications.
But think of the consequences.
It'll affect your profits if you lower your rates.
You need to take into account the reactions of the other gallery owners.
That may be true, but our situation's getting pretty desperate.
The problem with that is that it could really upset your best customers …

OFFERING COUNTER-ARGUMENTS
If you lower your commission, other galleries might start doing the same thing.
I think there's a strong argument for doing it.
We do need to have more young artists on our books.
We've got to do something if we want to survive.
But it wouldn't if we charged variable rates.
There are plenty of things you could do …

VOCABULARY

V1 ART AND ARTISTS
abstract, artist, art lover, cave painting, ceramics, collector, critic, contemporary, controversial, groundbreaking, landscape (painting), masterpiece, modern, mural, naturalistic, painter, performance art, preview, portrait (painting), pottery, realism, realist, retrospective, sculptor, sculpture, thought-provoking, traditional art, video art

V2 ADVERB-/ADJECTIVE COLLOCATIONS
absolutely unique, completely different, completely wrong, deeply moving, entirely unexpected, heavily criticised, highly praised, highly qualified, painfully shy, really excellent, totally different, totally unbelievable, totally unjustified, utterly impossible, utterly useless

V3 ADJECTIVES
absorbing, absurd, antique, appalling, bronze, charming, classical, critical, compelling, conservative, devastated, dismissive, dreary, dreadful, enormous, exhausted, exhilarating, fabulous, fascinating, gripping, heart-breaking, heat-resistant, hilarious, intellectual, laughable, monotonous, nail-biting, outstanding, passionate, picturesque, productive, radical, rectangular, repetitive, respectful, restful, ridiculous, shiny, stainless-steel, starving, tedious, touching, trendy, witty

G1 **1 Choose the correct adjective or adverb. Sometimes both choices are possible.**

1 Let's stay at home; it's *very / absolutely* freezing outside!
2 I was *really / absolutely* devastated when I heard the news.
3 This work of art is *absolutely / a bit* unique.
4 It's *really / very* important to have good friends.
5 Her new mobile is *slightly / extremely* unusual.
6 Be careful. The boss is *very / absolutely* angry.
7 These photographs are very *good / excellent*.
8 Mike's new house is really *enormous / big*.
9 Her latest book is extremely *interesting / fascinating*.
10 In August, Madrid is *hotter / more boiling* than Paris.
11 I'm absolutely *hungry / starving* – can we get something to eat?
12 Maria was a bit *devastated / upset* by her exam results.

G2 **2 There are seven adverbs/adverb phrases in the wrong position in the text. Find and correct the mistakes.**

Bridget Riley probably is the most famous living painter of op art (optical art). These are works which feature usually patterns that create illusions of movement and colour in the viewer's mind.
Riley studied in London and then had a number of jobs in art colleges and in the art department of an advertising agency. Her most famous works were painted in the 1960s. In these large paintings she used skilfully black and white lines to create amazing illusions. Her in London first big exhibition was in 1962. The paintings on display were so powerful that viewers complained frequently of seasickness or headaches.
In the 1970s and 1980s, Riley became inspired by Egyptian art. In the paintings from this period, she used imaginatively colour. She in the late 1980s, began to experiment with diagonal patterns.

3 Choose the correct word or phrase.

1 He *is mainly / mainly is* a singer, but he occasionally writes songs, too.
2 Michaela *opened carefully the envelope / opened the envelope carefully*.
3 *In 2004, I / I in 2004,* moved to Birmingham.
4 They *get home usually / usually get home* at 4 p.m.
5 You *certainly know / know certainly* lots about art!
6 We *often have seen / have often seen* foxes in our garden at this time of year.
7 What time *there did you get / did you get there*?
8 Jack was in a rush so he *finished his essay quickly / finished quickly his essay*.

KL **4 There is one word missing in these sentences. Complete them with words or phrases from the box. There are two extra words or phrases.**

could	if	into	may	start	wouldn't

1 The problem with that is that it really upset your best customers.
2 But it if we charged variable commission rates.
3 That be true, but our situation's getting pretty desperate.
4 You need to take account the reactions of the other businesses.
5 If you lower your commission, other galleries might doing the same thing.
6 We've got to do something we want to survive.

V1 **5 Find the following in V1.**

1 six people connected with art
2 four styles or periods of art
3 three adjectives describing opinion
4 two types of exhibition
5 the word for the best example of an artist's work

V2 **6 Choose the correct word in italics.**

1 The funeral was deeply *different / moving*.
2 Jo is *completely / painfully* shy so she hates parties.
3 Sorry – I'm utterly *useless / wrong* at Mathematics.
4 The model's behaviour was heavily *criticised / praised* in the press.
5 Although she is *highly / totally* qualified, she doesn't earn much money.
6 The sudden change in the weather was *heavily / entirely* unexpected.
7 A lot of people think the book's plot is *totally / deeply* unbelievable.
8 Jemma's painting was *highly / utterly* praised by the critics.
9 Your comments are *heavily / totally* unjustified.
10 The two works of art were totally *criticised / different*.
11 His answer was completely *qualified / wrong*.
12 It's *utterly / highly* impossible to live without food or water.

V3 **7 Complete the sentences with a word from V3.**

1 The book was absolutely _____ – I couldn't stop reading it till I got to the end!
2 His story was _____ – it really moved us.
3 The meal was absolutely _____ – we'll never go back to that restaurant.
4 I found his voice quite _____ – it nearly sent me to sleep!
5 She thought he was being overly _____ because he didn't have a nice word to say about anything that evening.
6 Her performance was _____ – we definitely recommend going to see her show.

GRAMMAR

G1 RELATIVE CLAUSES

Relative clauses give us information about something or someone in a main clause.

DEFINING RELATIVE CLAUSES

Use defining relative clauses to identify or define things, ideas, places, time and possessions.

> Mr Carson is the man **who taught us geography**.

Use a relative pronoun or adverb to introduce the relative clause. Use *that* for things and people, *which* for things, *who* for people, *where* for places, *when* for times, *whose* for possession.

In formal English we prefer to put prepositions before the relative pronoun. In informal English we normally put the preposition at the end of the clause.

> Parents need to know **with whom** their children are associating. (formal)
> Parents need to know who their children are mixing **with**. (informal)

Use *whom* instead of *who*, and *which* instead of *that* after prepositions.

> Children feel social pressure to conform to the peer group **with whom** they socialise.
> Parents need to encourage children to avoid situations **in which** they could be pressurised.

> ❗ Don't use prepositions with the relative adverbs *when* and *where*.
> 2011 was the year when she left home ~~in~~. ✗
> This is the school where I studied ~~at~~. ✗

If the relative pronoun is the object of the clause, we can omit it.

> Karl is the person (that) I told you about. (I told you about **him**.)

> ❗ We can't omit the relative pronoun if it is the subject of the clause.
> I'd like you to meet Steve, who used to be my boss.
> ~~I'd like you to meet Steve, used to be my boss.~~ ✗

NON-DEFINING RELATIVE CLAUSES

Non-defining relative clauses give us extra information which can be left out without affecting the main meaning of the sentence. They are more common in written English.

> The author lives in Oxford.
> The author, **who is elderly,** lives in Oxford.

These clauses have a comma before the clause, and after it if necessary.

> ❗ Don't use *that* in non-defining relative clauses.
> My new TV, ~~that~~ I bought last week, is broken. ✗
> My new TV, **which** I bought last week, is broken. ✓

In both spoken and written English we can use a non-defining clause to add a comment or opinion about the action or situation in the main clause.

> Everyone failed the test, **which was really unfair.**

G2 REDUCED RELATIVE CLAUSES

We can often replace a relative clause with a participle phrase (a phrase beginning with the past participle or *-ing* form of a verb).

> We read the text which had been sent by the suspect.
> = We read the text **sent by the suspect**.
> (passive meaning)

> He arrived late, which made us miss the train.
> = He arrived late, **making us miss the train**.
> (active meaning)

We can't replace a relative clause in this way if the relative pronoun is the object of the relative clause.

> ~~Karl is the person telling/told you about.~~ ✗

KEY LANGUAGE

KL GIVING AND REACTING TO ADVICE

GIVING ADVICE

I'd advise you to …
I think you need to …
Why don't you … ?
You could also …
You might consider …

If I were you, I'd …
It's vital/essential that you …
It might be a good idea to …
It'd be advisable to …
It might be worth …

REACTING TO ADVICE

Yes, that could be helpful.
OK, it's worth trying.
I like the idea, but …
I'm not sure, I could try it.

What's the point of doing that?
That sounds like a good idea.
That's really good advice.
Yes, I like the idea.

VOCABULARY

V1 PHRASAL VERBS CONNECTED WITH WORKING TOGETHER

break up, fall out (with), get down to, get on (with), get used to (+-*ing*), put up (with)

V2 PERSONALITY ADJECTIVES AND NOUNS

ambitious, ambition, authoritative, authority, conscientious, conscientiousness, controlling, control, creative, creativity, diplomatic, diplomacy, dynamic, energetic, energy, enthusiastic, enthusiasm, fair, impatient, indecisive, inflexible, knowledgeable, knowledge, objective, objectivity, observant, outgoing, practical, practicality, responsible, resourceful, resourcefulness

V3 WORD FORMATION

approve, approval, associate, association, behave, behavior, conform, conformity, continue, continuity, define, definition, disable, disability, propose, proposal, refuse, refusal, save, savior, secure, security, suggest, suggestion

V4 IDIOMS WITH MIND

be in two minds, be out of (your) mind, keep an open mind, make up (your) mind, peace of mind

V5 PSYCHOLOGY

assessment, case file, deduce, motive, profile, psychiatrist

G1 **1 Combine the information to make one sentence using a relative clause. If possible, do not include a relative pronoun.**
1 That's the man. I met him yesterday.
   That's _____.
2 This is the DVD player. It doesn't work very well.
   This is _____.
3 Janine is the woman. Her house was destroyed in the earthquake.
   Janine _____.
4 My sister lives in an old house. She's a doctor.
   My _____.
5 This is the computer game. I told you about it.
   This is _____.
6 The course is very difficult. It began in September.
   The _____.

2 Rewrite the sentences in more formal English.
1 I don't fully understand the problem that he's working on.
2 Protecting the environment is a cause that she really believes in.
3 This is the bill that we disagreed about.
4 This is the course which they applied for.
5 That hotel is the one that we often stayed in.
6 Constance is the architect who I work for.
7 That's the team that my brother plays football for.
8 Do you remember the project that we used to work together on?

3 There is a mistake in each sentence. Correct it.
1 Do you know the person about who I am talking?
2 This phone, that was very expensive, has never worked properly.
3 I'm visiting the place where I grew up in.
4 Michael is very intelligent, isn't very good at solving puzzles.
5 The students, are from many different countries, are learning English.
6 She's a woman that she never admits she's wrong.

G2 **4 Choose the correct word.**
1 This is one of the houses *designing / designed* by Le Corbusier.
2 There was a lot of rubbish *leaving / left* by the previous residents.
3 We noticed a girl *standing / stood* on the corner.
4 I always do the exercises *recommended / recommending* by my personal trainer.
5 We arrived early, *giving / given* us plenty of time to check in.
6 We live in a house *buying / bought* by my father in 1992.

KL **5 Complete the sentences with the phrases below.**
1 It might be _____ to speak to a lawyer.
2 Why don't you _____ your boss?
3 If I were you, _____ get some counselling.
4 It's essential _____ tell somebody about it.
5 I'd _____ you to ask for a refund.
6 You might _____ contacting a lawyer.
7 I think you _____ to see a doctor.
8 It's _____ that you talk to him

a consider
b vital
c a good idea
d I'd
e need
f advise
g talk to
h that you

V1 **6 Replace the phrases in italics with the verbs in V1.**
1 I *have a friendly relationship with* my neighbours.
2 It's hard to *become comfortable with* a new home.
3 My parents *separated* when I was quite young.
4 It's important not to *quarrel with* your colleagues.
5 My father won't *tolerate* bad behaviour.
6 Have you managed to *start* work on that project?

V2,3 **7 Match the definitions with a word from V2 or V3.**
1 able to use tact and sensitivity in dealing with others
2 act according to socially accepted standards
3 unable to make decisions quickly and effectively
4 be thorough and careful when doing a task
5 the state of being just and unbiased

V4 **8 Match the sentences.**
1 Carol deliberately doesn't form a definite opinion.
2 Michaela is crazy.
3 Now she's finished, Isabel feels calm and relaxed.
4 Cristina knows what she wants to do.
5 Serena can't decide what to do.

a She's in two minds.
b She's out of her mind.
c She keeps an open mind.
d She's made up her mind.
e She has peace of mind.

V5 **9 Complete the text with the correct form of words from V5.**

Speakers at next month's conference for the world's leading criminal profilers will include police officers, psychologists and [1]_____ from all over the world. Participants will be able to examine [2]_____ from a number of well-known criminal investigations. Presentations include lectures on psychological [3]_____ and the use of [4]_____ in terrorist cases. There will also be discussions on the analysis of [5]_____ and whether we can [6]_____ future criminal activity from youthful behaviour.

GRAMMAR

G1 REPORTED SPEECH

Use reported speech to report someone's words.
 'I'm hungry.'   She said she was hungry.

We use statement word order in reported questions. We don't put a question mark at the end.
 'How much is it?'
 She asked **how much it was**. ✓
 ~~She asked how much was it?~~ ✗

To report a *yes/no* question, we use *ask* + *if* or *whether*.
 'Is it expensive?'
 She asked **if it was expensive**.

When we use reported speech, we often make changes to the tense of the verb, to pronouns and to time adverbs. The table shows the most common changes:

direct speech	reported speech
tenses:	
present simple	past simple
present continuous	past continuous
present perfect	past perfect
past simple	past perfect
will	*would*
can	*could*
pronouns:	
I	he/she
we	they
my	his/her
our	their
time adverbs:	
today	then / that day
yesterday	the day before
tomorrow	the next day / the day
last week	after
	the week before

! The past perfect simple and continuous, and the modal verbs *could*, *would*, *might* and *should* do not change.

In some situations we can choose NOT to change the tense in reported speech. This can be because:
- the action or situation in the statement is still happening/true.
 'I'm expecting a baby.'
 She said she**'s expecting** a baby. (She's still expecting a baby.)
- the verb expresses a fact or situation that cannot change or is unlikely to change.
 'The city is beautiful.'
 He said the city **is** beautiful. (It's still true.)
- the verb comes after a time conjunction, e.g. *when, after*.
 'I started my job after I finished university.'
 He said he had started his job **after** he **finished** university.

! We do not change the tense or time adverbs if the reporting verb is in the present tense.
 He **says** he **is working** very hard **this year**.
 She **tells** us she **isn't earning** very much money **at the moment**.

G2 REPORTING VERBS

We often use particular verbs to report speech. The verbs show the attitude of the person speaking so they give a lot more information than *say*.
 'I think you really should apply for the job.'
 He **encouraged** me to apply for the job.

Different reporting verbs are followed by different structures.

infinitive with *to*	*offer, refuse, agree, promise*
object + infinitive with *to*	*advise, invite, warn, tell, encourage, persuade*
-ing form	*admit, regret, consider, deny, all verbs followed by a preposition, e.g. insist on, apologise for*

KEY LANGUAGE

KL CREATING IMPACT IN A PRESENTATION

TRIPLING (SAYING THINGS IN THREES)
… an important **industrial**, **commercial** and **cultural** centre.
… they help to create the **lively, friendly**, **cosmopolitan** atmosphere the city is famous for.

REPETITION
Toronto's getting **better** and **better** these days, as **more** and **more** people come from all over the world.

RHETORICAL QUESTIONS
So, **what** are the main sights of the city?
OK, **why** is the CN Tower worth seeing?

VOCABULARY

V1 ASPECTS OF CULTURE
anniversaries, architecture, attitudes, civil wars, climate, commemorations, cuisine, customs, dialects, faith/belief systems, geography, heritage, historical events, institutions, invasions, language, manners, monarchy, political system, revolutions, religion, rituals, rules of behaviour, rules of etiquette, the arts, sects, staple diet, specialities, superstitions, terrain, traditions, values

V2 ADJECTIVES
disappointed, excited, frustrated, hostile, inadequate, interesting, insufficient, intriguing, isolated, lonely, stimulated, unfriendly

V3 PREFIXES
anti-, counter-, inter-, mis-, multi-, post-, pre-, sub-

V4 SUFFIXES
-able, -ible, -ism, -less, -logy, -ment, -tion

V5 WORD FORMATION
antisocial, communication, counterculture, development, international, misunderstanding, multicultural, postwar, predate, responsible, sexism, sociology, subculture, timeless, valuable

G1 1 Complete the reported statements. Make changes to tenses, pronouns and time adverbs.

1 'I'm working in a café.'
   She said she _____ in a café.
2 'I lived in Berlin for three years.'
   He said he _____ in Berlin for three years.
3 'You should see a doctor.'
   She said I _____ a doctor.
4 'We'll see you here tomorrow.'
   They said they _____ us _____.
5 'I've been abroad with my wife and our children.'
   He said he _____ abroad with _____ wife and _____ children.
6 'My father received a tax bill yesterday.'
   He said _____ father _____ a tax bill _____.

2 Complete the reported statements. Do not change the tense if it is not necessary.

1 'I don't have a job at the moment.'
   This morning Caroline said _____.
2 'The weather here is always cold in the winter.'
   This afternoon the receptionist told us _____.
3 'We're going to France when we finish the course.'
   They said _____.
4 'I went to a terrible school when I was a child.'
   Michaela said she _____.
5 'We watched the final episode of *Emergency!* last night.'
   Last Wednesday, my friends said _____.
6 'Pollution from cars causes global warming.'
   We want to buy a smaller car because the scientist said _____.

G2 3 Choose the correct word.

1 The driver *warned / refused* me not to jump off the bus while it was moving.
2 Carol *refused / regretted* to pay the bill.
3 Our teacher *apologised for / offered* being late.
4 They've *offered / invited* to give me a trial.
5 My friends *persuaded / agreed* me to go to the park with them.
6 I'm afraid she didn't *agree / advise* to lend it to me.

4 Complete the sentences to report the statements.

1 'I'll carry your case.' He offered _____.
2 'I was really stupid to get married so young.' She regretted _____.
3 'Don't buy anything in that shop.' Mike warned _____.
4 'I'm really sorry that I shouted at you.' She apologised _____.
5 'We really think you should learn the guitar.' My parents encouraged _____.

KL 5 Use the notes to write sentences for a presentation about Cambridge. Use the techniques of tripling, repetition or rhetorical questions.

1 why / Cambridge / seeing ?
2 it / important educational / cultural / business centre
3 facilities / tourists / better each year
4 its buildings / parks / countryside / make it / beautiful place / live
5 the university / becoming / more popular / international students
6 what / main historical sights / city ?

V1 6 Complete the sentences with words from V1.

1 Most children learn a foreign _____ these days.
2 The financial and legal systems are vital _____.
3 I'm not keen on Indian _____ – I find it too spicy.
4 Buddhism is a popular _____ in Asia.
5 I love _____ in general, but my favourite is opera.
6 She loves the _____ of 16th-century Italy, especially Michelangelo's buildings.
7 Having a formal dance at the end of the year is one of the _____ of high school life in the USA.
8 I love places with a warm _____ – I hate the cold!

V2 7 Match the sentence halves.

1 I'm a happy person, but I live alone
2 My neighbours hate me – they shout at me
3 I feel frustrated when
4 Being surrounded by very intelligent people
5 We were really stimulated by
6 I couldn't work out who the murderer was

a and can be quite hostile.
b can make me feel inadequate.
c so it was very intriguing.
d so I sometimes feel isolated.
e I can't find the answer to a problem.
f all the exciting possibilities ahead of us.

V3,4 8 Complete the sentences with a suitable form of the word in brackets.

1 She owns a very _____ (value) watch.
2 It's OK – my children are very _____. (responsibility)
3 Budget airlines have made _____ (nation) travel much more affordable.
4 There are 20 different nationalities here – it's a very _____ (culture) area.
5 We had a fight over a stupid _____. (understand)
6 We will not tolerate _____ (social) behaviour here.
7 The castle is very old. It _____ (date) the surrounding buildings.
8 Really good music is _____ (time) – it appeals to people just as much today as it did in the past.

GRAMMAR

G1 CONDITIONALS: FIRST AND SECOND

FIRST CONDITIONAL

Form the first conditional in the following way:

If-clause	+	Main clause
if + present simple		*will/may/might/should*, etc. + infinitive without *to*

Use the first conditional to talk about real possibilities.

If you **ask** him, he'**ll be** happy to help you.

As long as and *provided that* mean *only if*. We often use these expressions to talk about rules or to make a bargain or promise.

You'll get a refund **provided that** you have a receipt. (= You'll get a refund only if you have a receipt.)

You'll be able to go **as long as** you finish your work.

SECOND CONDITIONAL

Form the second conditional in the following way:

If-clause	+	Main clause
if + past simple		*would/could/might*, etc. + infinitive without *to*

Use the second conditional to talk about an unreal situation in the present or future.

If you **had** good eyesight, you **wouldn't need** glasses. (= You don't have good eyesight.)

If you **were** invited to the party, **would** you **go**? (= You are unlikely to be invited to the party.)

We often use *supposing* (*that*) or *imagine* to talk about an imaginary situation.

Supposing/imagine you won the lottery, what would you buy?

G2 CONDITIONALS: THIRD AND MIXED

THIRD CONDITIONAL

Form the third conditional in the following way:

If-clause	+	Main clause
if + past perfect		*would/could/might* + *have* + past participle

Use the third conditional to talk about unreal situations in the past, i.e. situations that are contrary to the facts.

If you'**d been** there, you **would have seen** her. (= You weren't there so you didn't see her.)

If I **hadn't been** to university, I **wouldn't have got** this job. (= I did go to university so I did get this job.)

We often use the third conditional to talk about regrets or to criticise.

If I'**d studied** harder, **I could have gone** to university. (= I regret that I didn't study harder.)

If you'**d listened** to me, this **wouldn't have happened**. (= You should have listened to me.)

MIXED CONDITIONALS

We can combine the clauses from the second and third conditionals to talk about the present or past results of unreal situations.

- second + third conditional: past condition with present result

If-clause	+	Main clause
if + past perfect		*would/should/might/could*, etc. + infinitive without *to*

If you'**d brought** a map, we **wouldn't be** lost **now**. (= You didn't bring a map so now we are lost.)

- third + second conditional: present condition with past result

If-clause	+	Main clause
if + past simple		*would/might/could* + *have* + past participle.

If you **paid** attention in class, you **would have got** higher marks. (= You don't pay attention in class. You didn't get high marks.)

KEY LANGUAGE

KL PERSUADING, MAKING A CASE FOR SOMETHING

PERSUADING

Let's face it, the economy's not in good shape at the moment.
Everyone's suffering.
We don't want to be left behind.
It's true what you say, Stephanie, but we do need to …
That's a fair point, Stephanie, but look at the bigger picture.
I'm sure you agree with me, it's our job to manage change …
I've heard about these objections. My answer is simple.
Look, I think you'll agree, we've got some of the best and most experienced workers in the trade.

MAKING A CASE FOR SOMETHING

That's a very strong argument for …
Another reason is that …
I would argue that we'll be …
If some of our staff lose their jobs, it'll have a bad effect on production.
We'll have to reduce our workforce, maybe by 20 percent, but that'll help to lower our costs and make us more competitive. It's a hard world out there.
That's the way forward for us.
We don't have any other option.

VOCABULARY

V1 TECHNOLOGY

(breathing) apparatus, (household) appliance, (labour-saving) device, (internal combustion) engine, (computer) equipment, (clever) gadget, (cash) machine, technological, technology, technophobe

V2 TECHNOLOGY ADJECTIVES

cutting edge, durable, easy to use, environmentally friendly, green, handy, hard-wearing, long-lasting, non-polluting, obsolete, old-fashioned, out-of-date, practical, state-of-the-art, user-friendly

V3 PREFIXES (OPPOSITES)

dislike, **in**accurate, **in**appropriate, **in**convenient, **in**effective, **in**efficient, **in**equality, **in**sensitive, **mis**management, **mis**trust, **mis**understanding, **un**able, **un**likely, **un**necessary

G1 1 Complete the sentences with the correct form of buy, a, b, c or d.

a buy   **b** bought   **c** will buy   **d** would buy

1 I _____ you a new TV if you really needed it.
2 If you _____ me an expensive ring, I'll marry you.
3 I _____ lunch if you buy dinner.
4 If that phone isn't too expensive, I _____ it.
5 Joe _____ us a camera provided he can borrow it.
6 Supposing you _____ a big car, would you use it?
7 I _____ you a pet as long as you look after it.
8 Imagine you _____ a flat abroad – it'd be great!

2 There is a mistake in each sentence. Correct it.

1 If I'll go tomorrow, I'll call you.
2 Supposing we are rich, wouldn't it be fantastic?
3 I'd be much happier if I can play the piano.
4 As long as you would look after it, I'll let you borrow my dress tonight.
5 Jane will be able to take photos of the party tomorrow if she would bring her camera.
6 Imagine you lived to 100, won't it be amazing?

G2 3 Match the sentence halves.

1 If my mobile phone battery hadn't run out,
2 If the internet hadn't been invented,
3 If I hadn't found the tickets under the sofa,
4 If I hadn't bought a laptop computer,
5 If France hadn't had a revolution,
6 If airlines hadn't introduced cheap flights,
7 If we had invested in renewable energy sources,
8 If the shops had been open,

a we wouldn't be able to travel so often.
b I would have to go to internet cafés.
c we wouldn't be able to send emails.
d she would have bought you a present.
e we wouldn't have lost so many natural resources.
f we wouldn't have been able to go to the concert.
g it would have a king now.
h I would have sent you a text message.

4 Complete the sentences with a suitable verb form to make sentences using the third conditional or mixed conditionals.

1 If I'd seen you, I _____ to you. (I didn't talk to you.)
2 If I _____ more revision, I wouldn't have failed so many tests. (I don't do much revision.)
3 We would have visited our friends if we _____ time. (We didn't have time.)
4 Clare _____ the manager now if she hadn't lost that client. (She isn't the manager now.)
5 If I _____ to college, I would have a better job now. (I didn't go to college.)
6 There _____ so many wars if governments talked to each other more. (There have been a lot of wars.)

KL 5 There are mistakes in six of the sentences below. Add or delete a word to correct them.

1 We won't need as much as money, will we, to do that?
2 Let's face it, the company's not good shape at the moment.
3 It's what you say, but we do need to have a rethink.
4 I've heard about these objections plenty. My answer is simple.
5 I'm sure you agree with me, it's our job to decide what to change.
6 That's a point, but look at the bigger picture.
7 Look, I think you agree, we've got the most talented designers in the trade.
8 If some of our staff lose their jobs, it'll have a bad effect on production.

V1 6 Choose the correct word.

1 We sell a full range of domestic *apparatus / appliances*, from washing machines to cookers.
2 I've just bought an XJ56 – it's a *device / technology* for measuring distances between two points.
3 Did John get the *appliance / apparatus* he needs for his scientific experiments?
4 What *device / equipment* do you need for camping?
5 I've just found this little *engine / gadget* that helps you peel vegetables.

V2 7 Match the words and phrases in the box with the definitions below.

durable   environmentally friendly   handy
obsolete   state-of-the-art   user-friendly

1 easy for people to use
2 uses the most recent technology
3 will last for a long time
4 so old-fashioned that you can't use it any more
5 very useful and convenient
6 doesn't harm the planet

V3 8 Complete the sentences with one of the words in the box and the correct prefix *dis-*, *in-*, *mis-* or *un-*.

able   accurate   appropriate   efficient
likes   necessary   inequality   trust

1 Since the operation I've been _____ to walk.
2 Our party fights _____ in society.
3 Eleanor _____ spicy food – she never eats it.
4 The report is full of _____ information.
5 I _____ politicians – they never tell the truth.
6 Don't bring a gift – it's completely _____.
7 That company is very _____.
8 He wore a dirty T-shirt to my wedding. I think that's very _____ behaviour.

2 ENVIRONMENT

1 You are going to watch an interview with Dr Andrew McGonigle, a scientist who studies volcanoes. Discuss the questions in pairs.

1 What do you think his job involves?
2 Where do you think he works?
3 What dangers do you think he faces?

2 ▶ 2 Read the five topics he discusses. Watch the interview. Put the topics a–e in the order that Andrew talks about them.

a Information about the specific volcanoes he works with
b How volcanoes affect us
c The problems caused by natural disasters in Italy and how they work to reduce their impact
d How they study volcanic gases
e What his job involves and why he finds it interesting

3a Work with a partner and look at the notes below. Can you remember the missing information?

1 Andrew studies volcanoes to understand them and try to _____ eruptions.
2 Volcanoes provide an opportunity to study things which happen at the _____ _____ the Earth.
3 Volcanoes _____ us in lots of different ways.
4 Collecting samples in glass bottles provides _____ _____, but it's also very dangerous.
5 They currently use _____ _____ _____ to fly into volcanoes and collect data.
6 Both Etna and Stromboli have interesting ways of _____.
7 Stromboli shoots molten rocks a few _____ _____ into the air.
8 Vesuvius could be the most _____ _____ in Europe.
9 At the moment, evacuation in the Vesuvius area takes _____ _____.
10 The most important factor in working to reduce evacuation times is the dialogue between scientists and _____ _____.

3b Watch the interview again and complete sentences 1–10.

4a Look at the job titles below. Match jobs 1–5 with descriptions a–e.

1 an agronomist   a studies the spread of diseases
2 a seismologist   b studies fossils
3 an epidemiologist c studies soil and crops
4 a meteorologist   d studies the weather
5 a palaeontologist e studies earthquakes

4b Work with a partner. Which two jobs do you think would be most interesting? Why?

3 SPORT

1 Work with a partner and discuss the questions.

1 Do you play any sports?
2 Do you prefer team sports or individual sports?
3 In what ways do you think athletes prepare themselves for competitions, both mentally and physically?

2 ▶ 3 Dr Elizabeth Pummell is a sports psychologist. Watch the interview and answer the questions.

1 Which two of the following are the main focus of sports psychology?
   a Using principles of psychology to improve the way athletes perform.
   b Using participation in sport as a way of furthering the study of psychology.
   c Studying what it takes to win competitions.
   d Using sport as a way of treating psychological problems.
2 How important does Dr Pummell think the mind is in sport?
3 According to Dr Pummell, what lesson can we all learn from athletes?

3a Work in two groups:

Group A: Watch the video again and make notes on the questions.
1 Which two specific areas does she say that athletes want to work on?
2 Why are mental skills so important, according to athletes?
3 What four factors related to mental toughness does she give?
4 What does she encourage athletes to imagine themselves doing before a competition?

Group B: watch the video again and make notes on the questions.
1 What is important for sports to be like for young athletes?
2 What makes tennis mentally challenging?
3 What does she say about Roger Federer's mental toughness?
4 What is important for athletes to concentrate on?

3b Compare your notes with other students in your group.

3c Work with a partner from the other group and share information.

4a Choose one of the topics below, and prepare to talk about it. Think about the background to the situation and what you did in order to succeed.
• a time you stayed in control under pressure
• a time when you were nervous but succeeded
• a time when you were focused and determined

4b Work in groups. Share your experiences.

4 MEDICINE

1 Work with a partner and discuss the questions.

1 For what reasons might somebody have something implanted in their body?
2 How can scientists change the human body?

2a In her interview, Dr Tina Chowdhury, a scientist at Queen Mary University of London, talks about the topics below. Work with a partner and discuss what you think each one involves.

1 Information biology
2 Bionics
3 Biocompatibility
4 Microchip technology
5 Tissue engineering

2b ▶ 4 **Watch the interview and match each description below with the topics in Exercise 2a. What other information can you remember about each topic?**

a How well a device can stay in the body without degrading
b The study of why tissues break down and how they can be repaired
c Taking something from the human body and growing it in a lab
d Devices which improve how the brain works
e Building devices which can copy the functions of limbs or organs

3 Are these statements true or false? Watch the interview again to check your answers.

1 The ultimate purpose of bionic devices is to help people continue living their lives after an accident.
2 It is hoped bionic hearts will be used in the future.
3 With neurological problems such as Parkinson's disease the brain is getting bigger.
4 Tina thinks microchips should be used to help healthy people as well as patients.
5 Tissue engineering borrows tools from another area of study.

4 Discuss the questions in small groups.

1 Do you agree with Tina, that microchip technology should only be used with patients, not healthy people?
2 What might be some of the positive and negative effects of allowing healthy people to have microchip implants?

5 TRANSPORT

1 Work with a partner and discuss the questions.

1 Do you like travelling by train?
2 What's the longest train journey you've ever been on?
3 What are the advantages of travelling by train over other forms of transport?

2a You are going to watch an interview with Monisha Rajesh, a travel writer who recently wrote a book about her journey around India on trains. What do you think she might talk about? Choose four topics from the list.

a Why she decided to go
b The difficulties she had
c Why Indian trains are unique/special
d The trains and places she visited
e How much it cost
f The people she met
g Where she plans to go in the future

2b ▶ 5 Watch the interview. Which four topics in Exercise 2a did she talk about? What can you remember about each one?

3 Choose the correct answer (a, b or c). Then watch the interview again to check your answers.

1 Which of these was not a reason why she decided to travel by train?
   a she thought she'd be able to find out more about people than on planes
   b she wanted to visit the places she had visited when she was younger
   c she saw that trains went to places that planes don't
2 What was the most important factor when planning where to go?
   a the places they wanted to visit
   b the people they wanted to meet
   c the events they wanted to experience
3 What does she say about the way Indian people talk to you?
   a they often ask lots of personal questions
   b they won't talk to you unless you talk to them
   c it's important for them to know where you're from
4 What can you learn about Indian society from travelling by train?
   a the different classes of society
   b that people like to share
   c that there are 37 different classes
5 What does she say about the Lifeline Express?
   a they treat a limited number of health problems
   b it runs in the south
   c it helped raise her awareness of the importance of railways in India
6 What did she particularly like about the Konkan railway?
   a it goes from Mumbai to Goa
   b it's very beautiful
   c it travels over several high bridges
7 What happened with the members of parliament she met?
   a she never heard from them again and felt disappointed
   b the woman sitting next to her laughed at them
   c she thought she wouldn't hear from them again, but she did

4a You are going to plan a tour of your country and present it to the class. Work with a partner and decide on the following information.

• The 'theme' of your tour   • Places you will visit   • How you will travel

4b Present your tour to the class. Decide which tour you like best.

7 ARCHITECTURE

1 Work with a partner. Look at the three buildings in the photos and answer the questions.

1 The Mac   2 Park Hill   3 Sesc Pompeia

1 Where do you think each building is?
2 What do you think it's used for?
3 What adjectives would you use to describe each one?
4 Which one do you like best?

2 ▶ 7 Watch an interview with Laura Mark, a journalist for a magazine on architecture, and tick which four of the sentences (a–g) she says are unusual about the Sesc Pompeia building.

a It wasn't common at the time it was built for women architects to build large buildings.
b Lina Bo Bardi had already built many buildings like this.
c She changed a building that was there rather than building it from new.
d Before that, concrete had rarely been used on such a large scale.
e She built the walls from plaster.
f The windows look very different from the rest of the building.
g The building was popular at the time, but not now.

3a Work with a partner and look at the notes below. Can you remember the missing information?

1 The Sesc Pompeia is located in a _____ area of Sao Paulo.
2 One of its uses is as a place where people can play _____.
3 The organisation that built it, also built _____ other centres across Brazil.
4 Lina Bo Bardi worked with the local people in order to create a building which they _____.
5 The towers are _____ _____ high.
6 The colours of the windows were in _____ _____ to the material of the rest of the building.
7 Laura describes the appearance of the building as _____ _____.
8 Local people loved the building when it first opened and they still _____ it in the same way now.

3b Watch the interview again and complete the missing information.

4 Work in groups and discuss the questions.

1 Are there any unusual buildings in your city?
2 What are your favourite buildings? Why do you like them?
3 If you could design a building for your local area, what would you design?

8 GLOBALISATION

1a Match the adjectives in the box with their meanings below.

egalitarian   hierarchical   stifling
relationship-oriented   task-driven

1 a system where people are divided into levels of importance
2 focused more on results
3 a belief that everyone is equal and should have equal rights
4 a situation which stops you developing your own ideas and character
5 a belief that good contact with colleagues is important

1b Work in groups. Which words/phrases would you use to describe the way people communicate in your culture? Which other words/phrases would you use?

2 ▶ 8 Watch the interview with Richard Cook, who talks about working in a global environment, and put the quotes in the order he says them.

a '… and this is because they maybe have different ways of communicating or different styles of leadership.'
b 'Well, a global business environment can mean different things for different companies.'
c 'The biggest block for native English speakers working globally is that they believe they don't have to do anything differently when they communicate.'
d 'The implications for people working in a global environment are that it cannot be business as usual. There are big differences.'

3a Work with a partner. Can you remember Richard's answers to these questions? Make notes.

1 What different things can working in a global business environment mean to different companies?
2 What big differences are there between working in a global environment and 'business as usual'?
3 What different ways of communicating do the two cultures he refers to have?
4 What do native English speakers do when they communicate?
5 How does he suggest adapting the phrase *When in Rome, do as the Romans do?*

3b Watch the interview again and check your answers.

4a Work with a partner. You are going to give a short presentation on advice for people coming to work in your country. Make notes on these things, and think about how you are going to present your ideas.

• communication styles
• what people value most
• how to get the best out of people

4b Give your presentation to the class. Discuss which you liked the best.

9 ART

1 Work with a partner and discuss the questions.

movies   adverts   sculpture   pottery
theatre   street performance   jingles
modern art   graffiti   photography

1 Which of these things do you consider to be art? What are the other things?
2 Which of them do you like most/least?

2 You are going to watch an interview with Yulia Podolska, a sculptor. Before you watch, match the words in the box with their meanings 1–6 below.

carve   clay   maquette   marble   plasticine   sketch

1 a hard, white rock which becomes smooth when it is polished
2 a simple, quickly-made drawing which does not show much detail
3 a small scale model, or rough draft of a sculpture
4 a type of heavy, sticky earth that can be used for making pots and bricks
5 a soft substance that comes in many colours and is used by children for making models
6 make an object or pattern by cutting a piece of wood or stone

3a ▶ 9 Work in pairs. Put the stages of the sculpting process in order, then watch the interview and check your answers.

a She makes a bigger sculpture out of clay.
b She has an idea in her head.
c She uses that to make a cast out of plaster.
d She makes a maquette.
e She carves the sculpture in marble.
f She plays with plasticine or does a pencil sketch.

3b Watch the interview again and choose the correct option (a, b or c).

1 What inspired Yulia to become a sculptor?
   a her work as a doctor
   b a visit to a museum
   c her university professor in Kiev

2 Why is marble her favourite material?
   a you can make detailed sculptures with it
   b you can transform it into something very different
   c it's easy to use

3 Which of these is not a material she has used in her work?
   a plastic toys
   b rubber
   c ice

4 Why does she refer to Renaissance and contemporary collections in Italy and France?
   a she wants to create better pieces
   b she wants to create something different
   c she wants to create her own place within this world

5 Where does she get most of her ideas from?
   a her emotions and political situations
   b her relationships
   c the TV

6 What does she say about the stone she used for *The Cardinal*?
   a it was difficult to find
   b she knew what it would be as soon as she saw it
   c it was a difficult piece to carve

4 Work in groups and discuss the questions.

1 Yulia gives lots of examples of things that have inspired her. Can you think of an example of something which has inspired you to do something?
2 If you were going to create a piece of art (e.g. painting, sculpture, etc.), where do you think you'd get your ideas from?
3 Do you think people are born with artistic talent, or is it something that can be learnt?

▶ MEET THE EXPERT

10 PSYCHOLOGY

1a Work with a partner. How much do you know about the human brain? Do the quiz.

THE HUMAN BRAIN

I What percentage of the human brain is fat?
a) 5%   **b)** 20%   **c)** 60%

2 How much does the average brain weigh?
a) 500g–600g   **b)** 1.3kg–1.4kg   **c)** 2.5kg–2.7kg

3 What percentage of the brain is water?
a) 25%   **b)** 50%   **c)** 75%

4 What percentage of the body's blood and oxygen does the brain need?
a) 20%   **b)** 40%   **c)** 70%

5 What percentage of our brains do we usually use?
a) 10%   **b)** 50%   **c)** 100%

1b Check your answers with your teacher. Did you find any of the facts surprising?

2 ▶10 You are going to watch an interview with Dr Jack Lewis, a neuroscientist who studies the human brain. Watch the interview and put these topics in the order that he talks about them.

a Neuro-economics
b How neuroscience helps medicine
c Brain scans
d What neuroscience involves

3a Work with a partner and look at the notes below. Can you remember the missing information?

3b Watch the interview again and complete the missing information.

1 FMRI stands for Functional _____ Resonance _____.

2 At the smallest level, neuroscience studies how molecules _____.

3 At the highest level, neuroscience studies how _____ _____ cells communicate.

4 The two types of MRI scans are _____ and _____.

5 Looking at images activates the _____ of the brain, while listening to music activates the _____ of the brain.

6 Neuro-economics is concerned with how we make _____ decisions.

7 Neuro-economics tells us a lot about the _____ we make.

8 After strokes, some people are able to _____ parts of the brain to take over different functions.

9 Some types of chronic pain aren't generated by damage to the body, but inside the _____.

10 Brain scans help chronic pain sufferers to show people that the pain is really _____.

4 Work in groups and discuss the questions.

1 Why might someone have a brain scan?
2 Dr Jack Lewis talks about the benefits of neuroscience in treating stroke patients and dealing with chronic pain. What other benefits do you think it can bring to medicine?
3 How else can a better understanding of the human brain help us?

11 CULTURES

1 Work with a partner and discuss the questions.

1 Which foods and drinks are popular in your country?
2 Are there any traditional dishes you think people from other countries wouldn't like?
3 Which of these dishes have you tried? Did you like them?

chicken tikka masala   chop suey   fish and chips
fortune cookies   insects   McDonald's
roast beef   sweet and sour chicken

2 ▶11 Watch the interview with Anna Colquhoun, a culinary anthropologist, and match the names of dishes in Exercise 1 with the descriptions below.

1 Something British people would find disgusting _____
2 Two things brought to the UK by immigrants _____ and _____
3 A dish 'from abroad' that was actually invented in the UK _____
4 Two Chinese dishes popular in the USA _____ _____
5 US food popular in China _____

3a Watch the interview again and make notes in answer to these questions.

1 What does Anna's job involve?
2 Why is food important in our culture?
3 What processes move food across borders?
4 How does McDonald's reflect changing social relationships in China?
5 What is the actual effect of 'McDonaldisation' on food in Europe?

3b Compare your notes with a partner.

4 Work in groups amd discuss the questions.

1 Do you think that the 'McDonaldisation' of culture has led to more homogenous types of food, or, like Anna, do you think it's had the opposite effect? Can you think of any examples?
2 What other areas of culture might experience 'McDonaldisation'? Is this a good or bad thing?

154

COMMUNICATION ACTIVITIES

LESSON 1.4 EXERCISE 6A (P.13)

COUNSELLOR A
Summary of your conversation with Martin.
Problems
- He is unhappy because the flat is always untidy. He does more cleaning and washing-up than the other students.
- He thinks they spend too much money on food each week and a lot of food is wasted.
- He thinks that Stewart's friend, Tom, has stayed too long in the flat without paying any money.

Solutions
- He wants one flatmate to buy essential food for everyone else each Saturday at the local supermarket.
- Each flatmate should be responsible for cleaning the flat and washing the dishes on a certain day.
- Stewart's friend, Tom, must leave the flat immediately.

Martin's communication style
- He is very direct, 'I say what I think – some people don't like that.'
- He often puts up notices about cleaning the flat, washing the dishes and keeping the flat tidy, but no one pay any attention to the notices, he says.

LESSON 2.3 EXERCISE 10A (P. 21)

STUDENT A
Mount Vesuvius is an active volcano that overlooks the Bay of Naples in Southern Italy. It has erupted over 30 times. Its most famous eruption took place around 79 AD when the city of Pompeii (half a mile from the volcano) was wiped out and covered in lava and ash. The eruption lasted for two days. The city was rediscovered 1,700 years later and lead to an excavation. The site was very well preserved. Pompeii has since become a popular destination for tourists, scientists and historians.

LESSON 2.4 EXERCISE 5A (P.23)

STUDENT A: ENVIRONMENTALIST
You are an environmentalist.
You want the wind farm to go ahead as soon as possible. You are a member of an environmental pressure group 'Lovers of the Land' (LoL).
Your group is keen on renewable energy sources and supports the building of wind farms.
You think:
- there is an urgent need for sources of renewable energy.
- nuclear power is dangerous.
- the wind has been used as a clean and efficient source of power for centuries.
- the latest wind farms are much more efficient.
- the proposed wind farm is environmentally friendly.
- the wind farm sets a good example for other areas and countries.

You want to know what the disadvantages of wind farms are.

LESSON 5.1 EXERCISE 11A (P.47)

STUDENT A
Read this quote from a representative of the Campaign for Better Driving. Discuss the points in it with your group.

'I agree that we need to do something about the number of accidents and injuries on the roads today, but I don't agree with all these restrictions and safety features that the police want to introduce, you know, like speed cameras. They affect everybody and penalise the good drivers as well as the bad ones. It's a fact that driving fast doesn't cause accidents – it's driving badly that causes them, so I think we should be looking at bad drivers. Now, most crashes are caused by young men, so why don't we raise the age for learning to drive, say to 20 for women and 22 for men? Another possibility is to retest young drivers every two years until they're 30 – make sure they're driving well. I firmly believe that educating and monitoring young people is the way to solve this problem.'

LESSON 7.3 EXERCISE 10 (P.71)

STUDENT A

Read the information below and decide which points you think refer to the Millau Viaduct (above). Use the photo to help you. Then discuss with your partner the information you think refers to his/her bridge. Use the information to write a paragraph about the Millau Viaduct.

- Spans the River Tarn in the Massif Central mountains, France.
- Construction of the bridge started in 2001.
- It stretches from Karkoy Square in Istanbul to the Old Town.
- It is the tallest car bridge in the world. At its summit, it is 343 metres.
- The landing stage is used by steamboats and ferryboats every day.
- It is considered to be one of the engineering wonders of the world.
- It is located over an earthquake fault.

COMMUNICATION ACTIVITIES

LESSON 8.3 EXERCISE 8A (P.81)

STUDENT A
International Space Station
- artificial satellite in space – travels around the Earth 15.7 times per day
- ninth inhabited space station
- largest artificial body in space
- can be seen from Earth
- first launched 1998
- crew conduct experiments in Biology, Physics, Astronomy and Meteorology
- multinational programme – joint programme between five space agencies (Japanese, Russian, Canadian, European and American)
- one of most significant examples of international cooperation in modern history

LESSON 8.4 EXERCISE 5A (P.83)

STUDENT A
Chairperson
You will chair the debate about supermarket growth. You need to make sure everyone speaks and to stop people dominating the discussion. You may need to clarify points.
- Begin by welcoming the audience at home to the programme.
- Introduce each of the participants, and who they represent.
- Introduce the topic, which tonight is 'Supermarket superpower? The continued growth of a supermarket giant'.

Ask the panel the following general questions to start the debate.
- Should Smithsons come to your country?
- What effect will its arrival have on the economy? / employment? / other retailers? / shopping habits?

Bring the debate to an end and thank the guests and the audience at home for watching.

LESSON 11.3 EXERCISE 7A (P.110)

STUDENT A
Make sentences from these prompts.
- Offer to take notes and photocopy them.
- Warn your partners not to be late for the cinema this evening.
- Insist on buying your partners a coffee.

LESSON 11.5 EXERCISE 7A (P.114)

STUDENT A

What is a subculture?

A subculture is a group of people with a particular set of beliefs, ideas and behaviour, which makes them different from a larger culture. They may be different due to their race, gender or ethnic background. Subcultures are often defined by their opposition to the values of the larger culture to which they belong, although not all writers agree on this. Members of a subculture will often show their membership through a distinctive and symbolic use of style and dress. Therefore, the study of a subculture often consists of the study of the clothing, music and other visible signs used by members of the subculture to identify it. In addition, the ways in which these same symbols are interpreted by members of the dominant culture are important. Provided that the subculture is characterised by a systematic opposition to the dominant culture, then it may be described as a counterculture.

It may be difficult to identify subcultures because their style (particularly clothing and music) may often be adopted by mass culture for commercial purposes, as business is always looking for opportunities to make money. This process of cultural absorption may result in the death or evolution and development of the subculture, as its members adopt new styles.

A common example is the punk subculture of the United Kingdom, whose distinctive (and initially shocking) anti-fashion style of clothing was swiftly adopted by mass-market fashion companies once the subculture became a media interest. Nevertheless, many subcultures do constantly evolve, as their members attempt to remain one step ahead of the dominant culture. This process provides a constant stream of styles and ideas which can be commercially adopted by the mainstream culture. This activity seems to stimulate rather than kill the development of youth cultures.

LESSON 12.4 EXERCISE 7A (P.123)

UNION REPRESENTATIVE A (SEWING MACHINES DEPARTMENT)
Listen to the presentation of the CEO. Then, present the concerns of the workers in your department. They are worried that:
- the new machines will result in huge job losses. This will have a bad effect on staff morale.
- younger workers will be brought in to work on the new machines.
- they will lose money while they are being trained to operate the new machines.
- they won't be able to operate the new machines efficiently.
- the machines will not be as efficient as the supplier claims.

Add any other concerns you think they may have.

LESSON 1.4 EXERCISE 6A (P.13)

COUNSELLOR B
Summary of your conversation with Paul.
Problems
- His flatmates do not understand his problems. Law students are very competitive. He must study hard in the evenings to keep up with the other students. He has no time to socialise.
- He does not like Martin. Martin's habit of putting notices everywhere about cleaning the flat annoy him. He thinks Martin is too 'bossy'.
- He thinks the flat is too untidy, but it's not his fault.

Solutions
- Flatmates should not play music in the sitting room after midnight.
- The other flatmates should talk to Martin and ask him to be more 'relaxed'.
- They should pay someone to clean the flat once a week.

Martin's communication style
- He is polite, but does not have time to talk much to his flatmates: 'I must focus on my studies this year. It's very important for me to do well.'

LESSON 2.3 EXERCISE 10A (P.21)

STUDENT B

The volcano on the Indonesian island of Krakatoa erupted in 1883 and killed over 36,000 people. Most of those who died were drowned by a tsunami caused by the eruption. It erupted with 13,000 times the power of the Hiroshima nuclear bomb. The sound of the explosion is thought to be one of the loudest on record. People as far away as the eastern coast of Africa and Western Australia reported hearing the explosion. A new island at the site was seen in 1927 and was called Anak (Child of) Krakatau. Anak Krakatau has erupted in most years since then.

LESSON 2.4 EXERCISE 5A (P.23)

STUDENT B: LOCAL RESIDENT 1
You are a local resident.
You are very much in favour of the wind farm.
You live in the area and own some of the land needed for the wind farm. You represent a number of farmers. You will receive money because the wind farm will be built on your land.
You think:
- wind farms are beautiful structures.
- the wind farm will attract visitors to the area. It will be the biggest in the country.
- the wind farm will provide cheap power for the local community.
- building the wind farm will create jobs for local people.
- the wind farm will attract international interest and publicity.

You want to know what the disadvantages of the wind farm would be.

LESSON 5.1 EXERCISE 11A (P.47)

STUDENT B
Read this quote from a car manufacturer. Discuss the points in it with your group.

'A lot of people talk about understanding why crashes happen and educating people to stop them happening, but I don't agree with that. It just isn't possible to change people's behaviour – put some people behind the steering wheel of a car and you've got an accident waiting to happen. A car is a dangerous machine for everyone – the driver, passengers in the car and other road users, I mean other drivers, cyclists and pedestrians. I'm a great believer in using technology to solve problems, and we can certainly make cars safer. For example, we can have automatic speed limiters in cars so that the driver can't go above, say, 100km per hour. You can get better computer systems – we're trying to look at a system where the car senses how close it is to other vehicles, and it increases the distance. Another possibility might be making cars softer with external airbags to protect people both inside and outside the car if there's a crash. So, you see, there are lots of options. Engineering is the way to solve this problem.'

COMMUNICATION ACTIVITIES

LESSON 5.2 EXERCISE 5 (P.48)
STUDENT B

B Recent technological advances have meant that driverless cars are no longer a thing of the distant future. The cars are already street-legal in a number of American states, and one day in the future, driverless cars may become compulsory. In the next few years, the driverless cars won't be able to drive more safely than human drivers. However, with the advantages of no distractions, no drinking, better reflexes and better awareness of other vehicles, automated driving may overtake human driving in the next two decades.

The cars drive at the speed limit it has stored on its maps and maintains its distance from other vehicles using its system of sensors.

Driverless cars could have a significant impact on reducing traffic accidents and save on wasted commuting time and energy. The designers say that the cars will dramatically reduce human error, the number one cause of accidents. However, if something goes wrong, it may go badly wrong and if a decision has to be made quickly, the car computer will have to make the call.

There are a number of driverless car projects (e.g. Mercedes Benz, Bosch, Nissan, Toyota and Audi), but the biggest project currently is the Google driverless car project led by engineer Sebastien Thurn, Director of the Stanford Artificial Intelligence Laboratory and co-inventor of Google Street View. Google claim that driverless cars could reduce the number of cars on the road by 90 percent.

LESSON 7.3 EXERCISE 10 (P.71)
STUDENT B
Read the information below and decide which points you think refer to the New Galata Bridge. Use the photo to help you. Then discuss with your partner the information you think refers to his/her bridge. Use the information to write a paragraph about the New Galata Bridge.

- Spans the Golden Horn in Istanbul.
- Designed by British architect Norman Foster and French bridge engineer Michel Virlogeux.
- It was built to clear traffic jams round the town.
- It is over 300 metres high – taller than the famous Eiffel Tower in Paris.
- Its total length is 2,460 metres. Width: 32 metres.
- It is made with concrete and steel pillars.
- It was finished in 1994.
- The bridge was described as 'delicate as a butterfly' by its architect.

LESSON 8.3 EXERCISE 8A (P.81)
STUDENT B
Antarctic Treaty
- began 1961
- regulates international relations for Antarctic
- sets aside area as scientific preserve
- encourages freedom of scientific investigation and cooperation
- area to be used for peaceful purposes only
- headquarters in Argentina
- first arms control agreement established during the Cold War
- frequent consultation meetings take place among member nations

LESSON 8.4 EXERCISE 5A (P.83)
STUDENT B: LABOUR RELATIONS EXPERT
You need to listen carefully to the chairperson and other guests. Ask them to clarify anything you are not sure about. You are worried about the following:
- low wages
- rival businesses closing and unemployment
- poor working conditions, e.g. no breaks, overtime, etc.
- anti-union policies
- high staff turnover

LESSON 10.4 EXERCISE 7A (P.103)

STUDENT B

To:	Professor Bright
Subject:	Bullying at work

Dear Professor Bright,

I really need your help and advice.

I'm 30. I've just got a 'dream' job working in the clothing department of a large store. I'm good at the job, but maybe I'm too good; it certainly hasn't made me popular. My problem is, the younger staff don't like me and make nasty comments about me. They say I need to lose weight, and they criticise the way I dress and talk.

The manager's no help. She'll do anything to be popular with her staff. So when I complained the staff were making fun of me, she just said, 'Can't you take a joke?'

A couple of weeks ago, she said my timekeeping was bad. What did she expect? I live a long way from the store, and also I'm depressed and not sleeping properly. I don't want to leave this job, Vanessa. I just wish they'd stop bullying me.

How can I deal with this situation, Professor Bright?

To:	Professor Bright
Subject:	An adopted child

Dear Professor Bright,

I hope you can help me with my problem.

I got married when I was young, much too young. We didn't last very long, but, unfortunately, when we split up, we had just had a little baby boy. We didn't have much money at the time and neither of us had a job. Life was really hard, so we decided to have the baby adopted. That was 18 years ago.

Recently, I got a letter from my biological son. He said he'd often thought about his birth parents and wanted to meet us. I can't tell you how shocked and upset I was. It was so hard to give up my child for adoption. I've felt so guilty over the years.

Professor Bright, I don't want to upset my son's adoptive parents by meeting him. I'm sure they're very hurt because he wants to get in contact with me. Anyway, he won't be very impressed when he sees me. I live in a small apartment with my two children. We don't have much money – I live on welfare payments – but we're happy. My sons don't know they have another brother – the news will be a big shock for them.

I don't feel I'm strong enough, emotionally, to meet my adopted son. What do you think I should do, Professor Bright?

LESSON 11.3 EXERCISE 7A (P.110)

STUDENT B
Make sentences from these prompts.
- Invite your partners to dinner on Saturday evening.
- Apologise for interrupting too much.
- Refuse to share your sandwiches with your partners.

LESSON 11.5 EXERCISE 7A (P.114)

STUDENT B

What is youth culture?

With the development of post-World War II affluence and the subsequent baby boom in the United States and Europe, young people began to gain considerable influence and buying power. Throughout the 1950s, the growing numbers of young people in the USA and Europe began to greatly influence music, television and cinema, spurring the explosion of rock and roll in the late 1950s and a full-blown youth culture by the mid-1960s. Examples of the new youth cultures included mods, rockers and hippies. As teenagers and adolescents created their own identity and their disposable income increased, marketing companies focused their efforts on this emerging subset of society. Given this commercialisation, it is perhaps surprising that this activity did not kill off youth cultures. On the contrary, in the 70s and 80s, new youth cultures from the UK such as punk and goth developed and travelled around the world.

The tastes of young people began to drive fashion, music, films and literature. Corporations and businesses quickly took note and adapted to the shift by devising new marketing strategies. For young people, being more open to change and challenge, technology came more easily and their fashions changed more quickly than their adult counterparts. Baby boomers began to enter the workforce in the 1970s, and thereby had even greater influence, helping to innovate the computer revolution. Their children similarly provided the next generation of youth cultures. In the 90s and beyond, grunge style and hip-hop culture from America became popular around the world. Despite the fact that we live in an age of instant communication, it is still very difficult to predict what the next youth culture to sweep the world will be.

COMMUNICATION ACTIVITIES

LESSON 12.1 EXERCISE 8 (P.117)
STUDENT B

Call waiting

Vista del telefono trasmettitore Meucci.
(Dalla El. Rew.)

ANTONIO MEUCCI was an Italian inventor living in New York. In 1860, he demonstrated a device he called the teletrofono, for electronic voice communication. He had a description of it printed in New York's Italian newspaper. Between 1856 and 1870, he developed more than 30 different prototype telephones. He filed a caveat (a kind of intermediate patent) in 1871, a full five years before Alexander Graham Bell. After being injured in an accident, Meucci became ill and was unable to work so he did not have enough money to renew his caveat in 1874. When Bell registered his own patent in 1876, Meucci sued, but died before the case was finished. Bell won and was credited with the invention of the telephone. Finally, in 2002, the US House of Representatives passed a resolution that 'the life and achievements of Antonio Meucci should be recognised, and his work in the invention of the telephone should be acknowledged.'

LESSON 12.3 EXERCISE 12 (P.121)
GROUP A
Work out and note down all possible arguments to support the motion and include defences against points that might be brought up by the opposition. Decide who will say what, and in what order. Think of your own ideas but the following may help.
- People learn new skills.
- There are more advances in medical treatment.
- Housework is more convenient.
- Communication is easier.
- Modern technology can lead to future improvements in pollution.
- Most people have a higher standard of living than 20 years ago.

LESSON 12.3 EXERCISE 12 (P.121)
GROUP B
Work out and note down all possible arguments to oppose the motion and include defences against points that might be brought up by the opposition. Decide who will say what, and in what order. Think of your own ideas, but the following may help.
- People lose their jobs.
- People basically do not like change.
- Medical advances only help the rich.
- Modern technology has led to more pollution.
- Children cannot communicate as well as they could before.
- People may be richer, but they are not happier.

LESSON 12.4 EXERCISE 7A (P.123)
UNION REPRESENTATIVE B (CUTTING MACHINES AND DESIGN DEPARTMENTS)
Listen to the presentation of Union representative A, then present the concerns of the workers in your departments.
They are worried that:
- the older workers will lose their jobs.
- the company won't be able to afford to give good compensation if they lose their jobs.
- the company will not help them to find new jobs if they are made redundant.
- the company does not need to spend money on new machines. They expect economic conditions to improve soon.
- the company has made the wrong decision. The company doesn't have a production problem.

Add any other concerns you think they may have.

LESSON 1.4 EXERCISE 6A (P.13)

COUNSELLOR C
Summary of your conversation with Stewart.
Problems
- He wants to live cheaply and save money for his trips to Asia during the holidays.
- He would like to be more friendly with Paul as he likes and respects him.
- He does not know how to make friends with Paul. Paul is always so busy.
- He wants his friend, Tom, to stay in the flat until Tom gets a job.

Solutions
- He prefers to buy his own food and eat as little as possible.
- He will ask the other flatmates to be more understanding about Tom's situation.

Martin's communication style
- He does not communicate well with the other flatmates: 'I'm not a very confident person, that's my problem.'

LESSON 2.3 EXERCISE 10A (P.21)

STUDENT C

Eyjafjallajökull ('Ey-ya-fyah-dlah-yeuh-cudl'), whose name means 'Island Mountain Glacier' in Icelandic, erupted in the Spring of 2010. Although it was relatively small for a volcanic eruption, the eruption caused great inconvenience to the airline industry and passengers. The volcano ejected around 250 million tons of ash into the atmosphere. Air traffic in Europe was shut down because of concerns about the huge amount of ash in the sky. Many passengers in Europe were stranded. The shutdown lasted for a week and cost the airline industry more than $1 billion. 'Volcano tourism' quickly sprang up after the eruption, with local tour companies offering day trips to see the volcano.

LESSON 2.4 EXERCISE 5A (P. 23)

STUDENT C: LOCAL RESIDENT 2
You are a local resident.
You are completely opposed to the wind farm.
You live in the local area and run a hotel. The area is popular with tourists who want relaxing walking holidays.
You think:
- the wind farm will damage the tourist industry and affect local property prices.
- the machinery used creates a lot of noise pollution and wind farms are not as efficient as other ways of producing electricity.
- wind farms are ugly and ruin the landscape.
- the flashing lights on the towers and the shadows from the blades will disturb and upset people.
- it will take five years to build the wind farm. There are bound to be traffic problems.

You want to know what the disadvantages of the wind farm would be.

LESSON 5.1 EXERCISE 11A (P.47)

STUDENT C
Read this quote from the head of a traffic police unit. Discuss the points in it with your group.

> 'I obviously think that we can help to solve the problem of deaths and injuries on the road by changing the law. Sure, you can make cars safer, and you can educate people, but I think the only way to make a difference is to hit people where it hurts – fine them or take away their licence. So, I think we should have tougher penalties for drivers who break the law, so maybe they should automatically lose their licence for a year for speeding, or they should be given a really large fine for driving carelessly, something like that. Of course, we can try to change the way drivers behave by having lower speed limits and using more speed cameras. We could then use the money we get from the fines for more road safety classes, and advanced driving courses. But you've got to make people see that breaking the law when they drive is very serious.'

LESSON 8.4 EXERCISE 5A (P.83)

STUDENT C: GOVERNMENT REPRESENTATIVE
You need to listen carefully to the chairperson and other guests. Ask them to clarify anything you are not sure about. You also need to make the following points. You think Smithsons will bring the following benefits:
- an overall benefit to the economy
- lots of new jobs (it's a big employer)
- improvement in the environment in some areas through Smithsons' community work
- increased competition, which will encourage other retailers to do better
- up-to-date retail methods

LESSON 11.3 EXERCISE 7A (P.110)

STUDENT C
Make sentences from these prompts.
- Admit making a lot of mistakes in your life.
- Tell your partners to phone you at the weekend with any news.
- Encourage them to buy some designer clothes.

LESSON 12.1 EXERCISE 8 (P.117)

STUDENT C

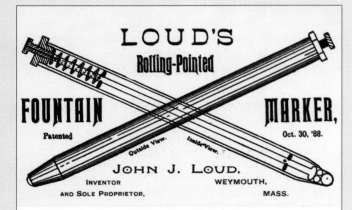

The write man

The problems of writing with a pen and ink were that they often leaked and the ink was slow to dry on the page. John J. Loud, an American leather tanner, recognised this problem and invented a new gadget for writing – a pen with a small rotating ball instead of a nib. He patented his invention on 30 October 1888. Although it still leaked, it could be used to mark rough surfaces such as leather. Loud, however, failed to exploit his patent commercially and it was left to the Hungarian Lazlo Biro, working with his brother, to patent the ballpoint pen between 1938 and 1943. Biro later licensed his pen to the Frenchman Marcel Bich, who called his company Bic. This is today the market leader in ballpoint pens. The company sells 15 million Bic Cristal pens per day.

LESSON 12.4 EXERCISE 7A (P.123)

CHIEF EXECUTIVE OFFICER (CEO)
Present the case for introducing the new machines. Your Production manager will add arguments when you finish. Then listen to the union representatives and lead the discussion on how to deal with the workers' concerns. Here are some ideas for your presentation. Add any information you wish.
The new machines will:
- reduce costs and increase workers' productivity.
- motivate workers because they'll produce more goods and make more money.
- help the company to compete against cheap imported clothing.
- enable workers to produce a wider range of products.
- make the production line more flexible. It will be able to respond more quickly to changes in fashion.

LESSON 12.4 EXERCISE 7A (P.123)

PRODUCTION MANAGER
Support your CEO by adding arguments at the end of his/her presentation.
Additional arguments: The new machines will:
- help the design department to produce more exciting designs.
- enable the company to make more expensive clothing.
- improve the quality of the clothes.
- result in a quicker delivery to customers because they will produce goods faster than the previous ones.
- be cheaper to run because they will need less maintenance.

LESSON 1.4 EXERCISE 6A (P.13)

COUNSELLOR D
Summary of your conversation with Carlos.
Problems
- His personality is different from the others. He's very sociable and extrovert. He wants to enjoy his time at university as well as study hard.
- He has problems with all three housemates. Stewart is not friendly. Carlos invited him to go to a Brazilian disco. 'Sorry, I don't have enough money,' Stewart answered. Paul is boring. 'He's always studying, never having any fun.' Martin is friendly and sociable, but too 'bossy' and puts up notices everywhere telling flatmates how to behave properly.
- Carlos loves Brazilian music and is unhappy he can't play it in the evening.

Solutions
- All the housemates should go out for a meal together once a week.
- Talk to Paul and explain that he's spending too much time studying.
- Ask Martin to be more relaxed and less 'bossy'.

LESSON 2.4 EXERCISE 5A (P.23)

STUDENT D: WILDLIFE GROUP REPRESENTATIVE
You are a wildlife group representative.
You are very hostile to the wind farm.
You are a member of a radical wildlife group Flora and Fauna Protection (FFP). You are strongly against the building of wind farms in areas of natural beauty.
You think:
- wind farms are dangerous to all wildlife.
- birds and bats are often killed when they fly into the blades of wind turbines.
- the habitat of many birds, animals and plants will be destroyed during the building of the farm.
- the proposed site is home to several rare species of butterfly.
- the area currently attracts a large number of scientists and naturalists who study the wildlife of the area.
- wind farms are an expensive and wasteful way of producing electricity.

You want to know what the advantages of wind farms are.

LESSON 8.4 EXERCISE 5A (P.83)

STUDENT D: OPPOSITION PARTY REPRESENTATIVE
You need to listen carefully to the chairperson and other guests. Ask them to clarify anything you are not sure about. You also need to make the following points.
You think Smithsons will have the following negative effects:
- be bad for the economy
- destroy jobs and small businesses
- use foreign suppliers, which is bad for local suppliers
- cause damage to the environment

LESSON 2.4 EXERCISE 5A (P.13)

STUDENT E: GOVERNMENT REPRESENTATIVE
You are a government representative.
You are a government minister in the Energy Department. You will welcome people to the meeting and lead the meeting.
You think:
- wind farms are a good idea and building new ones is a government policy.
- it is important, however, to listen to the opinions of local people. There is an election next year and you do not want to upset too many potential voters. As Sparrow Hill would be a very big wind farm it is important to make the right decision.

You want to know what the feelings of local people about the proposed wind farm are.

LESSON 8.4 EXERCISE 5A (P.83)

STUDENT E: CONSUMER GROUP REPRESENTATIVE
You need to listen carefully to the chairperson and other guests. Ask them to clarify anything you are not sure about. You also need to make the following points.
You think Smithsons will:
- benefit the consumer by lowering prices, which is good for poorer sections of society.
- give consumers a greater range of products at affordable prices.
- bring general improvement in quality.
- provide more international and up-to-date products.

SUPPLEMENTARY INFORMATION
LESSON 3.4 EXERCISE 7A (P. 33)

Lionel Messi, Argentinian footballer

- Born Rosario, Argentina, 1987. Moved to Spain at the age of 13 when Barcelona FC agreed to pay for his expensive medical treatment. Was suffering a lack of hormones which limited his growth.
- Considered to be the best footballer in the world and one of the greatest players in the history of the game.
- Became a star of the Barcelona team and Argentina national team. Set many records for goal scoring, helping his team to national and international championships.
- First footballer to win four FIFA Ballon d'Or awards.
- Made history by becoming the first player to score five goals in a Champions League match. Most goals in a calendar year (2012), beating the record of German footballer Gerd Müller, which had stood for 40 years.
- Playing style: a fast, attacking style. Quicker with the ball at his feet than any other footballer. Able to change direction rapidly.
- Diego Maradona, a famous Argentinian player, says about Messi, 'I see him as very similar to me,' he told the BBC, 'he's a leader and is offering lessons in beautiful football.'

Ye Shiwen, Chinese swimmer

- Born Hangzou, China, 1996
- She has performed exceptionally well in World Championships and the Olympic Games at a very young age (16).
- Gold medals in the 200 and 400 metres medley in the London Olympic Games in 2012. In the 400 metres race, she was five seconds faster than her previous best time. Swam the last 50 metres of the race faster than the men's winner Ryan Lochte. Set a World record in the 400 metres race and an Olympic record in the 200 metres.
- Started swimming aged six. Teacher noticed she had very big feet and hands – good for swimming.
- Was a member of the Chinese national team at age 12.
- Very tough training in China, financed by the Chinese Government. Had little contact with her parents between the age of 11–14 when training. Her mother said, 'I missed her a lot. We were allowed to see her only once a week ... But of course, it was all worthwhile. We are very proud of her.'
- Her father talked about the family's sacrifices in an interview, 'Chinese people believe that we have to give in order to earn. Give time and effort.'

Roger Federer, Professional tennis player

- Born Basel, Switzerland, 1981
- Considered by many experts to be the greatest player of all time.
- Holds many records.
- First Swiss man to win a Grand Slam title.
- Men's record for appearing in 24 Grand Slam titles.
- Won 17 Grand Slam titles.
- Only player to reach eight finals in the Wimbledon Tennis Tournament.
- Won Wimbledon seven times, equalling the record of Pete Sampras.
- Has also won five US Open titles.
- Has won every Grand Slam championship, including the French Open.
- Very sporting player. Won Sportsmanship award (voted by players) four times.
- A South African opinion poll voted him the second most trusted and respected person in the world, after Nelson Mandela.
- Style: versatile, creative, powerful play. Can play every shot in the book, and wins on all court surfaces – clay, grass and hard courts. McEnroe says, 'Federer's forehand is the greatest shot in tennis.'
- Set up the Federer Foundation in 2003. Helps young people in poor countries to take part in educational and sports projects.

Jessica Ennis-Hill, British field and track athlete

- Born in Sheffield, England, 1986.
- Had a perfect technique for hurdling by the age of 10. Won the National Schools Championships at the age of 14.
- Became interested in the heptathlon, which combines the high jump, long jump, shot put, javelin, 100-metre hurdles, 200-metre and 800-metre races. While training, went to Sheffield University and graduated in Psychology (2007).
- In 2008, had a bad ankle injury. Missed 2008 Beijing Olympics. Had a one-year break from competition.
- In 2009, won the world championships in the heptathlon and the world indoor pentathlon the following year.
- Competed in London Olympic Games in 2012. Great pressure because she was the 'Face of the Olympics'. Her image was on billboards and in the media everywhere – hopes of the nation were on her. Her first race was the 100 metres hurdles. She won easily and set a British record of 12.69 seconds.
- She was put forward as a role model for young students at a Californian high school. The presenter said to the students, 'Jessica Ennis as an international track star ... Last year, she took gold at the World Championships. Jessica Ennis is arguably the world's greatest female athlete. This young woman can fly and throw and jump. She's Wonder Woman.'

Lesson 4.1 EXERCISE 7A (P.37)

X-RAYS

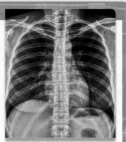

X-rays are images which are used to diagnose disease. They were discovered by Wilhelm Röntgen, a German scientist working in Munich, in 1895. He was working on a cathode ray tube* developed by one of his colleagues, when he noticed that it was projecting a green light on the wall. Strangely, the light was passing through some materials, including paper, wood and books. As he experimented by placing other materials in the way, he noticed that the outline of the bones in his hand was projected onto the wall. In the following weeks he continued to investigate the new rays, which he temporarily called 'X-rays'. Two months later, he published his paper 'On a new kind of X-rays', and in 1901 he was awarded the first Nobel Prize in Physics. Although the new rays would eventually be known as Röntgen rays, he always preferred the term X-rays. Today, Röntgen is considered the father of Diagnostic Radiology, a medical speciality using images to diagnose disease. Nowadays, radiologists can examine all areas of the body for different types of disease.

*A cathode ray tube is a piece of equipment which can produce an image on a screen, as in a television.

PENICILLIN

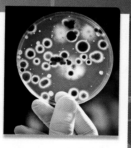

This was the first effective antibiotic. It was discovered by Alexander Fleming, who was a brilliant medical researcher at St Mary's Hospital, London. He was also careless and his laboratory was often untidy. In 1928, after returning from holiday, he noticed a glass dish that had some mould growing on it. His analysis of this and its effect on the bacteria in the dish led to the discovery of penicillin. This paved the way for the treatment of infectious disease. Fleming published his findings in 1929, but little attention was paid to them. He continued his research, but found it was difficult to grow penicillin mould and even more difficult to refine it.

Fleming shared the 1945 Nobel Prize in Physiology or Medicine with Ernst Chain, who worked out how to isolate and concentrate penicillin. Howard Florey also shared the prize for his work on mass producing penicillin. Fleming's accidental discovery marks the start of modern antibiotics. It is estimated that penicillin has saved nearly 200 million lives.

LESSON 4.4 EXERCISE 4A (P.43)

1 The clean-desk policy

RXZ has a clean-desk policy. This means that staff must not leave documents on their desk or on their computer screen when they leave work at the end of the day. A worker in the Research Department rushed away from her desk after receiving a call that her daughter had been taken ill at nursery. Very upset, she left immediately, leaving highly confidential research results on her screen overnight. She is a good researcher, very experienced at processing and analysing data. What action should the management take?

2 Gifts to doctors: a conflict of interest?

Up to now, RXZ has been giving expensive gifts to doctors who prescribe the company's brands, attend conferences run by the company or who give talks about RXZ's new and current drugs. For example, doctors who have been particularly loyal to the company's brands are sometimes given a week's cruise with their family on the Mediterranean. Many big pharmaceutical companies do the same thing. RXZ have learned that a newspaper is going to do an in-depth, critical article on the gifts that pharmaceutical companies make to doctors. Should RXZ introduce a policy of not giving gifts to doctors?

3 Negative results from trialling a new drug

RXZ's Research Department have been developing a promising new drug to treat obesity. But a recent series of tests have shown that it could have dangerous side effects for just a few patients. The company has invested millions of euros in the product and they are confident it will be a very profitable drug for years to come. They do not have many exciting drugs in the pipeline at present, so this drug is very important for the company's future. Should they ignore the side effects and not reveal the results of the trial?

4 Moving research overseas

RXZ have had a policy of testing new drugs and gathering data about them in European countries. The Head of Research and Development has proposed that, in future, they should test new products as much as possible in developing and emerging countries. It is easier and cheaper to get people to trial products in these countries, and also there is less red tape and bureaucratic obstacles. Many people in these countries are eager to take part in trials because this may be the only way for some of them to get the medicine they need. Should RXZ trial most of its drugs overseas in future?

5 Money or morality?

A group of young researchers in the company have been working on a drug that could be effective in treating a devastating disease that is common in some African countries. The company will need to invest a great deal of money to bring the drug to the market, and, when they do, they will never get a return on their investment. They are currently developing a new drug for diabetes which needs a lot more investment. If they can bring it to the market, it will have a big impact on their profits. Should they stop developing the drug for Africa and focus on the new drug for diabetes?

LESSON 4.5 EXERCISE 13 (P.45)

Herbal medicines

Information sources
Articles from well-known medical journals

Facts

- use plant extracts for remedies/medicines
- herbs have been used for thousands of years – ancient remedy
- three types of medicines: Western, Chinese, Indian
- safety: users need to take care – side effects from some herbs, also, they can interact badly with other drugs

Summary
Some herbal medicines have a harmful effect on the body.

But many benefits from herbs, as well.

Recommendations

- must be used with great care – get advice from a herbalist
- absolutely essential to tell your doctor if you are using herbal medicine
- make sure the herbal remedy is the correct product for you
- good idea for a herbalist to make a remedy specially for you
- don't believe all the claims you read on the packaging of a herbal product

LESSON 5.5 EXERCISE 7 (P.55)

Cargo Traffic at International Airports 2012 Numbers refer to freight in metric tonnes; 30 airports are included in the ranking.					
Rank	Airport	Location	Total cargo	Rank change	% change
1	Hong Kong International	Chek Lap Kok, Hong Kong	4,066,738		2.3%
3	Shanghai Pudong International	Pudong, Shanghai, China	2,938,157		-4.77%
4	Incheon International	Incheon, Seoul National Capital Area, South Korea	2,456,724	1	3.3%
5	Ted Stevens Anchorage International	Anchorage, Alaska, United States	2,463,696	1	-3.1%
9	Frankfurt	Frankfurt, Hesse, Germany	2,066,300	2	6.7%
13	Beijing Capital International	Chaoyang, Beijing, China	1,799,864	1	10%
16	London Heathrow	Hillingdon, London, UK	1,556,154		-0.9%

LESSON 9.3 EXERCISE 5B (P.90)

The table below shows the order of most adjectives before a noun.
(We don't usually use more than about three adjectives before a noun.)

Adjectives								Noun
Opinion	Size	Shape	Most other qualities	Age	Colour/ Pattern	Nationality	Material	Function/Class
beautiful				antique	colourful	Japanese	silk	paintings
	huge		well-known		dark		bronze	sculpture
			famous					art schools
			stainless				steel	plates
	enormous						metal	figure
	huge	fully-extended						wings
	small				brown		clay	figurines
			rich, aristocratic					family

LESSON 10.3 EXERCISE 1A (P.100)

A case where psychological profiling would have been difficult was that of Harold Shipman. He appeared to be a caring, well-respected doctor. Actually, he was an arrogant drug addict and mass murderer who killed approximately 236 people between 1971 and 1998. The people he killed were his elderly patients, so their deaths did not at first seem too suspicious. He was tried and imprisoned, but he hanged himself in prison in January 2004. A possible reason for his crimes was this: Shipman was devoted to his mother, Vera, who became ill with lung cancer when Shipman was very young. The family doctor injected Vera with morphine and she died aged 43. Shipman was only 17 years old.

LESSON 10.5 EXERCISE 8B (P.105)

In many parts of the world, it is becoming more common for parents to have only one child. An obvious reason for this is that people are tending to marry at a later age than they did some years ago. This is an important **area of discussion because some people think that being an only child is a big disadvantage in life.** Others take a different view. This essay discusses the arguments and considers whether, on balance, it is truly an advantage to be the only child in a family.

A major advantage of being an only child is that the child gets more attention and financial support from his or her parents. They will help the child with his or her homework, so that the child achieves above-average results at school. **In addition, because the only child is the sole focus of the parents' love, he or she develops more confidence and becomes more mature at an early age. Another advantage of being an only child is that they are on their own a lot more.** As a result, they learn how to occupy themselves and to become more independent than other children. They are also more able to cope with feelings of loneliness.

On the other hand, **some people argue that only children miss out on brother and sister relationships as they do not have siblings to share their joys and sorrows.** It is said that children who have siblings are less selfish and learn at an early age how to get on with other people – an important life skill. **Even though this is probably true, it is a fact that brothers and sisters often quarrel a lot.** Only children may well have quieter and more peaceful childhoods.

A recent study of China's one-child policy supports the view that there are disadvantages to being an only child. The study was published in *Science* by Professor Lisa Cameron and colleagues from Australian universities. It investigated the impact of one-child families in China. **The researchers compared the behaviour of Chinese people born before and after the one-child policy was adopted.** Their results showed that children born after the one-child policy, in other words 'only children', had certain characteristics. They were less willing to take risks, less conscientious, less trustworthy and more pessimistic. According to Professor Cameron, the amount of contact that subjects had with other children, such as their peers, did not affect the results of the study. **While this research seems to confirm that only children in China are at a disadvantage, this may not be the case in other countries.** The results, therefore, are not conclusive.

On the whole, in spite of the research on only children in China, evidence seems to suggest that it is an advantage to be an only child. However, the key point, surely, is that a child has the love and support of his or her parents. **This is the most important influence which will determine a child's development, happiness and future success in life.**

LESSON 11.3 EXERCISE 12 (P.111)

A Local cultures reflect ordinary people's feelings of appropriateness, comfort and correctness. Given the strength of local cultures, it is hard to argue that one global culture exists.

B Look, everyone's basically the same. I mean, at work nearly everyone wears the standard man's business suit with a coloured tie and a buttoned shirt. It's worn just about everywhere.

C Those who deny the importance of cultural diversity may refer to the universal business suit. But local variations have appeared. Iranian parliamentarians do not wear ties and Saudi diplomats alternate the business suit with traditional robes.

D You can see that most hotels in the world have become standardised. I mean, they now have western-style beds, toilets and showers. A lot of them have fitness centres and restaurants. They all fit a sort of global standard.

E The Davos group is an elite group of highly educated people operating in finance, media and diplomacy. They share common beliefs about individualism and market economy. However, they are too small a group to count as a coherent cultural system.

LESSON 1.1 RECORDING 1.1

1 Well, I have two phones, which I'm always checking for messages, but actually I love getting and making calls. It's just more personal than texting. I like hearing people's voices. I find there can be a lot of misunderstandings with SMS and messaging apps, even if you use emoticons. I guess I'm addicted to my phones. They are the last thing I check before I go to sleep and the first thing I look at in the morning!

2 I do use social media at the university for making arrangements with my classmates, but I tend to send a lot of SMS messages as well. I also like to use Facebook to keep track of all my friends around the world. It's funny, last month someone got in touch with me who I met on holiday two years ago. It was completely out of the blue and it was quite a surprise after all this time, but they tracked me down on Facebook. I also follow a few celebrities on social media. I think it's funny, but I know a lot of people think it's stupid.

3 I'm a big fan of social media, and I have my own blog, but I do send people real cards for birthdays and at Christmas. I really don't like those electronic greeting cards. They are so impersonal. A funny thing happened to me last year. I had lost touch with one of my friends from school, but I bumped into them by chance when I was shopping in Paris. We stay in contact by using one of the various messaging apps. They're really great.

4 I keep track of all my friends on Facebook. I also tend to Skype a lot as I'm a student studying abroad. I Skype with my family at least once a week. I can catch up with all the news from home. Sometimes the connection isn't very good though, which can make it difficult. Also, the time difference can cause problems, if I wake people up!

5 I'm afraid I'm a bit unusual, as I don't use a mobile phone. I mean, I have one but it's only for emergencies. No one knows the number. I'm not a technophobe, I just don't like phones. I tend to stay in touch with people by email, but really I prefer to speak to people face to face. I think technology sometimes gets in the way of real communication, but I suppose I'm a bit old fashioned. I mean I still send real Christmas cards to people through the post – snail mail I think it's called, ha, ha!

LESSON 1.3 RECORDING 1.2

1 Welcome to today's call in programme. As some of you may know, Deborah Tannen is most famous for her books *Talking from 9 to 5*, about women and men at work and *You Just Don't Understand*, about women and men in conversation. She has recently written a book about how sisters communicate called *You Were Always Mom's Favorite*. However, in today's programme we're focusing on an essay she has recently written for the *New York Times* about interrupting called 'Would You Please Let Me Finish', and I think a number of politicians might like to read it.

I'll just give a quick summary of what Professor Tannen thinks and then I'll take some calls. A lot of Professor Tannen's research has focused on the fact that conversation styles can vary greatly because of different factors – for example, your age, your gender, your culture. In this article she concentrates on the issue of interrupting, and how different ideas on what interrupting is and when it is good and bad can also vary greatly depending on gender, culture and so on. To back Tannen up, some recent surveys have shown that, surprise surprise, women tend to be interrupted more than men and that women who interrupt others are seen more negatively than men who do the same thing. However, it has also been found that there are more interruptions overall in conversations when all the people involved are women. Although these interruptions are often seen as 'talking along' with each other, rather than 'talking over' each other. OK, I'll take the first caller.

2 R = Rie, M =May

R: I've just made a nice pot of tea, May. Would you like a cup?

M: Oh, yes please.

R: How are you feeling at the moment? You said on the phone yesterday that it's been a bit rough recently.

M: I don't want to bore you, but the last few months have been terrible, Rie.

R: I'm sorry to hear that.

M: We've been married for nearly five years but it has all gone wrong. We've had so many arguments recently and he has moved out.

R: Oh, when did he leave?

M: This evening. He phoned me from a café at 5 p.m. and asked me to meet him there after work to talk about our problems. But by the time I arrived at the café he had left.

R: I'm sorry to hear that.

M: It was alright until he found out that I had booked a vacation with all the girls.

R: Well, you went on vacation every year with the girls before you got married.

M: Exactly. He's so controlling and it's my money. I should have known that it wouldn't have worked. And his mother hates me. When he introduced me to her, I knew I had seen her somewhere before. She had been a classmate of my mum and they had never been friends.

R: Oh, that's not good.

M: And we … we just don't do things together anymore. I've always been a sociable person but he just doesn't like going out with me. And when we do go out in a group, he always dominates the conversation and shows off. He thinks he knows everything and he's so insensitive. He interrupts me all the time in a group but when it's just the two of us he doesn't talk and doesn't listen. And he just won't talk about our relationship.

LESSON 1.4 RECORDING 1.3

C = Carol, J =Jean

C: I saw Marco in your office again this morning, Jean.

J: Yeah, it was the usual thing, he needs money. He shares a flat with two other students, as you know, and the problem is, he's been spending too much money once again – he can't pay this month's rent. The others aren't happy because they'll have to pay more than usual to stay in the flat.

C: Mmm, well, the way to sort it out, surely, is to tell him to get a loan from the Student Union.

J: I'm not sure it's the right thing to do, Carol. The trouble is, it's the third time he's run out of money. It's always the same story. He spends too much, can't pay the rent and then gets a loan from friends or the Student Union.

C: Mmm, he's not very good at managing his money, is he? He can't go on like that. You know, one way of dealing with this could be to look at his weekly expenses. Then work out a budget and tell him he's got to stick to it.

J: Mmm, good idea. I'll be seeing him again tomorrow, I'll suggest that. I've already advised him to contact his bank to pay for his rent by direct debit. That way, his rent will always be paid regularly.

C: Was he OK about that?

J: Yes, he thought it was a good idea. But unfortunately, he has another financial problem. You see, they have a lot of parties in his flat and during one of them, they broke an expensive lamp. The owner of the flat wants to charge them to replace it. Marco doesn't have the money to pay his share of the cost.

C: So, what are we going to do to help him?

J: It's not going to be easy, Carol, he's in a difficult situation. He doesn't have a lot of money for his everyday expenses, so he works part-time, quite long hours, to pay for his studies. But when he gets money, he likes to spend it. I told him I'd talk to you and we'd sort something out for him. What do you think?

C: Well, there's an obvious solution. We could talk to the owner of the flat and ask her to give Marco more time to pay for his share of the lamp. You know the owner, she's a reasonable person, I'm sure she'll be understanding.

J: Right. That makes sense to me. You know, if Marco sticks to his weekly budget and pays his rent by direct debit, we may not see him here so often.

C: Let's hope so.

LESSON 1.5 VIDEO RECORDING 1.1

James Hammond

Good evening everyone.

Did you know that in many surveys the worst phobia for many people is public speaking? Not spiders or rats or heights, but having to face an audience and talk to them.

How do people react when put in this situation? Well, there are a number of things which happen to our bodies when we are put in stressful situations, and making a speech is no different. Basically, your body goes into the classic 'fight or flight' response. In other words, your hands may sweat and your mouth may go dry. Your heart may beat faster and you may start feeling sick. You may sound strained – for instance, the audience will probably notice that you are speaking fast and that your voice is weak and with a higher pitch than normal. You will want to rush to the end of the talk and may even ignore the audience. There is a strong feeling of wanting to run away.

But making a speech to a group of people is in fact a great opportunity to impress them and really show what you can do, so why do so many people have a phobia about it?

Well, there are several reasons. Firstly, people feel they'll make mistakes and lose their way. Secondly, the speaker may fear that the audience won't like them personally. And finally, they may worry that the audience will not like or really understand what they're trying to say. All of these fears create a sense of looking a fool in front of other people, which is the main reason for all our worries and fears – no one wants to look a fool.

Now this response is more than just nerves. That's normal, and it would be strange not to feel nervous. Nerves will keep you alert and stop you feeling too relaxed. If controlled well, nerves can make the difference between an average speech and one which keeps people listening and wanting to hear more.

LESSON 1.5 VIDEO RECORDING 1.2

James Hammond

So how can we control our nerves and become more confident about making a speech? Well, the most important thing is to get your nerves to work for you rather than against you.

I intend to discuss a number of things you can do to help. First of all, I can say that rehearsal is essential. Nerves are caused by fear and being unfamiliar with things, so take time to practise your speech to feel comfortable with what you're going to say. Secondly, it's a good idea to know your introduction by heart. You'll feel most nervous at the beginning and may stumble over words. If you learn the beginning, this will become second nature and help you get into the main part of the speech more comfortably. Another good thing to do is begin with some kind of interest hook, such as an anecdote, or diagram or photo. This will engage the audience and help you get over the beginning of the speech. Take some deep breaths before you start. This'll help control your nerves. Breathe in slowly, count to three and then breathe out slowly. Finally, remember, you will always be more nervous than you look. You can 'trick' your mind in a few simple ways to help you – try and look confident and you'll become more confident. Stand in a relaxed way, hold your head up and smile. Look happy and enthusiastic, even if you're not!

One other thing is to focus on something other than yourself. Pay attention to the environment you're in to distract yourself. Notice the audience. For example, how are they dressed? Who's wearing glasses? Who's the most attractive? All of this will help to trick your mind into not noticing the situation you're in. The less you concentrate on how you're feeling, the more confident you'll become.

You should use plenty of eye contact, change the pace of your delivery, change the volume of your voice, and perhaps move around a bit. Don't worry too much about mistakes. A few mistakes are all right, they show the audience you're human. One way you can really engage with your audience is humour – tell a joke! If you aren't good at jokes, tell a story, or draw on your personal experience to connect with your audience.

The main rule about public speaking is that there are no rules! This seems a strange thing to say, but it's true – everyone is an individual and so you have to find what works for you in terms of delivering a speech. The most important thing is to control your nerves, build your confidence and learn to enjoy it!

LESSON 2.1 RECORDING 2.1

1   Well, I live in a detached house in a suburb of a major city. Mmm, what do I like about it? Mmm, well, for a start it's a friendly neighbourhood. I also like the access to all the facilities and shops, but what I really like is the fact that my local area is very green – you know, lots of parks and open spaces for the kids. The public transport connections are very good too, so I can be in the city centre in a very short time if I avoid the rush hour. So I guess you could say I have the best of both worlds! I suppose it's what people call a 'desirable area'. The only real problem, I think, is the mindless vandalism that goes on, you know, damage to cars and bus stops, which we all have to pay for in the end. It's bored young people with nothing to do. I suppose it's the price you pay for living in a city.

2   I live in a farm cottage on the edge of a very small village, almost a hamlet really, in the countryside. It really is very rural – about 25 kilometres to the nearest town. It's the peace and quiet I like really, and the fresh air. There aren't many vehicles on the roads – so no traffic congestion … the air's very clean, and there's very little noise and light pollution. The whole pace of life is much slower – no one rushes anywhere. Oh yes, and the fantastic views. The beautiful natural environment with the hills means I'm surrounded by magnificent scenery. There's a bit of trouble with a wind farm which could spoil it for some people, but I guess renewable energy is the future. The main environmental issue we have at the moment is abandoned cars. People are dumping old cars they don't want any more in the village at night. We then have to wait for ages before they're taken away.

3   I live in an apartment block in the city centre. It's the cosmopolitan atmosphere I like. There's always plenty to do, and such a wide range of shops. I can go out at any time of the day or night and get whatever I want, either food and drink or entertainment. The cultural activities are endless. I love the liveliness of the city and being surrounded by people all the time – you know, that constant buzz of activity. People talk about the crime rate in the city, but where I live there always seems to be loads of police, so I feel very safe. The one thing that gets me down is the amount of litter people drop on the streets. It's so unnecessary and just makes me feel depressed. Most of it could be recycled, it seems to me, if there were more recycling points. I guess a lot of people don't really care about the way the urban environment looks. I sometimes feel like saying to them, 'I have to live here with all your rubbish'. The council could do more to keep the streets clean as well, I suppose, but we all have to pay for it in higher taxes.

LESSON 2.3 RECORDING 2.3

P = Professor, S1 = Student 1, S2 = Student 2, S3 = Student 3, S4 = Student 4, S5 = Student 5, S6 = Student 6

P: Finally, to check you've all been listening, I'm going to ask you a question. So, what is a volcano? Yes, the young man in the red shirt.

S1: Erm … volcanoes are a natural way that the Earth has of cooling off … well, the Earth and other planets.

P: Yes that's right. OK. Do you have any questions for me? Yes, the woman in the green jacket.

S2: Professor, can I ask what the biggest volcano in the world is?

P: Right, that's easy. The biggest volcano on Earth is Mauna Loa in Hawaii and it's about 8.5 kilometres high – that's from the bottom of the ocean to its top. It's interesting that most of the volcanoes on Earth are found around the rim of the Pacific Ocean. But there are volcanoes around the coastline of Antarctica and there are even volcanoes underwater. There are probably more volcanoes and eruptions than people think. Out of an estimated 1,500 active volcanoes around the world, 50 or so erupt every year.

Another question … yes, you.

S3: Um, is it true that people can go inside volcanoes?

P: That's an interesting question. Obviously, you can't go inside an erupting volcano. As I told you, extremely high pressures under the Earth cause volcanoes to erupt – the pressure forces very hot lava up out of the volcano. Lava flows can have temperatures up to 1,250 degrees centigrade. But, actually, the answer to your question is yes. You can go inside volcanoes. Some people live inside volcanoes as some of them don't erupt for a long time. In the USA people live in three volcanoes, the most famous being the large volcano under Yellowstone National Park, which, incidentally, has been showing a lot of activity recently. Yes, the young man with the beard.

S4: Could you tell me if Vesuvius is an active volcano?

P: Well, an active volcano is one that has erupted in historical time. Vesuvius, which is east of Naples in Italy, famously destroyed Pompeii in ad 79 and it is the only volcano on the European mainland to have erupted within the last hundred years – I think it was 1944. So yes, it is an active volcano ... and a lot of people live near it. In fact, one in ten of the world's population live within volcanic danger zones. Another question ... yes?

S5: I'd like to know why volcanoes stop erupting.

P: That's a good question. There are three possible reasons. Maybe the heat runs out when the rocks are melted. Or the hot rocks – which, if you remember, we call magma, solidify on their way up. Or the magma can't generate enough pressure to crack the rock above it. OK, last question … yes?

S6: Do you know whether the Chilean Copahue volcano is safe for the local people?

LESSON 2.4 RECORDING 2.4

S = Switchboard, DR = Deborah Rydell, JR = John Reynolds

S: Good morning, Power Gas and Electricity, how can I help you?

DR: Good morning. Can I speak to John Reynolds, please?

S: Certainly. Who's calling, please?

DR: It's Deborah Rydell, from the Department of Energy.

S: Putting you through now.

DR: Hello, is that John?

JR: Speaking.

DR: Hi John, it's Deborah from the Energy Department. I wanted to have a chat with you about the wind farm proposal, you know, the one at Sparrow Hill.

JR: OK, Deborah. You're still in favour of it, I hope. You're not going to cancel it, are you?

DR: Well, it's not really my decision, John. Personally, there's no doubt in my mind that wind farms are the future, although some of my colleagues seem to think we should be doing more with nuclear power. It's much more cost effective at the moment, they say.

JR: Well, that's one way of looking at it, but we need to think long term. We just can't go on in the same old way.

DR: You're absolutely right, because oil and gas will run out eventually. Well, really, my reason for calling, John, is that I'd like to know when you think we should have the first public meeting about Sparrow Hill. You know, to stop any rumours.

JR: Well, it's a bit too early. I'm totally convinced that we should wait until we get further with the process, as there's likely to be a lot of trouble about this.

DR: You have a point, but don't you think we should have a meeting and put our case early? I mean, I'm sure we'll be able to get some supporters to attend. I was wondering if holding a public meeting sooner rather than later could really help.

JR: Mmm, I see what you mean, but I'm just worried that it could get very noisy – you know a lot of people feel strongly about this sort of thing. Though ... thinking about it, I'm interested in knowing what sort of local support you think we're likely to get. It could also be a great chance to see how people who live in the area really feel.

DR: Yes, exactly. I just think if we want it to get public approval, we need to persuade people it's right for the area from the start, and this would be a good opportunity.

JR: That's very true, because without local support we're probably not going to get much further very quickly.

DR: OK, I'll sort out a venue for some time in July and organise some publicity and security. I think that's important in case things get out of hand.

JR: I'd go along with you there, because some of these environmental groups can get quite violent. But, don't worry, I'm sure it will be OK. I really believe all the really great ideas are unpopular at first.

DR: Yes, OK, John. Goodbye.

JR: Goodbye.

LESSON 2.5 RECORDING 2.5

L = Lecturer, S = Student

L: It's not easy to design a good questionnaire, Paula. I'm not surprised you're having problems. How can I help?

S: Well, a few tips would be useful. I mean, what are the key points?

L: Erm, OK, when you design your questionnaire, remember two things. Firstly, you need to ask the right questions so you get the information you're looking for. And secondly, you want to make sure you get enough data to analyse. You need as many questionnaires as possible to be completed and returned to you. OK?

S: OK, so I have to choose good questions and get as many responses as possible.

L: Exactly. Now would you like me to give you a few tips about the wording of questions? Of course, the type of question depends on what the aims of the questionnaire are, but there are certain rules, I'd say ...

S: Oh, yes?

L: Mmm, first of all, use simple, short sentences. And avoid questions which are too long. Some people just won't bother to answer them if they're long, and other people just won't understand them.

S: OK, short and snappy questions, I've got it.

L: Another thing, Paula. Try to use open and closed questions in your questionnaire. Mix them if possible.

S: Hold on, can you explain, erm, open and closed questions?

L: Sure. Open questions, well, they allow people to answer as they wish, for example, if you ask people, 'How do you feel about the quality of the teaching you received?' it's an open question. You'll probably get a variety of answers. But closed questions are questions to which the answers are given, so the person answering has a limited choice. For example, a question like, 'How satisfied are you with your course? a) satisfied, b) not satisfied, c) don't know. Circle the appropriate answer.' Well, that's a closed question; the choices are given to you. OK?

S: Right. I suppose you get more information with open questions.

L: Yes, you do, but it takes a lot longer to analyse all the answers!

S: Yeah, I can see that.

L: Oh, a word of warning about open questions. Ask for only one piece of information at a time. For example, if you ask, 'What is your opinion of the course materials and teaching method?', that's not really a good question. It's really two questions, and it would be better to use two separate questions, not one, to get your information.

S: I see, OK.

L: Another thing about questions. All questions should be clear and well structured. In other words, respondents should be able to see the point of the question; they shouldn't be thinking, 'What on earth does that mean?' Also, it's good to start with fairly simple questions which people can answer easily. This encourages them to complete the questionnaire.

S: Yes, I see! OK, I've got all that.

L: One final piece of advice. Before designing your questionnaire, you need to look ahead and think carefully about how you're going to analyse the data. People often forget to do this when they design a questionnaire, and they find out they can't analyse the data very easily. It's too late then!

LESSON 2.5 RECORDING 2.6

D = Donna, E= Eduardo, S= Sophie

D: OK, let's talk about the questions we'll put in our questionnaire. Eduardo, you've done some work on this, what have you come up with?

E: OK, well, I think we all agree that we need to get some basic data about the respondents in our sample. You know, we'll need to know their age, sex, marital status, that sort of thing. And their educational qualifications, of course.

D: Yes, and also get something about their current employment situation. Are they employed or still students?

E: Exactly. And I'd add a question about their nationality – that could be very useful for us to know.

D: True, let's get that as well. OK, the next thing is ... what issues do we want to include? Sophie, I think you've got some ideas about that.

S: Yeah, I've done a bit of research, the key issues are ... let's see ... in no particular order: nuclear power; climate change; air pollution; real food, in other words, there's a lot of concern about genetic engineering of food products – GMOs. Those are the four key issues. OK?

D: It's a good list. How about protecting rainforests?

S: It's an important issue, I agree, but I think four issues are enough.

D: OK, we'll go with those. Now, what other questions ...

LESSON 2.5 RECORDING 2.7

D = Donna, E = Eduardo

D: Now, what other questions shall we include? Any suggestions, Eduardo?

E: Yes. We'll need to know how important each issue is for our respondents; that'll be the first question. So, I think we should ask them to rank the issues in order of importance, with one being the top issue. And then we should have a second question asking them to give reasons for their choice. Of course, that would be an open question, and the answers might be more difficult to analyse.

D: Yes, but it'd be a useful question, so let's include it. Anything else?

E: We'll need to find out how *aware* they are of all the issues, and how *worried* they are about them. Those could be questions three and four. Probably for question four they could fill in a chart with headings like 'very worried', 'fairly worried', 'not worried at all', and they put ticks in the appropriate boxes to show their opinion.

D: Great idea. Just one final point. I'd like to have a question asking if they're prepared to help us, you know, by working in the office, interviewing people, taking part in campaigns, or raising money for us – that's very important. Let's put one in – a final question – to find out if they want to join us. Right, time to get started writing the questionnaire.

LESSON 3.2 RECORDING 3.1

I = Interviewer, KC = Kevin Coles

I: How long have you been doing karate?

KC: OK. My time in karate is just over 32 years now. I started back in 1981 in my final year at university down in Bath and I've been training ever since on the basis of something like between two and five times a week. So, 32 years in karate. Like, we say it takes about five to six years to get to black belt – that's what we say is the beginning of karate. So I achieved my black belt in 1987 and since then I've been working my way as a black belt through the various levels and I'm now at the fifth level of black belt.

I: What gives you the most satisfaction in teaching karate?

KC: Well, I think I'm going to sum it up with one word. Impact ... having an impact on people – our students – students who now these days range from four to ... I was going to say 64, but we've had someone of 73 in one of our clubs.
We can measure progress through different belts – something which was introduced in the West. These days people need to measure their achievement and that's good. It's a way to distinguish different levels. And when students achieve their new belt ... I take tremendous joy in seeing their reaction, you get smiling faces, you get some children coming up and saying, 'Wow, it's the best day of my life.' I mean, for the adults it may be simply an expression of relief – the fact that they've got through an exam 20 years after having left school and not taking anything of this like before.
But I'd like to take that a step further. I take greatest satisfaction from witnessing the change in a student's approach and attitude. When I see students who cross a barrier from just doing movements to feeling or living their karate, then I feel

great – we've made a change somewhere, and I can think of a number of incidences where I've had, say, children who are floppy and not really with it, and after a certain level something snaps – all of a sudden they are down in their stances, they're breathing, they're concentrating, they're looking, things are working, and for me that's a case of … well, between us, them and me, we've made a change.

LESSON 3.2 RECORDING 3.2

I = Interviewer, KC = Kevin Coles

I: Is it a hobby or is it more of a way of life?

KC: Yeah, this is a classic question, really. I mean, for most people who do it these days it's undoubtedly a hobby. Mmm, for some, lessons learnt in karate can be part of their life, it can become part of their life if they do it for longer and longer.

I: Why do people start karate?

KC: The majority of the new starters these days are children and either they are attracted themselves by the glamour and excitement of karate, the martial arts, they've seen it on TV, they've enacted it on their Playstation games, they see the noise, the excitement, they see the fast-flowing kicks and so on. Or it may be because their mum or dad has encouraged them to attend. And there could be the twin attractions there of karate instilling discipline and control in their children. As is increasingly the case these days, maybe things don't work at home, parents are out at work more often. Maybe the school doesn't instil discipline. Very often these days teachers are restricted in terms of what they can say and do and parents bring their children and say 'sort them out'. And the kid can also, from a parent's perspective, their child can also learn stuff which enables them to look after themselves, and that's an admirable aim in itself because everyone's fearful of their child being out of their sight.

LESSON 3.3 RECORDING 3.3

1 I studied sports psychology as part of my course at university.
2 We can meet outside the university at six o'clock.
3 Did you see the game where the captain broke his ankle?
4 Tennis players tend to suffer a lot of wrist injuries.
5 We saw all the tennis players who had arrived early at the courts.

LESSON 3.4 RECORDING 3.4

Yuna Kim is a South Korean figure skater. She was born in Gumpo, South Korea in 1990. She's a truly remarkable sportswoman and some people say she's the greatest modern sportswoman. Let me tell you about her. When she was still very young, her coaches noticed she had the perfect body for skating. However, she had to overcome difficulties to develop her talent. There's no doubt she's a very determined person because at that time, there were not many public ice rinks in South Korea, so she had to practise very early in the morning or late at night. The rinks were so cold that she risked injuries. In spite of this, at the age of 12, she won the senior figure skating title in the South Korean championships. An outstanding achievement for such a young person. She was the youngest woman ever to win the championship. After that, she won many international championships. She won her first World Championship title in 2009 and at the 2010 Olympic Games she won a gold medal. Yuna Kim's skating programmes were given the highest scores since the International Skating Union had judged the competition. You can watch her astonishing performance in the competition on YouTube. Experts have described it as 'amazing', 'breath-taking' and 'phenomenal'. She seemed to skate faster than the other competitors, her jumps were higher and more artistic. She moved more elegantly and more athletically than the other skaters in the competition and she appeared to hear the rhythms better than everyone else.

After her success in the Olympics, she worked hard to promote ice skating in South Korea and also to ensure that her country won the bid for the Winter Olympics in 2018. She presented television programmes and also wrote books on her sport giving advice to young skaters.

In 2013, she took part in the South Korean Ladies Championship. She won the competition and, once again, people admired her extraordinary technical skills, her artistry and elegance.

She is a role model not only for young people in South Korea but also for skaters all over the world. She is one of the highest-paid female athletes in the world. Because of her fame, her beauty and, above all, her admirable personal qualities, she is asked to endorse all kinds of products. She was a UNICEF Goodwill Ambassador and often represents South Korea at international events. What's also extraordinary about her is that's she's so versatile. She's a fine singer and has recorded a number of songs written by Korean pop stars. There seems to be no end to Yuna Kim's remarkable talents. She is undoubtedly a superstar.

LESSON 3.5 RECORDING 3.5

L = Lecturer, S1 = Student 1, S2 = Student 2, S3 = Student 3

L: Right, thank you very much for coming and I hope you found the session useful. Now, if there are any questions, I'll be here for a few minutes if anyone wants to discuss anything.

S1: I have this essay to write and I'm finding it a real struggle. Could you give me a few tips?

L: Sure. Gosh, where do I start? OK, well, a common mistake new students often make is about the purpose of an essay. An essay is basically a question which needs an answer. Erm, I mean, it isn't an opportunity for you to show how much you know about a particular subject. So, if you don't actually answer the question, you'll fail the task, however good your writing is. A lot of people forget this.

S1: I see, that makes sense. So what's the best way of preparing to write an essay, do you think?

L: Well, the first thing I would do is analyse the title. I think it's helpful to underline any key words and work out what you're actually being asked to do. Then decide what kind of structure the title indicates to you. For example, is it a for-and-against essay or are you being asked to compare and contrast, or even offer solutions to a problem?

S1: OK, thanks. That's good. Then, what do you recommend I do next?

L: Well, then I think you should make some notes. Start by writing the exact title at the top of a new sheet of paper to focus your attention, and then brainstorm your ideas. I find it's helpful for students to get into the habit of starting with the topic area and just noting down any topic vocabulary which comes to mind.

S1: Oh, OK. That's a good idea. What next?

L: Well, I suggest that you ask yourself questions such as, what do I already know? What do I need to find out? Get all your ideas down on paper, however crazy they may seem. Then, organise your notes – it's really important that you have a clear and logical structure in your mind before you start writing.

S1: Yeah, I think that's one of my problems, getting to that. Thank you very much.

L: That's OK.

S2: I was wondering if you could give me some advice on how I should go about actually writing the essay?

L: Sure … a good approach to writing is what I call the beginning, middle and end approach. I think that good essays tend to follow this.

S2: Oh, right. What does that mean?

L: Right, I'll explain. I think at the beginning or in the first paragraph you should restate the question in your own words and introduce the topic. The next two, three or four paragraphs are the middle or main part of the essay where you state the arguments for and against the proposition, or offer solutions to the problem. The third part and final paragraph is a conclusion where you should refer back to the question and offer your own opinion if that is appropriate.

S2: That's useful, thanks very much. Is there anything special about academic writing that we should think about?

L: Mmm, let's think. Yes, firstly, most questions involve some kind of comparison and contrast, if only looking at the for and against of something, or assessing which solution to a problem is better. Secondly, good academic writing will have a logical argument and guide the reader through the argument, using examples and supporting the points you make with examples where necessary and appropriate. You should also put similar ideas in a single paragraph, you know, all the reasons for a particular thing, that sort of thing.

S2: OK, great, thanks.

S3: Could I ask about the language itself?

L: Mmm, good point. Most important – academic writing tends to be neutral in tone.

S3: Neutral? What exactly do you mean?

L: Well, you need to stand back and to appear to look at the question from a distance to be emotionally detached. A good way of achieving this is to leave yourself out of your writing – don't keep writing 'I think', but instead use phrases like 'it is clear that' and 'it is obvious that', 'this shows that', 'it is true that' and so on. You can put in your own experience, but it's often better to make this sound more general by introducing personal opinions and experiences with phrases like 'for many people', and 'a lot of men, women, younger people find …'. Passive structures are often used because they help to give that distance and objectivity. Finally, you should avoid abbreviations and contractions if it's a formal academic essay.

S3: Well, thanks very much. You've really been helpful. I think I'm ready to make a start now.

L: No problem, I hope it helps.

LESSON 4.1 RECORDING 4.1

Well, yes, there is certainly a lot of training and it takes a long time to become qualified. There's a lot to learn. You do need to be good at science, there's no doubt about that. Oh, and not mind the sight of blood! Seriously though, I think many people forget that it is after all a job about people, and being able to deal with people. There is a very human side to being a good doctor. It's a sociable job. For me … well, I try to make a real effort to engage with patients, simple things like remembering names. Some of my colleagues think I spend too long with patients, and that I'm not efficient. Sometimes it can be difficult with certain cases – you know we call them hypochondriacs – they like to come to the doctor, but are not really ill. It can be difficult to be sympathetic sometimes, as they are time wasters, and doctors are busy people, you know!

Some doctors go a lot further and like to lecture people about their lifestyles. I don't think you can do that too much, but you can chat to patients and find out what is going on in their lives. It is a good idea to be open-minded as far as treatments are concerned. I'm constantly surprised by what does and doesn't work with different patients. Some patients respond to treatments which have no effect on others. In my experience, some of the alternative treatments really do work and doctors should consider them, although western science is sometimes still very sceptical.

One thing I do feel, is that doctors today need to think about money. You can't just keep giving out tablets and medicine all the time. They are very expensive. Another thing which …

LESSON 4.2 RECORDING 4.3

The pharmaceutical industry has a problem at the present time because the very common diseases throughout the world such as high blood pressure, asthma, diabetes and so on have huge markets with potentially very large profits for successful drugs, but the people who are paying for the drug, such as insurance companies and state health services, do not wish to pay more than they have to for an effective treatment. That is why so much money goes into marketing as well as into development and testing of drugs.

There are still very large areas of medicine where new drugs are desperately needed. For example, it would be wonderful if we had more anti-malarial drugs because many of the existing preparations have become less effective as time has gone on and the malaria parasite has become resistant to them. Ideally, we need a vaccine against malaria so that all the people in a particular malarial country can be immunised and thereby protected. This of course needs to be combined with measures to reduce mosquitoes and so on. But these countries where there are huge needs for effective new treatment are generally poor and can't afford the huge cost of new drugs. So the pharmaceutical companies are less keen to develop new treatments which will not be very profitable. This type of development really depends upon support from international agencies such as the World Health Organisation, the World Bank, the European Union and similar organisations. Working in partnerships with university departments, the agencies can try to produce treatments and develop them to a stage where a pharmaceutical company would be interested in bringing them to the market.

LESSON 4.2 RECORDING 4.4

J = Jan   T = Tom   S = Susan

J: So, Tom, you're in charge of arrangements. Can you give us the details?

T: Sure, Jan. All the support team are flying out to Kampala at 5 p.m. on Friday. We are flying from Heathrow. We're all meeting at check-in at 3 p.m. Everyone has been emailed and all the arrangements have been made.

J: Thanks, Tom. OK, Susan, how's it going with the support team in Uganda?

S: Well, they've purchased half a million mosquito nets and these are the long lasting insecticide-treated nets.

J: Great. And what's happening with the celebrities?

S: The Ugandan team will be waiting for the celebrities in the hotel reception on Monday morning at 9 a.m. when the celebrity bus arrives.

J: So the Ugandan team are getting to the hotel at nine?

S: No they'll be there before nine.

J: OK. Good.

S: Then we'll be filming the celebrity interviews for the fundraising appeal all Monday morning and then we'll be distributing the first batch of mosquito nets with the celebrities on Monday afternoon. Tom and I will be working in Uganda all next month, helping with the distribution of the rest of the nets.

J: Great. And what are the celebrities doing?

S: Some of the celebrities are going to spend a few days sightseeing, but no arrangements have been made yet.

J: Well, everything's looking good … and based on the money we've raised so far and the support we've had, I think we're going to raise a lot more money than last year.

LESSON 4.3 RECORDING 4.5

1   Well, in terms of sight, I think 100 years from now we will probably have a genetic way to fix diabetes, which is the number one cause of blindness in this country. And as diabetes accounts for 10% of the health budget, it's a good area for researchers to focus on. I also think we'll have succeeded in preventing some eye diseases – maybe with a pill. I think we'll definitely be able to transplant the optic nerve and the area at the back of the eye and will possibly be able to clone eyes from skin cells. People ask me if scientists will make a bionic man or woman soon. Well, they have already made a bionic eye.

2   By 2120, engineers will have developed a 'smart suit', or a sort of special 'airbag' … and when you're skiing or doing other vigorous activities and you start to fall then the suit would quickly adjust to help protect you.

3   I believe that in the not too distant future, scientists will have created personal virtual computer models that will be constantly updated to record injuries, accidents or diseases or illnesses that you suffer from. It will be kept in cyberspace and your doctor will probably be able to access it from anywhere in the world. I also think they will have invented tiny robots that you swallow which will perform surgery. The robots would go right to the problem area and use lasers or stitches or produce a healing material which will help patients recover from their injuries quickly.

4   I think cancer will be treated differently. Instead of trying to totally destroy the cancer from the outside, I think we will have found something very small that can get into the cell. Mind you, I think we'll probably have a whole different set of diseases that we'll be worrying about. I agree with those who say that cancer probably won't be a big problem in 100 years.

5   In terms of imaging technology, I guess that in 100 years, three-dimensional imaging (and I mean things like CAT scans and three-dimensional ultra sound) will be huge. X-rays and radiation will certainly not disappear completely, but we will have found ways to use lower amounts of radiation.

6   100 years … well, in 100 years people will probably be living on other planets or out in space. I think by then we will have developed a way to protect astronauts from radiation exposure, and those methods could be used to help prevent damage in people exposed to radiation and it will be easier to care for them.

LESSON 4.4 RECORDING 4.6

S = Sandra, H = Hans

S: I know the doctor well, Hans, he's very popular with all his patients. He's a good listener, very sympathetic, knowledgeable, up-to-date with treatments – just what you want for a family doctor.

H: Yeah, that's what I've heard too. And he did some great work for us when he was trialling our new products for arthritis and diabetes. We've used him a lot for our research – he's very reliable and writes good reports.

S: We've got to be careful how we deal with this. We want to support him, but we need to look at the implications of doing it. If we support him too strongly, the press may get hold of the story. They'll start digging around and perhaps suggest we do this sort of thing all the time, I mean, not informing patients, using them as guinea pigs.

H: Yeah, it could be really bad for our reputation. What do you think we should do then?

S: Well, I don't know. I suppose we could offer the patient some sort of financial compensation and persuade her not to make a fuss. But it's a risky option. One consequence could be she'll start negotiating with us. Asking for more cash. We don't want to get into that scenario, do we?

H: No, we certainly don't. How about if we meet her, say we're really sorry, and explain that the doctor was trying to give her the very best treatment available? We could say it's a wonderful drug and it's had great results in clinical trials. The doctor was very busy at the time and he simply forgot to tell her that the drug was still being trialled.

S: It might work, but it has a serious disadvantage.

H: Oh, what's that?

S: Well, will she believe it's a wonder drug? It seems she had some bad side effects when she took it. She often felt dizzy and her blood pressure went up. According to her, she didn't feel at all well.

H: Mmm, that could be a big problem for us. It would have a huge impact on our profits if that information was made public. It would also result in other patients coming forward with complaints.

S: Yes, it would be very damaging. But let's

face it, all drugs have side effects, she's just been unlucky. I think we need to go softly with this one. We should talk to her, be very honest. And remind her that she has a wonderful doctor to treat her. I think she's been with him for some years.

H: True, but she's not very happy with him at the moment.

S: It's understandable, I suppose.

LESSON 4.5 RECORDING 4.7

My name is Jeffrey Davies and I'm a business consultant. My job is to advise individuals and companies on ways in which they can improve their performance in terms of work processes, team building and better customer and client service.

I use the Internet all the time – for research, for contact-building and networking, and generally for keeping up to date with trends and issues in areas of business that are relevant to my work. In terms of research, I read a lot of studies and articles written by academics and researchers on topics that are linked to what I do – work-place efficiency, staff training and development, and so on. There is a huge amount of material out there, of course, and the hard part is finding out what I need to learn about and not spending time reading through what I already know. I follow a number of management professionals online – their blogs and articles – and I often look up the reading which they recommend. I also often use an RSS news feed. This lets me know if there are any new and relevant blogs, articles and other publications that'll be useful to me.

As far as networking goes, services like LinkedIn and more specialised professional sites are very useful for making new contacts, letting people know what I do and sharing information with other professionals. In some cases it leads to new working relationships – working with other consultants in order to share our experience and offer an expanded service to potential clients. You can learn a great deal from fellow professionals in this way. It's so important to keep up to date with trends and issues in business, and the Internet offers so much with its truly global reach. The problem, always, is the sheer amount of information and the lack of time to wade through it. So people who can design really good information selection systems – which filter out key content and let you access it quickly and easily – are going to make a lot of money in future, I'm sure!

LESSON 4.5 RECORDING 4.8

Remember, anyone can create a website, so there's a lot of information out there and it's not easy to know if your source of information is reliable and appropriate for your research. But I can give you some tips to help you. First, consider who has made the website. Is the author a recognised authority on the subject? Can you trust the person behind the website? So, look for clues which point to the credibility of the writer or the organisation who created the website. Secondly, you need to know why the website was created and what its purpose is. For example, if you want to find factual information about a new drug, you'll want to know if the webpage is produced by the company making the drug or by an independent research group. The

information from the independent research group may be more trustworthy.

Thirdly, you need to consider whether the website is providing facts or if it is clearly giving the author's opinion. If it's providing facts, ask yourself what evidence the author gives to back up his or her facts.

My next tip is about the age of the website. You'll want to know how old the website is and if it's been well maintained. It's important that the information you obtain is up-to-date. You don't want to use out-of-date information in your research.

My fifth tip concerns the need to check the information you find. Does the writer indicate where their information comes from? Can you check the information from other sources, for example, from an encyclopedia, an authoritative report or article or from some published statistics? Finally, see if the website provides links to other relevant information. And if it does, check that all the links work. You may also want to check if the website has a real postal address and telephone number so that you can respond to the author or organisation. You know, evaluating website information is all about critical thinking. You need to be constantly asking yourself questions while you read a webpage so that you can decide if you want to use the information in your research.

LESSON 5.1 RECORDING 5.1

1 I'm afraid I've had a lot of bad experiences, and this was more of the same. It's not that it is inefficient, it's just for me there is too much waiting around. The last time was a nightmare. Admittedly, it did involve a stopover, and a missed connection, but even so it seemed like everything went wrong. I'm just glad I didn't use one of the budget carriers – it could have been even worse. The weather started it all. A fogbound runway meant nothing was leaving, and it's true you couldn't see a thing. When we were finally cleared for departure, it took almost 15 minutes to walk to the gate! I had priority boarding and I'd booked an aisle seat, so that was OK, but there was a lot of turbulence shortly after take off, which scared a lot of people. Then the transit lounge was closed due to a security alert, and when I finally arrived at my destination – guess what? Lost baggage! My luggage had gone to Hong Kong instead of Jakarta!

2 It's a great way to travel, really. You can work easily on board and the fares are reasonable if you can book early enough. I know a lot of people complain, and for some people it has a bad image. You know, they are always going on about the delays because of signalling problems and engineering work, but I guess I've been lucky. Having said that, the last journey I made was almost a disaster as there was a last minute platform alteration, so I had to run like crazy, but luckily I made it. It seemed to be something to do with the change to the winter timetable and some late running due to the weather. It is supposed to be a high-speed line, but it wasn't that day, I'm afraid. It hasn't put me off though. Given the choice, it's how I like to travel.

3 The main problem is it is very unpredictable as a way to travel – sometimes it's fantastic, fast and door to door – but other times it can be awful, although getting out of the city is

better since they introduced the congestion charge. It just depends. Last week I had a terrible journey. There was a long tailback due to a big accident. They talked about it on the news – a multi-vehicle pile up, so that really delayed things. Because of the lane closures it caused a bottleneck, so the traffic was very slow. You know, crawling along-slower than walking – and very stop/start. After about 45 minutes we started to move properly again, but then there was another problem. Someone had a breakdown. It looked like a puncture, and was blocking the carriageway, and right near a junction as well! I don't know – some days nothing goes my way, but as I say, at other times it's just the best way to travel!

4 It's not something I have used often, but a few times, and generally I like it. It can be very relaxing, and comfortable. The last time was a bit different though. Well, there had been engine trouble on the previous crossing so everything was delayed. The Captain was very apologetic and we did get an upgrade to a first class cabin. Of course, by this time it was low tide and we had to wait again – delayed sailing they call it. Once we finally left the harbour there was more rough weather, because of the time of year. Most of the passengers and crew were ill. It wasn't pleasant, I can tell you. We docked about twelve hours late, and I was glad to get back on dry land. As voyages go, it was one of the worst!

LESSON 5.2 RECORDING 5.2

Space tourism using ordinary rocket ships has been talked about for a number of years. We've all heard about Virgin's plans to send rich people into space. But recently a range of new technologies to help people into space has been suggested. In today's technology report, we're going to look at two of them. The first is the space train or Orbital Maglev. A train carriage would be levitated by magnets and would be contained inside a vacuum tube. The final 20km of the 1,609km-long track would point upwards, launching the carriage into space. The space train is the idea of Dr George Maise and Dr James Powell, who is one of the inventors of the superconducting Maglev. It is hoped that this system could significantly reduce the cost of putting space tourists and commercial cargo into space.

Let's move on to another idea to get people into space. Let's look at the space elevator, which was first talked about over 100 years ago. The idea is to use a cable tied to a base station to send elevators climbing into space at a fraction of the cost of rocket-based launch systems. A thin cable made from light material would stretch from a base station near the Equator to a point 95,560 km into space. The Earth's rotation and a weight on the upper end of the cable would keep the line tight and elevators travelling as fast as trains would be sent up into space. Tokyo-based construction company Obayashi Corporation is hoping to have a space elevator capable of carrying 30 passengers a time working by 2050.

LESSON 5.4 RECORDING 5.3

And now some news for all you tourists who are planning to go to the beautiful city of Beauciel for a vacation. The results of a survey about the transport system in the city have just been published. They make interesting reading. As many people know, Beauciel has serious transport problems. According to the survey, there are too many cars in the city, traffic jams at peak times, insufficient car parks, too much noise, especially from motorbikes, and slow, unreliable buses. Residents also mentioned on-street parking, which slows down traffic, especially the buses.

For most people in the survey, that's over 80 percent, traffic jams are the biggest problem. At peak times in the morning and evening, there are often serious traffic jams when people enter and leave the city. Over 75 percent of the residents consider there are too many cars in the city.

Many residents, about 70 percent of those surveyed, feel the city needs more car parks. There is only one car park near the city centre, and that is always full early in the morning. The other car parks, dotted around the city, are generally small and insufficient for the number of cars.

Many residents, roughly 60 percent in the survey, mentioned the unacceptable noise levels, not just from cars but also from motorcycles. This is having a bad effect on people's quality of life.

Just over 45 percent drew attention to the problem of on-street parking. There are too many private cars parked on the streets. This causes problems for people who have to park on the roads such as ambulance drivers, taxis, school buses, road maintenance vehicles, and so on.

The unreliable bus services were criticised by 40 percent of the residents. Many complained also about the time it takes by bus to travel across the city from east to west. The journey, a distance of about five kilometres, usually takes more than an hour.

The survey results have come at the right time. The city planners are now considering how to solve the problems and have set up a website where people can give their opinions and voice their complaints. That's all from me. I'll be back again tomorrow morning at 11 o'clock.

LESSON 5.4 RECORDING 5.4

F = Francoise, K = Kirsten, D = Daniel

F: OK, I'd like to move on. But first, let me recap, please. We've talked about having bicycle lanes. We think it's a good idea and we'd like to discuss it at the next planning meeting. But Kirsten, you're not convinced it's worth doing, right?

K: Well, I know it's been tried in other cities and hasn't really worked.

F: So, just to confirm, you won't support the proposal if it goes to a vote.

K: Exactly.

F: Right. Now what about our biggest problem? How to get from the harbour to the city centre. It took me almost an hour yesterday to get there. It's not good enough, the journey's only three kilometres, and the bus was stopping every five metres. It's so frustrating, especially when the weather's hot. What do you think, Daniel? What's the answer?

D: Mmm, it's a big problem getting from east to west, no doubt about that. In the long term, we'll need to have a tram system or build a ring road. But either solution will cost a lot of money, and there'll be environmental problems. What do you think, Kirsten?

K: You're right, a ring road or tram system, they're long-term solutions. Do we need

to spend time discussing them? I think we should focus on a short-term solution. I'd like to have more exclusive bus routes, and more buses for that matter. And let's get rid of on-street parking on the busy routes.

D: Well, they're interesting ideas. Right, Francoise?

F: Yes, very interesting. A better bus system is definitely worth considering. But still, I'd like to discuss the ring road proposal at the next meeting. If we could build that ring road, a lot of cars would go round the city instead of through it. And that'd greatly reduce traffic congestion. OK?

D: Well, OK. I suppose you're right.

F: OK, do we essentially have agreement, then?

K: OK

F: Right, I'll now sum up. We talked about bicycle lanes and agreed to discuss this proposal at our next meeting. But Kirsten is not in favour of them. We think a short-term solution could be to improve the bus system, have more buses and stop on-street parking on some routes. And we'd also like to discuss a long term solution at the meeting, building a ring road which will take cars round the southern part of the city. Everyone happy with my summary?

K: Yeah, fine.

LESSON 6.1 RECORDING 6.1

J = Jenny, E = Erika, P = Paul, M = Michael

J: Now, if everyone's got a coffee, I think we should begin. Has everyone read this month's book and seen the film?

E/P: Yes, sure.

J: Well, Michael, I suppose as you chose this book for us to read, you should start us off. Why did you choose it?

M: Yes, well … OK. I chose it because we have a book and a film which I think people will have strong opinions about. Also his latest book Inferno has just come out – again seems to be dividing opinion. Critics are often not keen, but people buy his books. He is one of the world's most read authors. I thought I would choose one of his earlier works and the one which perhaps made him so popular. Well, The Da Vinci Code by Dan Brown. What can I say? I really thought it was brilliant! It's a real page turner. I read the whole thing in a day. I thought the film was great too, but I suppose I just really like Tom Hanks. He's a fantastic actor.

P: Really??!! I thought it was dreadful!

M: Oh come on, Paul!

P: All that stuff about the Louvre being a museum, which is in Paris, which is in France. I felt insulted. And what was all that romantic stuff in the middle? No, I'm sorry, it's not my kind of thing. And in the film Tom Hanks looks nothing like the main character in the book, Robert Langdon, should. It's ridiculous. Jenny, what did you think?

J: OK Paul, I agree that was a bit odd, but you must agree the plot was riveting, all those twists and turns? I couldn't put it down.

P: Really, Jenny, I'm surprised at you. It was really tedious. And the ending was a real let down. After 500 pages nothing really happened. I found that Stephen King book we read last month much more tense, and at least the characters were written with some imagination.

E: I agree with you, Paul – I just couldn't get into it. It was really dull and just not thought-provoking, which I was surprised about, considering the subject matter. And as for the

film – oh dear, what a disappointment. It was just awful. In fact, I think the film is worse than the book, if that's possible!

M: Come on, Erika, it's a thriller. It's light and easy to read, just a good story.

E: Well, not for me. It was very hard going at the beginning and then I just gave up. There were just too many people in it for me. And all those really short chapters about the different people – I suppose that was to make it easier to follow, except that for me it didn't work. I don't know if it was the way it was written.

J: Well, for me it certainly lived up to all the hype – I'd definitely read one of his others now. I agree with Michael. It was really gripping. I couldn't wait to see what would happen next.

P: Not me. I mean, I like a good mystery but this was definitely overrated.

E: Yes, just awful … anyway, let's agree to differ on this one, but it's my turn to choose for next month and it's going to be something a bit less lightweight. How about a classic, perhaps something by Charles Dickens, you know, with interesting characters?

J: Great. A lot of his stories have been made into films as well.

M: Yes, I've never read any of his, but I'm sure I've seen some of the film versions.

J: Sounds good.

LESSON 6.2 RECORDING 6.2

1 Which film has had the biggest impact on me … mmm … I'd have to say Jack Nicholson's performance in One Flew Over the Cuckoo's Nest. Trying to choose just one of Nicholson's great performances is difficult and he was amazing in The Shining. But he is heroic, funny and menacing as McMurphy who ends up in a prison ward for the mentally ill and leads a fight against Nurse Ratched. This film isn't only great entertainment. It goes much deeper than this and gives us a wonderful insight into society. Everything about the film is brilliant: the plot, direction, filming, casting and of course, the acting. Rarely can a film make you laugh and gasp with horror and shock at the same time. Rarely can a film leave you so entertained yet thinking about its disturbing scenes. The book by Ken Kesey is brilliant, but I believe the film is better than the book.

2 I really enjoyed the Japanese film Zatoichi which starts as a straightforward samurai movie, turns into a comedy and ends as a dance scene. I love it mainly because the lead actor and director is Takeshi Kitano, who some may know as Beat Takeshi. Kitano is famous as an actor, director, comedian, kid's TV favourite, novelist, poet, cartoonist and painter, and he seems to have made a film that combines a number of his talents. Kitano plays the blind masseur Zatoichi who turns out to be incredibly skilled with a sword. He wanders into a town harassed by a criminal gang and helps two geishas take revenge on the men who murdered their parents. I loved Kitano's performance as the chuckling, shuffling, friendly masseur who turns into a revenging warrior when required. He makes an intensely likeable main character while speaking very few words throughout the film.

3 In terms of visual impact, I think I'd have to say Crouching Tiger Hidden Dragon with excellent performances from Michelle Yeoh and Zhang Ziyi, two of Asia's greatest actresses. This movie

has breathtaking fight scenes and contains beautiful landscapes. The cinematography is outstanding and I think it won an Oscar for art direction. I also loved the beautiful musical score, and especially the use of the cello. The film was based on a novel by novelist Wang Dulu, but I can't say which I preferred as I haven't read the book. The film was a Chinese, Hong Kong, Taiwanese, American co-production directed by Ang Lee. The dialogue is in Mandarin with subtitles and in my opinion that version is much better than the version with English voiceovers.

4 I've enjoyed many of the Sherlock Holmes films and Holmes is the most portrayed movie character, with more than 70 actors playing the part in over 200 films. I enjoyed watching Peter Cushing and Christopher Lee portraying Holmes and also recent versions with the brilliant Robert Downey Jnr. I also like the modern series set in New York which stars Lucy Liu as Dr Watson. But to be honest, I prefer the books, which made a huge impression on me when I first read them, and the reason's simple. Sherlock Holmes himself is a fascinating person … someone we can all admire. He's got a brilliant intellect and incredible analytical powers. He's also got amazing powers of observation – just by looking at people, he can deduce all kinds of things about them and their lives. He's supremely talented as a detective and can solve the most difficult cases. But he has human failings as well. He has character flaws, like he can be very arrogant – especially in his relations with his sidekick, Dr Watson. Watson accompanies him on most cases, and he isn't stupid, but Holmes is so brilliant! And he's a very courageous person, especially when dealing with some very dangerous men. He's knowledgeable and he's talented musically. He often plays the violin when he's in an unhappy mood. He's very believable as the main character in the stories. When I was young, my uncle used to read extracts from the stories to me, and he could quote pages of the stories by heart. I love Sherlock Holmes and I've re-read the stories many times.

LESSON 6.2 RECORDING 6.3

One book that has made a huge impression on me is 'The Great Gatsby' by the American writer, F. Scott Fitzgerald. It's always been my favourite novel. I've re-read it many times and each time I find new meaning in it. There have been two impressive films based on the novel: one with Robert Redford and Mia Farrow and a more recent one with Leonardo di Caprio and Carey Mulligan.

The book is about a wealthy man, Jay Gatsby, who tries to win back the love of Daisy, a beautiful woman he first met when he was young and penniless. Instead of marrying Gatsby, Daisy marries a rich man, Tom Buchanan, from her own social class and years later, Gatsby, who's now very wealthy, wants to revive their romance. The narrator of the story, Nick Carraway moves to Long Island where his cousin, Daisy lives. He rents a small house, close to the magnificent mansion of Jay Gatsby. Gatsby holds lavish parties every Saturday. Hundreds of people come to them, and most of them are not invited and have never met their host. Nick is surprised to receive a written invitation to one of the parties, even though he's never met Gatsby. In a key scene, Nick wanders around the party and meets a man who turns out to be Gatsby. Later on, Gatsby uses his friendship with Nick to meet Daisy again, the woman he

loved and lost. The story doesn't have a happy ending for Gatsby. He manages to have a romantic relationship with Daisy. However, she chooses to remain with her husband rather than start a new life with Gatsby.

I like this book for several reasons. First, it's extremely well written. Fitzgerald is so skilful at describing the characters and their emotions. And his language is very evocative. You really get the feel of how upper class people lived in the 1920s in America. He sees this as a period of declining social and moral values. People are greedy and pursue pleasure and money at all costs. The novel holds a mirror up to this corrupt society.

I find the main characters, especially Jay Gatsby, absolutely fascinating. Gatsby has a romantic view of life. He believes that you can repeat the past and achieve happiness. He is a mysterious person. There are all kinds of rumours about his past. As the story unfolds, you are not sure about his character. He is undoubtedly charismatic with a charming smile, but you wonder if he is not what he seems. For example, he did not inherit his fortune, as he says, but made money from selling alcohol, which was illegal at the time. Your feelings about him change as you learn more about his past. The characters in the book are all richly drawn and that is one of the book's greatest strengths. I have a favourite bit of dialogue about Gatsby which reveals his character. Nick says to him, ' You can't repeat the past.' Gatsby replies, 'Of course, you can. Of course you can.'

The 'Great Gatsby' was published in 1926, just a few years after the Great War. The novel had a great impact. This was not just because of the novel's fascinating plot, but because it poses interesting questions like: 'Can you get back the past?' 'Is there such a thing as 'true love?' It was also, I think, because in the novel, Fitzgerald depicted brilliantly and accurately the lives and behaviour of wealthy people in America.

LESSON 6.3 RECORDING 6.4

1 When I was in elementary school I was a devoted reader and a good student. I used to read in bed for an hour every night before I fell asleep. And at school I would go to the library every afternoon. I loved reading. Then my dad lost his job and we kept moving schools. As soon as I got used to the new school and new friends I would have to leave. And finally I ended up in a school where reading was not cool, certainly not for boys. My grades got worse and I would only read one or two books a year. When I left school, I joined a band and started composing songs. I started reading again because reading helped me understand the world and understand myself, and helped me find ideas for my songs.

2 I used to read more than one book at a time and sometimes I'd have three or four on the go. But in recent years, I've mainly stuck to one book at a time, although if I'm reading a hardcover I'll sometimes have a paperback on the side to bring on the train or to read in the bath. And that's my favourite place for reading – the bath – and if it's a really good book I'll keep reading till the water goes cold. Life would be a much less interesting place if I didn't read.

3 As a child I loved to read and I would read in bed almost every night. But now I seem to have lost my love of reading. I used to love it. And I mean love it. I was a bookworm. I used to read, like, a whole novel in one day or less than a day. I loved imagining myself in the book. But now I've lost interest in them – even

my favourite books that I would read over and over. To be honest, I think it's down to the Internet. I seem to have lost my attention span and focus. I used to read entire books in one sitting, now I put them down to check my phone, forget about them, only read the beginning and then lose interest.

4 I didn't use to read a lot. It once took me a year to read Martin Johnson, the ex-England Rugby Captain's autobiography. I used to read a page a night and I would get bored really quickly. I hated reading at school because I'm dyslexic. However, I'm reading a lot more now. Recently, I've been reading the Lee Childs novels and I read two chapters a night and actually I'm really proud of myself.

5 Before I became a librarian, I used to read pretty exclusively within the fantasy/sci-fi genres. Even now those are my go-to book choices. However, I try to continuously remind myself to read across as many genres as possible because advising readers is a big part of my job. And actually I really enjoyed reading George Eliot's *Middlemarch*. It's not the sort of book I would normally read, but it had everything – great characters, great stories and great descriptions of the scenery and countryside. It was warm and funny and gripping. I'm reading more now than I did when I was younger … and I'm reading different genres as well.

LESSON 6.3 RECORDING 6.6

I used to read in bed for an hour every night before I fell asleep.

LESSON 6.4 RECORDING 6.7

J = Jerry, F= Francesca

J I've got a great idea for a film, Francesca. I'm sure it'll be a winner.

F Really? OK, try it out on me. Imagine I'm the management listening to your pitch. If it's really good, we can work on it and enter the competition.

J OK, I'm confident you'll like my idea.

F I hope so.

J OK, I'll start. Good morning, everyone, I'm sure you'll find our concept exciting and original. I'll start with the storyline. Two women are returning from college to their parents' houses. On the way, they find the road's closed, with a notice saying 'Do not enter'. A local man explains that there was an awful murder last night at the house on the hill. The women are in a hurry. They ignore the notice and go down the road. They're never seen again. I think you'll agree, it's a really interesting and creative idea. Of course, we'll have to work out the details. It's just a storyline at the moment. But it's got a lot of potential and it could be a real winner. A woman disappears and no one knows what's happened to her. It's really … intriguing.
Turning now to the actors. We'd like to get stars, if possible – young actors who've already proved themselves. We're thinking of Naomi Watts and Jennifer Lawrence – the one who was in *Hunger Games*. They're both really attractive and good actors. They'd be perfect. The budget, I think, would allow us to use well-known actors. They're bound to appeal to the audience who'd go to the film.

F OK, so, who is our target audience? Who do we have in mind?

J I'd say the twenty-to-forty-year-old group.

175

They're the ones that go regularly to the cinema. They'll love our concept. It's got such a wide appeal:, two female characters, mystery and danger. It's biggest selling point would be that it's a thriller and also a horror film. OK, to summarise, our concept has a fascinating storyline. We think it's got tremendous potential. The audience will want to know what's happened to the two women. Have they disappeared for ever? That's the mystery the film will solve. There'll be all kinds of twists and turns in the plot, and a lot of human interest. We really believe in our concept and hope we've managed to convince you too … What do you think, Francesca? Do you like the idea?

F I absolutely love it, It's a fantastic plot. Well done!

J Great, I thought you'd like it.

F I do. You've convinced me totally. Nice presentation too. Let's start working on it because the management will ask a lot of questions and expect more details. I'd say we've got a winner, Jerry, with this concept.

J OK, let's meet tomorrow after work in the canteen. OK with you?

F Fine. See you roundabout six.

LESSON 6.5 RECORDING 6.8

1 I went to a lecture on English Literature. To make her key point, the lecturer quoted two lines from the American poet Robert Frost, 'Home is where you go to and they can't turn you away.' She repeated the two lines several times during her talk to make her points. I heard that presentation 25 years ago and I still remember the quote. Her presentation was truly outstanding.

2 The lecturer was talking about trends in the current economic climate. Her presentation could have been boring, but the slides she used to illustrate her points were striking and incredibly imaginative. So everyone listened to her very intently.

3 There was another presenter at the conference on the current economic climate. He started by telling us an anecdote, something about a train coming through a tunnel and almost crashing when it came out the other side. He took about two minutes to come to the punchline. He took so long to tell the story that the audience were amused and listened carefully for the rest of his talk.

4 The presenter had worked for years for the BBC. His talk was on 'how to give an effective presentation'. He spoke in a low but powerful voice which carried to the back of the room without the need of a loudspeaker. He had such a magnificent voice that his presentation was memorable.

5 It was the best presentation I've ever heard. The speaker used all kinds of rhetorical devices, you know, techniques to get across his ideas in a memorable way, like tripling – that's using words in threes – contrasting ideas, repetition, alliteration, quotes from literature. It was an amazing demonstration of how to make a presentation effective.

LESSON 6.5 VIDEO RECORDING 6

Presenter

Hi everyone. The film you're going to see tonight is The Girl with the Dragon Tattoo. It's based on the first of three Swedish novels written by Stieg Larsson and it features two main characters, an investigative journalist Mikael Blomkvist and a female researcher, Lisbeth Salander. The books were a huge success internationally. Their sales to date have been well over $100 million. The film has been equally successful. One critic, comparing it to the book wrote, 'This mystery is just as devastating, suspenseful and satisfying on screen.' And another one wrote, 'This dynamite thriller shivers with suspense. In a word, wow!'

OK, I'll start by outlining the plot of the film. It's very complicated and I hope my summary will make it easier for you to understand the twists and turns in the story. After that, I'll talk about the two main characters. And finally, I'll suggest a couple of reasons why the film has been so popular and highly praised.

Right, let's start with the plot. The film's about an investigation by a journalist, Mikael Blomkvist. He's hired by a millionaire, Henrik Vanger, to find out what happened to Vanger's niece, Harriet, who disappeared 40 years ago. Henrik suspects that someone in the family, the powerful Vanger family, murdered Harriet.

In his investigation, Mikael gets help from a young female researcher, Lisbeth Salander. She's a computer hacker, very anti-social and looks like a punk. They soon realise that Harriet's disappearance isn't a single event, but rather linked to a series of terrible murders in the area. They begin to discover a dark and appalling family history, and when they do this, they put themselves in great danger.

So, I've given you an idea of what the film's about. Moving on now to the two main characters: Mikael Blomkvist and Lisbeth Salander. They're an interesting contrast. On the one hand, there's Mikael, the journalist, played by Daniel Craig, who's better known for playing James Bond in the Bond films. Mikael's a serious person, with a journalist's curiosity and a strong social conscience. He's 20 years older than Lisbeth. On the other hand, there's Lisbeth Salander, by far the most interesting character in the film. Who wouldn't find her fascinating? A small woman, at times she looks like a frightened animal. But at other times, she's strong, single-minded and stubborn. She's a very troubled person because she had a difficult childhood. Physically, she's very attractive in an unusual way. She has shiny black hair, yet her skin is pale like porcelain china. She has a tattoo, nose ring and many ear rings. Often a victim, she always takes revenge on her enemies. So why has the film been so successful? Probably for two reasons. The main characters are played by two extraordinarily talented actors, Daniel Craig and Rooney Mara – they're perfect for their roles. And the second reason is that the film's based on a superb novel that millions of people have enjoyed. OK, I hope you've found my presentation useful and informative. Let's watch the film!

LESSON 7.2 RECORDING 7.2

S1 = Student 1, S2 = Student 2, S3 = Student 3, M = Marta,

S1: What do architects find interesting when designing buildings?

M: A good question. I'd say the most interesting thing relates to our role as an architect. In most cases, what are architects trying to do? I mean, we're trying to design an ideal place to meet human needs. That's really our main motivation. It's our 'duty' if you like, to create a place that integrates interior design with the needs of the people who'll be using the building. It's, how can I say, a relationship in which the individual and the place are integrated. They depend on each other.

S2: What type of architecture has particularly impressed you in terms of solving problems?

M: That's an interesting question. I've lived in and visited a lot of hot climates and I really like the way that Islamic architecture deals with the problem of extreme heat. Houses are often built around a central open courtyard which ventilates them. And they often have a central basin or fountain, which provides a cooling effect and the soothing sound of falling water. When you visit the old mosques and palaces, which did not have electricity, you notice that the temperature is often just right. I sometimes use some of the central features of Arab architecture, which include patios, open courtyards and water features, when designing hotels. Those features are really useful in regulating heat and cooling buildings during long, hot summer days.

S3: What's your next project?

M: Well, it seems that affordable housing is the new buzzword and we've just won a contract to deliver 300 housing units on sites in and around Copenhagen. These will be very reasonably priced and a large proportion will be reserved for essential workers such as nurses, police officers and teachers. Most affordable housing looks very boring but our project offers a huge variation of housing sizes and configurations. The project is based on a prefab basis module of wood which surrounds a central core for a wet room or shower and technical installations and a staircase. Then the modules can be put together horizontally and vertically like building blocks. We're really looking forward to getting started.

LESSON 7.4 RECORDING 7.3

C =Carlos, G = Gabriela, R = Richard

C: Let's talk about our plans for the ground floor. Gabriela, What ideas do you have?

G: Well, I need a little more time to think about it, but seeing that space won't be a problem, in my opinion, it's vital we have some sort of sports facility on the ground floor. Also we'll need an area where people can relax.

C: How about you, Richard? What do you think?

R: I agree with Gabriela, she's right. It's absolutely essential to offer a facility for people who want to forget work for a while, just, you know, chill out, and the ground floor's the best place to provide it. But I'm not sure what sort of facility it should be.

C: So, Gabriela, any ideas?

G: Mmm, well, people are very health conscious these days, they do want to relax, they're often very stressed. So … we've got to offer them something, that's for sure. Off the top of my head, I suggest we have a games room on the ground floor – you know, table tennis, snooker, that sort of thing. It'd be very popular with some of our guests.

C: Mmm, I don't know, Gabriela. We certainly need some kind of area where people can take it easy, let their hair down a bit. But I'm not sure a games room is the answer. I mean, is it really the right choice for a business hotel?

G: OK, maybe not a games room, but we should offer them something to help them relax, maybe a sauna, a jacuzzi, a sun deck. Don't you agree, Richard?

R: Yeah, a sauna, why not? And, erm, I've just thought of something. It might be a good idea to have an aerobics and dance studio.

Of course, we'd have to find out first if our guests really wanted that kind of facility. We could also consider having a stand with free newspapers for guests – that'd be popular.

C: Mmm, I like that idea, Richard, aerobics and dancing. It'd probably appeal to all age groups. And it'd be good to offer guests free newspapers. Nice idea. But we need to think this through. There are plenty of options to meet the needs of groups who want to keep fit, and others who'll want to wind down. Let's talk about it tomorrow and get ideas from the rest of the team.

G: Right, they'll have plenty of ideas. Let's see what they come up with.

LESSON 8.1 RECORDING 8.1

M = Michel, Mi = Mike, A= Astrid, J = John, Ma = Maria

M: I'm Michel, from France. Globalisation's definitely made the world smaller, but I don't think it's a fairer place. I think it has benefits for developed world consumers, but not for workers in poorer countries. It often means things like child labour and other abuses of human rights. There are some benefits but they're not evenly distributed. It's contributed to the gap between the rich and poor countries. Globalisation exploits the poor and has no respect for local cultures.

MI: Hi, this is Mike from the USA. Globalisation is just another aspect of evolution. It's a new name for an old process. Surely the coming of the railways and industrialisation hundreds of years ago was globalisation? It enables products to be produced wherever it is most efficient to do so. I think it means great social and economic progress for developing countries. I don't understand this anti-globalisation movement and feeling. Surely free markets and the free movement of people, goods and services are beneficial to economies all over the world?

A: This is Astrid, from Sweden. I think it's true that globalisation has connected the world with great technological advances in communications. Television and the Internet have improved people's lives all over the world. For me personally, globalisation is a good thing but it has also pushed rich and poor further apart. Globalisation is basically an economic movement. Manufacturing goes to the cheapest places. Companies maximise profits by exploiting workers as a way of reducing costs. Globalisation is mostly about corporate greed.

J: John, from the UK. Globalisation benefits everyone, including people in developing countries. It allows me personally to work from home in the UK with clients and colleagues all over the world. Globalisation isn't just benefiting big corporations. It also benefits small businesses like my own. Technology and cheaper transport mean I can compete with large corporations who used to have a monopoly on faraway markets.

MA: I'm Maria, speaking from Colombia. You know, when the result of globalisation is damaging the environment, it's a bad thing. It's clear to me that global warming and climate change are the direct results of globalisation. Industry and big business have no respect for the environment – they're only interested in making money. I don't see any benefits for workers in poor countries who are just exploited by globalisation.

LESSON 8.2 RECORDING 8.2

R = Radio presenter, G = Gina, P = Paulo, C = Carlos, I = Iwonna

R: On today's programme four international recruitment managers give advice to university leavers who wish to work for global companies. Gina, could you start us off please?

G: Certainly. I meet a lot of employers who recruit graduates, and most of them say they value individuals who are comfortable working in global teams and who are willing to work with people from different backgrounds and cultures. They want people who have the ability to think quickly and intelligently. It's about taking an active interest in the world around them and having a global mindset. That's what will catch the eye of global recruiters. These global graduates need to be able to show they've thought about the global challenges and opportunities facing companies.

P: I agree with you, Gina. They need to demonstrate that they have global skills. They need to understand the communication styles of the cultures they've come from, for example are their cultures direct or indirect, are they formal or informal. And they need to demonstrate curiosity and patience and be respectful about how people from other cultures communicate. It's about having more awareness about yourself and the culture you come from. If they are in a confusing situation they need to take a step back and not take things personally. The challenge is to stay open to other ways of communicating and not to make quick judgments about people. It's about putting yourself in their shoes. At the same time, treat people as individuals and don't stereotype them. The key words to think about are flexibility and adaptability. You can try to act appropriately by watching what other people do and mirroring their behaviour. If you try to respect and adjust to the way another person communicates, then that will help put them at ease and help you to avoid miscommunication. Trust your intuition and have confidence that you will act with sensitivity.

C: Maybe I can come in here Paulo, and give an example of how you can adapt and adjust. If I'm communicating with someone who has a more indirect communication style than me, then I should remember that they may be giving me hints rather than explaining clearly what they want. And they may not appreciate a very direct answer as this may be interpreted as rude. In this situation I would adapt my behaviour by paying more attention to how I phrase things and by softening my style to make sure information and facts don't come across too directly. And I could think about speaking to them in private as that might avoid embarrassment. I would also look out for body language and non-verbal clues as to what they are trying to express. Iwonna, would you like to come in here?

I: That's a really useful example Carlos. I'd like to give our listeners a practical example as well. Let's take the classic example of attitudes to meetings. Let's consider a meeting between people from two different cultures. In the first culture, the individual and their contributions and achievements are highly valued. People from this culture want a focussed, facts only, get it done, listen to me type meeting. However, in the second culture, the team is highly valued, and consensus, deciding something together, is a vital step in decision-making and it might take time to get to a decision. This culture also wants to make the other person look good and is not focussed on grabbing the spotlight or speaking up in meetings. People from the second culture don't speak up and people from the first culture just think people from the second culture never say anything. So good ideas go unspoken and misunderstandings grow. And the problem can get worse when one is looking at virtual communication and tele conferencing between people in different time zones, and where there is a shortage of time and meetings cannot drag on. If you want to work for a global team, you need to think about how you would react in situations like these, and you need to be able to adapt, whichever culture you come from …

LESSON 8.3 RECORDING 8.3

J = Jane, T = Tomas, M = Maria

J: Well, I'm delighted with the outcome of the annual report on our charity and we can say our clean up from the oil spill was a great success. But let's catch up on our plans for our latest environmental campaign … and I have to say I'm sorry for being out of touch last week but I had my computer fixed yesterday and hope to catch up with emails this week. So, can you bring us up to speed, Tomas?

T: Yeah. I had the web team update the site with news about the global campaign last week and we got the figures approved by Finance.

J: Right. One other thing I forgot to say … Hamza called me and, unfortunately, he had his car stolen so he won't be able to make the meeting!

T: Oh dear!

M: That's a shame.

J: OK, well back to the new campaign. So now it's just a case of having it all signed off by the legal team. Maria, can you deal with that?

M: Sure. When do we need it by?

J: Oh, no rush. The original deadline is fine – we're well ahead of schedule.

LESSON 8.4 RECORDING 8.4

P = Presenter, CEO = Bob Craven

P: Good evening everyone and welcome to this week's edition of In the Hot Seat, with me, Louise Falcon. Tonight my guest is Bob Craven, chief executive of the supermarket giant Smithsons.

CEO: Good evening, everyone.

P: Welcome to the programme, Bob. It's good to finally have you on the show to answer a few questions.

CEO: It's my pleasure, Louise.

P: Could I start off by asking you about the success of Smithsons – why do you think it's so successful?

CEO: Well, Louise, I think it's because of our range of products and because we have always meant good value for money.

P: Yes, but what do you mean by good value? Surely in some markets, and for some people, you are very expensive?

CEO: Well, I don't think so actually. Basically, what I'm saying is the customer is at the heart of our business. We always charge lower prices than our competitors.

AUDIO SCRIPTS

P: Ah, yes, but some people accuse you of using low prices to force the competition out of business.

CEO: Sorry, I don't know what you mean, Louise.

P: Well, there've been examples where you have destroyed small businesses by keeping prices low, which of course you can do because of your size.

CEO: That's ridiculous, Louise. What we're doing is offering the consumer a choice … and part of that choice is lower prices. And we're proud of that. Now, you could force people to use higher priced competitors to keep them in business, but that doesn't seem right to me. What I really want to say is that we believe in the customers' right to choose where they shop.

P: I see, but let me ask you …

CEO: Or to put it another way, businesses come and go. The world changes. Nothing lasts for ever.

P: OK, but don't you think that some people might think that's a rather arrogant thing to say when you consider the impact on people's lives. If you don't mind, I'd like to move on now to your staff. There have been criticisms of the fact that as a company you pay low wages, and also there are accusations that some of your clothing suppliers may use child labour and sweatshops.

CEO: Right, well, I can't comment on our suppliers, but what I can tell you is that in many markets our workers are paid over the minimum wage and as a company we do a lot for charity.

P: Could you explain that in more detail, please? What do you actually do for charity?

CEO: Certainly. I can tell you that Smithsons gives about 2.5 percent of its profits to local community projects.

P: Could you be more specific? Because many people have claimed they haven't seen the results of these community projects.

CEO: Yes, well, er, for example, if we build a new store, we, er, also, er, set aside money for a community centre or park. People like Smithsons, Louise. We do a lot for people.

P: Yes, but what about the negative impact of Smithsons?

CEO: Sorry, I don't follow you.

P: OK. Let me rephrase that. What I'm talking about is economic and social damage which big multinational companies like yours can do around the world.

CEO: Could you give me an example?

P: Yes, the fact that as a company you are anti union. You don't let employees join workers' organisations.

CEO: Yes, that's true. We don't think that unions are a good idea for staff or the company as a whole.

P: But why not? What I mean is … what are you worried about?

CEO: I don't think we're worried at all. I'm sorry, I don't see what you mean by all this damage you talk about. I see only benefits. Perhaps in some ways we are victims of our own success. We are almost too successful, but that's down to our customers. Statistics show that in the markets we have entered recently it is actually the poorest sections of society who benefit most. To be more precise … we really appeal to everyone and alienate no one.

P: Right. Another question for you now …

LESSON 9.1 RECORDING 9.1

1 Well, I'm a big fan of contemporary art – you know, really up-to-date things. I like video art – the stuff many people think is a bit crazy. I'm really into that sort of thing. I think some of it … some of it is really stylish, but you wouldn't, or couldn't have it in your home. I suppose I like art which is controversial. I also like the idea of mixing artistic styles and types of art together. A friend of mine took me to a great performance art exhibition which I loved. With the music, lights and the movement it was so impressive – out of this world. It was a bit like dance in some parts. I also enjoy sculpture, but really weird stuff made from strange materials. I know it's not for everyone, but I really like it.

2 It's much more traditional art which I like, big museums and galleries. I like classical art, I suppose, you know, landscapes and portraits – the typical masterpieces. But recently I've got very interested in Asian art. I saw this exhibition of Chinese art which was incredible. It was so beautiful. It really took my breath away. I'd seen a lot of stuff in books and then I saw a TV documentary about the exhibition. It really lived up to my expectations when I saw it. The reality was even better than I hoped. Some of the pottery was amazing, especially when you think how old it is. The whole exhibition inspired me to find out more about art from around the world.

3 I like modern art, and particularly abstract art. At the moment, I also really like Pop Art – all that stuff from the 60's which was inspired by advertising and comic books. I went to see a great exhibition last month. It was a bit expensive, and I had to queue to get in, but it was worth the effort and the cost. I suppose I'm lucky being in London, as we seem to get a lot of high profile exhibitions and retrospectives. This was a once-in-a-lifetime opportunity. It's funny, but I wasn't interested in art at all when I was younger. It's something which I've become fascinated by during the last couple of years. I'm thinking of joining one of the big museums as a member, as then you get invited to previews, and it's a lot cheaper. I remember going on a school trip to Paris once to see the masterpieces in the big museums, but I found that classical art rather dead and disappointing, and the galleries were just too crowded and full of people taking photos, rather than looking at the art!

LESSON 9.4 RECORDING 9.2

V = Vanessa, R = Russell, D = Dennis

R: One of the things we're considering, Dennis, is to lower our commission. At the moment, we charge 50%, that's confidential by the way. But if we lowered the commission, we'd attract quite a few younger artists and that could be helpful for us.

D: Maybe, but consider the implications. At the moment, your artists are paying 50% and not complaining, they're accepting your terms of sale. If you lower your commission, other galleries might start doing the same thing, then you'll be in a price war. How do you feel about lowering commissions, Vanessa?

V: Well, I think there's a strong argument for doing it. We do need to have more young artists on our books, I've said it for some time. It'd be a way of attracting them. It'd be quick and very effective.

D: But think of the consequences, Vanessa. It'll affect your profits if you lower your commission rate. Also, you need to take into account the reactions of the other gallery owners. They won't be pleased if they hear you're price-cutting. They'll start doing the same thing and that won't be in anyone's interests.

V: That may be true, but our situation's getting pretty desperate. We've got to do something if we want to survive.

D: Well, the effect of a lower commission rate will be harmful to your business, in my opinion.

R: I've had a few thoughts about this, Dennis. You say that it'll affect our profits. But it wouldn't if we charged variable commission rates, I mean, charge different rates to different artists. Keep the rates we've got for artists who are popular with collectors and people who pay top prices, but give up-and-coming artists a lower rate. How about that?

D: The problem with that is it could really upset your best customers, the cash cows, if I can put it like that, who are keeping your gallery afloat.

R: Mmm, I don't know, maybe you're right. OK, well then, what are we going to do if we don't lower our commission?

D: You've got a lot of options, believe me. There are plenty of things you could do that'll get more people coming to your gallery and improve your bottom line. You can't do all of them. Some, I'm sure, you'll reject immediately. You'll have to make up your minds and choose the best ones. Some will be expensive, others won't cost too much. I've jotted down some ideas for you. Let's talk about them. I hope you'll feel some are worth considering.

LESSON 9.5 RECORDING 9.3

If you go on a fairly long holiday, maybe to a faraway destination, I think it's a really good idea to write a travel blog. You see, one advantage of doing it is you can create a social environment with your blog. What do I mean by that? Well, you'll create a group of people who are interested in what you're doing. Your family and your friends can read your diary entries and respond to them, so they become part of your holiday. With your blog, you can keep in touch with a much bigger group of people, you won't need to buy dozens of postcards to let them know what you're doing. So you'll save money, that's always a good thing, I'm sure you'll agree.

Blogs are a great way of telling your family and friends about your holiday and how it's going, you know, the interesting places you're visiting, the people you're meeting. And everyone who's following you will know you're safe because they're constantly reading your messages. They'll also be able to look at your photos and videos. Oh, one other advantage I want to mention, your travel blog is a permanent record of your trip – something you can look at again when you're back home.

So, I'm encouraging you all to write a travel blog – it's good practice for improving your writing – and you can tell everyone about the amazing experiences you're having and maybe even about things that have gone wrong, especially if they're funny and not too serious.

LESSON 10.1 RECORDING 10.1

Ambitious - ambition
Authoritative - authority
Conscientious - conscientiousness
creative – creativity
diplomatic – diplomacy
energetic – energy
knowledgeable – knowledge
objective – objectivity
practical – practicality
resourceful – resourcefulness

LESSON 10.1 RECORDING 10.2

Good morning, everyone. Our topic today is group dynamics. I want to talk about how groups develop over a period of time. So I'll describe the stages that groups often go through.

Erm, first of all, I'd like to mention an academic who did some interesting early work on groups. His name's Kurt Lewin, you spell Kurt, scientifically, so he's important. He published his results during the 1940s and 1950s. And he created the term 'group dynamics' to describe how groups and individuals act and react in changing situations.

OK, the next really important contribution came from a researcher, Bruce Tuckman. Tuckman developed a theory about groups in 1965. He argued that groups went through four stages. Now I'd like to look briefly at each of the stages in turn.

First, 'Forming'. This is the stage when the group pretends to get on well with each other and everyone seems to be happy. It's a kind of honeymoon period.

Next is the 'Storming' stage. As the name suggests, at this stage, members of the group are less polite to each other and they try to resolve their issues, even if they lose their tempers at times. Individual group members may fall out with each other as the true personalities of group members become clearer at this time.

'Norming' is the stage after that. Members get used to each other at this stage. They begin to trust each other, share information and are much more productive as they get down to the job of working together.

The final stage is 'Performing'. The members of the group have common goals. The atmosphere in the group is good. They work efficiently together and cooperate effectively with each other.

These are the four stages in Tuckman's original theory about how groups develop. I should say that later on he added a fifth stage. He called it 'Adjourning'. That's the stage when the group breaks up. Of course, some groups never even reach the 'Norming' stage. If they don't trust each other, and members find they cannot put up with each other, the group may break up early, before the 'Norming' stage.

Tuckman's theory is useful and of practical value. Think for a moment about pop groups, or bands you know. A classic example for me, although not from my generation (laughs) is The Beatles, for example. They went through all five stages. During the 'Performing' stage, they were very effective, and wrote and performed some of their best songs, but eventually John Lennon moved away from the group and after Paul McCartney left, the band began to break up. You can also think of successful football teams which go through those stages. After early struggles, they have a period of success, with a core of the same team members, although a few individuals will leave and join. This stable team may do well and win championships and trophies. Then the team breaks up – for whatever reason – perhaps due to the age or the ambition of the players. Finally, a very contemporary example would be in reality TV, where the way the group works together is often the most interesting part of these sorts of programme, and why people watch them. So Tuckman's model is a good one, and it's useful for analysing group dynamics.
Now are there any questions so far …?

LESSON 10.4 RECORDING 10.3

PB = Professor Brown, M = Michelle

PB: OK, let's go to my next caller, who's in Preston.
M: Hello Professor, my name's Michelle.
PB: Hi Michelle. How can I help?
M: It's about my husband, Jack. You see, he's retired now, he hasn't worked for over a year. And the problem is, he's got nothing to do all day except spend money and, well, he's spending an awful lot of money.
PB: Oh dear! That must be worrying.
M: Mmm. You see, he's run up a lot of debts, he owes people money all over the place, and if he goes on like this, well, we'll have to sell our house.
PB: Michelle, I can see you're very upset. Can you tell me a little bit more? What's he spending his money on?
M: Well, you see, Jack spends a lot of time on the internet. He's bored, I suppose, and then he continually buys things. Usually it's really expensive stuff, top brand clothes, designer sunglasses, that sort of thing. A few weeks ago, he bought a Rolex watch on eBay. It cost a fortune – over £7,000.
PB: Mmm, I'd say he's addicted to spending money. There are so many forms of addiction, Michelle, and so often we find that the addict isn't aware they're addicted. That seems to be your husband's problem. Once he understands he's addicted to spending, it'll be possible to help him get rid of the addiction.
M: Yes, you're right, he is addicted. And it's a terrible problem. We just can't afford that level of spending. He's already up to the limit on three credit cards, we've no savings left in the bank, and he's just taken out a personal loan.
PB: And doesn't this level of debt worry him?
M: Well, no. It doesn't seem to, no.
PB: Well, you can't go on like that. What was he like before he retired, Michelle? Was he always a big spender?
M: Yes, he was. He always loved giving parties, going out on the town, helping his friends if they needed money – that sort of thing. Actually, early on in our marriage, he went bankrupt – it was an awful time for us. You know, I sometimes wonder why I stay with him, and when things get really bad, I've even thought of leaving him.
PB: Perhaps it's because you still love him.
M: I suppose I do. You know it's not easy to leave someone you've been with a long time – even if they are ruining your life. I'm so confused, Professor. What do you think I should do?

LESSON 10.4 RECORDING 10.4

PB = Professor Brown, M = Michelle

PB: Well, it's obviously very difficult for you, Michelle. No wonder you're confused and upset.
M: Mmm, I don't know which way to turn, to be honest. That's why I've phoned you – I need some good advice.

PB: Right, first of all, you need to talk to someone about the debts you have. A real professional.
M: Mmm, yes, that could be helpful, I suppose. But I don't know anyone who does that sort of thing.
PB: Well, I do, Michelle. At the end of the programme, I'll give you the name of someone who can advise you how to deal with your debts.
M: Great, thanks very much.
PB: Now, you could also contact your local Citizens Advice Centre – their services are free. If possible, you should both go there. OK?
M: Well, I like the idea but … I don't think it'd work, both of us going there, I mean. I know Jack'll find some excuse not to go, I'm sure he won't like the idea.
PB: OK, then, fair enough, let's look at some other things you could do. Can I ask you, do you have a joint account with your husband?
M: Yes, we do – our account's in both our names. Always has been.
PB: Well, you know, it might be a good idea to have a separate bank account. Just for the time being, until your husband gets his finances in order. Why don't you suggest it to him?
M: Oh, I don't think so, what's the point of doing that? There's no way he'd agree to it. We've had a joint account all our married life.
PB: OK, we'll forget about that one. Do you use the internet a lot a home?
M: Yes, almost every day.
PB: Great! Well, if I were you, I'd look at some of the sites offering help for people in your situation. I can give you the addresses of some of the reputable ones. Also, it might be worth contacting a finance company. They could help you with your debts. If you decide to do that, you should contact your bank for a name. They'll be able to recommend a suitable company. OK?
M: Yes, I'll check some websites and maybe ask my bank to recommend a finance company. That sounds like a good idea to me. But what about my husband's spending problem? What can I do about it?
PB: Well, it's vital that you do something about his overspending, Michelle. Or should I say, it's vital your husband does something about it. Why don't you have a serious talk with him? Try to persuade him to join a counselling group. I'll give you the name of an organisation that's helped many people like your husband to control their spending. It meets every two weeks and it doesn't cost anything to join.
M: You know, that's really good advice. Jack likes meeting new people – he'd probably go regularly to that sort of counselling session. Yeah, I like that idea. Thanks very much, Professor. You've been really helpful.
PB: Good. Michelle, I've one final bit of advice. You might consider getting some counselling yourself. You've had a tough time recently, life's been difficult for you. It might help you to have a few sessions with a counsellor. Just an idea.
M: Counselling? For me? I don't think so. It's my husband who needs counselling, not me. He's the one with the problems. No, I've got too much on my mind at the moment. I don't have time for that.
PB: OK, just a suggestion. I agree it's your husband who really needs counselling. It's essential that he changes his behaviour. If he doesn't, you'll be very unhappy and it'll end in tears.
M: Yes, that's what I'm worried about. Anyway, thanks a lot for your advice.

PB: Good. My staff will contact you and pass on all the information you need. Goodbye Michelle, and good luck!

LESSON 11.1 RECORDING 11.1

1 When I'm outside Turkey, travelling for my job, I miss the smell of strong Turkish coffee, and the smell of the food. I really miss our typical Turkish breakfast of white cheese, bread, eggs, honey and olives. I think also of the rain in my home town, and holidays where my family and relatives come together. I miss the prayers we hear five times a day from the mosques. I also think Turkish hospitality is wonderful. I miss visiting friends, relatives and neighbours and the way that Turkish people really try hard to make their guests feel comfortable. Another thing I miss about Turkish culture is the respect for older people.

2 When I lived abroad, I missed cycling to places. I didn't see many people on bikes, everyone used cars all the time, even for short distances. Children were taken to school by their parents, and my host father drove to a nearby petrol station to get his newspaper. I thought about getting a bike, but there were no cycle paths in my area, and I felt I'd be a kind of 'outsider' if I cycled to work in the morning.
I also missed small local supermarkets where you can walk to do your shopping. In Germany, we have many small supermarkets in all parts of cities or towns, and you can get everything you need there. They are not huge and anonymous, like the big supermarkets in some other countries.
Talking of food, I missed German bread and German rolls. Bread tastes a lot better in my country, I can tell you.

3 When I worked abroad what I missed most was certain emotional aspects of our culture, not material ones. I certainly missed the Russian style of friendship. In my country, people will discuss all kinds of very personal problems, even intimate problems with you. And they expect friends to forget their own problems and do everything to help you out. But outside Russia, I noticed people are more individualistic, and even with good friends, the conversations are more superficial, they take less time, and people tend to be more focused on their own problems.
Also, I miss Russian jokes and loud laughter. Russians often organise parties at someone's home, old friends come together and spend hours eating and drinking around a big table, discussing things, singing, dancing. One final thing. I missed our traditional Russian winter, going down snow covered hills on a toboggan with my young son, skiing and skating, playing snowballs and making snow maidens with our fluffy snow.

4 What did I miss when I was abroad? Definitely the food. In Cameroon, everything we eat is fresh, no processing, artificial stuff or colouring. I remember we had to literally chase the chicken, kill it, and then cook it. It took almost the whole afternoon. And then I missed the spices. We took the tomatoes, basil and peanuts straight out of the field, it was wonderful! When we wanted a treat, all we had to do was go to the mango or guava or avocado tree and pick it. And if we wanted a snack, we would go to the cornfield to get some corn. I tell you, I had no problem keeping slim.
The weather, I missed that too. Cameroon is a tropical country, so we have some very good

weather. Believe it or not, what I missed most was the sun of course, but also the tropical rain. I tell you, when it beats down on top of a tin roof, it produces a sound that's like a lullaby, it makes you feel sleepy.

5 I feel comfortable living in foreign countries, especially in Europe. I like the variety of cultures you meet just travelling a few hundred kilometres. But I miss something that just isn't there. It's the sound of my typically Italian language where I grew up. It took me a long time to realise its effect on me. When I hear people speaking my Italian dialect, then I let myself dive into a very private comfort zone. It's a blend of feelings consisting of love, trust, comfort and being 'home'. For me, I've lived and worked in various places around the world, but I've never experienced that anywhere else, except in my home country. I'm studying in England now and I definitely miss not being able to express my ideas as soon as they come into my mind. I just can't communicate easily and precisely what I think in English, and that frustrates me.
Of course, I miss knowing where to go to find what I need. Being Italian, it means I miss good food, the sun and friendly people. I miss so much, but I'm really enjoying being in England.

6 I've travelled all over the world. What do I miss? Well, the first thing that comes to mind is the more relaxed atmosphere we have in the streets, you know, socialising and meeting friends for coffee or dinner. It's a very spontaneous culture. You don't need to make arrangements a long time in advance. You just phone a friend, and then meet them at home or outside only a few minutes after your phone call.
I should mention our drink, I miss it a lot when I'm overseas. It's called *mate*, it's a traditional drink in a special container. You pour a kind of green tea herb (called *yerba mate*) into the container, you add boiling hot water and then sip the tea. It's a kind of ritual. You pass the container around with a group when you get together at someone's home – it's a bit like the Indian tribes used to pass round the 'pipes of peace'. You chat, have fun and talk philosophically about life, the state of the world and so on. Friendship and bonding are very important in Argentina. I missed all that socialising when I was in England and the United States.

LESSON 11.2 RECORDING 11.2

I = Interviewer, L = Lars, S = Sofia, H = Hugo
I: Thanks for all coming today. Who's come the furthest? Lars?
L: Well, I've just finished studying at Hokkaido University but I'm now working for a bank in Tokyo – so it's not me.
H: It can't be me, either. I'm teaching English here in Tokyo.
I: Sofia, how about you?
S: Yep, must be me. I've come from Fukuoka, which for your listeners, is on the Southern island of Kyushu.
I: Well, thanks for coming all this way Sofia. Can you tell us about your experience of living in Japan and culture shock?
S: Well, I arrived here one month ago, and I'm studying Japanese on a scholarship from Nihon Keizai University. I'm staying in a dormitory provided by the university.
I: And are you enjoying it?
S: I'm having such a good time. People have been incredibly welcoming. I've been invited

back to peoples' homes and they've cooked for me. I've met up with people for language exchange – where we've had lunch together and then gone shopping. I've met a lot of people – Japanese and foreigners – through the Fukuoka Now website. I just love Japanese food, especially sushi. It's all so different from home, but it's fantastic. The only problem I've had is that I've got quite big feet and I just can't buy women's shoes here that fit me.
I: Hahaha. It sounds like you're having a great time. Hugo, I know your experience has been slightly different.
H: Yes, you're right. I've been here three months now and, as I said, I'm teaching English here in Tokyo. I have a very small room and I feel a bit lonely. Also I get frustrated by the giggling and whispered comments when schoolchildren pass me. I've stopped going out into the countryside because when I went out into the countryside children would stare at me. I'm just not fitting in at the moment. Sometimes the Japanese are quite indirect with their requests and suggestions, and I don't know what they are really trying to get at.
I: Sorry to hear that Hugo. How about you Lars?
L: Well, as I said, I've just finished studying at Hokkaido University in Sapporo in the north of Japan. I studied economics and I'm now working for a bank in Tokyo. So I've been in Japan for five years. Hokkaido is really beautiful. The winter landscapes are stunning and the people in Hokkaido are wonderful. If you go there, look out for the volcanoes, the frozen sea and the famous ice sculptures. And I really recommend going cross country skiing to appreciate the scenery.
I: And what has been your experience of culture shock, Lars?
L: Well, I think I can now appreciate all the strengths of both Japanese culture and my own culture. I think you don't have to worry too much about obeying rules. It's more important to remember your manners, behave and speak with respect and realise that humour crosses all barriers. Your stay in this wonderful country is so much more relaxing if you just have a sense of humour.
I: And finally, for those planning to come to Japan, is it safe?
H: Definitely.
L: Yes.
S: Obviously, crime does happen, but it's been a really great experience to live in a place that feels so safe.

LESSON 11.3 RECORDING 11.3

1 When my wife and I were on holiday in Istanbul, Turkey, we decided to visit a market. My wife persuaded me to travel there by *dolmus* – one of the small minibuses which hold about 20 passengers. We sat in the middle of the bus, and after about ten minutes, an old woman came from the back seats, tapped me on the shoulder and put two coins in my hand, muttering something in Turkish. I didn't understand, but thanked her and put the coins in my pocket. A few minutes later, the bus driver stopped and spoke to the old woman. She pointed at me, and didn't look very pleased. The bus driver started waving his arms about and shouting at me in broken English, 'You bad person. You get off my bus, you don't give me money.' I suddenly realised that the woman had given me the coins to pass on to the driver to pay for the journey. I was so embarrassed.

I admitted taking the money and apologised for not giving it to him. He just wouldn't listen. He warned me not to get on his bus again. I regretted travelling by *dolmus* and we never did it again. During the rest of our holiday, we travelled by taxi and ferry-boat!

2 I made a terrible social gaffe in Spain the first time I went there for work purposes. I'd refused to do the orientation programme because I'd been to Malaga for a week a few years before – it was great: sunny beaches and loads of other expatriates – I really enjoyed myself. But when I went there for a week to work it was totally different. I'd arrived in the afternoon and there was a car to take me to the hotel from the airport. I'd missed lunch so I had a snack at about three o'clock. Then, knowing that my hosts had insisted on picking me up at nine o'clock and that I'd agreed to meet them in the hotel lobby, I thought I would have my supper before going out for the evening. Big mistake! I hadn't realised that the Spanish eat very late. So there I was in a very nice restaurant having to choose a meal at 11 o'clock when I felt stuffed full from my supper earlier. They encouraged me to order lots of different dishes. I tried to eat but couldn't manage more than two or three mouthfuls. My hosts thought I must be unhappy or ill. I could see that they were very concerned so I decided to tell them the truth. They nearly fell off their chairs laughing and told me to forget about eating any more food. In a funny way, my social gaffe worked out OK in the end because everybody was laughing so much that we were able to talk business in a friendly atmosphere. But I never went anywhere new ever again without a full briefing

LESSON 11.4 RECORDING 11.4

Hello, everyone. My name's James and I'm from Canada. This morning I'm going to talk to you about my fascinating home town of Toronto. I've divided my presentation into three parts. First of all, I'll start with some background information, then I'll move on to the main sights. Finally, I'll outline some other experiences a visitor should try when they come to Toronto. If you don't mind, we'll leave questions to the end.

OK, I'll start with some basic information. Toronto is the capital city of the province of Ontario, and it's situated on Lake Ontario. Until 1934, it was called York. It's got a population of approximately 2.4 million, so it's a fairly large city. It's an important industrial, commercial and cultural centre.

Toronto's getting better and better these days, as more and more people come from all over the world to settle here. They enrich our city greatly with their skills and talents and they help to create the lively, friendly, cosmopolitan atmosphere the city is famous for.

LESSON 11.4 RECORDING 11.5

So, what are the main sights of the city? Well, there are many things to see, but let me focus on three: the CN tower, City Hall and Casa Loma. OK, why is the CN Tower worth seeing? Well, it's a tall building, a very tall building. Actually, it's one of the tallest structures in the world; it's 1,815 feet high. Built in 1976 by Canadian National Railways, it overlooks the city and you can see it wherever you are in the city. It's

truly gigantic, incredible, and awe inspiring. Go up the tower and you get a fantastic view of the city. And if you're very brave, why don't you stand on the glass floor, 342 metres off the ground, then look down? And if you can do that, why not take the elevator and go on up to the Sky Pod? That's another 34 storeys higher! Another great sight is the City Hall. There was a worldwide competition in the 60s to design it, and a Finnish architect, Viljo Revell, won the competition. Unfortunately, he died before it was opened in 1965. It's beautifully designed, and far ahead of its time. Now it's a very popular tourist attraction, in fact it's probably the most popular attraction. In front of it is Nathan Phillips Square. The Square is an entertainment venue, it offers free concerts, ice skating and on New Year's Eve, a huge celebration takes place there.

Finally, Casa Loma. What can I say about this extraordinary castle? It was called a 'rich man's folly'. People thought Sir Henry Pellatt, the owner, was crazy to spend so much money on building the castle in 1914. It cost 3.5 million dollars, a huge sum in those days. And he went bankrupt trying to maintain and develop it. Ten years later, its value was just 27,000 dollars. It has so many interesting architectural features: 60 large rooms, an immense Great Hall, where 2,000 people can be entertained, a beautiful library, secret underground passages and magnificent gardens. It's a MUST place to visit.

LESSON 11.4 RECORDING 11.6

Finally, I'll talk about some things a visitor should definitely do when they come to Toronto.

Well, how about trying some waffles for breakfast? They're sort of pancakes – with maple syrup – delicious, and typically Canadian food.

Secondly, if you like sports, you should go to see a hockey game – an ice hockey game - featuring the local Maple Leaf team. They've won many championships and are one of the top ice hockey teams in North America. Hockey is physical, fast and exciting. It's a rough game, a contact sport, but thrilling and skilful.

I'd also like to suggest that visitors should try and experience the Caribana festival, which takes place every year from mid July to early August. It is one of North America's largest street festivals and is based on the Trinidad carnival. The first one took place in 1967, when the city's Caribbean community celebrated the 100th anniversary of Canada. It just got bigger and bigger so that today it attracts more than a million visitors.

To sum up, I'd just like to say that Toronto is a modern, exciting, and welcoming city just waiting to be explored. I do hope you will be able to add it to your list of destinations and we look forward to showing you the very best which Toronto has to offer.

That's all from me. Any questions?

LESSON 11.4 RECORDING 11.7

It's got a population of approximately 2.4 million, so it's a fairly large city. It's an important industrial, commercial and cultural centre. Toronto's getting better and better these days, as more and more people come from all over the world to settle here. They enrich our city greatly with their skills and talents and they help to create the lively, friendly, cosmopolitan atmosphere the city is famous for.

So, what are the main sights of the city? Well, there are many things to see, but let me focus on three: the CN tower, City Hall and Casa Loma. OK, why is the CN Tower worth seeing? Well, it's a tall building, a very tall building. Actually, it's one of the the tallest structures in the world; it's 1,815 feet high.

LESSON 11.4 RECORDING 11.8

P = Presenter, M = Mary Robinson

P: ... and welcome to today's edition of *Daybreak*, where my guest is Professor Mary Robinson, the author of a new book on improving reading skills.

M: Hello, Pam, and good morning everyone.

P: Yes, hello, Mary, and thanks for joining us. Perhaps we could start with you telling us a bit about why you wrote the book?

M: Yes, sure. Well, I've noticed that among the sort of students I meet at the university, there seems to be a decline in the amount of reading they do, both for their studies and for pleasure. This is a real shame because there is a clear link between the amount you read and your ability to express yourself. Also, it seems that reading is the best way of acquiring knowledge. For example, research into how people acquire knowledge has shown that people who watched more TV were more likely to get general knowledge questions wrong, and this is independent of intellectual ability.

P: Really, how interesting.

M: Yes, it seems the more reading you do, the better, whatever it is. Reading increases vocabulary, improves your general knowledge and keeps your memory and reasoning abilities working well.

P: That's got to be a good thing! So what tips can you give for improving reading?

M: Obviously, it depends on the sort of reading you're doing. However, I think students are often not selective enough about what they choose to read and then they focus too much on details. It's very important to get an overall idea about what you're reading and to make full use of any headings and subheadings to help guide your reading, and stop you wasting time reading unnecessary information. Also, I think it's crucial to engage with what you read. People often think of reading as a one way process, but in fact it should be a two way process ...

P: Can you explain what you mean there?

M: Of course. To be an effective reader, you should always be thinking about what the writer may say next, and also questioning what you read. Think about if you agree or disagree with what you're reading, with the opinion of the writer, with their logic, conclusions and arguments ... that sort of thing.

P: Right. Anything else?

M: Well, one particular problem that I've noticed is foreign students who focus too much on unknown vocabulary. This can make reading very time-consuming as they constantly stop to look up words in their dictionaries.

P: Yes, I see. In fact, I think people often do that in their own language too.

M: When they're studying, indeed. However, often, you can work out the meaning of the word by reading on and looking at the context it's used in, or at least make an educated guess. For people who want to improve their reading speed, a good tip is to use your finger, but not to follow the words on the line. No, the secret here is to move your finger down the page as you read, as this will train your eyes to move more quickly down the text and keep you moving forward.

P: That's a good tip. Well, thank you very much, Professor, and good luck with the book.

M: Thank you, Pam.

LESSON 12.1 RECORDING 12.1

1 I really detest GPS. Actually, I have one myself. (laughs). I will admit they are very practical – and they can stop a lot of arguments, about which is the quickest, or fastest way to get somewhere when you are driving, but they can get people into trouble. I think they are an example of people putting too much faith in technology. They don't trust their instincts. They would sooner rely on a state-of-the-art gadget than what their own eyes tell them. These people who end up driving through rivers or get stuck in tiny, narrow streets – ridiculous. And then there are the people who mistype the destination and end up going to a completely different place! Then again, you could say GPS is dangerous, when people try and race them, you know by trying to get to the destination faster than the arrival time the GPS says. There are also those drivers who look at the screen rather than the road ahead, but I suppose this is people who are a danger rather than the technology. Whatever happened to maps and atlases? At least they gave you an overview. I really think GPS has given people a worse sense of direction, and some people have just lost their common sense! But, I have to agree that they are very handy!

2 What's my favourite piece of technology? That's easy, my tablet computer. It's really great. I know it's cutting edge, the very latest model and all that, but what I don't like is that it takes a long time to charge. Also, I have other gadgets from the same company, but they all have different chargers. I've got so many – why they can't just have one? I've no idea – it's a real pain. It's really easy to use and it seems durable. I did drop it, but it didn't break, unlike my last smart phone. That wasn't at all hard-wearing – the screen cracked pretty soon after I got it and I had to get a replacement. I suppose I love gadgets – the trouble is that because technology changes so fast these days they go out of date very quickly – they become obsolete almost as soon as you buy them. I guess I am a bit of a slave to my machines, as I panic if I don't have them with me. Yes, I'm a technology addict!

3 I suppose the last piece of technology I bought was a shredder, you know, for shredding documents and things like that. Everyone kept telling me to buy one because they, … because of identity fraud – other people finding out information about you and using it to, I don't know, to steal from your bank account or get a passport in your name, that kind of thing. So I've just bought a shredder, and it's all right. It was cheap enough and it's pretty user friendly, but I don't like it … the idea, I mean. I don't like the idea of having to destroy important documents so other people can't use them. It's just that it shows what kind of a world we live in now, I suppose, and I don't want

to believe it. The other thing about the shredder that I don't like is the fact that it isn't very environmentally friendly – it uses quite a lot of electricity, which isn't very green to start with, and apparently, you can't put shredded paper in the recycling bin. I think it's different from council to council, but where I live, they won't take shredded paper because the pieces are too small and can't be sorted mechanically for recycling.

LESSON 12.3 RECORDING 12.2

L = Lia, P = Paulo

L: I think we all agree that the discovery of penicillin changed the world and if Edward Jenner hadn't discovered vaccines, there would be far more fatalities every year than there actually are. And I think it's vital that we move forward with golden rice. If the authorities hadn't blocked the introduction of golden rice we could have saved many from blindness.

P: I think many people are uneasy about GM foods, Lia. If wheat grew in the desert, we wouldn't have needed to develop GM crops in the first place as we would have had enough food. And another thing. I saw on a TV programme the other day that a person would need to eat seven kilos of cooked rice every day in order to get sufficient vitamin A.

L: Well Paulo, in the first place, GM crops are about improving health as well as providing enough food. And secondly, according to the latest scientific evidence, it seems that a large amount of vitamin A can be obtained by eating sixty grams of cooked golden rice and that's grams not kilos.

LESSON 12.4 RECORDING 12.3

J = Jessie, C = Carol

J: It's pretty obvious the way the wind's blowing, isn't it, Carol? I mean, why they want to buy these new machines.

C: Yeah, no doubt about it. They want to cut costs and reduce the workforce – what other reason would they have?

J: That's the way I see it too. They just want to squeeze more work out of us and reduce the labour bill. Then the profits will look a bit healthier.

C: Exactly, You know, I don't fancy my chances having a job here in six months' time. Not at my age, I'll be one of the first to go.

J: Well, I don't know, you may be lucky. Both of us may be able to survive. We work pretty fast and we've got a lot of experience. But I must say, I don't like the idea of working on some really complicated new machines. I'm not sure I'll be able to. I'm doing good work on the ones we have now. Like you, I'm used to them and no one's complained about my work. But I'll take months to get the hang of these new ones. I'm not sure I'll be able to do it.

C: I feel the same. I don't want to spend weeks on a training course to master the machines.

J: We're not the only ones who feel like that. There are a lot of unhappy and worried people here at the moment. Everyone wants to know what's going on and the rumours are flying around.

C: Yeah, it's about time the management told us exactly what their plans are – then we'll know where we stand.

LESSON 12.4 RECORDING 12.4

S = Stephanie, D = Don

S: You know, Don, a lot of people, and I'm one of them, don't think we need to spend a load of money on new machines at the moment. We're still making a profit, not as much as before, true, but let's face it, the economy's not in good shape at the moment. Everyone's suffering.

D: It's true what you say Stephanie, but we do need to modernise our production line. Our competitors are up-dating their equipment, and we need to do the same. We don't want to be left behind. That's a very strong argument for spending some money on the latest machines. Another reason is that the new machines will enable operators to produce a wider range of goods and earn more money. Don't forget, their pay depends on how many items they produce.

S: We won't need as many workers, will we, to do that?

D: I would argue that we'll be using our resources more efficiently. Of course, we'll have to reduce our workforce, maybe by 20%, but that'll help to lower our costs and make us more competitive. It's a hard world out there.

S: If some of our staff lose their jobs, it'll have a bad effect on production. Staff will be unhappy and then we'll begin to have problems, serious problems. It'll affect the culture of our company. You know, one happy family, the staff are our biggest asset.

D: That's a fair point, Stephanie, but look at the bigger picture. You know the saying, you can't make an omelette without breaking eggs. I'm sure you agree with me, it's our job to manage change, to help staff to adapt to the new situation, even if it's painful for some of them.

S: You know, some of our colleagues don't think we need the new technology. Who's to say that the new machines … they're very complicated, can we be sure they'll do the job for us?

D: I've heard about these objections. My answer is simple. The manufacturer has assured us that the machines will increase the output of each worker by 20–50%. That's good enough for me. Their equipment is reliable and they don't make claims they can't back up.

S: Yeah, but will the older workers, we've got plenty of them, learn how to use the new machines? I'm not so sure.

D: Look, I think you'll agree, we've got some of the best and most experienced workers in the trade. They'll learn how to use the machines if we give them plenty of time to train on them. That's the way forward for us. We can't compete with these cheap imports unless we use the most up-to-date technology. We don't have any other option.

S: I don't know if I share your opinion. You may be surprised by the resistance they show. People don't like change. In any case, there are other options …

D: Oh?

S: Yeah, Well, firstly, we could stay as we are, we're making a profit in difficult economic conditions …

Intermediate, Upper Intermediate and Advanced levels

David Cotton studied Economics at the University of Reading and did an MA in French Language and Literature at the University of Toronto. He has over forty-four years teaching and training experience, and is co-author of the successful *Market Leader* and *Business Class* course books. He has taught in Canada, France and England, and has been visiting lecturer in many universities overseas. Previously, he was Senior Lecturer at London Metropolitan University. He frequently gives talks at EFL conferences.

David Falvey studied Politics, Philosophy and Economics at the University of Oxford and did his MA in TEFL at the University of Birmingham. He has lived in Africa and the Middle East and has teaching, training and managerial experience in the UK and Asia, including working as a teacher trainer at the British Council in Tokyo. He was previously Head of the English Language Centre at London Metropolitan University. David is co-author of the successful business English course *Market Leader*.

Simon Kent studied History at the University of Sheffield, and also has an M.A in History and Cultural Studies. He has over twenty-five years' teaching experience including three years in Berlin at the time of German reunification. Simon is co-author of the successful business English course *Market Leader*. He is currently Senior Lecturer in English as a Foreign Language at London Metropolitan University.

Elementary, Pre-intermediate and Advanced levels

Gareth Rees studied Natural Sciences at the University of Cambridge. Having taught in Spain and China, he currently teaches at the University of the Arts, London. As well as teaching English, he is an academic English course leader, and unit leader on courses in cross-cultural communication for the London College of Fashion. He has also developed English language materials for the BBC World Service Learning English section, and he makes films which appear in festivals and on British television.

Ian Lebeau studied Modern Languages at the University of Cambridge and did his MA in Applied Linguistics at the University of Reading. He has thirty-five years' experience in ELT – mainly in higher education – and has taught in Spain, Italy and Japan. He is currently Senior Lecturer in English as a Foreign Language at London Metropolitan University.

Far left: Simon Kent
Centre left: David Falvey
Centre: Gareth Rees
Centre right: Ian Lebeau
Far right: David Cotton

Pearson Education Limited
Edinburgh Gate
Harlow
Essex CM20 2JE
England
and Associated Companies throughout the world.

www.pearsonelt.com

First published 2014
Seventh impression 2018
ISBN: 978-1-4479-4863-6
Set in Optima
Printed by L.E.G.O. S.p.A, Italy

Acknowledgements
The Publisher and authors would like to thank the following people who gave us valuable feedback during the development of the material:

Australia: Caroline Mueller; **France:** Carine Buret; **Poland:** Dorota Rejman **Russia:** Elena Smetkina, Lyudmila Delyagina; **Turkey:** Emine Yetgin; **UK:** Elizabeth Davies, Lyudmila Delyagina, Sarah Mattin, Nicholas Northall, Jane Sealy-Thompson.

Photo acknowledgements
The publisher would like to thank the following for their kind permission to reproduce their photographs:
(Key: b-bottom; c-centre; l-left; r-right; t-top)
akg-images Ltd: Interfoto 37cl; **Alamy Images:** Adrian Muttitt 110tr, Alex Federowicz 46t, Alex Segre 110tl, Chris Willson 116cl, David Levenson 82-83tc, M-dash 17br, Paul Carter 52bl, Peakscape 152tc, Powered by Light / Alan Spencer 47bl, RubberBall 116br, The Photolibrary Wales 22-23b, TianYin Li 85cr, VIEW Pictures Ltd 152tl; **Atelier Tekuto. Architect: Yasuhiro Yamashita:** Makoto Yoshida 69tl, Sergio Pirrone 69tc; **Bridgeman Art Library Ltd:** The Sower, 1888 (oil on canvas), Gogh, Vincent van (1853-90) / Rijksmuseum Kroller-Muller, Otterlo, Netherlands / De Agostini Picture Library 86-87b; **Corbis:** Adam Stoltman 164bl, Armin Weigel / dpa 90bc, Denis Balibouse / Reuters 80tr, epa / Rolf Vennenbernd 56t, Fraser Hall 95tr, Gyro Photography / amanaimages 70cr, Hughes Herve / Hemis 95cr, Jean-Louis Atlan / Sygma 119tl, Kacper Pempel / Reuters 69c, Lukasz Nowosadzki / Demotix 69cl, Martial Trezzini / epa 84br, Massimo Borchi / Atlantide Phototravel 152tr, Niels Quist Petersen / Demotix 90-91b, Ocean 112tl, Paul Souders 16t, 161cl, Rafe Swan / cultura 36t, Reed Kaestner 66t, Rob Howard 13cl, Steve Chenn 118t, Wolfgang Kaehler 50tr, 51tl; **Datacraft Co Ltd:** 60cr; **DK Images:** Jon Cunningham / Rough Guides 71tl, Martin Richardson / Rough Guides 71cl, Steve Gorton 45tr; **FLPA Images of Nature:** Imagebroker 18br; **Fotolia.com:** 13cr, 42br, 46b, 72cl, 102bl, 105cl, 112cr, 116cr, 116bl, 154tc, 155cl, 158tr; **Getty Images:** AFP 33bl, 90tc, Alexis Boichard / Agence Zoom 26t, Barcroft Media 18cr, 74tl, Bloomberg 72-73b, 80t, 80br, 122b, Christian Science Monitor 80cr, David M. Benett 91tl, FlickrVision 106t, John Giustina 12b, Hulton Archive 37cr, Jack Guez / AFP 86t, Jamie Grill 102tr, Jasper Juinen 164cl, José Rodrigues 108tr, Justin Sullivan 158tl, Kevin C. Cox 30tr, Mario Tama 91cl, Mondadori 160tl, Oleg Nikishin 32cr, Paul Gilham 35tl, Pool 82-83bc, Popperfoto 27c, Robert Marquardt / WireImage 107cr, Science & Society Picture Library 37c, 37r, 117cr, Transcendental Graphics 33br, Trevor Humphries / Hulton Archive 33bc; **Magnum Photos Ltd:** Henri Cartier-Bresson 88cl, Robert Capa / International Center of Photography 88br; **Nature Picture Library:** Constantinos Petrinos 19tl, Jeff Rotman 6t; **Pearson Education:** 14bl, 21b, 31b, 41b, 51b, 67t, 77b, 91b, 101b, 111b, 124; **Photoshot Holdings Limited:** David Osborn 21t, Guillem Lopez 125tc, Tibor Bognar 66br; **Yulia Podolska:** 153bl; **Press Association Images:** Alastair Grant / AP 31tr, AP 100tl, Chen Xie / AP 51tr, Chris Young / The Canadian Press 113br, Ed Wray / AP 157bl, Mike Egerton / PA Archive 164br, S&G / / EMPICS Sport 32br; **Reuters:** Bobby Yip 69b, 69bl, Erik De Castro 121b; **Rex Features:** 69tr, 69cr, Action Press 34br, c.Col Pics / Everett 64br,

65tr, Courtesy Everett Collection 57cr, David Bagnall 82-83c, Image Broker 106br, Monkey Business Images 67br, Stuart Clarke 27br, The World of Sports SC 32bl, 164cr, View Pictures 90tr; **Shutterstock. com:** A-R-T 48cr, Allies Interactive 37br, Andrey Kuzmin 96t, Anton Chalakov 122-123c, baza178 54cr, donatas1205 88b, Francisco Javier Alcerreca Gomez 70tr, Gaspar Janos 155cr, Godruma 37bl, Goldenarts 107tl, Gordan 27b, Henrik Larsson 38cr, HunThomas 70-71bc, iordani 13bl, jannoon028 24bl, Kodda 92b, Kzenon 28br, locrifa 62b, Molodec 115cr, Monkey Business Images 42t, radoma 13, 25bl, Alexander Raths 165c, ririro 28r, Sergii Rudiuk 107bl, StockLite 13br, Stuart Jenner 8br, swatchandsoda 123b, Tancha 100c, Tyler Olson 43b, ValeStock 113bl, vita khorzhevska 28tl, Vitezslav Valka 111cl, wonderisland 165tc, XR 78-79bc; **Sozaijiten:** 78tl; **SuperStock:** Photononstop 52-53b, Radius 112b; **The Kobal Collection:** Columbia / MGM / Scott Rudin Prod. 64cr, Fox 2000 Pictures / Dune Entertainment / Ingenious Media / Haishang Films 56bc, MGM 116t, New Line / Saul Zaentz / Wing Nut 57cl, Orion / Ken Regan 101tr, Summit Entertainment 56br; **TopFoto:** 100tr, The Granger Collection 162cl; **Tuca Vieira:** 76t

Illustrated by: Kerry Hyndman

Cover images: Front: **Corbis:** Ocean bc

All other images © Pearson Education

Every effort has been made to trace the copyright holders and we apologise in advance for any unintentional omissions. We would be pleased to insert the appropriate acknowledgement in any subsequent edition of this publication.